Where to Wear 2003

THE *BLACK BOOK* FOR
NEW YORK SHOPPING

Fairchild & Gallagher
NEW YORK • LONDON

PUBLISHERS
Jill Fairchild & Gerri Gallagher

WRITER
Laura Brown

COPY EDITOR
Jim Fallon

FACT CHECKER
Jamie Fallon

DESIGN/PRODUCTION ARTIST
Jeff Baker

Where to Wear, New York, 2003 Edition

ISBN 0-9715544-0-4

Copyright © 2002 Fairchild & Gallagher
Manhattan maps © 2000 Eureka Cartography
Original design and Manhattan maps
courtesy of Graphic Image, Inc.
Printed and bound in Canada.

All rights reserved.
Every effort has been made to ensure the accuracy of the information
in this book. However, the publisher and authors make no claims to,
and accept no liability for, any misrepresentations contained herein.
No part of this book may be used or reproduced in any
manner whatsoever without written permission, except in the
case of brief quotations embodied in critical articles and reviews.
For information, contact *Where to Wear* in New York or London at:

666 Fifth Avenue
PMB 377
New York, NY 10103
TEL 212-969-0138
FAX 914-763-0056
E-MAIL wheretowear@aol.com

571 King's Road, London SW6 2EB
TEL 020 7371 9004
E-MAIL wheretowear@onetel.net.uk

www.wheretowear.com

Table of Contents

Manhattan Overview Map	vi
Introduction	vii
Where to Wear New York 2003	1
Best Picks	2
Noteworthy Newcomers	2
In-Store Restaurants	3
Restaurants	3
Clothing & Shoe Size Equivalents	8
Alphabetical Store Directory	9
Stores by Category	239
Stores by Neighborhood/Area Maps	263
Health & Beauty	299
Barbers	300
Haircuts—Unisex	300
Haircuts—Children	300
Hair Salons	301
Hair Removal	303
Beauty Treatments	303
Eyebrow Grooming	305
Manicures/Pedicures	305
Day Spas—Women	306
Day Spas—Men	308
Fitness Studios	309
Pilates/Mat Classes	311
Yoga	311
Massage Therapists	312
Tanning Salons	313
Bridal Consultants	313
Make-up Artists	313
Personal Shoppers	314
Repairs & Services	315
Dry Cleaners	316
Mending & Alterations	317
Custom Design Tailors	318
Boutique Clothing Storage	318
Shoe Repair	318
Leather Repair (Handbags & Luggage)	319
Trimmings (Ribbons, Buttons, etc.)	319
Thrift Shops	320
Fashion Speak	321

Introduction

Dear New York Shopper,

Welcome to *Where to Wear*, the world's most detailed and authoritative directory of clothing and accessory stores. *Where to Wear* annually updates its collection of global guides, making your travels through the world's fashion cities a breeze. We pioneered in 1999 with *Where to Wear New York*, and we have since added *London*, *Los Angeles*, *Paris* and *San Francisco*. This year we are introducing *Where to Wear Italy* which includes Florence, Milan and Rome.

The 2003 edition of *Where to Wear New York* has all the information you'll need to look and feel great. We describe over 800 different clothing and accessories stores, ranging from the global celebrity names of Madison Avenue and SoHo to out-of-the-way treasure-houses. *Where to Wear* shows visitors where to begin and New Yorkers where to go next. If you want the best vintage value or the bonniest baby boutique, you'll find them using *Where to Wear*.

Where to Wear is the only shopping guide written by a team of top fashion journalists. We have our fingers on the pulse of the ever-changing fashion world. We've tromped through each and every store to discover what's fabulous, functional, frumpy, fancy or frightful in them this season. We tell you what the store and its merchandise are all about and who its target customer is, and we list the address, phone number and opening hours. We've marked those stores that merit special consideration with a star (☆), and occasionally we have something sweet (or not so sweet) to say about the staff's helpfulness or attitude. Please let us know if you disagree.

And to make your life even simpler we have included ten pages of user-friendly maps and two separate indexes grouping the stores both by category and by location. Shopping has never been easier! In addition, you'll find the best addresses for beauty treatments, fitness studios, day spas, couture dry cleaners, shoe repair shops, specialty stores (for beads, ribbons, etc) and much else.

Life is not all shopping, of course, so you will also find a list of in-store restaurants and other delightful lunch spots. It's an eclectic list, chosen by our experts for your fun and convenience.

So rev up your credit card and get going, and make sure to keep *W2W* in your handbag, briefcase or backpack.

—Jill Fairchild & Gerri Gallagher

Jill Fairchild Melhado, daughter of fashion world legend and *W* magazine founder John Fairchild, worked as an intern at *Glamour* magazine, *GQ* and *Vogue*. Ms. Fairchild has worked for Ailes Communications, a television production company, and in the late Eighties she founded and ran her own accessories company.

Gerri Gallagher is a freelance editor who has lived in Europe for 15 years. She was the managing editor of Fairchild Publication's *W Europe* from 1990 to 1993 and is currently associate editor of *Tatler* magazine in London.

Where to Wear 2003

Best Picks

Noteworthy Newcomers

In-Store Restaurants

Restaurants

Clothing & Shoe Size Equivalents

Where to Wear New York 2003

Best Picks

Alexander McQueen
Alife Rivington Club
A.P.C.
Barneys New York

BCBG by Max Azria
Betwixt
Borrelli
Cadeau

Century 21
Decollage
Domenico Vacca
Doyle & Doyle

Eres
Eugenia Kim
Eye candy
Flight 001

Foley & Corinna
Forward
Gap
Gas

Gucci
Ina
Intermix

J. Mendel
Jeffrey New York
Jussara Lee

Keni Valenti
La Petite Coquette
Lacoste

Language
LeSportSac
Liz Lange Maternity
Loehmann's

Manolo Blahnik
Marc Jacobs
Martin
Me & Ro

Me Too
Peter Elliot Kids
Pookie & Sebastian
Prada

The Puma Store
Ralph Lauren
Reem Acra
Resurrection Vintage

Rugby North America
Seize sur Vingt (16/20)
Shelly Steffee
Steven Alan

Takashimaya
37 = 1
Tse Cashmere

Urban Outfitters
Vera Wang
Yona Lee

Zara International
Zitomer

Noteworthy Newcomers

Adidas
Alexander McQueesn
Alife Rivington Club
Ann Klein

Basiques
C. Ronson
Cadeau
Chanel (Accessory store)

Chelsea Girl
Decollage
Domenico Vacca
Doyle & Doyle

Edmundo Castillo
Flying A
Francis Hendy

Gas
Helen Marien
Lynn Park NY
Maud Frizon

Me Too
No. 436
Puma
Reem Acra

Shelly Steffee
Sorelle Firenze
Stella McCartney
37 = 1

Triple Five Soul
Y & Kei water the earth
Yona Lee

Where to Wear New York 2003

In-Store Restaurants

American Café at Lord & Taylor   212-391-3344
424 Fifth Avenue, 5th Fl.   bet. 38/39th Street

Au Bon Pain at Macy's   212-494-3959
Broadway at Herald Square, 8th Fl.   bet. B'way/34th Street

Blanche's Organic Café at DKNY   212-223-3569
655 Madison   at 60th Street

Café SFA at Saks Fifth Avenue   212-940-4000
611 Fifth Avenue   bet. 49/50th Street

Café 745 at Bergdorf Goodman Men   212-339-3326
745 Fifth Avenue   bet. 57/58th Street

40 Karats at Bloomingdale's   212-705-2000
1000 Third Avenue, 3rd Fl.   bet. 59/60th Street

Fred's at Barneys   212-833-2200
10 East 61st Street, 9th Fl.   bet 5th/Madison Ave.

Le Train Bleu at Bloomingdale's   212-705-2100
1000 Third Avenue, 6th Fl.   bet. 59/60th Street

Nicole's at Nicole Farhi   212-223-2288
10 East 60th Street   bet. Madison/5th Ave.

On Five at Bergdorf Goodman   212-872-8843
754 Fifth Avenue   bet. 57/58th Street

Showtime Café at Bloomingdale's   212-705-2000
1000 Third Avenue   bet. 59/60th Street

The Tea Box at Takashimaya   212-350-0180
693 Fifth Avenue   bet. 54/55th Street

Restaurants

The following is a select list of restaurants perfect for lunching during your shopping spree.

UPPER EAST SIDE (61ST-96TH STREETS)

East 60's

Amaranth (Bistro)   212-980-6700
21 East 62nd Street   bet. Madison/5th Ave.

Bilboquet (French Bistro)   212-751-3036
25 East 63rd Street   bet. Madison/Park Ave.

Ferrier (French Bistro)   212-772-9000
29 East 65th Street   bet. Madison/Park Ave.

Jackson Hole (Burger Joint)   212-371-7187
232 East 64th Street   bet. 2/3rd Ave.

La Goulue (French Bistro)   212-988-8169
746 Madison Avenue   bet. 64/65th Street

Where to Wear New York 2003

Le Charlot (French Bistro) — 212-794-1628
19 East 69th Street — bet. Madison/Park Ave.

Nello (Italian Bistro) — 212-980-9099
696 Madison Avenue — bet. 62/63rd Street

Serafina (Italian Pizzeria) — 212-702-9898
29 East 61st — bet. Madison/Park Ave.

East 70's

EJ's Lucheonette (Glorified Diner) — 212-472-0600
1271 Third Avenue — at 73rd Street

The Gallery at The Carlyle Hotel — 212-570-7192
(Omelettes, Salads, and Sandwiches)
35 East 76th Street — bet. 76/77th Street

J.G. Melon (Hamburger Joint) — 212-744-0585
1291 Third Avenue — at 74th Street

Le Petit Hulot (French Bistro) — 212-794-9800
973 Lexington Avenue — bet. 70/71st St.

Mezzaluna (Pizzas and Pasta) — 212-535-9600
1295 Third Avenue — bet. 74/75th Street

Orsay (bistro) — 212-517-6400
1057 Lexington — at 75th Street

Swifty's (American Bistro) — 212-535-6000
1007 Lexington Avenue — bet. 72/73rd Street

East 80's and 90's

E.A.T. — 212-772-0022
(Gourmet Sandwiches and Salads)
1064 Madison Avenue — bet. 80/81st Street

Island (Italian Bistro) — 212-996-1200
1305 Madison Avenue — bet. 92/93rd Street

Jackson Hole (Hamburger Joint) — 212-427-2820
1270 Madison — at 91st Street

Sarabeth's (Tea Room) — 212-410-7335
1295 Madison — bet. 92/93rd St.

Upper West Side

Café Luxembourg (French Bistro) — 212-873-7411
200 West 70th Street — bet. Amsterdam/West End Ave.

Isabella's (Italian) — 212-724-2100
359 Columbus — at 77th Street

Nick & Toni (Mediterranean) — 212-496-4000
100 West 67th Street — bet. B'way/Columbus Ave.

Sarabeth's (Tea room) — 212-496-6280
423 Amsterdam Avenue — bet. 80/81st Street

Shun Lee Café (Chinese) — 212-769-3888
43 West 65th Street bet. Columbus/Central Park West

Time Café (Brunch, Salads, Sandwiches) — 212-579-5100
2330 Broadway at 85th Street

Vince and Eddie (American Bistro) — 212-721-0068
70 West 68th Street bet. Columbus/Central Park West

MIDTOWN/FIFTH AVENUE (42ND-61ST STREETS)

Bice (Northern Italian) — 212-688-1999
7 East 54th Street bet. Madison/5th Ave.

Bricco (Italian) — 212-245-7160
304 West 56th Street bet. 8/9th Ave.

California Pizza (Pizza, Pasta, and Salads) — 212-755-7773
201 East 60th Street bet. 2/3rd Ave.

California Pizza (Pizza, Pasta, and Salads) — 212-869-8231
234 West 42nd Street bet. 7/8th Ave.

DB Bistro (French Bistro) — 212-391-2400
55 West 44th Street bet. 5/6th Ave.

Fresco by Scotto on the Go (Italian) — 212-754-2700
40 East 52nd Street bet. Madison/Park Ave.

Mme. Romaine de Lyon (Omelettes) — 212-758-2422
132 East 61st Street bet. Park/Lexington Ave.

Baby Blue @ the Royalton Hotel (Fusion) — 212-869-4400
44 West 44th Street bet. 5/6th Ave.

Rue 57 (French Bistro) — 212-307-5656
60 West 57th Street at 6th Ave.

FLATIRON/NOHO/CENTRAL VILLAGE

Borgo Antico (Tuscan Fare) — 212-807-1313
22 East 13th Street bet. 5th Ave./University Place

City Bakery (Salad, Sandwich, Pastry) — 212-366-1414
3 West 18th Street at 5th Ave.

Cosi Sandwich Bar (Great Sandwiches) — 212-598-9300
3 East 17th Street bet. B'way/5th Ave.

Indochine (French Vietnamese) — 212-505-5111
430 Lafayette Street bet. Astor Place/4th Street

Marquet Patisserie (Bistro) — 212-229-9313
15 East 12th Street bet. 5th Ave./University Place

Time Café (Brunch, Salads, Sandwiches) — 212-533-7000
380 Lafayette Street bet. East 4th St./Great Jones

Thè Adore (Pastries, Salads, Sandwiches) — 212-243-8742
17 East 13th Street bet. 5th/University Place

T Salon (Soups, Salads, Sandwiches)   212-358-0506
11 East 20th Street   bet. B'way/5th Ave.

CHELSEA / WEST VILLAGE

Amy's Bread (Sandwiches)   212-462-4338
75 Ninth Avenue   bet. 15/16th Street (Chelsea Market)

Chelsea Bistro & Bar (French Bistro)   212-727-2026
358 West 23rd Street   bet. 8/9th Ave.

Corner Bistro (Burger Joint)   212-242-9502
331 West 4th Street   at 8th Ave.

Cosi Sandwich Bar   212-505-7978
257 Park Avenue South   bet. 20/21st Street

EJ's (Diner)   212-473-5555
432 Sixth Avenue   bet. 9/10th Street

Le Madri (Italian)   212-727-8022
168 West 18th Street   at 7th Ave.

Markt (Belgian Brasserie)   212-727-3314
401 West 14th Street   at 9th Ave.

Pastis (French Bistro)   212-929-4844
9 Ninth Avenue   at Little West 12th

Petite Abeille   212-604-9350
(Soups, Waffles, and Sandwiches)
107 West 18th Street   bet. 6/7th Ave.

Tartine (French Bistro)   212-229-2611
253 West 11th Street   at West 4th Street

SOHO / NOLITA

Balthazar (French Bistro)   212-965-1414
80 Spring Street   bet. Broadway/Crosby

Boom (Italian)   212-431-3663
152 Spring Street   bet. Wooster/Broadway

Bot (Italian)   646-613-1312
231 Mott Street   bet. Prince/Spring

Café Habana (Cuban)   212-625-2002
17 Prince Street   at Elizabeth

Café Gitane (French Bistro)   212-334-9552
242 Mott Street   bet. Prince/Houston

Downtown   212-343-0999
(Harry Cipriani's Soho Location)
376 West Broadway   at Broome

Fanelli's Café (Burgers)   212-431-5744
94 Prince Street   at Mercer

Felix (French Bistro) — 212-431-0021
340 West Broadway — at Grand

Mezzogiorno (Italian) — 212-334-2112
195 Spring Street — at Sullivan

Rialto (French American) — 212-334-7900
265 Elizabeth Street — bet. Houston/Prince

Rice (Thai/Asian) — 212-226-5775
227 Mott Street — bet. Prince/Spring

Thom's @ the Thompson Hotel — 212-219-2000
(Modern American)
60 Thompson Street — bet. Broome/Spring

TRIBECA / LOWER MANHATTAN

Bouley Bakery (New French) — 212-964-2525
120 West Broadway — at Duane

Bubby's — 212-219-0666
(Soups, Burgers, Salads, and Sandwiches)
120 Hudson Street — at North Moore

Franklin Station Café (Malaysian) — 212-274-8525
222 West Broadway — bet. Franklin/White

Nobu Next Door (Japanese) — 212-334-4445
105 Hudson Street — at Franklin

The Odeon (Bistro) — 212-233-0507
145 West Broadway — bet. Duane/Thomas

Seaport Soup Company — 212-693-1371
(Soups & Sandwiches)
76 Fulton Street — at Gold

Spartina (Mediterranean) — 212-274-9310
355 Greenwich Street — at Harrison

Tribeca Grill (New American) — 212-941-3900
375 Greenwich Street — at Franklin

Clothing & Shoe Size Equivalents

Children's Clothing

American	3	4	5	6	6X
Continental	98	104	110	116	122
British	18	20	22	24	26

Children's Shoes

American	8	9	10	11	12	12	1	2	3
Continental	24	25	27	28	29	30	32	33	34
British	7	8	9	10	11	12	13	1	2

Ladies' Coats, Dresses, Skirts

American	3	5	7	9	11	12	13	14	15
Continental	36	38	38	40	40	42	42	44	44
British	8	10	11	12	13	14	15	16	17

Ladies' Blouses & Sweaters

American	10	12	14	16	18	20
Continental	38	40	42	44	46	48
British	32	34	36	38	40	42

Ladies' Hosiery

American	8	8.5	9	9.5	10	10.5
Continental	1	2	3	4	5	6
British	8	8.5	9	9.5	10	10.5

Ladies' Shoes

American	5	6	7	8	9	10
Continental	36	37	38	39	40	41
British	3.5	4.5	5.5	6.5	7.5	8.5

Men's Suits

American	34	36	38	40	42	44	46	48
Continental	44	46	48	50	52	54	56	58
British	34	36	38	40	42	44	46	48

Men's Shirts

American	14	15	15.5	16	16.5	17	17.5	18
Continental	37	38	39	41	42	43	44	45
British	14	15	15.5	16	16	17	17.5	18

Men's Shoes

American	7	8	9	10	11	12	13
Continental	39.5	41	42	43	44.5	46	47
British	6	7	8	9	10	11	12

Alphabetical Store Directory

Abercrombie & Fitch

Abercrombie & Fitch is an American icon, and for very good reason. It combines outdoor utilitarianism with all-American spirit—cargo and parachute pants, denim, printed tees, knits, sweats, outerwear and accessories—all with the instantly recognisable A&F logo. Also, every now and then, look out for naughty slogan T-shirts. Check out their cool kid's division named "Abercrombie" and don't forget to pick up a copy of their hip catalog while you're at it.
800-432-0888   www.abercrombie.com

Lower Manhattan   **212-809-9000**
199 Water Street   at South Street Seaport
NYC 10038   Mon-Sat 10-9, Sun 11-8

Aboud Mimi

This small, simple store features a selection of shoes for men and women. Women can choose from designs by Florence Girardier, Luc Berjen, Zita Maria and Aboud Mimi. A small collection of English handmade and hand-stitched shoes for men are surprisingly well-priced at $175-250 a pair. Accessories include bags by Keri Krop.

SoHo   **212-253-8557**
137 Thompson Street   bet. Prince/Houston
NYC 10012   Mon-Sun 11-7

A. Cheng

Past tours of duty at Gap and Tommy Hilfiger gave designer Alice Cheng the savvy—and commercial sense—she needed to open her own shop. Cheng's collection caters predominantly to professionals who want easy-to-wear clothing. Best buys: her signature shirt dress as well as skirts, pants, jackets, silk print tops, and feminine button-down shirts.   www.achengshop.com

East Village   **212-979-7324**
443 East 9th Street   bet. Ave. A/1st Ave.
NYC 10009   Mon-Fri 12-8, Sat & Sun 12-7

add

Stocking the wares of over 40 designers, this small accessories boutique is packed with hats, handbags, knock-out costume jewelry, and an abundance of shawl styles that will add the right degree of je ne sais quoi to any outfit—especially if you like pink! Check out satin evening purses, raffia totes, and fashionable day bags by Francesco Biasia, Franchi, Mitzi Baker, Inca and Neal Decker, and Bettina Duncan. Hat styles include fancy dress numbers, adjustable straw boaters, madras caps and panamas by labels like Kokin, Karl Donoghue, Annabel Ingall and Amsterdam's Bronte. Great for the races.

SoHo   **212-539-1439**
461 West Broadway   bet. Houston/Prince
NYC 10012   Mon-Sun 11-8

Aerosoles

Addison On Madison
A dress shirt shop for men looking for great value for money. Choose from over 400 different styles at an average price of $75. Manufactured in Italian cotton, shirts come in a full cut with a relaxed fit. Accessories include neckties, bow ties, pocket squares and cufflinks.

Upper East Side	212-308-2660
698 Madison Avenue	bet. 62/63rd St.
NYC 10021	Mon-Sat 10:30-6:30

A Détacher
Owner/designer Monica Kowalska's collection, with its high-concept Japanese sensibility, is, in her words, "art fashion for adults." The result is a clean, minimalist line of monochromatic dresses, pants, skirts, blouses and more. Kowalska uses linear cuts (not form-fitting) and a basic color palette of black, white and gray. Head to the back of the shop and discover handbag designer Dillen's fantastic, Hermès-like, custom order accessories. Also amuse yourself with a quirky collection of homewares.

NoLiTa	212-625-3380
262 Mott Street	bet. Houston/Prince
NYC 10012	Tues-Sat 12-7, Sun 1-6

Adidas
The coolest three stripes in the sports world, Adidas has had a firm hold on everyone from athletes to the style set for over 80 years. And it just keeps getting better. Responding to the feverish demand for boutique sportswear, the label recently opened its third—after Tokyo and Berlin—Originals Store in SoHo. Hipsters (and the occasional genuine athlete) head here for the newly reinvented and super-hip Originals line. Shiny polyester tracksuits beloved by the streetwise set, limited edition sneakers, casualwear—the whole world of retro Adidas is here for you. Too cool for school.

SoHo	212-777-2001
136 Wooster Street	bet. Prince/Spring
NYC 10012	Mon-Sat 11-7, Sun 12-5

Aerosoles
Aerosoles designs orthopedically correct shoes that deliver, not surprisingly, more comfort than fashion (not that there's anything wrong with that). Looks run from business casual to sporty weekend. Find easy-to-wear pumps, boots, oxfords, sneakers, flats and cushioned-sole sandals that emphasize stretch, movement and flexibility. 800-798-9478 www.aerosoles.com

Upper East Side	212-751-6372
1155 Second Avenue	at 61st St.
NYC 10021	Mon-Sat 10-8, Sun 12-6
Upper West Side	212-579-8659
310 Columbus Avenue	bet. 74/75th St.
NYC 10023	Mon-Sat 9:30-8, Sun 11-6

Afterlife

NoHo　　　　　　　　　　　　　　　　　**212-358-7855**
63 East 8th Street　　　　　　　　bet. B'way/University Pl.
NYC 10003　　　　　　　　　　　　Mon-Sat 9:30-9, Sun 12-7

Afterlife

When you walk into a shop with live mannequins in the window grooving to pumping rock music, you know you're not in for a standard shopping experience. This huge club-like store, currently expanding, provides downtown boys and girls with instant fashion hits in the form of cool screenprint tees (designed by owner Richard Gultry), novelty jeans, accessories…even vintage records. "I wanted to create a fashionable shopping and entertainment experience," Gultry says—and he has. Treat yourself to a glass of complimentary white wine, as a "thank you for stopping in" but do restrain yourself from modeling your purchases in the window…

SoHo　　　　　　　　　　　　　　　　　**212-625-0767**
450 Broadway　　　　　　　　　　　　bet. Houston/Prince
NYC 10012　　　　　　　　　　　　　Mon-Sat 11-8, Sun 12-6

Agent Provocateur

Welcome to the underworld. No-one has given designer lingerie such a kick in the pants as Agent Provocateur, the masters of kinky chic. London's most exclusive lingerie label, started almost a decade ago by Vivienne Westwood's son Joe Corre and wife Serena Rees, perfectly marries shameless eroticism and naughty exhibitionism—which is probably why their little nothings are craved by every supermodel, and superstar, on the planet. The long wait for a New York outpost is finally over with this SoHo store, a chic retail bordello with a comely staff in nurse uniforms and a world of equally naughty, retro-inspired knickers. It's the perfect place to dispatch your boyfriend to pick up the signature lingerie, also chokers, leopard print stilettos, or perhaps a bottle of AP's saucy fragrance. Sexy with a capital S…

SoHo　　　　　　　　　　　　　　　　　**212-965-0229**
133 Mercer Street　　　　　　　　　　　bet. Spring/Prince
NYC 10012　　　　　　　　　　　　　Mon-Sat 11-7, Sun 12-5

agnès b.

Effortlessly stylish women have long shopped at agnès b. to snare some Parisian bon ton (fashionability without trendiness). The classic and clever ready-to-wear collection offers pants, jackets, sweaters, suits and skirts that are simple, chic and feminine—and some of the best T-shirts around. New and very cool is Madame B's collaboration with boxing label Everlast, b.Everlast, elegant urban streetwear like hooded sweatshirts and tanks.　　　　　　　www.agnesb.fr

Upper East Side　　　　　　　　　　　　**212-570-9333**
1063 Madison Avenue　　　　　　　　　　bet. 80/81st St.
NYC 10028　　　　　　　　　　　　　Mon-Sat 11-7, Sun 12-6

Flatiron　　　　　　　　　　　　　　　　**212-741-2585**
13 East 16th Street　　　　　bet. 5th Ave./Union Sq. West
NYC 10003　　　　　　　　　　　　　Mon-Sat 11-7, Sun 12-6

Alexander McQueen

SoHo
76 Greene Street
NYC 10012

212-925-4649
bet. Spring/Prince
Mon-Sun 11-7

agnès b. homme

agnès b. homme caters to the monsieurs (or wannabe monsieurs) of the world seeking simple looks with that particular Parisian edge. Choose from a ready-to-wear collection of suits, dress pants, shirts, khakis and jeans—all up, a one-stop foolproof wardrobe. It's simple clothes with that covetable French elegance. Sizes run small. www.agnesb.fr

SoHo
79 Greene Street
NYC 10012

212-431-4339
bet. Spring/Broome
Mon-Sun 11-7

Aldo

Calling all twentysomethings: This is your funky footwear home! Shop for streety looks like Cher-worthy platforms, wedges, rubber or wooden soles, boots, sassy stilettos and sandals in bursts of raspberry pink, purple, blue, and orange, (black and white, too). Affordably priced footwear with attitude to spare. www.aldoshoes.com

Upper East Side
157 East 86th Street
NYC 10028

212-828-3725
bet. 3rd/Lex. Ave.
Mon-Sat 10-8, Sun 12-7

Midtown East
730 Lexington Avenue
NYC 10022

212-832-1692
bet. 58/59th St.
Mon-Sat 10-9, Sun 11-8

Midtown West
15 West 34th Street
NYC 10001

212-594-6255
bet. 5/6th Ave.
Mon-Sat 10-9, Sun 11-8

NoHo
700 Broadway
NYC 10003

212-982-0958
at East 4th St.
Mon-Sat 10-9, Sun 11-8

SoHo
579 Broadway
NYC 10012

212-226-7974
bet. Houston/Prince
Mon-Wed 10-8, Thur-Sat 10-9, Sun 11-7

☆ Alexander McQueen

Fashion's dark prince, who first drew international attention showing his now famous "bumsters" in London churches, is now a bona fide international brand, following backing by fashion powerhouse Gucci. After opening his first store in Tokyo, McQueen's New York outpost, located in the überfashionable meatpacking district, is a deliberate trip into the recesses of his mind. "It's supposed to be a spaceship environment, so everything hovers. It's very ethereal," he says. The single-floor store showcases McQueen's complete women's collection: sinuous suits, sharp pants, his signature leather corsetry, death-defying shoes, logo sunglasses and the now cult "McQueen's" jeans, as well as his new capsule collection of bespoke suits for those men who want their own taste of McQueen edginess

Chelsea 417 West 14th Street NYC 10014
212-645-1797 bet. 9th Ave./Washington Mon-Fri 10-8, Thur 10-9 Sat 10-7, Sun 12:30-6

Alexandre de Paris

An established French retailer of hair accessories, including chignon pins, hairnets, headbands, hair forks, combs and barrettes. Each item is hand-made to posh perfection and styles run from simply beaded to fabulously bejeweled. A private line of hairbrushes and sunglasses also available.

Upper East Side 971 Madison Avenue NYC 10021
212-717-2122 bet. 75/76th St. Mon-Fri 10-6, Sat 10-6

Alexandros Furs

Choose from a collection of quality avant-garde and classic fur coats—from sporty fox and raccoon to luxurious mink, sable or lynx. Alongside the house label, they also carry luxe designs from Ekso. Other outerwear includes cashmere overcoats and reversibles. Alexandros also offers storage, cleaning and remodeling.

Midtown East 5 East 59th Street, 2nd Fl. NYC 10022
212-702-0744 bet. Madison/5th Ave. Mon-Fri 10-6, Sat 10-5 (closed Saturdays July & Aug)

Chelsea 213 West 28th Street NYC 10001
212-967-1222 bet. 7/8th Ave. Mon-Sat 10-6 (Sun 10-6 October thru Feb)

Alexia Crawford Accessories

A tiny boutique packed to the rafters with accessories. Dress up a dull outfit with one of Crawford's delicate jewelry designs, or opt for a silky, diaphanous scarf or shawl with matching evening bags. Styles run from young and trendy to classic and sophisticated. Great prices.

www.alexiacrawford.com

SoHo 199 Prince Street NYC 10012
212-473-9703 bet. Sullivan/MacDougal Mon-Thur 11-7, Fri, Sat 11-8, Sun 11-6

Alfred Dunhill

Dunhill, like many other British brands, is aiming to inject some spark into its classic suits and accessories for the sophisticated fellow and this just-redecorated store shows off its new look with red walls, dark wood floor and lots of leather trim. Think of an English gentlemen's club for the Guy Ritchie set. The main floor is home to accessories, great leathergoods, fragrances, jewelry and cigars. Saunter up to the second floor, which boasts a discriminating collection of suits, shirts, ties, knitwear, sportswear and outerwear, all with the new dunhill' label. Off-the-rack suits run from $1,400 to $1,700, while a custom suit will run you from $2,200 to approx $5,000.   800-860-8362   www.dunhill.com

Alife Rivington Club

Fifth Avenue   **212-753-9292**
711 Fifth Avenue   bet. 55/56th St.
NYC 10022   Mon-Sat 10-7, Thur 10-8, Sun 12-5

Alice Underground
Take a trip into Alice's world and discover a vast selection of secondhand clothing and other serendipitous goodies. Shop for vintage looks from the 40's to the 70's, including reconditioned vintage leather, dresses, sweaters, saucy lingerie, shoes, retro scarves, and jewelry. Don't overlook the bargain bins in the back stuffed with a random selection of merchandise. All up, it's the place to go for that Kenny Rogers T-shirt you've always wanted...

SoHo   **212-431-9067**
481 Broadway   bet. Broome/Grand
NYC 10012   Mon-Sun 11-7:30

Alicia Mugetti
Alicia Mugetti specializes in romantic damsel dresses designed in rich velvets and crushed satins. Find them in beautiful colors and feminine, floor-length silhouettes. Lush fabrics and Renaissance looks—all very Knights of the Round Table (or the princesses they woo, anyway).

Upper East Side   **212-794-6186**
999 Madison Avenue   bet. 77/78th St.
NYC 10021   Mon-Sat 10-6

Alife
Get Alife! An eclectic, defiantly downtown mix of footwear, clothing, graffiti paraphernalia, design books, and the ever-vital stuffed animals. Check out zip-front sweaters designed by graffiti guru ESPO, cult Tsubi jeans, local designer tees, patched sweatshirts, shirts, industrial accessories and edgy shoes ranging from modern-looking sneaks by Snipe and Converse to men's Tseubos, a cross between an orthopedic sneaker and Prada shoe. Every two months, they also feature progressive installations by up-and-coming artists.   www.alifenyc.com

Lower East Side   **646-654-0628**
178 Orchard Street   bet. Houston/Stanton
NYC 10002   Tues-Sun 12-7

☆ Alife Rivington Club
Confirming the Lower East Side's new status as the sneaker capital of the world, along comes the older brother to Alife. Alife Rivington Club looks like a cross between a Savile Row tailor and Athlete's Foot, with limited edition sneakers back-lit and displayed reverently in cherrywood cases. Obscure and dead-cool, look out for classic retro Adidas and contemplate kicking your sneaker addiction from the gorgeous Italian leather couch that lines an entire wall. Then, forget it and buy two pairs.

Lower East Side   **212-375-8128**
158 Rivington Street   bet. Clinton/Suffolk
NYC 10002   Tues-Sun 12-7

Alixandre

Alixandre
Run by three generations of the Schulman family, Alixandre delivers honest, reliable and knowledgeable service, as well as an outstanding selection of fur coats. Find top quality shearlings, broadtails, minks and sables from designer Oscar de la Renta. Appointments suggested between Memorial Day and Labor Day. www.alixandrefurs.com

Midtown West 212-736-5550
150 West 30th Street, 13th Fl. bet. 6/7th Ave.
NYC 10001 Mon-Fri 9-5, Sat 9-1:30

Allan & Suzi
Allan & Suzi are masters at mixing vintage pieces with current fashions to create totally original style. Find discounted designer garb by Jean Paul Gaultier, Vivienne Westwood, Versace, Prada and Yohji Yamamoto plus vintage pieces by Courrèges, Pucci, and Pierre Cardin. The shop's atmosphere and fab merchandise are sure to send tingles up your spine but, like so many vintage stores these days, these retro pieces don't always come cheap.

Upper West Side 212-724-7445
416 Amsterdam Avenue at 80th St.
NYC 10024 Mon-Sat 12-7, Sun 12-6

Allen Edmonds
For over 75 years, the customer has come first at Allen Edmonds. Find over 200 styles of dress and corporate classics, casual weekend shoes, as well as fashion-forward lifestyle footwear. Great care has gone into obtaining the perfect balance between quality and price.
800-235-2348 www.allenedmonds.com

Midtown East 212-308-8305
551 Madison Avenue bet. 55/56th St.
NYC 10022 Mon-Fri 9-7, Sat 9-6, Sun 12-5

Midtown 212-682-3144
24 East 44th Street bet. Madison/5th Ave.
NYC 10017 Mon-Fri 9-7, Sat 9-6, Sun 12-5

Allure Lingerie
A super-sweet neighborhood lingerie shop featuring brands like Only Hearts, Hanky Panky, Hanro, Wolford, LeJaby, Pluto and Cosabella (the best thongs around). Find a great selection of seamless bras, panties and thongs, as well as hosiery by DKNY and Wolford. Robes and slippers are also available.

Upper East Side 212-860-7871
1324 Lexington Avenue bet. 88/89th St.
NYC 10128 Mon-Fri 11-7, Sat 11-6

Alpana Bawa
Alpana Bawa's signature is vibrant colors and brave geometric and floral patterns in separates and accessories in hand-embroidered wool, silk, cotton or nylon. There are also cotton men's shirts, embellished with prints and

American Eagle Outfitters

embroidery, favored by out-there actor types like Willem Dafoe. www.alpanabawa.com

SoHo 212-965-0559
41 Grand Street bet. W. B'way/Thompson
NYC 10013 Mon-Sat 11-7, Sun 12-6

East Village (outlet) 212-254-1249
70 East 1st Street bet. 1/2nd Ave.
NYC 10003 Thur-Sat 1-7

Alskling
Alskling means "darling" in Swedish and the clothes are indeed that. This shop boasts an enormous collection of dresses, especially their signature slip dress in an array of prints, as well as easy-to-wash pants, tops and skirts. The super-soft and romantic look might be too cutesy for some, although there are adorable floral dresses for tots up to 3 years old.

Upper West Side 212-787-7066
228 Columbus Avenue bet. 70/71st St.
NYC 10023 Mon-Sun 10-7

Amarcord Vintage Fashion
This airy shop sells vintage clothing lovingly hand-picked by owners Patti Bordoni and Marco Liotta. These passionate Italian expatriates collect many of their pieces direct from Europe through word-of-mouth and "top secret" sources. Find both non-designer prized pieces, as well as winning looks by Cacharel, Gucci, Roberto Cavalli, you name it. Everything is in great condition (especially the classic handbags) and attractively priced. Unlike so many other vintage emporiums, they only pick the best, and they color code them, too.

East Village 212-614-7133
84 East 7th Street bet. 1/2nd Ave.
NYC 10009 Tues-Sun 12:30-7:30

American Colors
Henry Lehr's private-label line, "American Colors," features casual basics like capri pants, shirts, khakis, shorts and plenty of tanks and T-shirts — all made in America and garment dyed in a rainbow of colors (hence the name). The merchandise is machine washable and dryable; i.e, thankfully low-maintenance.

NoLiTa 212-334-2656
232 Elizabeth Street bet. Prince/Houston
NYC 10012 Mon-Sun 11-7

American Eagle Outfitters
After an Abercrombie alternative? Then head to AEO, which targets the same high school and collegiate shopper searching for affordable, all-American, casual lifestyle clothing. Jeans, graphic T-shirts, sweaters, khakis, outerwear, shoes and accessories all look wholesome and are guaranteed not to offend parents. After all, they're probably paying the bill. 888-232-4535 www.ae.com

Amsale

Lower Manhattan   **212-571-5354**
89 South Street   at the South Street Seaport
NYC 10038   Mon-Sat 10-9, Sun 11-6

Amsale

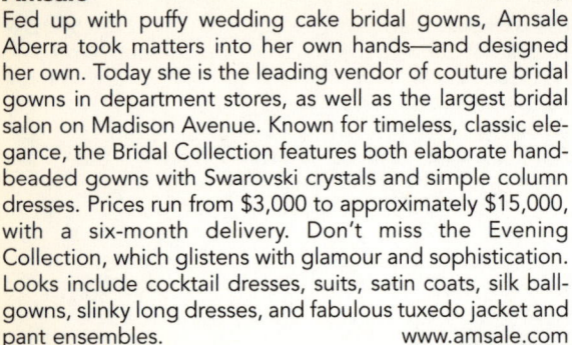

Fed up with puffy wedding cake bridal gowns, Amsale Aberra took matters into her own hands—and designed her own. Today she is the leading vendor of couture bridal gowns in department stores, as well as the largest bridal salon on Madison Avenue. Known for timeless, classic elegance, the Bridal Collection features both elaborate hand-beaded gowns with Swarovski crystals and simple column dresses. Prices run from $3,000 to approximately $15,000, with a six-month delivery. Don't miss the Evening Collection, which glistens with glamour and sophistication. Looks include cocktail dresses, suits, satin coats, silk ballgowns, slinky long dresses, and fabulous tuxedo jacket and pant ensembles.   www.amsale.com

Midtown East   **212-583-1700**
625 Madison Avenue, Mezzanine level   at 58th St.
NYC 10022   Tues-Sat 10-6, Thur 10-7

Amy Chan

Fashion girls make the pilgrimage here for the adventurously edited collection of pieces from young, edgy designers like L.A.'s Alicia Lawhon. The progressive retailer even hosts an occasional open house for new names to show their wares. The result? You'll be guaranteed to find something no one else has (which, in fashion, is vital). As a designer, Chan made her name with a quirky assortment of handbags—and they're still here in force, including her signature mosaic bag, where small acrylic tiles are heat-sealed onto colorful saris, pinstripes, floral motifs, denim or other fabrics. Prices run from $130 to $400.

NoLiTa   **212-966-3417**
247 Mulberry Street   bet. Prince/Spring
NYC 10012   Mon-Sun 12-7

Amy Downs Hats

Amy Downs is one of New York's most creative milliners; her style is deliberately and eclectically "downtown". Shop for headwear with names like Twister or Happy Family, or choose from a collection of polar fleece and wool hats, hunting caps, straw boaters, funky felts, fun furs, bold berets, wool ski hats and more.

East Village   **212-358-8756**
227 East 14th Street   bet. 2/3rd Ave.
NYC 10002   Tues-Sat 1-7

Andy's Chee-Pees

A vintage store for style swingers in search of fun, one-of-a-kind fashion hits. Find collectible denim, swing clothes from the 40's and 50's, biker and bomber jackets, jeans, old police leather jackets, Hawaiian shirts, a complete line of unisex dickeys in bold bright colors, party wigs, vintage jewelry and more. For the 18-35 crowd desperate for some nostalgia—or something eye-catching to wear to a costume party.

NoHo
691 Broadway
NYC 10012

212-420-5980
bet. 3/4th St.
Mon-Sat 11-9, Sun 12-8

Angelo Lambrou

What do the First Lady of Botswana and 'Nsync have in common? They both wear clothes by Angelo Lambrou—and that's about it. Exotic fabrics and colors, combined with a passion for draping and bias cutting, are key to the Lambrou look. Check out a ready-to-wear collection of tailored suits, dresses, sleek leather pieces and coats. But the highlight here is eveningwear, which runs from intricately beaded gowns to short, sheer sexy dresses (which are not what 'Nsync wears). Prices run from $900 to $5,000. Custom couture and bridal also available.

East Village
96 East 7th Street
NYC 10009

212-460-9870
bet. Ave. A/1st Ave.
Tues-Sun 1-8

Anik

Young, professional women shop here for fashionable career clothing that doesn't scream corporate bland-o. It's the home of hip designers like Chaiken, Theory, Alice & Trixie, Bella Dahl, Only Hearts and Easel, plus such accessories as cute beaded belts. With their huge top selection, it's easy to look stylish at work and cool at the weekend.

Upper East Side
1355 Third Avenue
NYC 10021

212-861-9840
bet. 77/78th St.
Mon-Sat 11-8, Sun 11-7

Upper East Side
1122 Madison Avenue
NYC 10028

212-249-2417
bet. 83/84th St.
Mon-Sat 10-8, Sun 11-7

Anna

One of New York's best-kept secrets, this is the kind of boutique that fashion-obsessed East Village girls wish they could keep to themselves. Sorry, we have to spread the love. Owner/designer Kathy Kemp sells her collection of addictive striped wrap dresses, girlish double-layered skirts, smocked tops, customized sweatshirts and carefully chosen, complementary vintage pieces. The look is feminine, fantastically offbeat, and no item costs more than $200.

East Village
150 East 3rd Street
NYC 10009

212-358-0195
bet. Ave. A/B
Mon-Sat 1-8, Sun 1-7

Anna Sui

At the heart of every Anna Sui collection comes "the celebration of the nouvelle hippie." This downtown icon made her name with boho pieces that are saucy and sweet at the same time. Her SoHo treasure trove is inspired by a myriad of decades—but the 60's and 70's are clearly the favorites. Choose from a head-to-toe collection featuring dresses, skirts tossed with crochet pieces, romantic blouses, chunky coats, sexy denims, patchwork and even dainty underwear. Devotees include Nicole Kidman, Madonna and all of Anna's many model friends. Accessories include fanciful, decorative shoes, handbags and jewelry—and if you really want to feel the Sui love, check out the cute-goth make-up and the fragrance.

SoHo 212-941-8406
113 Greene Street bet. Prince/Spring
NYC 10012 Mon-Sat 11:30-7, Sun 12-6

Anne Fontaine

French designer Anne Fontaine has built a company around a single brilliant idea: make the white shirt a chic and indispensable part of every woman's wardrobe (although black and cream have also recently crept into the line). Find luxurious, dressy shirts from tailored button-downs to pin-front camisoles, all in feminine silhouettes and materials like organdy, stretch cotton, piqué and poplin. Prices from $80 to $325. With each purchase, discover a rose sachet tucked into your shirt. Lovely. www.annefontaine.com

Upper East Side 212-639-9651
791 Madison Avenue at 67th St.
NYC 10021 Mon-Sat 10-6, Sun 12-5

SoHo 212-343-3154
93 Greene Street bet. Prince/Spring
NYC 10012 Mon-Sat 11-7, Sun 12-6

Anne Klein

Established and elegant, Anne Klein has a tradition of dressing women for more than 30 years. But it's upped the ante of late by appointing designer Charles Nolan, launching a chic advertising campaign with model Bridget Hall and positioning itself as a fashion-oriented collection rather than simply a career-driven bridge line. Visit this, the company's first signature flagship, for the complete Anne Klein New York collection—think simple pieces like silk jersey tops and taffeta pants—plus the sportier AK Anne Klein line. The signature lion's head logo is in evidence, both on accessories and in the store's dramatic décor.

SoHo 212-965-9499
417 West Broadway bet. Prince/Spring
NYC 10012 Mon-Wed 10-7, Thur-Sat 10-8, Sun 12-7

Ann Taylor

Gone forever are the days when Ann Taylor catered solely to young professionals. The new version is for everyone from corporate women to chic urbanites of all ages (like Christy Turlington, who is the face of the latest ad campaign). Find suits and separates for the office,

Ann Taylor Loft

sportswear for weekends and understated cocktail dresses for evening. In addition, shop a terrific selection of private-label shoes, an extensive petite section and accessories. We can't guarantee you'll leave resembling Christy, sadly!   800-677-0300   www.anntaylor.com

Upper East Side — 212-988-8930
1055 Madison Avenue — at 80th St.
NYC 10028 — Mon-Fri 10-8, Sat 10-6, Sun 12-6

Upper East Side — 212-832-9114
645 Madison Avenue — at 60th St.
NYC 10022 — Mon-Fri 10-8, Sat 10-7, Sun 12-6

Upper East Side — 212-861-3392
1320 Third Avenue — bet. 75/76th St
NYC 10021 — Mon-Fri 10-8, Sat 10-6, Sun 12-6

Upper West Side — 212-721-3130
2380 Broadway — at 87th St.
NYC 10024 — Mon-Sat 10-9, Sun 12-6

Upper West Side — 212-873-7344
2015-17 Broadway — at 69th St.
NYC 10023 — Mon-Sat 10-9, Sun 12-7

Midtown East — 212-308-5333
850 Third Avenue — at 52nd St.
NYC 10022 — Mon-Fri 10-8, Sat 10-6, Sun 12-5

Midtown East — 212-949-0008
330 Madison Avenue — at 43rd St.
NYC 10017 — Mon-Fri 9-8, Sat 10-7, Sun 12-5

Midtown West — 212-642-4340
1166 Sixth Avenue — at 46th St.
NYC 10036 — Mon-Fri 9-8, Sat 10-7, Sun 12-6

Midtown East — 212-922-3621
575 Fifth Avenue — at 47th St.
NYC 10017 — Mon-Fri 10-8, Sat 10-7, Sun 11-6

Lower Manhattan — 212-480-4100
4 Fulton Street — at South Street Seaport
NYC 10038 — Mon-Fri 10-8, Sat 11-8, Sun 10-7

Ann Taylor Loft

There's Ann Taylor for dressier occasions and then there's Ann Taylor Loft for perfect weekend clothing. The Ann Taylor woman shops here for casual basics like sweater sets, pants, cotton and silk shirts, dresses and accessories—all up, relaxed and practical pieces at lower price points than the weekday Ann Taylor line.

Upper East Side — 212-472-7281
1492 Third Avenue — bet. 84/85th St.
NYC 10028 — Mon-Sat 10-9, Sun 11-6

Upper East Side — 212-772-9952
1155 Third Avenue — at 68th St.
NYC 10021 — Mon-Sat 10-8, Sun 11-7

Midtown East — 212-883-8766
150 East 42nd Street — at Lex. Ave.
NYC 10017 — Mon-Fri 9-9, Sat 10-8, Sun 11-6

Annika Inez

Midtown East 212-308-1129
488 Madison Avenue at 52nd St.
NYC 10022 Mon-Fri 10-8, Sat 10-7, Sun 12-5

Midtown West 212-399-1078
1290 Avenue of the Americas at 52nd St.
NYC 10104 Mon-Fri 9-9, Sat 10-8, Sun 11-6

Midtown West 212-244-8926
35 West 34th Street bet Fifth/Sixth Ave.
NYC 10001 Mon-Sat 10-9, Sun 11-7

NoHo 646-602-1582
770 Broadway at 9th St.
NYC 10003 Mon-Sat 10-9, Sun 12-6

SoHo 212-625-0427
560 Broadway bet. Prince/Spring
NYC 10012 Mon-Sat 10-8, Sun 12-6

TriBeCa 212-809-1435
2 Broadway bet. Beaver/Whitehall
NYC 10004 Mon-Fri 8-7

Annika Inez

A fab little secret on the Upper East Side, Annika is a destination for chic beaded jewelry made by Swedish store owner Annika Salame, using vintage beads from the Thirties to the Seventies. The store is simple and uncluttered, all the better to display this small collection, which also includes wooden heart necklaces, hair ornaments and simple silky tops by LA designer Stacey Bees. Great for gifts—or just to spoil yourself. www.annikainez.com

Upper East Side 212-717-9644
243 East 78th Street bet. 2nd/3rd Ave.
NYC 10021 Mon-Wed 11-7, Thur-Fri 12-8, Sat 11-7

Anthropologie

The grown-up sibling of Urban Outfitters, this is a massive store packed with an eclectic selection of apparel and home furnishings aimed at a slightly older customer with hippie leanings (no surprises that it's big in L.A.). Find sportswear and casual basics that more often than not are ethnically inspired. Labels include Anthropologie, Bella Dahl, Billy Blues, Free People, Michael Stars, and Marimekko. Also, a vast selection of affordable housewares from Indian-style tableware to luxurious Provencal bath lotions and potions. 800-309-2500 www.anthropologie.com

SoHo 212-343-7070
375 West Broadway bet. Broome/Spring
NYC 10012 Mon-Sat 11-8, Sun 11-6

Flatiron 212-627-5885
85 Fifth Avenue at 16th St.
NYC 10003 Mon-Sat 10-8, Sun 11-7

Antique Boutique

Antique Boutique sells just that: vintage fashion, from the Forties to the Eighties. There are jeans by Levi's, Wrangler, and Seventies classic Jordache, rayon shirts, dresses, halter

A.P.C.

tops, leathers, Hawaiian shirts, raincoats, T-shirts, and just about anything else with a retro feel. A favorite among the growing ranks of vintage obsessives.

NoHo   **212-995-5577**
712-714 Broadway   bet. 4th/Astor Place
NYC 10003   Mon-Thur 11-9, Fri & Sat 11-10, Sun 12-8

Antoin

A reliable neighborhood store packed with hip shoes. Although you won't come across any heavy-hitter designer labels, you're still guaranteed to find lots of designer looks like stilettos, fashionable mules, and everything in between. Names include Petra, Rinaldi and Enzo Burini alongside Antoin's house label. But be warned: despite their lack of designer names, these shoes don't come cheap.

Upper East Side   **212-249-6703**
1110 Lexington Avenue   bet. 77/78th St.
NYC 10021   Mon-Fri 9-8, Sat-Sun 11-8

Anya Hindmarch

This quirky London handbag designer turns out sophisticated and witty collections of Italian-crafted designs. Choose from classics in scratch-resistant, luxurious leathers, evening numbers in couture satins and velvets, and cotton or silk bags with playful, vintage photographic images of dogs, bartenders, and drive-thru wedding chapels. Resort bags are printed with kitsch maps of the Cote D'Azur or St Barths. Each bag carries (stamped or hand-sewn) a dainty "bow" logo. The fashion crowd are still carrying last year's personalized bags, complete with photos of their owners' choosing. Pay $180-$260 for print bags and $400-$1,400 for leather handbags (for pony hair, expect to pay up to $2,000). Small leathergoods, jewelry, wallets, travel and make-up bags also available.   www.anyahindmarch.com

Upper East Side   **212-750-3974**
29 East 60th Street   bet. Park/Madison Ave.
NYC 10022   Mon-Sat 10-7

SoHo   **212-343-8147**
115 Greene Street   bet. Prince/Spring
NYC 10012   Mon-Sat 11-7, Sun 12-6

☆ A.P.C.

A.P.C., an abbreviation for Atelier de Production et Creations, is a favorite among fashion insiders seeking urban basics that are cool without trying. Owner/designer Jean Touitou produces a chicly understated collection of lightweight dress shirts, cool sweatshirts, chinos, sweaters and outerwear. They also have a fantastic selection of underground CDs and some of the coolest jeans (approximately $109-$120) around. Staff are super-cool, but friendly.   www.apc.com

SoHo   **212-966-9685**
131 Mercer Street   bet. Prince/Spring
NYC 10012   Mon-Sat 11-7, Sun 12-6

The Apartment
This hip space blazed a new trend through the retail scene: store as reality entertainment, where the customers (and occasionally, models) play the role of performer/observer and the shop and merchandise become the stage and props. As one would expect, The Apartment's primary focus is on groovy furniture, kitchen equipment and bathroom fixtures; however, cutting-edge clothing and accessories from Hidden, Not Tom, Dick and Harry, and the Apartment T-shirt line can be found among the housewares.

Soho   **212-219-3661**
101 Crosby Steet   bet. Prince/Spring
NYC 10012   Mon-Sat 11-7, Sun 12-6

April Cornell
While most people come to April Cornell for her lovely table and bed linens, she also features a collection of dresses, jackets, skirts, nighties and hats for women and children in delightful combinations of Indian-inspired fabrics.   www.aprilcornell.com

Upper West Side   **212-799-4342**
487 Columbus Avenue   bet. 83/84th St.
NYC 10024   Mon-Sat 10-8, Sun 11-7

Arche
A super-popular family-owned French company known for comfortable, spongy leather shoes in a myriad of colors and styles. They might not be terribly refined for the grownups but the thick rubber soles and clunky heels—printed with everything from Klimt paintings to zebras to American flags—continue to do it for younger customers.

Upper East Side   **212-439-0700**
995 Madison Avenue   at 77th St.
NYC 10021   Mon-Fri 10-7, Sat 10-6, Sun 12-5

Upper East Side   **212-838-1933**
1045 Third Avenue   bet. 61/62nd St.
NYC 10021   Mon-Fri 10-7, Sat 10-6, Sun 12-5

Midtown West   **212-262-5488**
128 West 57th Street   bet. 6/7th Ave.
NYC 10019   Mon-Fri 10-7, Sat 10-6, Sun 12-5

SoHo   **646-613-8700**
123 Wooster Street   bet. Spring/Prince
NYC 10012   Mon-Sat 11-7, Sun 12-6

NoHo   **212-529-4808**
10 Astor Place   bet. B'way/Lafayette
NYC 10003   Mon-Fri 10-7, Sat 10-6, Sun 12-5

Arleen Bowman
Arleen Bowman sells casual sportswear with a capital C. Her collection features signature two-pocket shirts in perforated suede, linen, silk, cotton and velvet plus relaxed skirts, pants and coats. In addition, find traveling suits, sweaters, dresses, T-shirts, tops and jeans from Garfield & Marks,

Margaret O'Leary, Lileth, Cambio, Womyn and 3 Dots. Accessories include shoes, jewelry and handbags.

West Village — 212-645-8740
353 Bleecker Street — bet. West 10th St./Charles
NYC 10014 — Mon-Sat 12-7, Sun 1-6

Arthur Gluck Shirtmakers

Gluck specializes in custom shirts at reasonable prices ($200). Hand-sewn monograms and mother-of-pearl buttons are a trademark. Orders take approximately one month. www.shirtcreations.com

Midtown West — 212-755-8165
47 West 57th Street — bet. 5/6th Ave.
NYC 10019 — Mon-Thur 9-5, Fri 9-2

Ascot Chang

One of New York's finest shirt-makers, Ascot Chang caters to some of the world's nattiest dressers with made-to-measure suits and overcoats, too. Choose from 2,000 luxurious fabrics and know that your purchase will last forever. If your wallet isn't that flush, Chang also features off-the-rack shirts, sportcoats, blazers and overcoats. Furnishings, pajamas and silk robes available. Custom-made suits start at $1,700, while shirts start at $90. www.ascotchang.com

Midtown West — 212-759-3333
7 West 57th Street — bet. 5/6th Ave.
NYC 10019 — Mon-Sat 9:30-6

Assets London

One of the cooler—and more colorful—stores on the Upper West Side, Assets sells a youthful edit of labels like Philosophy di Alberta Ferretti, Diane von Furstenberg, Jill Stuart, the hipper-than-hip DieselStyleLab and lots and lots of D&G. Also browse cool sneakers and the odd pair of ridiculously fashionable designer sunglasses. For bored boyfriends, there's a couch and a monitor playing catwalk videos (Gisele in a swimsuit should keep their interest).

Upper West Side — 212-874-8253
464 Columbus Avenue — bet. 82/83rd St.
NYC 10024 — Mon-Sat 11-8, Sun 12-7

TriBeCa — 212-219-8777
152 Franklin Street — bet. Hudson/Varick
NYC 10013 — Mon-Sat 10-7

A. Tempo

A super-girly store for that knockout party dress. A great selection features beaded and sequined evening dresses, flowy chiffon column dresses, and floor-length skirts paired with spaghetti-strap tops. Embellish your fancy outfit with coordinating accessories like beaded purses, jewelry, shawls and a ton of diamante hair ornaments.

Upper West Side — 212-769-0368
290 Columbus Avenue — bet. 73/74th St.
NYC 10023 — Mon-Sat 11-8, Sun 12-7

A. Testoni

An established footwear retailer from Bologna, Italy, A. Testoni features high-quality leather shoes that are the epitome of understatement. For men, find hand-made and bench-made dress shoes, as well as slip-ons and loafers. For women, styles run from loafers and boots to pumps and eveningwear. Check out the "Duckling" line, a casual, rubber-soled moccasin in suede or leather retailing from $245-$365. Handbags, briefcases, scarves, ties, belts and luggage also available. Expensive. 877-testoni.

Fifth Avenue   **212-223-0909**
665 Fifth Avenue   bet. 52/53rd St.
NYC 10022   Mon-Fri 10-7, Sat 10-6:30, Sun 12-5

A.T. Harris Formalwear

A brilliant source for renting a tuxedo, especially for weddings. Expect to pay $145 to $195 for a 24-hour rental. Shirts and the necessary black tie accoutrements are also available. www.atharris.com

Midtown East   **212-682-6325**
11 East 44th Street, 2nd Floor   bet. Madison/5th Ave.
NYC 10017   Mon-Fri 9-6, Thur 9-7
Sat 10-4 by appointment

Athlete's Foot

It's a festival of sneakers for every sport on the planet—be it aerobics, tennis, running, basketball or just plain posing. You'll find every top brand, including Adidas, New Balance, Nike and Reebok, although don't expect the staff to be too knowledgeable about the product. Children's sizes from toddler to size 6. www.theathletesfoot.com

Upper East Side   **212-223-8022**
1031 Third Avenue   at 61st St.
NYC 10021   Mon-Sat 10-8, Sun 11-6

Upper West Side   **212-579-2153**
2265 Broadway   bet. 81/82nd St.
NYC 10024   Mon-Sat 10-8, Sun 11-6

Upper West Side   **212-961-9556**
2563 Broadway   bet. 96/97th St.
NYC 10025   Mon-Sat 10-9, Sun 11-6

Midtown East   **212-317-1920**
655 Lexington Avenue   at 55th St.
NYC 10022   Mon-Sat 10-8:30, Sun 12-6:30

Midtown East   **212-867-4599**
41 East 42nd Street   bet. Madison/Vanderbilt Ave.
NYC 10017   Mon-Sat 9-8:30, Sun 11-6

Midtown West   **212-768-3195**
1568 Broadway   at 47th St.
NYC 10036   Mon-Sat 9-10, Sun 10-9

Midtown West   **212-629-8200**
46 West 34th Street   bet. 5/6th Ave.
NYC 10001   Mon-Sat 9-9, Sun 10-8

Midtown West 212-947-6972
390 Fifth Avenue bet. 35th/36th St
NYC 10018 Mon-Sat 9-9, Sun 9-8:30

NoHo 212-260-0360
60 East 8th Street at B'way
NYC 10003 Mon-Sat 9:30-10, Sun 12-7

Atomic Passion

Don't mess with the folks at Atomic Passion, this legendary, kitsch-heavy vintage store. "Buy or Die" reads their business card, which also boasts a skull and crossbones in case you didn't get the message. Luckily, buying is easy (if you have time to rummage through racks and racks of clothes) at this laid-back shop, which carries an eclectic mix of clothing, a huge amount of shoes, handbags and sunglasses. If you can see beyond the endless strands of Christmas lights and fake fruit on the ceiling, that is…

East Village 212-533-0718
430 East 9th Street bet. Ave. A/1st Ave.
NYC 10009 Mon-Sun 1-9

Atrium

Atrium stocks the proverbial alphabet of streetwear designer labels. Find sportswear and casual clothes like jeans, tanks, sweaters, and T-shirts by Diesel, Miss Sixty, Seven, DKNY, Iceberg, Hugo Boss, G-Star and Evisu.

NoHo 212-473-9200
644 Broadway at Bleecker
NYC 10012 Mon-Sat 10-9, Sun 11-8

Au Chat Botté

A venerable East Side children's shop that features top-of-the-line European clothing brands and luxurious bassinets and crib furnishings. It's recognized for its fine quality traditional clothing, so your child will be beautifully dressed in everything from hand-smocked dresses and dainty blouses to rompers and knit outfits. From newborn to size 4.

Upper East Side 212-722-6474
1192 Madison Avenue bet. 87/88th St.
NYC 10028 Mon-Sat 10-6

Avirex

Rappers and Red Baron wannabes get their sporty leather looks from Avirex. Since 1975, Jeff Clyman has been fashioning hides for sports legends, rock stars, actors and aviators (he's an official supplier to the U.S. Air Force). His colorful collegiate jackets, motorcycle numbers, oversized baseball bombers, jeans and T-shirts (heavily logo'd with the Avirex name) are sold at this SoHo shop. Don't miss the bright yellow bomber at the back of the store, surrounded by other encased model planes. www.avirex.com

SoHo 212-925-5456
652 Broadway bet. Bleecker/Bond
NYC 10012 Mon-Sat 11-7, Sun 12-6

Avitto

In the heart of Soho, Avitto offers footwear styles that cover all the bases. Women can choose from mules, pumps, slingbacks, evening shoes and a large boot selection, while the fellas can browse business and casual shoes from sandals to $800 alligator lace-ups. Labels include Gianfranco Ferré, Alberto Zago, Byblos, Yoriko Powell, Avitto, Trussardi, Rodolfo Zengarini and Calvin Klein.   www.avitto.com

SoHo **212-219-7501**
424 West Broadway bet. Prince/Spring
NYC 10012   Mon-Thur 11-8, Fri, Sat 11-8:30, Sun 11-8

A/X Armani Exchange

This 10,000-sq. ft. emporium caters to the fashion conscious in search of casual basics with the ever-vital Armani logo. Find jeans, T-shirts, pants, sweaters, jackets and outerwear that are relaxed and hip—the denim skirts are especially cool. Think an upscale designer Gap—especially since it's just launched Armani's famously well-fitting jeans collection, which hasn't been available in the U.S. until now. Prices are surprisingly reasonable and quality is up to the lofty Armani standards.   www.armaniexchange.com

Fifth Avenue **212-980-3037**
645 Fifth Avenue at 51st St.
NYC 10022 Mon-Sat 10-8, Sun 10-7

SoHo **212-431-6000**
568 Broadway at Prince
NYC 10012 Mon-Sat 10-8, Sun 11-7

Baby Blue Line (BBL)

Korean designer Eunjoo Lee adds more diversity to NoLiTa with her collection of sportswear and informal eveningwear. Her design philosophy: cater to all body types and make clothes comfortable and easy-to-wear. Many of her dresses, skirts and tops incorporate custom-made screen prints and unique fabrics like crushed, wrinkled silks. Although the clothes are well-priced, the look probably won't appeal to everyone.

NoLiTa **212-226-5866**
238 Mott Street bet. Prince/Spring
NYC 10012 Mon-Sun 12-7

Bagutta

A spacious downtown boutique with seriously fabulous clothes from the world's top designers, including Ann Demeulemeester, Dolce & Gabbana, Jean Paul Gaultier, Stella McCartney, Christian Dior (they love Dior here), Roberto Cavalli, Marn, and Olivier Theyskens. Look out for saucy, frilly dresses from hot, new New York designer Zac Posen. The atmosphere is relaxed and the sales staff knowledgeable.

SoHo **212-925-5216**
402 West Broadway at Spring
NYC 10012 Mon-Sat 11-7, Sun 12-6

Bambini

Bakers 👫
In the tourist wasteland around the Empire State Building, there are a few clothing and shoe shops not aimed at the itinerants. One of the longest denizens, the shoe store Baker, recently moved a few doors down to this larger, updated location. Suiting the area, its offerings are more mass than class, focusing on such labels as Steve Madden, Guess, Diesel and its own Bakers line and designs from bowling-style sneakers to fringed, suede calf-length boots. Fashionable footwear at middle-market prices.

Midtown East   **212 279-7016**
1 East 34th Street   at 5th Ave.
NYC 10001   Mon-Fri 9-8:30, Sat 10-9, Sun 10-7

Baldwin Formalwear 👨
Need a tux? Specialists Baldwin give you the option of buying or renting. Find top designer labels like Ralph Lauren, Christian Dior, Oscar de la Renta, and Perry Ellis. Pay $110 and up to rent and $300-plus to buy. In addition, find all the necessary black-tie amenities like neckwear, vests and cummerbunds, as well as shoes by Fredericko Deleon.   www.nyctuxedos.com

Midtown West   **212-245-8190**
52 West 56th Street, 2nd Fl.   bet. 5/6th Ave.
NYC 10019   Mon-Fri 9-7, Sat 10-5

Bally 👫
The Swiss brand Bally is another of those venerable companies trying for a new image, with mixed success. Creative director Scott Fellows (who is rumored to be leaving at the end of the year) has come up with a women's collection full of cool classics like pencil skirts, wrap leather jackets, comfortable knitwear, shearlings, suedes and storm coats, while his menswear is young, sleek and Prada-esque. It may have all been too hip for the staid Bally customer, however. Stripes and interlocked "B's" adorn Bally's luggage and handbag collection in colors like turquoise blue, buttery yellow and olive gray/green. As for the footwear, check out their riding boots and fantastically chic (and fantastically expensive) cross logo trainers.
    800-332-2559   www.bally.com

Midtown East   **212-751-9082**
628 Madison Avenue   at 59th St.
NYC 10153   Mon-Fri 10-6:30, Thur 10-7
    Sat 10-6, Sun 12-5

Bambini 👨
Every child should be so lucky to be all dressed up in a jaunty Bambini outfit. There is everything from casual and back-to-school basics to party and dress wear. Bambini is packed with Italian brand names featuring traditional looks in pants, dresses, shirts, sweaters, tees, rompers and more. Highlights include their private-label shoes and hand-knit sweaters. From newborn to size 8.

Banana Republic

Upper East Side   212-717-6742
1367 Third Avenue   at 78th St.
NYC 10021   Mon-Sat 10-6:30, Sun 12-5

Banana Republic

Banana Republic remains a one-stop shop for great-looking, affordable basics that are more chic than trendy. Feel-good fabrics and clean sensible shapes are the label's hallmarks in suits, sportswear, cashmeres, shoes and accessories. Their T-shirts are second-to-none and their flat-front "Martin" pants are an instant classic. Head to the sale corner where you can find cute skirts for as low as $15.   888-277-8953   www.bananarepublic.com

Fifth Avenue (Flagship Store)   212-974-2350
626 Fifth Avenue   at Rockefeller Center
NYC 10022   Mon-Sat 10-8, Sun 11-7

Upper East Side   212-570-2465
1136 Madison Avenue   bet. 84/85th St.
NYC 10028   Mon-Sat 10-7, Sun 12-6

Upper East Side   212-288-4279
1110 Third Avenue   at 66th St.
NYC 10021   Mon-Sat 10-8, Sun 11-7

Upper East Side   212-360-1296
1529 Third Avenue   at 86th St.
NYC 10028   Mon-Sat 10-9, Sun 11-7

Upper West Side   212-787-2064
2360 Broadway   at 86th St.
NYC 10024   Mon-Sat 10-9, Sun 11-7

Upper West Side   212-873-9048
215 Columbus Avenue   bet. 69/70th St.
NYC 10023   Mon-Wed 10-8, Thur-Sat 10-9, Sun 11-7

Midtown East   212-751-5570
130 East 59th Street   at Lex. Ave.
NYC 10022   Mon-Fri 9:30-8:30, Sat 9:30-8, Sun 10-7

Midtown East   212-490-3127
107 East 42nd Street   at Grand Central
NYC 10017   Mon-Fri 8-9, Sat 10-8, Sun 11-6

Midtown West (Flagship)   212-244-3060
17-19 West 34th Street   bet. 5/6th Ave.
NYC 10001   Mon-Sat 10-8:30, Sun 11-7

Flatiron (M)   212-366-4630
114 Fifth Avenue   bet. 17/18 St.
NYC 10011   Mon-Fri 10-9, Sat 10-8, Sun 11-7

Flatiron (W)   212-366-4630
89 Fifth Avenue   bet. 16/17th St.
NYC 10003   Mon-Fri 10-9, Sat 10-8, Sun 11-7

Chelsea (M)   212-645-1032
111 Eighth Avenue   bet. 15/16th St.
NYC 10011   Mon-Sat 10-9, Sun 12-7

West Village   212-473-9570
205 Bleecker Street   at 6th Ave.
NYC 10012   Mon-Sat 10-8, Sun 11-7

Barbara Feinman Millinery

SoHo (W)   **212-925-0308**
550 Broadway   bet. Spring/Prince
NYC 10012   Mon-Sat 10-8, Sun 11-7

SoHo (M)   **212-334-3034**
528 Broadway   at Spring
NYC 10012   Mon-Sat 10-8, Sun 11-7

Barami

Barami should be the first stop for cost-conscious corporate women seeking contemporary style. Rifle through suits with matching coordinates, tailored shirts, separates and accessories, all domestically manufactured and in fashionable, well-priced styles.   www.barami.com

Upper East Side   **212-988-3470**
1404 Second Avenue   at 73rd St.
NYC 10021   Mon-Sat 11-8, Sun 12-6

Midtown East   **212-980-9333**
136 East 57th Street   at Lex. Ave.
NYC 10022   Mon- Fri 9-9, Sat 10-8, Sun 12-6

Midtown East   **212-682-2550**
375 Lexington Avenue   at 41st St.
NYC 10017   Mon-Fri 8-7:30, Sat-Sun 11-6

Midtown West   **212-967-2990**
485 Seventh Avenue   bet. 36/37th St.
NYC 10018   Mon-Fri 7:30-7:30, Sat 10-6, Sun 12-6

Fifth Avenue   **212-949-1000**
535 Fifth Avenue   at 45th St.
NYC 10017   Mon-Fri 8-8, Sat 10-7, Sun 12-6

Barbara Bui

This enormous, minimalist shop serves as a backdrop for this cool Parisian designer's monochromatic ready-to-wear collection. Bui's forte is her extensive range of beautifully tailored pants, ranging from bootleg to man-tailored—"I always make at least three cuts of pants, for different bodies", she says—but you can also choose from a huge number of jackets, skirts, sweaters, dresses, form-fitted tees (shrink-wrapped—very groovy), outerwear and shoes. A tip: wait for the sales, when the pricey numbers are reduced by 50%.   www.barbarabui.fr

SoHo   **212-625-1938**
117 Wooster Street   bet. Prince/Spring
NYC 10012   Mon-Sat 11-7, Sun 12-6

Barbara Feinman Millinery

All of Barbara Feinman's toppers are made on the premises at this special little hat shop, and she is always happy to educate a customer in the art of hand-blocked hats or to do a custom fitting. Fedoras, cloches, panamas, cowboy hats and lampshade hats come in such fabrics as straw, raffia, canvas, denim, felt, velvet and velour. Accessories include moderately priced handbags and jewelry.

Barbara Shaum

East Village
66 East 7th Street
NYC 10003

212-358-7092
bet. 1/2nd Ave.
Mon-Sat 12:30-8, Sun 1-7

Barbara Shaum

Barbara Shaum is the haute sandal specialist, having been whipping up beautiful woven versions for almost 50 years. But she has experienced something of a reinvention thanks to king-of-cool Calvin Klein, who last year paired his men's collection with Shaum's gladiator- or thong-style custom-made creations. Since then she's hit the big leagues, with her shoes on the fabulous feet of model Iman, photographer and trend-maker Steve Meisel and designer Ralph Lauren. Prices run from $200 to $500. Belts also available.

East Village
60 East 4th Street
NYC 10003

212-254-4250
bet. Bowery/2nd Ave.
Wed-Fri 1-8, Sat 1-6

☆ Barneys New York

Oh, Barneys, hallowed be thy name! This too-chic-to-speak fashion emporium is God's gift to shopping. In addition to excellent beauty—check out the new Foundation level on the lower ground floor (get it?)—and accessories departments, it boasts five floors of perfectly edited and ultra-hip women's and men's wear, from cute-cool Cacharel to conceptual Yohji Yamamoto. Young fashionistas head at light-speed to the 7th and 8th floor Co-op for the hippest denim, swimwear, lingerie, shoes and accessories from such labels as the cult Marc by Marc Jacobs, girly Tocca, Jill Stuart, Paul & Joe and a special section devoted entirely to Miu Miu shoes. Other departments include outerwear; designer shoes—from Manolos to Michel Perry; lingerie; Barneys' private label (designed by hot new designer Behnaz Sarafpour); a maternity line, aptly named "Procreation;" a newborn and toddler section, and Chelsea Passage, a tabletop and gift department. Then there's a vintage department and a fully-fledged luxury bridal salon that features over 60 unbelievably chic bridal styles. In contrast, the men's store is an oasis of calm, where classic types can go for suits from the likes of Oxxford, Ralph Lauren Purple Label, Hickey-Freeman, Kilgour French Stanbury and Huntsman and coolsters can choose from such designers as Armani, Dolce & Gabbana, Prada and Helmut Lang. Other departments include men's furnishings, made-to-measure suits and dress shirts, designer shoes, sportswear, rainwear, outerwear, special sizes, casual wear, formalwear, shoes and, phew, accessories. If you are nearly dropping from shopping, find sustenance at Barneys fabulous in-store restaurant Fred's, which is the latest "in" spot for fashionistas. And did we tell you about the twice-yearly warehouse sales? Legendary. 888-222-7639 www.barneys.com

Upper East Side
660 Madison Avenue
NYC 10021

212-826-8900
at 61st St.
Mon-Fri 10-8, Sat 10-7, Sun 11-6

☆ Barneys Co-op

Just when you thought it couldn't get any better, along comes the joy that is Barneys younger, hipper (if possible) sister, Co-op. And there are now two locations—the spanking new 7,000-square-foot store on Wooster Street in Soho and the established location in Chelsea. Head to either for all the looks you will find on the seventh and eighth floors of the department store like—take a deep breath—Theory, Seven, MRS, Alice and Olivia, Diane von Furstenberg, Magda Berliner, 2katayone and Marc by Marc Jacobs, plus Kiehl's and Somme Institute skincare. The first floor houses accessories, jewelry and cosmetics, while the lower level carries jeans, shoes and T-shirts. Basically, it's hipster heaven. www.barneys.com

Chelsea	**212-593-7800**
236 West 18th Street	bet. 7/8th Ave.
NYC 10011	Mon-Fri 11-8, Sat 11-7, Sun 12-6

SoHo	**212-965-9964**
116 Wooster Street	bet. Prince/Spring
NYC 10012	Mon-Sat 11-7, Sun 12-6

Basic Basic

As the shop's name none-too-subtly suggests, you can find great basic contemporary junior clothing here. Choose from a great selection of T-shirts by Petit Bâteau, 3 Dots (great colors and original styles) and Juicy Couture, as well as jeans by Buffalo and Juicy. Cute skirts, dresses, sweaters and pants complete the easy-breezy assortment.

NoHo	**212-477-5711**
710 Broadway	bet. Washington Pl./4th St.
NYC 10003	Mon-Sat 11-8, Sun 12-7

Basiques

A sweetly chic clothing and linen store, with every item imported from France and Italy. The jaunty clothing lives up to the basique name, with simple, pre-packaged white shirts, navy shirtdresses and classic black tanks retailing for $65. The linen collection is more decorative, featuring classic prints and embroidery. The colors are simple—French blue, red, black and white—and the staff charming.

West Village	**212-414-1783**
380 Bleecker Street	bet. Perry/Charles
NYC 10014	Mon 12-7, Tues-Sat 12-8, Sun 12-6

Bati

A nice'n'handy neighborhood shoe store featuring the latest in footwear designs from European labels like Bati, No Name, Sebastian, Giancarlo Paoli, Pura Lopez and Enrico Antinori. Styles include boots, flats, pumps, mules, sandals and wedges in trendy fabrications and shapes. Prices run from $60 to $500 for the fancy stuff.

Upper East Side	**646-497-0581**
1052 Third Avenue	bet. 62/63rd St.
NYC 10021	Mon-Sat 11-7:30, Sun 12-6

BCBG by Max Azria

Upper West Side   **212-724-7214**
2323 Broadway   bet. 84/85th St.
NYC 10024   Mon-Sat 11-8, Sun 12-7:30

☆ BCBG by Max Azria

Designer Max Azria chose the name BCBG because it stands for "bon chic, bon genre," Parisian slang for "good style, good attitude." And that's the secret to BCBG's phenomenal success: the perfect balance of classic style with chic, cute detailing. It's impossible not to find something that makes you look fabulous in here—from lightly beaded party dresses and figure-hugging pants to flirty, floaty tops. What Azria does so well is take the current trends and make them accessible—and desirable—to every cool girl in town, especially those who didn't marry a millionaire. Accessories include shoes, handbags like killer evening clutches, eyewear, and jewelry.   www.bcbg.com

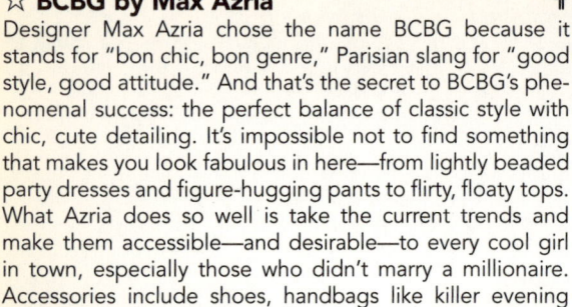

Upper East Side   **212-717-4225**
770 Madison Avenue   at 66th St
NYC 10021   Mon-Sat 10-7, Thur 10-8, Sun 12-6

SoHo   **212-625-2723**
120 Wooster Street   bet. Prince/Spring
NYC 10012   Mon-Sat 11-7, Sun 12-6

Beau Brummel

The perfect shop for the busy executive, offering suits, furnishings, sportswear, casual wear, outerwear and accessories from classic-cool European labels like Cerruti, Allegri, Gran Sasso and Canali, as well as private label. On the spot tailoring, excellent service and a relaxed atmosphere actually make suit shopping a pleasure rather than a pain...   www.beaubrummel.com

SoHo   **212-219-2666**
421 West Broadway   bet. Prince/Spring
NYC 10012   Mon-Wed 11-6:45
    Thur-Sat 11-7:30, Sun 12-7

Bebe

If you're a flaunt-it kinda girl, then Bebe is the store for you. Its sexy pieces are heavy on the Lycra and are no doubt devilishly effective! Pants, skirts, dresses, navel-baring tops, tanks, tees and cute accessories make up the saucy collection. Only for the young, the brave...and Britney Spears wannabes. Sizes 0-12.   www.bebe.com

Upper East Side   **212-517-2323**
1044 Madison Avenue   bet. 79/80th St.
NYC 10021   Mon-Fri 10-8, Sat 10-7, Sun 11-6

Upper East Side   **212-935-2444**
1127 Third Avenue   at 66th St.
NYC 10021   Mon-Fri 10-8, Sat 10-7, Sun 11-6

Midtown East   **212-588-9060**
805 Third Avenue   at 50th St.
NYC 10022   Mon-Fri 10-8, Sat 10-7, Sun 12-5

Flatiron 212-675-2323
100 Fifth Avenue at 15th St.
NYC 10011 Mon-Fri 10-8, Sat 10-7, Sun 11-6

Bebe Thompson

Children's wear that will have the customers positively cooing. Look out for casual basics and dress-up wear from Claude Velle, Lili Gaufrette, Lilly Pulitzer, Chevignon and Kenzo Jungle and party dresses by Rosetta Millington. Snuggly pajamas, bathing suits, outerwear, knits, bonnets, socks and hair accessories will have your child looking adorable (and well-dressed, of course) from head to toe. From newborn to 16 years.

Upper East Side 212-249-4740
1216 Lexington Avenue bet. 82/83rd St.
NYC 10028 Mon-Fri 10-6, closed weekends

Behrle

All hail the leather queen! Designer Carla Dawn Behrle turns out sexy clothes in vibrant brights and neutrals with an awesome fit. No wonder her custom-made pieces are coveted by flaunt-it celebrities. Leather pants are her forte—rocking it in every style from boot- and straight-leg to hip huggers and capris. Other sex-o-matic items include bustiers, jackets, skirts and shirts. The customer has three buying options: off-the-rack (it fits you perfectly), special order (it fits, but you'd rather have it in a different color, or it needs a small alteration), and, finally, custom (any design, fit or color your heart desires). Expect a one- to two-month delivery. Custom, sadly, is only for men.

TriBeCa 212-243-8877
89 Franklin Street bet. Church/B'way
NYC 10013 By appointment only

Belgian Shoes

Belgian Shoes are pretty much what they say: distinctive, hand-made loafers that continue their fine tradition of being Waspy status symbols. The range is incredible: every look imaginable, from suede to leather to positively quirky crushed velvet. If you feel the need for a royal crest or crown (no wardrobe is complete!) they will add one just for you. Once hooked, you may end up collecting every one of their 50 color combinations. Sizing is unusual and runs two to three sizes below normal. Expect to wait 12 to18 months for special orders.

Midtown East 212-755-7372
110 East 55th Street bet. Park/Lex. Ave.
NYC 10022 Mon-Fri 9-4:30, Sat 10-3

Benetton

Italian label Benetton is a truly global brand that sells rainbow colored, energetic casual clothes for men and women. Best are the sweaters ($44-$68) in every style and color imaginable but it also does a nifty line in work suits, A-line skirts ($48-$78), T-shirts, jeans, wool coats ($178-

$218), awesome swimwear, intimates, shoes and accessories. Benetton gives true meaning to the term "lifestyle" label because these are clothes purpose-built for easy living. 800-535-4491 www.benetton.com

Fifth Avenue — **212-317-2501**
597 Fifth Avenue — bet. 48/49th St.
NYC 10017 — Mon-Sat 10-7, Thur 10-8, Sun 12-5

NoHo — **212-533-0230**
749 Broadway — bet. 8th St./Astor Pl.
NYC 10003 — Mon-Sat 10-9, Sun 12-8

Midtown East — **212-818-0449**
666 Third Avenue — at 42nd St.
NYC 10017 — Mon-Sat 10-7, Sun 12-5

Chelsea — **646-638-1086**
120 Seventh Avenue — at 17th St.
NYC 10011 — Mon-Sat 11-7, Sun 12-6

SoHo — **212-941-8010**
555 Broadway — bet. Spring/Prince
NYC 10012 — Mon-Sat 10-8, Sun 11-7

Ben Thylan Furs

Ben Thylan's extensive styles run the gamut from sporty to dressy. Its specialty: fur-lined or fur-trimmed water-repellent coats. These all-weather classics can be lined in any fur of your choosing, including mink, fox or sable. Cashmere, wool and camel's hair coats are also available. Services include color and fashion consultations, as well as storage and cleaning. www.benthylanfurs.com

Chelsea — **212-753-7700**
345 Seventh Avenue, 24th Fl. — bet. 29/30th St.
NYC 10001 — Mon-Fri 9-5, Sat 9-1
by appointment only

Beretta

Renowned the world over for its guns, Beretta also manufactures fine hunting, sporting and weekend wear—think an Italian version of Holland & Holland, or a real-life version of "White Mischief." Tweeds, lodens, fine cashmeres and wools make up the collection of classic sportswear fit for a king—or a safari.

Upper East Side — **212-319-3235**
718 Madison Avenue — bet. 63/64th St.
NYC 10021 — Mon-Sat 10-6

Bergdorf Goodman

Bergdorf's is the bee's knees in luxury retailing, from a first floor devoted to handbags, classic to adventurous jewelry, hosiery and accessories to five upper floors stocked with the chic to the edgy, including Richard Tyler, Alexander McQueen, Valentino, Chloé, Michael Kors, Chanel and Calvin Klein. The "Level of Beauty" is a lower-level cosmetics planet featuring exclusive beauty and skincare treatments, fragrances, spa products, Michael George's flower shop, Morganthal Federics' optical shop and the "Buff Spa" nail salon (fantastic pedicures and somewhere to rest your shopping bags). Other departments include designer and contemporary shoes (praise be—a whole room devoted to Manolo Blahnik!), lingerie, eveningwear, contemporary sportswear, suits, bridal, custom, outerwear and a genius gift and tabletop shop. The John Barrett Hair Salon, which delivers a great blow-out, and Susan Ciminelli Day Spa are housed on the ninth floor.   800-964-8619

Fifth Avenue 212-753-7300
754 Fifth Avenue bet. 57/58th St.
NYC 10019 Mon-Sat 10-7, Thur 10-8, Sun 12-6

Bergdorf Goodman Men

A huge, 45,000 square foot emporium which still somehow manages to have the feeling of an intimate and exclusive gentleman's club. It might have something to do with the classic labels in stock: Turnbull & Asser, Charvet and Ferragamo shirts and ties and traditional suit collections by Oxxford, Canali, Hickey-Freeman and Luciano Barbera. Not that they compromise cool: you'll also find Armani, Jil Sander, Etro and the sex appeal of Gucci. Custom lines include Saint Andrews, Kiton, Sartoria Attolini, Domenico Spano and Oxxford. Mark the sales in your calendar now—they're fantastic.   800-964-8619

Fifth Avenue 212-753-7300
745 Fifth Avenue at 58th St.
NYC 10022 Mon-Sat 10-7
Thur 10-8, Sun 12-6

Berk

If you want to make a cunning cashmere purchase, invest in one of Berk's sweaters and be assured you'll be swanning about in it for a lifetime. That's because the Ballantyne label sold here is world-renowned for top quality and craftmanship. Choose from classic styles like crew necks, turtlenecks, cardigans and twin sets in 60 glorious colors (can we have them all—please?) plus capes, stoles and accessories. Great velvet slippers, too.

Upper East Side 212-570-0285
781 Madison Avenue bet. 66/67th St.
NYC 10021 Mon-Sat 10-5:30

Best of Scotland

And it is. A top floor retreat that sells Scottish cashmere sweaters at terrific prices. They carry a full range of styles for men and women, from sizes 32 to 58, at prices which average an amazing 50 percent below retail. Crew necks priced at $390 uptown on Madison Avenue retail for around $190, so get in here fast! Delicious cashmere overcoats, lush scarves and mufflers are also available.

Fifth Avenue 212-644-0403
581 Fifth Avenue, Penthouse bet. 47/48th St.
NYC 10017 Mon-Sat 10-5:30

Betsey Bunky Nini

This well-edited store carries expensive European designers perfect for Upper East Siders looking for clothes with kick—an easy hybrid of ethnic and preppy. Best buys are found in the extensive sportswear and sweater selection—but there also are jackets, suits and eveningwear by labels like Cividini, René Lezard, Ines Raspoort, Peter Cohen, Piazza Sempione, Gunext and Paul Smith. Invest in some floaty Alberta Ferretti and you'll never look back. Accessories include handbags and jewelry.

Upper East Side   **212-744-6716**
980 Lexington Avenue   bet. 71/72nd St.
NYC 10021   Mon-Sat 10:30-6
Thur 10:30-7, closed Sunday

Betsey Johnson

Betsey Johnson's world is a fun, flirtatious and often completely far-out place to be. Johnson—who just celebrated her 60th birthday and is best known for cartwheeling down the runway at the end of her shows—sells wild, sexy designs that have dazzled and shocked women for over 20 years. Although she leans toward the over-the-top, her signature bias-cut slip dresses and coordinating girly cardigans are a sellout every year. Then there are the slinky micro minis, biased skirts, curvy pants, velvet and animal print pieces and fun holiday and special occasion dresses. Check out the outrageous shoes, which look like something Pebbles Flintstone would wear on a hot date with Bam-Bam.   www.betseyjohnson.com

Upper East Side   **212-734-1257**
1060 Madison Avenue   bet. 80/81st St.
NYC 10028   Mon-Sat 11-7, Sun 12-7

Upper East Side   **212-319-7699**
251 East 60th Street   bet. 2/3rd Ave.
NYC 10022   Mon-Sat 11-7, Sun 12-7

Upper West Side   **212-362-3364**
248 Columbus Avenue   bet. 71/72 St.
NYC 10023   Mon-Sat 11-7, Sun 12-7

SoHo   **212-995-5048**
138 Wooster Street   bet. Houston/Prince
NYC 10012   Mon-Sat 11-7, Sun 12-7

☆ Betwixt

Teen-shopping can be hell, what can we tell you, but Betwixt is there for you…It's a fabulous "tweens" lifestyle shop that totally meets the "I wanna be cool" priorities of in-between girls. Perfect for slumber-worthy intimates, stretchy print lace dresses, glittery tube tops and satin tanks, while the T-shirt rack and jeans selection will cause a feeding frenzy over such bestselling labels as Diesel, Hollywood, Miss Sixty, Killer, Roxy and Itsus. A separate dress-up area does the trick for special occasions like bar mitzvahs and graduations. You may have trouble extracting your teen from the front section, though, where she'll be loading up on glittery necklaces, earrings and rhinestone-encrusted sunglasses.

West Village   **212-243-8590**
245 West 10th Street   bet. Bleecker/Hudson
NYC 10014   Mon-Fri 11:30-6:30, Sat 11-6, Sun 12-5

Bicycle Habitat

On your bike! Bicycle Habitat features mountain, road and suspension bikes from manufacturers such as Specialized and Trek, priced from $250 to $3,000. High-end brands include Bontrager and Klein, with price tags that run from $1,000 to $4,000—don't forget to buy a lock! Lycra-lovely biking wear is available, as well as a lifetime service guarantee on all their bikes, bicycle repair classes and group bike rides. www.bicyclehabitat.com

SoHo   **212-431-3315**
244 Lafayette Street   bet. Prince/Spring
NYC 10012   Mon-Thur 10-7
Fri 10-6:30, Sat & Sun 10-6

Bicycle Renaissance

A fantastic selection of mountain, road and hybrid bikes from makers like Specialized, Cannondale, Trek and Klein. Price tags run from $330 to $4,000. Clothing, accessories and workshops make this a full-service—and freewheeling—destination.

Upper West Side   **212-724-2350**
430 Columbus Avenue   at 81st St.
NYC 10024   Mon-Fri 10:30-7, Sat 10-6, Sun 10-5

Big Drop

Big Drop is way cool. Indie rock plays as you check out progressive clothing for the 18-to-35 crowd from a funky mix of young designers: Earl Jeans, Juicy Couture, Vanessa Bruno, Big Drop, John Richmond, Joie, Tracy Reese, Easel, Inc. and more. Hip additions to the new West Broadway store include Development, Ya-ya, Petrozillia and Martin. They have a great range of equally funky handbags, too.

Upper East Side   **212-988-3344**
1321 Third Avenue   bet. 75/76th St.
NYC 10021   Mon-Sat 11-8, Sun 12-7

SoHo   **212-966-4299**
174 Spring Street   bet. Thompson/W. B'way
NYC 10012   Mon-Sat 11-8, Sun 12-8

SoHo   **212-226-9292**
425 West Broadway   bet. Prince/Spring St.
NYC 10012   Mon-Sat 11-8, Sun 12-8

Billy Martins

Ride 'em, cowboy! Straight to Billy Martins. This western-themed store is the best place around for handcrafted cowboy boots and fancy belts. Urban cowgirls and buckaroos will also find everything from suede jackets and skirts to cowboy shirts, jewelry and belt buckles. These are high-priced statement pieces that will get you back to your Ponderosa in complete style. 800-888-8915 www.billy-martin.com

Upper East Side   **212-861-3100**
220 East 60th Street   at 3rd Ave.
NYC 10022   Mon-Fri 10-7, Sat 10-6, Sun 12-5

Bis

Bis 👤

Keep an eagle eye on Bis because every other day this secondhand clothing store receives a delivery of designer merchandise straight from the bulging closets of well-dressed, well-heeled New Yorkers. Clever women head here for high-end European and American labels in tip-top condition—and fabulous prices. It's not uncommon to spot an Armani beaded evening jacket for $300 (retail price $1,500), a Hermès handbag for $900 (retail price $2,600) or a Michael Kors cashmere for $250 (retail price $1,250). You'll also find the occasional vintage piece like a Pucci dress. www.BisBiz.com

Upper East Side **212-396-2760**
1134 Madison Avenue, 2nd Fl. bet. 84/85th St.
NYC 10028 Mon-Thur 10-7
Fri & Sat 10-6, Sun 12-5

Bisou-Bisou 👤

Kiss kiss! No, not a fashion editor greeting but the English translation of this store name. French designer Michele Bohbot sees her clothing as being "about a woman who is not a child, but not really a woman—she is somewhere in between." This adds up to modern sportswear—with a hint of lace—that includes stretch pants, tight tops, dresses, skirts, shoes and accessories like cute fringed belts. Best to buy as separates to coordinate with your existing wardrobe rather than as a top-to-bottom look. Expect to pay $88 to $190 for pants, $165 to $299 for jackets and $38 to $120 for tops. Be warned: these are fashions for the young and lean. www.bisou-bisou.com

SoHo **212-260-9640**
474 West Broadway bet. Houston/Prince
NYC 10012 Mon-Sat 11-8, Sun 12-7

Blades Board and Skate 👨👩👦

In-line skating is still one of the hippest sports around and nowhere can you find the requisite cool accessories better than Blades. The selection includes in-line skates, skateboards, snowboards and ice skates, as well as the obligatory protective gear. Top it off with matching clothing and accessories and you're ready to roll. In-line skate rentals are $21.65 a day with a $200 deposit. Helpful, nice sales staff.
www.blades.com

Upper East Side **212-996-1644**
160 East 86th Street bet. 3rd/Lex. Ave.
NYC 10028 Mon-Fri 10-8, Sat 10-7, Sun 10-6

Upper West Side **212-787-3911**
120 West 72nd Street bet. Columbus/B'way
NYC 10023 Mon-Sat 10-9, Sun 11-7

Midtown West **212-563-2488**
901 Sixth Avenue at Manhattan Mall at 32nd St.
NYC 10001 Mon-Sun 10-8

Bloomingdale's

Chelsea 212-336-6299
23rd Street and West Street at Chelsea Piers, Pier 62
NYC 10011 Mon-Sat 10-8, Sun 10-7

NoHo 212-477-7350
659 Broadway bet. 3rd St./Bleecker
NYC 10012 Mon-Sat 10-9, Sun 11-7

Bloomers

Comfy, cosy and covetable, this store sells children's clothing and sleepwear alongside their selection of women's nighties, pj's, and robes. Mothers can shop one side of the store for easy pieces from Hanro, Pluto, Cherry Pie, Treesha Inc, At Home, House Inc. and Only Hearts, then head to the other to please the kids. Find playwear and sleepwear from Skibby Doodles, Sweet Potato, Marimekko and more as well as baby accessories and rugs. Sizes for clothing from 3 months to 6X and for sleepwear to Size 16.

Upper East Side 212-570-9529
1042 Lexington Avenue bet. 74/75th St.
NYC 10021 Mon-Sat 10-6:30, Thur 10-7

Bloomingdale's

Every New York tourist wants to experience the mythical Bloomingdale's and they should, at least once anyway. After all, it would be a dull shopper who didn't even want to take a glance at Harrods on his or her first ever visit to London, or at Galeries Lafayette in Paris. So, Bloomies is a must. But make sure you're high on energy because it can be an exhausting adventure for even the pro shopper—the crush of people extends well past the first floor and it's incredibly easy to get lost in the plus-size section when you're actually looking for shoes. But you must persist! The store continues to be a fashion trendsetter with innovative merchandising concepts and sales extravaganzas. Boulevard Four showcases the latest designer fashions for women by Armani, Calvin Klein, Chanel, Donna Karan, Ralph Lauren and others, while the contemporary selection includes Marc by Marc Jacobs (they have the best range in the city), Trina Turk, Theory, Helmut Lang and William B. Men's fashions run from designer suits and formalwear to sportswear and casual wear from Joseph Abboud, Canali, Donna Karan, Hugo Boss and Kenneth Cole, as well as their own private label. Also find one of the largest—and most intimidating—cosmetics floors and accessories departments around and three floors of home furnishings and decorative accessories. An added plus is the outstanding service departments, which include personalized shopping, in-store TicketMaster, hotel delivery and bridal registry. For shoppers in need of a bite, or some shopping respite, choose from four in-house eateries. One warning: choose well, because returning goods can be a nightmare. 800-777-0000
www.bloomingdales.com

Midtown East   **212-705-2000**
1000 Third Avenue   bet. 59/60th St.
NYC 10022   Mon-Fri 10-8:30, Sat 10-7, Sun 11-7

Blue Bag

This is one of the cuter shops among the world of handbag boutiques that is NoLiTa. Husband-and-wife team Marnie and Pascal Legrand cover the gamut of designs from basic totes to whimsical one-offs to great looking wallets. Don't miss their nylon reversible tote by Ocaba, available in three sizes—and yes, in blue. Wear it one day as a relaxed shoulder tote and the next as a sporty look-a-like Hermès Kelly bag. New arrivals constantly, and in summer, they stock cool swimsuits, too. Prices run from $75 to $400.

NoLiTa   **212-966-8566**
266 Elizabeth Street   bet. Houston/Prince
NYC 10012   Mon-Sat 11-7, Sun 12-7

Bolton's

Easy access shopping, all over Manhattan. Head here for a selection of wardrobe staples that include business suits, blouses, sportswear, lingerie and accessories, all at discount prices. Buyer beware: you'll find yourself searching high and low for that designer label.

Upper East Side   **212-223-3450**
787 Lexington Avenue   bet. 61/62nd St.
NYC 10021   Mon-Fri 9:30-8:30, Sat 10-7, Sun 11-7

Upper East Side   **212-722-4419**
1180 Madison Avenue   at 86th St.
NYC 10028   Mon-Fri 10-8, Sat 10-7, Sun 12-6

Upper East Side   **212-639-9298**
1191 Third Avenue   bet. 69th/70th St.
NYC 10028   Mon-Fri 9-8, Sat-Sun 10-6

Midtown East   **212-980-6148**
800 Third Avenue   at 51st St
NYC 10018   Mon-Fri 9-7, Sat 10-7, Sun 11-6

Midtown East   **646-865-0898**
109 East 42nd Street   at Lex. Ave.
NYC 10017   Mon-Tues 9-7, Wed, Thur, Fri 9-8
           Sat, Sun 10-6

Midtown East   **212-684-3750**
4 East 34th Street   bet. Madison/5th Ave.
NYC 10016   Mon-Fri 9-7, Sat 10-7, Sun 11-6

Midtown West   **212-935-4431**
27 West 57th Street   bet. 5/6th Ave.
NYC 10019   Mon-Fri 10-8, Sat 10-7, Sun 12-6

Midtown West   **212-245-5227**
110 West 51st Street   at 6th Ave.
NYC 10020   Mon-Fri 8-6:30, Sat & Sun 10-6

Midtown West   **212-307-5089**
1700 Broadway   at 54th St.
NYC 10019   Mon, Tues & Fri 9-7
           Wed-Thur 9-8, Sat 10-7, Sun 10-6

Bond 07

A super-cool accessories wonderland where hip girls will be spoilt for choice. Think groovy eyewear from Selima Optique (plus a prescription glasses service), hats, handbags, vintage pieces, antiques, perfumes, shoes and jewelry, plus frilly lingerie and clothing from owner Selima Salaun's lingerie and ready-to-wear collection to European and hip downtown designer labels like Alice Roi, Cacharel, Mint and Australian dress queen Collette Dinnigan.

NoHo   **212-677-8487**
7 Bond Street   bet. B'way/Lafayette
NYC 10012   Mon-Sat 11-7, Thur 11-8, Sun 12-7

Bonpoint

If you're the type to play show-off with your child, the exclusive, French Bonpoint is the store for you. Luxury fabrics, attention to detail and impeccable tailoring are the keys to its well-earned reputation for the perfect fancy dress-up clothes—beautiful hand-smocked dresses, traditional blouses, shirts, pants, outerwear, swimwear and accessories, all at haute couture prices (maybe buy a size-up, in case they grow out of them in a month!) There also is a selection of casual clothes. Newborn to size 16 girls/8 boys. Could they make clothing for adults, please?

www.bonpoint.com

Upper East Side   **212-722-7720**
1269 Madison Avenue   at 91st St.
NYC 10128   Mon-Thur 10-6, Fri 10-5, Sat 11-5

Upper East Side   **212-879-0900**
811 Madison Avenue   at 68th St.
NYC 10021   Mon-Thur 10-6, Fri 10-5, Sat 11-5

☆ Borrelli

Drop-dead elegant menswear that will have the women swooning, just ask fans Harrison Ford and Robert Redford. The Neapolitan shirtmaker carries over 2,800 fabrics (!). You can buy off-the-rack or order 100% handmade shirts fitted with mother-of-pearl buttons at a cost of $290-$675 with an eight-week delivery time. Borrelli also boasts a collection of elegant suits, sport coats, leathers, cashmeres, knits and men's furnishings. Expensive, but worth every single penny.

Midtown East   **212-644-9610**
16 East 60th Street   bet. Madison/5th Ave.
NYC 10022   Mon-Sat 10-7, Sun 12-6

Bostonian

Men head here for the selection of affordable footwear, which runs from business wear to weekend casual. The Bostonian label offers classic lace-ups to dressy loafers, while there are sporty looks from the likes of Kenneth Cole and casual styles from such labels as Timberland, Ecco, Clarks and Rockport. Pay from $89 to $189.

www.bostonian.com

Bottega Veneta

Midtown East   212-949-9545
363 Madison Avenue   at 45th St.
NYC 10017   Mon-Fri 9-6:30, Thur 9-7, Sat 9-6, Sun 12-5

Bottega Veneta

Bottega Veneta has long been one of the most glamorous, gorgeous accessories labels in the world—and now it's even more so since it was acquired by the Gucci Group. Its classics include the "Intrecciato" collection of woven leather handbags and shoes and their Venetian loafers. Seriously fashionable are their leather "Accordion" boots. Under new creative director Tomas Maier they've cut back for now on their clothing collection to focus on what they do best—belts, bags and shoes—but a few knits and other clothing pieces will still be produced as accent pieces. Look out for Maier's new men's line, due next spring.   877-362-1715 www.bvlux.com

Midtown East   212-371-5511
635 Madison Avenue   bet. 59/60th St.
NYC 10022   Mon-Sat 10-6, Thur 10-7

Botticelli

Happily located in the bustling Midtown area, Botticelli stocks Italian leather shoes under its own label. Find classic shoes for work, casual loafers for weekend wear and weatherproof boots for city living or country getaways. Other styles include sandals, mules, sling-backs, fur-lined loafers, fashionable boots and evening shoes. Prices run from $195 to $595.

Fifth Avenue   212-221-9075
522 Fifth Avenue   bet. 43/44th St.
NYC 10036   Mon-Fri 10-7:30, Sat 10-7, Sun 12-6

Fifth Avenue   212-586-7421
666 Fifth Avenue (enter on 53rd St.)   bet. 5/6th Ave.
NYC 10103   Mon-Sat 10-7, Sun 12-6

Fifth Avenue (W)   212-582-6313
620 Fifth Avenue   at Rockefeller Center
NYC 10020   Mon-Sat 10-7, Sun 12-6

Boudoir

Indonesian owner Hanni Shagranum's store was inspired by the decadence of 18th-century boudoirs. But this store is perfect for the modern day, too: Shagranum encourages Old World lingering with such New World amenities as cappuccinos, complimentary home delivery and cellphone recharging. As for the clothes, there are hard-to-find collections by Japanese designer Atsuro Tayama, Alessandro Dell'Acqua, Samantha Treacy (ex-Diane von Furstenberg), Markus Lupfer and cult French name Martine Sitbon. Cute striped tops a la Cacharel are a must. Accessories and lingerie are also available.

NoLiTa   212-965-9925
244 Mulberry Street   bet. Prince/Spring
NYC 10012   Tues-Fri 11:30-7:30, Sat 12-7, Sun 12:30-6

Boyd's Madison Avenue

Head to Boyd's for top-of-the-line European hair accessories like headbands, elaborate combs, clips, chignon pins, mink twisters, barrettes...you name it. Brand names include Alexandre de Paris, Vuille and Francois Huchard. They also have excellent health and beauty products, including an extensive collection of cosmetics and perfumes, plus the ubiquitous pashmina shawls selling for $90, jewelry and lingerie. Be warned: sales staff can be outright aggressive and goods are a little on the glitzy side.

Upper East Side　　　　　　　　　　**212-838-6558**
655 Madison Avenue　　　　　　　　bet. 60/61st St.
NYC 10021　　　　　　　　　　　　Mon-Fri 8:30-7:30
　　　　　　　　　　　　　　　　Sat 9:30-7, Sun 12-6

Bra Smythe

We all know that buying a bra is never a funfest, but Bra Smythe makes it a little easier. Choose from over 1,500 styles with bra sizes that range from A to DDD cups. Custom fittings and alterations are their specialty. Also find a good selection of undergarments from Hanro, Lise Charmel, Aubade, Chantelle and Wacoa and swimwear by Karla Colletto and Domani.

Upper East Side　　　　　　　　　　**212-772-9400**
905 Madison Avenue　　　　　　　　bet. 72/73rd St.
NYC 10021　　　　　　　　　　　Mon-Sat 10-7, Sun 12-5

Bridge

Bridge occupies two adjacent shops—the first sells lower-priced merchandise, predominantly leather jackets, while the other, slightly (and we do mean slightly) fancier one houses slick looks in leather jackets, pants and coats. Labels include Red Kid and Ducksport. Prices are generally good.

Lower East Side　　　　　　　　　　**212-979-9777**
98-100 Orchard Street　　　　　　bet. Broome/Delancey
NYC 10002　　　　　　　　　　Mon-Fri 10-5:30, Sun 9-5:30

Brief Encounters

The racily-named Brief Encounters features a vast selection of American and European lingerie covering everything from trusty basics to sexy, seductive underpinnings for hot nights. Labels include Lise Charmel, LeJaby, Gemma, Chantelle, On Gossamer, Mystere and Cosabella. Custom fitting is also available.

Upper West Side　　　　　　　　　　**212-496-5649**
239 Columbus Avenue　　　　　　　　　at 71st St.
NYC 10023　　　　　　　　Mon-Fri 10-7, Sat 10-6, Sun 1-6

Brioni

For over 50 years this classic Italian hand-tailored menswear house has dressed Hollywood's biggest stars, from Clark Gable and Gary Cooper to the latest James Bond, Pierce Brosnan. Classic sensibility, luxury fabrics and European styling define Brioni, which offers suits off-

Brooks Brothers

the-rack or custom-made, patterned dress shirts, neckwear, sportswear, separates and outerwear. The women's collection features suits, slim skirts and fitted sheared minks. 800-444-1613 www.brioni.it

Midtown East   **212-376-5777**
57 East 57th Street   bet. Park/Madison Ave.
NYC 10022   Mon-Sat 9-6

Midtown East   **212-355-1940**
55 East 52nd Street   bet. Park/Madison Ave.
NYC 10022   Mon-Sat 9:30-6

Brooks Brothers 👤👩👤

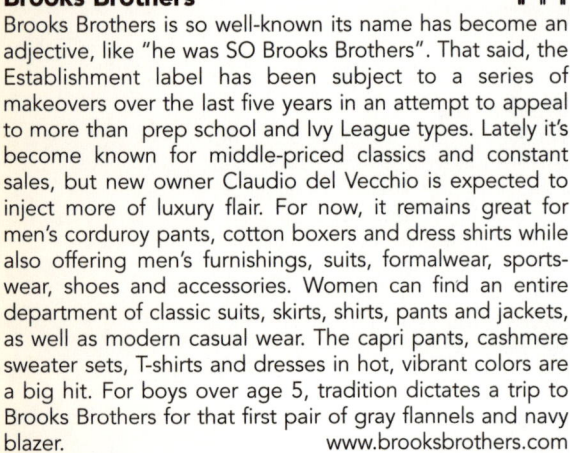

Brooks Brothers is so well-known its name has become an adjective, like "he was SO Brooks Brothers". That said, the Establishment label has been subject to a series of makeovers over the last five years in an attempt to appeal to more than prep school and Ivy League types. Lately it's become known for middle-priced classics and constant sales, but new owner Claudio del Vecchio is expected to inject more of luxury flair. For now, it remains great for men's corduroy pants, cotton boxers and dress shirts while also offering men's furnishings, suits, formalwear, sportswear, shoes and accessories. Women can find an entire department of classic suits, skirts, shirts, pants and jackets, as well as modern casual wear. The capri pants, cashmere sweater sets, T-shirts and dresses in hot, vibrant colors are a big hit. For boys over age 5, tradition dictates a trip to Brooks Brothers for that first pair of gray flannels and navy blazer. www.brooksbrothers.com

Midtown East   **212-682-8800**
346 Madison Avenue   bet. 44/45th St.
NYC 10017   Mon-Sat 9-7, Thur 9-8, Sun 12-6

Fifth Avenue   **212-261-9440**
666 Fifth Avenue   bet. 52/53rd St.
NYC 10103   Mon-Fri 10-8, Sat 10-7, Sun 11-7

Bruno Magli 👤👩

Worn by savvy, older fellows everywhere, the watchwords for this 63-year-old Italian footwear retailer: "The secret to a handsome shoe lies in all the invisible components." Head here for a menswear collection of rubber-soled shoes, formal patent leather pumps, lace-ups and loafers. Women can choose from classic pumps, open-toed sandals and slingbacks in supple leathers and suedes. But it's really best for the guys. www.brunomagli.com

Fifth Avenue   **212-752-7900**
677 Fifth Avenue   at 53rd St.
NYC 10022   Mon-Fri 10-6:30, Thur 10-7
  Sat 10-6, Sun 12-6

Bu and the Duck 👤

Cool name—Lord knows what it means—but Bu and the Duck sells fashionable trappings for your pampered child. Inspired by American styles of the 30's, owner Susan Lane has created a clothing and toy collection that captures the innocence of children with wonderful crocheted sweaters from Peru, cotton dresses with matching crocheted tops, linen overalls, miniskirts, and shirts made from kimonos. Accessories include Italian handmade shoes, delicately hand-embroidered quilts by Judy Boisson, stuffed animals, hair accessories and Bambini products to keep diaper rash at bay. From newborn to 6 years. www.buandtheduck.com

TriBeCa 212-431-9226
106 Franklin Street bet. W. B'way/Church
NYC 10013 Mon-Sat 10-7, Sun 10-4

Buffalo Chips USA
A specialist in handmade Western footwear from well-known Texan boot makers like Stallion, Ammons, Liberty and Tres Outlaw (pink cowboy boots, anyone?). Clothing-wise, look out for rocker, cowboy and biker leathers—not to mention tanks inscribed with "boy beater." Ranch jackets, chaps, leather-laced pants, cowboy hats, silver belt buckles and alligator and lizard belts complete the yee-hah selection. Don't forget to check out their table of bargain boots marked down 50%.

SoHo 212-625-8400
355 West Broadway bet. Broome/Grand
NYC 10013 Mon-Sat 11-7, Sun 12-6

Built by Wendy
Think the Marc Jacobs school of cool (except before Marc Jacobs was doing it). Downtown's indie girl Wendy Mullin set up shop to showcase her fun, hip and, even better, affordable clothes. This artsy lady is coolly confident with color, and has just the right dose of retro chic: think cute cords, funky blouses, edgy slogan T-shirts and stripy tops. Mod girls, school girls…cool girls, this is the place for you. And don't be fazed by the extremely large dog!

SoHo 212-925-6538
7 Centre Market Place bet. Broome/Grand
NYC 10012 Mon-Sat 12-7, Sun 1-6

Burberry
The British house of Burberry's signature plaid-lined trench-coat (designed for "safety on land, on air or afloat") has ruled the elements for over a century But since its funky makeover three years ago—remember when the plaid was rampant everywhere from umbrellas to bikinis?—creative director Christopher Bailey has kept the tradition, but added the cool. And its new, massive Manhattan flagship, due to open this fall, is meant to showcase all that is the reborn Burberry: fantastic rainwear, of course, as well as beautiful leathers, trench-inspired dresses, great knits, better-than-ever accessories from bags to shoes and casual wear under the Burberry London and the more expensive Burberry Prorsum labels. For men, there are classic English suits, jackets and casual wear, plus butter-soft leathers and knits. Don't forget to browse Burberry's new children's line

for your tots. The SoHo store, opened earlier this year, has a younger, hipper edge with hardwood floors and exposed ducting and offers an edited-down selection of the collections. 800-284-8480 www.burberry.com

Midtown East (opening Autumn 2002)
9 East 57th Street bet. 6th/Madison Ave
NYC 10022 Mon-Fri 9:30-7, Sat 9:30-6, Sun 12-6

SoHo 212-925-9300
133 Spring Street bet. Greene/Wooster
NYC 10012 Mon-Sat 11-7, Sun 12-6

Burlington Coat Factory

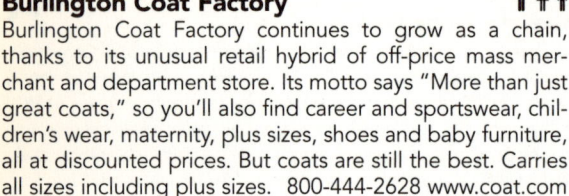

Burlington Coat Factory continues to grow as a chain, thanks to its unusual retail hybrid of off-price mass merchant and department store. Its motto says "More than just great coats," so you'll also find career and sportswear, children's wear, maternity, plus sizes, shoes and baby furniture, all at discounted prices. But coats are still the best. Carries all sizes including plus sizes. 800-444-2628 www.coat.com

Chelsea 212-229-1300
707 Sixth Avenue at 23rd St.
NYC 10011 Mon-Sat 9-9, Sun 10-6

C. Ronson

Charlotte Ronson, a member of social page favorites the Ronson family, recently opened this cooler-than-cool store to showcase her collection of hip streetwear. A huge blown-up picture of her over-stuffed closet provides a grungy backdrop to her sportswear, which shares an aesthetic with Marc by Marc Jacobs and Daryl K. Think teeny terry shorts, zip-up jackets, hooded sweatshirts, thermal shirts with cord elbow patches, wife beater tank tops, striped T-shirts, and chunky espadrilles, plus a small collection of jewelry, including feather bracelets. www.charlotteronson.com

NoLiTa 212-625-9074
269 Elizabeth Street bet. Houston/Prince
NYC 10012 Mon-Sat 11-7, Sun 12-6

Caché

More shopping mall than city chic, Caché is best for special-event eveningwear. Although it covers the latest trends, expect much of it to be manufactured in synthetic fabrics. Looks include spaghetti-strap dresses, tiny sequined tops and snug-fitting outfits perfect for club-hopping. A massive selection of coordinating jewelry rounds out the collection. 800-788-cache www.cache.com

Midtown East 212-588-8719
805 Third Avenue bet. 49/50th St.
NYC 10022 Mon-Fri 10-7, Sat 10-6, Sun 12-6

☆ Cadeau

Cadeau is an incredibly fashionable maternity brand. Why? Well, it might have to do with the fact that owners Emilia Fabricant and Chrissy Yu both worked at Barneys New York,

Calypso St. Barths

for both the cult Co-op and as a women's designer buyer, respectively. "The modern styles, manufactured in Italy, are about allowing a woman to be herself throughout her pregnancy without having to give up her sense of style," Fabricant says. Hear, hear.

NoLiTa 212-674-5747
254 Elizabeth Street bet. Houston/Prince
NYC 10012 Tues-Sun 11-7

Calvin Klein

Where would we all be without our Calvins? Klein reinvented American casual and continues to set the trends in slickly minimal city pieces that strike a perfect balance between uptown polish and downtown chic. With his precise cuts and monochromatic palettes (you want black, you got it) Klein is the effortless master of cool. The best destination for sleek-chic suits, clingy knits, shirts, dresses, skirts, relaxed sweaters and beautifully basic eveningwear. Then there are the shoes, accessories, jeans, underwear and home furnishings All up: Calvin Heaven. 877-256-7373

Upper East Side 212-292-9000
654 Madison Avenue at 60th St.
NYC 10021 Mon-Sat 10-6
Thur 10-7, Sun 12-6

Calypso Enfant

A cuter-than-cute children's shop that carries top-of-the-line French clothing. For *les petits enfants*, find an adorable layette selection, irresistible sailor outfits, jumpers, pleated skirts, dresses, knits with matching hats, outerwear, shoes and accessories. You'll also discover fabulous clothing for your *plus grands enfants*. Like the whimsical Calypso St. Barths, which caters to adults, this is an outpost for spirited clothes in bursts of bright color, featuring looks from bustle skirts and pants to embroidered shirts and cute accessories. Newborn to 12 years.

NoLiTa 212-966-3234
426 Broome Street bet. Lafayette/Crosby
NYC 10012 Mon-Sat 12-8, Sun 12-6

Calypso St. Barths

Born in, you guessed it, St. Barths, this tropical store is a magnet for Boho moms and model types on the hunt for bright, resort-friendly clothes by young French and American designers. Bursts of pinks, blues, reds and oranges (but never black) and bohemian, ethnic prints rule. Find flirty, girly looks in silk-sleeved shirts, cashmere sweaters, filmy blouses, T-shirts, Dr. Boudoir's customized tank tops and swimwear and sarongs by Matilde. Buy up and head to the Caribbean immediately! And don't forget to pick up a bag, a boa and a bottle of their signature mimosa perfume—it's absolutely gorgeous.

Upper East Side 212-535-4100
935 Madison Avenue bet. 74/75th St.
NYC 10021 Mon-Sat 10-6, Sun 12-6

49

Calypso Homme

SoHo   **212-274-0449**
424 Broome Street   bet. Crosby/Lafayette
NYC 10013   Mon-Sat 12-8, Sun 12-6

NoLiTa   **212-965-0990**
280 Mott Street   bet. Houston/Prince
NYC 10012   Mon-Sat 11:30-7:30, Sun 12-6:30

Calypso Homme

This store takes the Calypso aesthetic and translates it, in a thoroughly non-girly way, for the fellows. Think colorful shirts, knits, shorts, flip-flops and swimwear. The perfect stop for when you are heading with your gorgeous, Boho wife or model girlfriend (see above) to—where else?—St Barths!

SoHo   **212-343-0450**
405 Broome Street   bet. Crosby/Lafayette
NYC 10013   Mon-Sat 11-7, Sun 12-6

Camouflage

Buy these labels and you won't want to camouflage them one bit: Helmut Lang, Paul Smith, Etro, Michael Kors, John Smedley and Byblos, just for starters. A door apart, one space offers casual, younger clothing, while the other carries more sophisticated pieces. Head here for outerwear, cool cashmeres and accessories.

Chelsea   **212-741-9118**
139/141 Eighth Avenue   at 17th St.
NYC 10011   Mon-Sat 12-8, Sun 12-6

Camper

This defiantly quirky Spanish shoe company is on the road to world domination. Nothing here is standard, from the four gigantic fiberglass lamps that hang above a footwear runway or the company's lofty design mission: to develop shoes so "pure" that every step feels as though you're walking barefoot. No stilettos here then! Rather, you'll find ultra-hip, immediately recognizable shoes that are scratch-resistant, equipped with light rubber soles and special linings to absorb perspiration. The coolest styles—sneakers that look like rugby boots in strong color combos of black and beige.

SoHo   **212-358-1841**
125 Prince Street   at Wooster
NYC 10012   Mon-Sat 11-8, Sun 12-6

Canyon Beachwear

Go east! That's what this California institution did and they've brought some hot swimwear with them. Shop for bikinis, thongs, one-pieces, tankinis and everything in between in the best color selection around. European and American brands include Dolce & Gabbana, Bachata, Pin Up Stars, Huit, Luce di Sole, Manuel Canovas, Ann Cole, Calvin Klein, Delfina and Domani. Sarongs, matching cover-ups, sandals, beach totes and lotions complete the amazing range. Sizes run from 0 to 22. www.canyonbeachwear.com

Upper East Side   917-432-0732
1136 Third Avenue   bet. 66/67th St.
NYC 10121   Mon-Sun 11-7, Wed, Thur 11-8, Sun 11-6

Capezio

Shall we dance? Well, twirl your way to Capezio, which since 1887 has caressed the feet of legendary dancers like Anna Pavlova, Fred Astaire and Bob Fosse. Today the company has expanded its horizons to cover other dance wear, including leotards, leg warmers, leggings, tights, jazz pants and knits by pro makers like Danskin, City Lights, Marika, Baltog and, of course, Capezio. They're perfect for ballerinas of all sizes and skills. Footwear includes ballet slippers, tap, jazz and toe shoes.   www.capeziodance.com

Upper East Side   212-758-8833
136 East 61st Street   bet. Lex./Park Ave.
NYC 10021   Mon-Fri 10-7, Sat 10-6, Sun 12-5

Upper East Side   212-348-7210
1651 Third Avenue, 3rd Fl.   bet. 92/93rd St.
NYC 10028   Mon-Fri 9-6, Sat 9-4

Midtown West   212-245-2130
1650 Broadway, 2nd Fl.   at 51st St.
NYC 10019   Mon-Fri 9:30-7, Sat 9:30-6:30
                                                                   Sun 11:30-5

Midtown West   212-586-5140
1776 Broadway, 2nd Fl.   at 57th St.
NYC 10019   Mon-Fri 10-7, Sat 10-6, Sun 12-5

Carolina Herrera

The ever-graceful Carolina Herrera is the epitome of uptown sophistication. Her signature style focuses on slim silhouettes with luxurious details—silk shirts with fur cuffs are a fabulous example. Find pencil skirts below the knee, beautifully cut pants, glorious cashmeres, supple suedes, sleek wool coats and other beautiful fur pieces, like a hooded lynx coat. In eveningwear, Herrera designs unapologetic "entrance-makers"—remember Renée Zellweger at last year's Oscars? A knockout. She's also the perfect provider of a classic tuxedo suit and some of the most covetable white shirts you'll find. Getting married soon? Ascend a grand staircase that leads to her bridal boutique, home to a stunning selection of empire and column gowns, A-line and full skirts, from chic simplicity to lavish embroideries of crystals, sequins, and lace. Classic accessories include handbags, sunglasses and scarves.

Upper East Side   212-249-6552
954 Madison Avenue   at 75th St.
NYC 10021   Mon-Sat 10-6

Cashmere Cashmere

Cashmere—you can never have too much! A great source for Italian and Scottish cashmere in classic styles, including twinsets, turtlenecks, cardigans, crew necks and pants.

Accessories include socks, cape shawls, stoles, gloves, scarves and blankets. Prices run from $325 to $1,200.

Upper East Side   **212-988-5252**
965 Madison Avenue   bet. 75/76th St.
NYC 10021   Mon-Thur 10-6, Fri & Sat 10-5

Cashmere New York

Jet-setters buy up gorgeous Scottish and Italian sweaters here, all of which meet the highest standards of quality and design. Choose from over 50 glorious shades in styles from basic turtlenecks and twinsets to dressier satin-trimmed and beaded sweaters. They also sell day and eveningwear ensembles like capri pants paired with a cashmere camisole or a taffeta long skirt worn with a silk/cashmere beaded top.

Upper East Side   **212-744-3500**
1100 Madison Avenue   bet. 82/83rd St.
NYC 10028   Mon-Sat 10-6:30

Upper East Side   **212-517-3600**
1052 Lexington Avenue   at 75th St.
NYC 10021   Mon-Sat 10-6:30

Catherine

Designer Catherine Malandrino really loves America. In the past, her playful and flirty collections have been inspired by everything from the Jazz Age in Harlem to the Wild West. Her Stars-and-Stripes collection from a few years ago is still sported by patriotic fashionistas. "Clothes should float around the body, make a woman feel as if she is walking in a dream," she says. That's what her spirited, colorful SoHo store feels like, too. It showcases an eclectic mix of clothing with girly rock 'n roll attitude (yes that is possible—Mary J Blige is a big fan). This is not the place to come for suits—Malandrino hates them. Accessories include quirky-cool hats and silk embroidered and beaded shawls.

SoHo   **212-925-6765**
468 Broome Street   at Greene
NYC 10013   Mon-Sat 11-7, Sun 12-6

Catimini

This French import brings to New York its playful collection of comfortable children's pants, jackets, separates and outerwear, all in screen-printed fabrics full of whimsy and charm. It's fun, casual clothing that children will love wearing. From 6 months to size 10/12.   www.catimini.com.au

Upper East Side   **212-987-0688**
1284 Madison Avenue   bet. 91/92nd St.
NYC 10128   Mon-Sat 10-6, Sun 12-5

Celine

Celine is the ultimate brand for uptown girls. The established French label, designed by luxe sportswear king Michael Kors is the ultimate in luxurious yet casual dressing. Kors is a guru to young socialites who want their hip with a

Cerruti

healthy dose of discretion. Styles run from sporty rugged tweeds, sophisticated shirting, checkered skirts and reversible coyote fur to evening looks of long, pleated gowns and slip dresses. Celine shoes, in classic colors with witty details, are some of the best around. You'll wear them forever. Great sales, too. www.celine.com

Upper East Side 212-486-9700
667 Madison Avenue bet. 60/61st St.
NYC 10021 Mon-Sat 10-6, Thur 10-7

Central Park West
The Upper West Side's best destination for cool, trendy clothes with a great selection of flirty dresses, skirts, tanks, tees, shorts, sweaters and jeans by hot labels like Theory, Nanette Lepore, Juicy, Jet, Denim Doctor, Grassroots and Michael Stars. Also a great range of boutique jean lines. Perfect to play around with—and in.

Upper West Side 212-579-3737
2124 Broadway bet. 74/75th St.
NYC 10023 Mon-Fri 11-7:30, Sat 11-7, Sun 12-6

☆ Century 21
Century 21 has risen from the ashes, and bargain hunters everywhere are thanking their lucky stars. Located at the edge of Ground Zero, Century 21, one of the city's cult retail destinations, is back with its refurbished interior, fresh inventory and the best prices anywhere. A polyglot mix of shoppers flocks here for heavily reduced designer clothing from Prada to Polo Sport. Check out Italian designer suits from $250 to $700, wedding dresses from $130 to $375, Polo sweaters from $40 to $70, designer outerwear from $300 to $750, and—yes!—Marc by Marc Jacobs denim and T-shirts for as little as $50. Other merchandise includes intimates, cosmetics, luggage, housewares, bedlinens (Donna Karan, Ralph Lauren and more, all at fabulous prices), appliances and electronics. Take a deep breath and go nuts...

Lower Manhattan 212-227-9092
22 Cortland Street bet. Church/B'way
NYC 10007 Mon-Fri 7:45-8
Thur 7:45-8:30, Sat 10-8, Sun 11-7

Cerruti
This fashion house has been on a roller-coaster ride ever since founder Nino Cerruti sold it to the Italian group Fin.part last year. First Cerruti was succeeded by ex-Burberry head Roberto Menichetti, who lasted only six months. Now Istvan Francer is at the design helm of the house for its signature Cerruti line and will show his first collection for spring 2003. Meanwhile, the Cerruti 1881 label continues to be designed by an in-house team and to focus on what made Cerruti great in the first place—discreetly glamorous clothes in luxurious fabrics and neutral colors like charcoal and beige. The four-floor boutique features both ready-to-wear collections and men can

53

choose from classic and modern suits, sportswear, outerwear, tuxedos, shoes and accessories. The women's collection features suits, pleated skirts, dresses, classic coats, knits, as well as a sophisticated collection of shoes made exclusively for Cerruti by Manolo Blahnik. But it might be best to wait a season to see what the real Cerruti will look like. www.cerruti-femme.com

Upper East Side   212-327-2222
789 Madison Avenue   at 67th St.
NYC 10021   Mon-Sat 10-6, Thur 10-7

Cesare Paciotti
Sex-o-matic! With their signature silver dagger logo stamped or affixed to much of their footwear, you'll never forget you're wearing a pair of Cesare Paciotti shoes. No-one else will either and that's the point. The collection showcases sexy stiletto heels, pumps, flats and boots, with toes as pointed and sharp as a…dagger. For men, find a slightly tamer selection of shoes and boots better suited to artsy pursuits than to Wall Street. www.cesare-paciotti.com

Upper East Side   212-452-1222
833 Madison Avenue   bet. 69/70th St.
NYC 10021   Mon-Sat 10-6

Champs
Whether it's golf, soccer, basketball, racquet sports, running, billiards or the extremely athletic darts, Champs is happy to accommodate you. Find a large sneaker department for the whole family, as well as team logo'd jerseys and sweats. Best for boys and men.   800-991-6813
www.champssports.com

Fifth Avenue   212-239-3256
1 West 34th Street   at 5th Ave.
NYC 10001   Mon-Sat 8-9, Sun 11-7

Midtown West   212-757-3638
1381-99 Sixth Avenue   at 56th St.
NYC 10019   Mon-Sat 9-9, Sun 11-6

Lower Manhattan   212-406-6944
89 South Street   at South Street Seaport
NYC 10038   Mon-Sat 10-9, Sun 11-8

Chanel
The very definition of French chic. Since Coco Chanel designed the world's first little black dress and adorned it with her signature pearls, Chanel has ruled the fashion world. The famous interlocking C's are the most recognizable fashion logo on the planet, and the clothes remain the ultimate status symbol. Designer Karl Lagerfeld lives by strict design standards, claiming his clothes must be "beautiful, wearable, understandable and interesting all in one." Although a Chanel design is classic, Lagerfeld never fails to make it hip, too—be it a groovy sweatshirt with a print of Madame Chanel or furry logo'd boots. The collec-

tion favors slim suits by day and blouse-and-skirt combinations by night. Other looks include lean bouclé coats worn over dresses, tweed jacket and skirt ensembles, too-chic-to-speak eveningwear, luxury separates and addictive shoes. The *ne plus ultra* is, of course, the quilted Chanel handbag, a true icon in the fashion world even if it has been sidelined temporarily by offerings from Prada, Gucci or Vuitton. New to Madison Avenue is their store devoted exclusively to accessories—a paradise of gorgeous Chanel baubles... www.chanel.com

Upper East Side   **212-535-5505**
737 Madison Avenue   at 64th St.
NYC 10021   Mon-Fri 10-6, Sat 10-5

Upper East Side   **212-535-5828**
733 Madison Avenue   at 64th St.
NYC 10021   Mon-Fri 10-6, Sat 10-5

Midtown East   **212-355-5050**
15 East 57th Street   bet. Madison/5th Ave.
NYC 10022   Mon-Wed, Fri 10-6:30
    Thur 10-7, Sat 10-6

SoHo   **212-334-0055**
139 Spring Street   at Wooster
NYC 10012   Mon-Sat 11-7, Sun 12-6

Charles Jourdan

This notable French shoe designer is perfect for that pair of "statement" shoes. A Charles Jourdan design boasts color, sex appeal and, most importantly, high heels. Find evening shoes, chic pumps, platforms, wedges, boots, flats and sandals. Prices run from $165 to $300.   800-997-2717
www.charles-jourdan.com

Midtown East   **212-421-6270**
612 Madison Avenue   bet. 58/59th St.
NYC 10022   Mon-Sat 10-7, Sun 12-5

Chelsea Girl

Owner Elisa Casas has got a Fifties thing goin' on, judging from this cult store, which stocks a great range of sundresses in bright colors from the Twenties right through to the Seventies—visited regularly by celeb vintage fans like Claire Danes, Winona Ryder and Debra Messing. Accessorize your retro look with kitschly coordinated print shoes and handbags that Lucy Riccardo would love. Also available are those vintage store staples, beaded cashmere cardigans. Be warned: Fifties dresses are best on Fifties-size waists. Breathe in!   www.chelsea-girl.com

SoHo   **212-343-1658**
63 Thompson Street   bet Broome/Spring
NYC 10012   Mon-Sun 12-7

Cheo Tailors

Oriental carpets, oak cutting tables and bolts of luxurious European fabrics suck you into one of the world's finest tailors. Favored by social register types, Mr. Cheo specializes in a Savile Row style—jackets are cut slim with minimal padding, pants are full cut and sit naturally on the waist and everything (measuring, cutting, sewing and fittings) is done by Mr. Cheo himself. Six to eight week delivery, with an average cost of $3,500.

Upper East Side   **212-980-9838**
30 East 60th Street   bet. Madison/Park Ave.
NYC 10022   Mon-Fri 10-6 by appointment

Cherry

Girls love Cherry—and so they should! Recently moved from the Lower East Side, the store features an eclectic mix of merchandise, from modernist furnishings to retro clothing and accessories. Their vintage collection spans the 50's to the 80's with leather jackets, denim, Pucci print shirts, suedes, shirts and accessories from, among others, Gucci, Courrèges, Missoni and Yves Saint Laurent. It's the shoes here that will ruin you—many a fashion girl has been known to spend a week's rent on that perfect pair of boho boots.

West Village   **212-924-1410**
19 Eighth Avenue   bet. West 12th/James
NYC 10014   Mon-Sat 12-10, Sun 11-5

The Children's Place

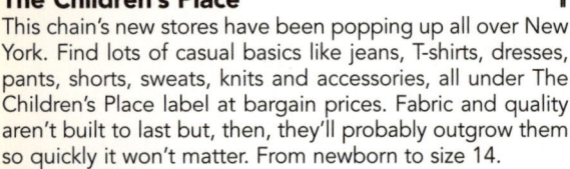

This chain's new stores have been popping up all over New York. Find lots of casual basics like jeans, T-shirts, dresses, pants, shorts, sweats, knits and accessories, all under The Children's Place label at bargain prices. Fabric and quality aren't built to last but, then, they'll probably outgrow them so quickly it won't matter. From newborn to size 14.

Upper East Side   **212-831-5100**
173 East 86th Street   bet. Lex./3rd Ave.
NYC 10028   Mon-Sat 8:30-9, Sun 10-6

Upper West Side   **917-441-9807**
2187 Broadway   at 77th St.
NYC 10024   Mon-Fri 8:30-8:30, Sat 9-8:30, Sun 10-5

Upper West Side   **917-441-2374**
2039 Broadway   bet. Amsterdam/70th St.
NYC 10023   Mon-Fri 8:30-8:30, Sat 9-8:30, Sun 9-6

Midtown West   **212-398-4416**
1460 Broadway   bet. 41/42nd St.
NYC 10035   Mon-Fri 9:30-7, Sat 10-7, Sun 11-6

Midtown West   **212-268-7696**
901 Sixth Avenue   bet. 32/33rd St.
Level C2   at Manhattan Mall
NYC 10001   Mon-Sat 8:30-8, Sun 10-6

Flatiron   **212-529-2201**
36 Union Square East   at 16th St.
NYC 10003   Mon-Fri 10-7, Thur 10-8, Sat 10-5, Sun 11-5

Chloé

Phoebe Philo, who succeeded her former boss Stella McCartney as Chloé's designer a year ago, goes from strength to strength. She has kept the naughty attitude but added a serious dose of sophistication. Basically, the Chloé girl has grown up. Philo is inspired by everything from bohemian style icon Talitha Getty to pretty-girl Brigitte Bardot. Chloé addicts flock here for brilliantly tailored pants, slouchy, sexy blouses and, in summer, itsy-bitsy bikinis. It's all body-conscious without being tarty. Philo has also broadened the accessory range because, unlike staunch vegetarian McCartney, she's willing to work with leather. And don't forget to check out See by Chloé, the cute diffusion line, and look out for what will no doubt be a dead-sexy lingerie line coming soon.

Upper East Side 212-717-8220
850 Madison Avenue at 70th St.
NYC 10021 Mon-Sat 10-6

Christian Dior

At the base of the LVMH tower sit the glamorous 6,000 square foot digs of Christian Dior, a world of John Galliano's imagination. And his imagination is a trip—his collections roam the world and meld ethnic influences, costume, history, hip-hop...anything epic creative force Galliano absorbs. Each Dior collection clearly displays his passion for design, his mastery of fabric and complex cutting methods. The clean and modern ground floor is devoted to handbags, small leathergoods, scarves, eyeglasses, cosmetics and fragrances, as well as a bravely chic shoe salon at the back. A dramatic, angular staircase leads up to the ready-to-wear floor, where there are casual items like denim and knitwear, formal daywear, beautiful eveningwear and furs. Galliano's signature bias-cut dresses are the ultimate in gorgeous evening dressing. Think Nicole Kidman at the Oscars and dream... www.dior.com

Midtown East 212-931-2950
21 East 57th Street bet. Madison/5th Ave.
NYC 10022 Mon-Sat 10-6, Thur 10-7, Sun 12-6

Christian Louboutin

Enter this boudoir-like boutique and coo over the designer's fanciful, red-soled shoes. "Black soles are for widows, beige soles are for the Milanese, but red soles are for those who want to flirt and dance," he says. Louboutin also celebrates offbeat detailing, which includes using silk fabrics from French tie manufacturers, dainty rose petals and even old postage stamps. Find mules, embroidered flats, gray flannel spectator pumps, ponyskin boots and killer evening stilettos. His range of handbags is also wonderfully distinctive—one you'll pay for! Prices range from $380 to $650.

Upper East Side 212-396-1884
941 Madison Avenue bet. 74/75th St.
NYC 10021 Mon-Sat 10-6

Christie Brothers Furs

A discount retailer of luxury fur coats with a selection of mink, shearling and Russian sable, as well as cashmere and

Christopher Totman

microfiber coats which can be custom-lined and fitted with the fur of your choosing. In-house storage facilities are also available.

Chelsea   **212-736-6944**
333 Seventh Avenue, 11th Fl.   bet. 28/29th St.
NYC 10001   Mon-Fri 8:30-6 and by appointment

Christopher Totman

Christopher Totman melds the worlds of New York and South America in clothing that involves an extensive use of handwork with ethnic flavor—colorful Guatemalan stripes, hand-loomed fabrics, circular crochets and alpaca knits. Choose from his trademark single-seam long skirt ("LaLunaskirt"), gauze shirts, dresses, hand-knit pima cotton sweaters and more. Super-comfy (and super-cool) Birkenstock sandals also available.

NoLiTa   **212-925-7495**
262 Mott Street   bet. Houston/Prince
NYC 10012   Mon-Sat 11-7, Sun 12-6

Chuckies

Not the swankiest name, but don't be fooled: this cool boutique features a fabulous range of cutting edge, covetable footwear from such designer labels as Jimmy Choo, Sergio Rossi, Casadei, Miu Miu, Giuseppe Zanotti, Helmut Lang, Marc Jacobs, Richard Tyler and Dolce & Gabbana. An excellent source for fun, funky and glamorous shoes and boots that you won't find anywhere else.

Upper East Side   **212-593-9898**
1073 Third Avenue   bet. 63/64th St.
NYC 10021   Mon-Fri 10:45-7:45
    Sat 10:45-7, Sun 12:30-6

SoHo   **212-343-1717**
399 West Broadway   bet. Spring/Broome
NYC 10012   Mon-Sat 11-7:30, Sun 12-7:30

Church's English Shoes

When it comes to men's shoes, no one does it better than the English and Church's shoes are among the best. For 125 years, it has been recognized worldwide for classic, bench-made shoes, which is why fashion powerhouse Prada bought the company. Choose from two collections with styles that include plain-toed oxfords, banker shoes, slip-ons, tie-up wingtips, traditional five-eyelet bluchers, loafers and moccasins. Prices run from $180 to $800. Six-month delivery for custom orders. Great sales. At press time, the store was planning to move to a new location, so call 411 for their new address.   800-221-4540
    www.churchsshoes.com

Midtown East   **212-755-4313**
428 Madison Avenue   at 49th St.
NYC 10017   Mon-Sat 10-6, Sun 12-5

Clifford Michael Design

Circle
A newish NoLiTa store with a very marked Asian flavor. Designer Christopher Totman—who owns another store across the street (see above)—dreams up the most exquisite kimono fabric wrap tops and jackets in jewel-like colors, perfect with a pair of beaten-up jeans. Sadly, they are not cheap, but they look the business. A NoLiTa girl's favorite—and rightly so.

NoLiTa	**212-966-3093**
279 Mott Street	bet. Houston/Prince
NYC 10012	Mon-Sat 12-7:30, Sun 12-6:30

Citishoes
Citishoes is popular with Midtown executives, as well as tourists staying at neighboring hotels. Men will find a good selection of brand name dress shoes by Alden, Cole Haan, Kenneth Cole, Santoni and Allen Edmonds, as well as casual comfort shoes by Mephisto, Ecco and Rockport.

Midtown East	**212-751-3200**
445 Park Avenue	bet. 56/57th St.
NYC 10022	Mon-Fri 9:30-6:30, Sat 10:30-5:30

City Cricket
This adorable children's shop offers an exclusive selection of merchandise with a magical appeal. Find cute knitted sweaters and one-of-a-kind handmade blankets and quilts in unusual fabrics and playful designs. Other items include children's indoor and outdoor furniture like upholstered wing chairs, hand-painted tables and chairs, antique wicker and bent willow twig chairs. www.citycricket.com

West Village	**212-242-2258**
215 West 10th Street	at Bleecker
NYC 10014	Mon-Sat 11-7, Sun 12-5

Claire Blaydon
A bright, sunny store filled with Blaydon's signature collection of restructured knitwear, jersey tops, lacy dresses, skirts and accessories. She uses delicate trimmings and silk-embroidered borders to perk up the fronts, collars and cuffs of all her tops, making each a one-of-a-kind piece. While some may balk at the price of a trimmed T-shirt ($95), check out her stylish, body-hugging cashmere/angora pieces. Accessories include jewelry, handbags, hats and gloves.

NoLiTa	**212-219-1490**
202A Mott Street	bet. Spring/Kenmare
NYC 10012	Mon-Sat 12-7, Sun 12-6

Clifford Michael Design
The place to hit for special-occasion dressing. If you're the bride, the mother-of-the-bride or just an invited guest, head upstairs and select your appropriate wedding attire. When your invitation says "black tie," doll yourself up in an elaborate gown, tuxedo, evening suit or sexy cocktail

Club Monaco

dress. Coordinating handbags and silk scarves are also available. Downstairs is home to leathers and shearling outerwear. www.cliffordmichael.com

Upper East Side **212-888-7665**
45 East 60th Street bet. Madison/Park Ave.
NYC 10022 Mon-Fri 10-6:30, Thur 10-7
Sat 10-6, Sun 12-5

Club Monaco

Chic basics that look to the catwalks for inspiration. Club Monaco, a Canadian-based company owned by fashion tycoon Ralph Lauren, is a fantastic source for high-fashion pieces and the latest runway looks with a sportswear edge. The color palette is monochromatic, but you can be sure you'll walk out with that perfect black sweater or easy-chic jeans. A consistently good source for fresh young looks at affordable prices—and their sales are amazing. www.clubmonaco.com

Midtown West Side—Flagship n/a at press time
37 West 57th Street bet. 5th/6th Ave.
NYC 10019 n/a at press time

Upper East Side **212-355-2949**
1111 Third Avenue at 65th St.
NYC 10021 Mon-Sat 10-8, Sun 11-6

Upper West Side **212-579-2587**
2376 Broadway at 87th St.
NYC 10024 Mon-Sat 10-8, Sun 12-6

Flatiron **212-352-0936**
160 Fifth Avenue bet. 20/21st St.
NYC 10010 Mon-Sat 10-9, Sun 11-7

SoHo **212-533-8930**
121 Prince Street bet. Wooster/Greene
NYC 10012 Mon-Wed 11-8, Thur-Sat 11-9, Sun 11-7

SoHo **212-941-1511**
520 Broadway at Spring
NYC 10012 Mon-Sat 11-9, Sun 11-7

Clyde's on Madison

In a city packed with cosmetic/drug/beauty stores, Clyde's is a standout. This redesigned luxury emporium features the finest American and European brands of cosmetics, fragrances, hair- and skin-care products and aromatherapy, as well as toys, gift baskets, candles, Alexandre de Paris hair accessories and more. It also offers such services as a pharmacy, an on-premise herbalist and a nutritionist.
800-792-5933 www.clydesonmadison.com

Upper East Side **212-744-5050**
926 Madison Avenue bet. 73/74th St.
NYC 10021 Mon-Fri 9-7:30, Thur 9-8, Sat 9-7, Sun 10-6

Coach

Coach is one of the fastest-growing accessories brands around and the fashion crowd is now proud to carry their signature totes and mince around in their cool sandals and

Comme des Garçons

espadrilles. Shop for briefcases, handbags, travel bags and small leathergoods, manufactured in clean, chic and functional shapes. Their handbag collection includes shoulder bags, sleek clutches, cotton-twill travel totes and a collection of canvas bags trimmed in leather. There also is a selection of leather jackets, wallets, belts, gloves, shoes, watches and umbrellas.   800-444-3611 www.coach.com.

Upper East Side   212-879-9391
1145 Madison Avenue   at 85th St.
NYC 10028   Mon-Sat 10-8, Sun 11-6

Upper West Side   212-799-1624
2321 Broadway   at 84th St.
NYC 10024   Mon-Sat 10-8, Sun 11-6

Midtown East   212-754-0041
595 Madison Avenue   at 57th St.
NYC 10022   Mon-Sat 10-8, Sun 11-6

Midtown East   212-599-4777
342 Madison Avenue   bet. 43/44th St.
NYC 10017   Mon-Sat 10-8, Sun 11-6

Fifth Avenue   212-245-4148
620 Fifth Avenue   at Rockefeller Ctr.
NYC 10020   Mon-Sat 10-8, Sun 11-7

SoHo   212-473-6925
143 Prince Street   at West B'way
NYC 10012   Mon-Sat 10-8, Sun 11-6

Lower Manhattan   212-425-4350
193 Front Street   at South Street Seaport
NYC 10038   Mon-Sat 10-8, Sun 11-6

Cole Haan

Cole Haan delivers a brilliant footwear collection of modern classics that embrace fashion. Both sexes will find smart-looking loafers, snappy mules, driving moccasins, oxfords, sensible sandals and boots. Prices start at $145 and run to approximately $1,000. Best buys are Cole Haan's line of fabulously comfortable sports shoes, developed with help from parent company Nike and equipped with its Nike Air technology. Coordinating accessories include classy handbags in all leathers, luggage, belts, socks and leather jackets.   800-488-2000 www.colehaan.com

Upper East Side   212-421-8440
667 Madison Avenue   at 61st St.
NYC 10021   Mon-Sat 10-7, Thur 10-8, Sun 12-6

Fifth Avenue   212-765-9747
620 Fifth Avenue   at 50th St.
NYC 10020   Mon-Sat 10-7, Thur 10-8, Sun 12-6

Comme des Garçons

If you suffer from fashion's cruelest afflictions—avant-garditis and conspicuous consumption—get yourself to Comme des Garçons. Known for her high-concept designs, cult Japanese designer Rei Kawakubo's collection is long on intellectualism. Enter through an aluminum tunnel into a parallel universe: an interior of white foam-covered walls houses pieces from the basic to the absurd and textiles that are wondrous in color and quality. Best accessory bets: her fabulous logo'd bags and wallets that look good on everyone.

Chelsea   **212-604-9200**
520 West 22nd Street   bet. 10/11th Ave.
NYC 10011   Tues-Sat 11-7, Sun & Mon 12-6

Conrad's Bike Shop
Conrad's is for elite cyclists who take their sport seriously. It offers clothing, shoes, accessories, components and, of course, bicycles from top brands like Colnago, Serotta, Seven, DeRosa and Eddy Merckx. Price points range from $1,200 to $7,000. Best for pro racing bikes.

Midtown East   **212-697-6966**
25 Tudor City Place   at 41st St.
NYC 10017   Mon-Sat 11-7

Cose Belle
Designer Shannon McLean specializes in clean, simple designs manufactured in luxury fabrics. Located in a penthouse showroom, Cose Belle features pants, dresses, sweaters and evening and bridal gowns. It's classic clothing with sporty elegance. Her muse? A modern Audrey Hepburn.

Upper East Side   **212-988-4210**
7 East 81st Street, 4th Fl.   bet. Madison/5th Ave.
NYC 10028   Mon-Fri 10-6:30 by appointment only

Costume National
Italian designer Ennio Capasa's aesthetic is a dark one: an androgynous world of lean, mean and sleek silhouettes where sexy black rules. Each collection is extremely edgy but always accessible and wearable. Capasa cuts a mean pair of pants, but the standouts are his sexy evening tops, often with cut-out backs or shoulders. Also, this store is one of the best places in the city to come for a slick, modern suit and killer leather pieces. Then there are his sinuous, earthy-toned shoes and kick-ass boots.   www.costumenational.com

SoHo   **212-431-1530**
108 Wooster Street   bet. Prince/Spring
NYC 10012   Mon-Sat 11-7, Sun 12-6

Couture by Jennifer Dule
Designer Jennifer Dule specializes in women's custom tailoring for "after five," special occasion and bridal dressing. Bring a photograph from a magazine and she'll copy it to a "T" or change it to your specifications. Pants average $550, while suits start at $1,600. An elaborate satin evening gown with lavish detailing will run you $3,500+.

Flatiron   **212-777-2100**
133 Fifth Avenue, 3rd Fl.   at 20th St.
NYC 10003   by appointment only

C. P. Shades

Simple, carefree and comfortable clothing designed with down-to-earth practicality, with everything guaranteed to withstand the rigors of wash and wear. All dresses, skirts, pants and separates are manufactured in easy-care fabrics.
800-900-9581 www.cpshades.com

Upper West Side   **212-724-9474**
300 Columbus Avenue   at 74th St.
NYC 10023   Mon-Sat 11-7, Sun 12-6

SoHo   **212-226-4434**
154 Spring Street   bet. Wooster/W. B'way
NYC 10012   Mon-Sat 11-7, Sun 12-6

Crouch & Fitzgerald

Crouch & Fitzgerald has sold brand name leathergoods since opening its doors in 1939. The selection covers handbags, luggage, small leathergoods, briefcases and belts from such labels as Ghurka, Longchamp, Tumi, Hartmann and its own Crouch & Fitzgerald line.

Midtown East   **212-755-5888**
400 Madison Avenue   bet. 47/48th St.
NYC 10017   Mon-Fri 9-6, Sat 9-5

Crunch

This hip gym chain also has its own shop packed with the "Crunch" collection of fleece jackets, Lycra outfits, leggings, mesh hockey jerseys, sweats, hats, unisex jazz pants, bodywear and sportswear, perfect for working out or just posing.   www.crunch.com

Upper West Side   **212-875-1902**
162 West 83rd Street   bet. Columbus/Amsterdam
NYC 10024   Mon-Thur 5:30-11, Fri 5:30-10, Sat & Sun 8-9

Midtown East   **212-758-3434**
1109 Second Avenue   bet. 58/59th St.
NYC 10022   Mon-Thur 5-11, Fri 5-10, Sat 8-9

Midtown West   **212-869-7788**
144 West 38th Street   bet. 7th/B'way
NYC 10018   Mon-Fri 5:30-10, Sat & Sun 8-6

Midtown West   **212-594-8050**
560 West 43rd Street   at 11th Ave.
NYC 10036   Mon-Fri 6-10, Sat & Sun 9-7

Flatiron   **212-475-2018**
54 East 13th Street   bet. B'way/Univ. Pl.
NYC 10003   Mon-Fri 6-10, Sat & Sun 8-8

West Village   **212-366-3725**
152 Christopher Street   bet. Washington/Greenwich
NYC 10014   Mon-Fri 6-11, Sat & Sun 8-9

SoHo   **212-420-0507**
623 Broadway   at Houston St.
NYC 10012   Mon-Fri 6-11, Sat 8-8, Sun 9-8

NoHo   **212-614-0120**
404 Lafayette   bet. Astor/E. 4th St.
NYC 10003   Mon-Fri open 24 hrs., Sat to 9, Sun 8-9

Cynthia Rowley

Designer Cynthia Rowley's frilly, flirty clothes swing with unabashed girliness. Detailing emphasizes ruffles, ruching, eyelets and other retro touches and twists. Good girls will love her full-skirted dresses nipped at the waist, knits, tops with dainty detailing, print dresses and coats, while bad ones will go for Rowley's leather and coquettish pieces frequently worn by the fashion-forward "Sex In The City" girls. Accessories include handbags, shoes and eyewear.

SoHo — 212-334-1144
112 Wooster Street — bet. Prince/Spring
NYC 10012 — Mon-Sat 11-7
Thur & Fri 11-8, Sun 12-6

Daffy's

One of New York's largest—and loudest—discount chains, Daffy's carries clothing for the entire family with discounts up to 80% on sportswear, outerwear, workout apparel, underwear, accessories and shoes. If you're lucky, you might even come across a designer label like Tommy Hilfiger, Versace or Guess. Daffy's claims their prices are so low that "you'll be tempted to haggle them up." www.daffys.com

Midtown East — 212-376-4477
125 East 57th Street — bet. Lex./Park Ave.
NYC 10022 — Mon-Fri 10-8, Sat 10-7, Sun 11-6

Midtown East — 212-557-4422
335 Madison Avenue — at 44th St.
NYC 10017 — Mon-Fri 8-8, Sat 10-6, Sun 12-6

Midtown West — 212-736-4577
1311 Broadway — bet. 33/34th St.
NYC 10013 — Mon-Fri 10-9, Sat 10-8, Sun 11-7

Flatiron — 212-529-4477
111 Fifth Avenue — at 18th St.
NYC 10003 — Mon-Sat 10-9, Sun 12-7

SoHo — 212-334-7444
462 Broadway — at Grand
NYC 10012 — Mon-Thur 10-8
Fri & Sat 10-9, Sun 12-7

Dana Buchman

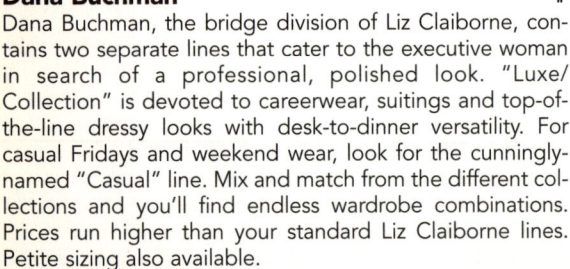

Dana Buchman, the bridge division of Liz Claiborne, contains two separate lines that cater to the executive woman in search of a professional, polished look. "Luxe/Collection" is devoted to careerwear, suitings and top-of-the-line dressy looks with desk-to-dinner versatility. For casual Fridays and weekend wear, look for the cunningly-named "Casual" line. Mix and match from the different collections and you'll find endless wardrobe combinations. Prices run higher than your standard Liz Claiborne lines. Petite sizing also available.

Midtown East — 212-319-3257
65 East 57th Street — bet. Madison/Park Ave.
NYC 10022 — Mon-Sat 10-6, Thur 10-8, Sun 12-5

Danskin

Danskin equals second-skin. Check out their signature exercise, dance and activewear which include leotards, leggings, unitards, tanks, sweatpants and ballet and jazz shoes. But since you need clothes to wear on the way to ballet class, too, you can choose from Danskin's selection of fashionable street-wear such as short skirts, slim-fitted dresses and slinky tops. www.danskin.com

Upper West Side 212-724-2992
159 Columbus Avenue bet. 67/68th St.
NYC 10023 Mon-Wed 10-8, Thur-Sat 10-9, Sun 11-6
Barbara Gee Danskin Center (outlet)

Upper West Side 212-769-2923
2282 1/2 Broadway bet. 82/83rd St.
NYC 10024 Mon-Sat 10:30-7:30, Sun 1-6
Barbara Gee Danskin Center (outlet)

Upper West Side 212-769-1564
2487 Broadway bet. 92/93rd St.
NYC 10025 Mon-Sat 10:30-7:30

Daphne

Va-va-voom clothing for the voluptuous woman: bias-cut dresses, shirts and jackets in easy-wear fabrics like wool, rayon and cotton blends. There also is a good collection of accessories including hand-painted silk scarves, jewelry and stylish hats. www.daphne1.com

Upper West Side 212-877-5073
467 Amsterdam Avenue bet. 82/83rd St.
NYC 10024 Mon-Sat 12-7, Sun 12-6

Darryl's

An extremely handy Upper West Side source to hit for your day-to-day wardrobe needs. They carry everything from career and eveningwear to casual and relaxed basics. There are suits, separates, pants, knits, twinsets and accessories from labels like Georges Rech, Silvia Sharrel, Momenti and Pablo.

Upper West Side 212-874-6677
492 Amsterdam Avenue bet. 83/84th St.
NYC 10024 Mon-Fri 11-7, Thur 11-8, Sat 11-6, Sun 12-6

David Aaron

Who would guess that the fashionable David Aaron and funky Steve Madden footwear lines are designed by the same team? David Aaron will satisfy anyone in search of Prada looks without Prada prices, with chic black ponyskin mules, driving moccasins, fun sandals, slip-ons, evening pumps and boots. Pay anywhere from $79 to $179 and have everyone think you're wearing designer when you're not.

SoHo 212-431-6022
529 Broadway bet. Spring/Prince
NYC 10012 Mon-Thur 11-8, Fri & Sat 11-8:30, Sun 11-7

Davide Cenci

Davide Cenci's mission statement is comfort, warmth, lightness and balance. The Cenci label focuses on luxurious fabrics, impeccable tailoring and subtle colors in suits, sportswear, shirts, sweaters, outerwear, accessories and a made-to-measure department. Off-the-rack suits begin at $1,200 and made-to-measure start at $2,100. Also find Tod's footwear. www.davidecenci.com

Upper East Side
801 Madison Avenue
NYC 10021

212-628-5910
bet. 67/68th St.
Mon-Sat 10-6:30, Thur 10-7:30

DDC Lab

DDC Lab is a techno-flavored parallel universe that looks like a space station where you can buy stuff. It contains a relaxed coffee bar, a magazine section, blaring rock music in the background and a clothing line for the edgy, designer denim-addicted crowd. High-tech, functional fabrics are their forte, driven by denim streetwear in finishes from stretch to tie-dyed. There also are hip basics like stretch leather pants, T-shirts, jackets and corduroys. Cool accessories include 70's and 80's styled vintage sunglasses and futuristic watches. Be prepared to spend—a pair of jeans alone will run you $160-$210.

Lower East Side
180 Orchard Street
NYC 10002

212-375-1647
bet. Stanton/Houston
Mon-Wed 11-7
Thur & Sat 11-8, Sun 12-6

Deco Jewels, Inc.

Deco's Janice Berkson travels far and wide in search of 40's and 50's Lucite handbags and lovingly restores them to pristine perfection. Prices start at $200. Vintage costume jewelry and cufflinks from the 1800s to the 1960s round out the gorgeous assortment.

SoHo
131 Thompson Street
NYC 10012

212-253-1222
bet. Prince/Houston
Mon-Sat 12-8, Sun 12-7

☆ Decollage

Decollage is different with a capital D. Owners Leah Forester and Heather Rich both walked away from fashion PR jobs to create this highly original retail-cum-showroom concept in a rickety townhouse in the West Village, covered with chinoiserie wallpaper and showcasing vintage and new pieces from a ruthlessly edited selection of like-minded designers. Hot name Zac Posen provides one-of-a-kind dresses while the store also stocks Alice Roi, Lainey Keogh knitwear and gorgeous Damaris Evans jewelry from London. The idea behind Decollage is to give artists an outlet for their more avant-garde work—in their very succinct words: "a fashion gallery." Go take a tour.

West Village   212-352-3338
23 Eighth Avenue   bet.12th/James
NYC 10014   Mon-Fri 10-5 (by appointment)

Delfino

Delfino's motto is that there's a bag for every outfit (only one?) and this stylish little shop houses a selection of all sizes and shapes in eye-popping colors, wild animal textures, as well as basic leathers. Labels include Longchamp, Ginkgo, Hervé Chapelier, Francesco Biasia, France's Bronti Bay and Mandarina Duck.   www.delfinoshop.com

Upper East Side   212-517-5391
1351A Third Avenue   bet. 77/78th St.
NYC 10021   Mon-Fri 10:30-8, Sat 10-7:30, Sun 12-7

Midtown West   212-956-0868
56 West 50th Street   at Rockefeller Center
NYC 10112   Mon-Fri 10:30-8, Sat 10:30-7, Sun 12-6

Detour

Sexy, slinky and somewhat pricey, Detour is a destination for the younger set in search of hip, tight-fitting outfits, including tees, jeans, skirts, dresses, leather jackets and racy ensembles perfect for club-hopping—because that's what Detour girls do!

SoHo   212-979-6315
472 West Broadway   bet. Houston/Prince
NYC 10012   Mon-Sun 11-8

SoHo   212-966-3635
154 Prince Street   bet. W. B'way/Thompson
NYC 10012   Mon-Sun 11-8

SoHo (M)   212-219-2692
425 West Broadway   bet. Prince/Spring
NYC 10012   Mon-Sun 11-8

D&G

If Dolce and Gabbana is about sensuality, its younger line, D&G, is pretty much all about sex. (A hooded sweatshirt emblazoned with the words, "Certified Sex Instructor" anyone?) Two floors of sportswear, eveningwear and casual wear are packed with flashy-cool pieces—super-tight pants, sexy minis, distressed jeans, rugged furs, chiffon florals, lots of sheer lace, pencil-thin leathers, smart suits and VLBDs (very little black dresses). The designers say the D&G woman "takes incredible joy at dressing up aimed at perplexing, teasing, having fun and, of course, showing herself." And how. Men aren't left out, though, and can choose from everything from classic Italian suits to screaming floral shirts, leather pants, jeans and logo'd T-shirts (check out their saucy take on I ❤ NY). Not for the timid. www.dolcegabbana.it

SoHo   212-965-8000
434 West Broadway   bet. Prince/Spring
NYC 10012   Mon-Fri 11-7, Thur 11-8, Sat 11-6, Sun 12-5

Denimax

Denimax
Three floors dedicated to coats and jackets in fur, shearling, leather, cashmere and microfiber in every style from basic leather jackets to luxury rabbit and mink coats. You can spend as little as $300 or as much as $100,000 if your heart is set on sable—and you are filthy rich.

Midtown East   212-207-4900
444 Madison Avenue   bet. 49/50th St.
NYC 10022   Mon-Fri 9-6, Sat & Sun 12-5

Dernier Cri
Another brilliant addition to the primo Meatpacking District shopping area. Owner Stacia Valle, the former tour manager for Third Eye Blind, has assembled an eclectic collection of clothes, accessories and, basically, incredibly cool stuff from designers specializing in that very thing: rocking casual by Luella Bartley, cool drama from London's Preen, Circle by Mara Hoffman and Tata Naka. Accessories are for the fashion fearless, including Kooba bags and Caprice Crane jewelry. Flick through vintage Rolling Stone magazines and Mick Rock photo books, spritz yourself with Sarah Horowitz perfume, and emerge radiant (and, more importantly in this neighborhood, very, very cool).

Chelsea   212-242-6061
869 Washington   bet. 13/14th St.
NYC 10014   Tues-Sat 11:30-10, Sun 12:30-6:30

Destination
After a serious designer clothes fix at Jeffrey (just one block away), make this your destination for hot new accessories, from hats and shoes to handbags and jewelry, by a great selection of labels. Best are an eclectic mix of jewelry (from feminine, delicate pieces to hard-core punk) by Stefano Poletti and Serge Thoroval and stylish handbags from labels like Jacques Le Corres.

Chelsea   212-727-2031
32-36 Little West 12th Street   bet. Washington/9th Ave.
NYC 10014   Mon-Sat 12-8, Sun 12-7

Diana & Jeffries
Away from the midtown retail frenzy, Diana & Jeffries is a slightly chaotic world of useful, street-smart looks, including handmade sweaters, cashmeres, sundresses, sequined spaghetti tops, hip-hugger jeans and T-shirts from labels including Theory, Nanette Lepore, Carol Horn, Cambio, Juicy and 3 Dot.

Upper East Side   212-831-0531
1310 Madison Avenue   bet. 92/93rd St.
NYC 10128   Mon-Sat 11-7, Sun 1-7

Upper West Side   212-874-2884
2062 Broadway   bet. 70/71st St.
NYC 10023   Mon-Sat 11-8, Sun 1-7

Diane von Furstenberg

Diane von Furstenberg invented the wrap dress and slick, city girls everywhere (like the Hilton sisters) are forever grateful. This store-cum-showroom—check out the Warhol of von Furstenberg on the wall—is a world of DVF, offering plenty of dresses (wraps, of course) in her signature prints and solid colors, flirty ruched tops, silk shirts, bias-cut georgette and matte jersey skirts, slim-fitting ultrasuede pants and jeans. Coordinating accessories include beaded handbags and shoes. Be forewarned, though: while the shop is well worth the trek, it's practically in New Jersey.

West Village   **646-486-4800**
385 West 12th Street   bet. Washington/West Side Highway
NYC 10014-1723   Mon-Wed, & Fri 11-7, Thur 11-8
Sat 11-6, Sun 12-5

Diesel

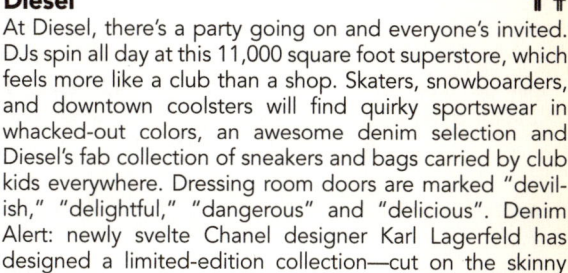

At Diesel, there's a party going on and everyone's invited. DJs spin all day at this 11,000 square foot superstore, which feels more like a club than a shop. Skaters, snowboarders, and downtown coolsters will find quirky sportswear in whacked-out colors, an awesome denim selection and Diesel's fab collection of sneakers and bags carried by club kids everywhere. Dressing room doors are marked "devilish," "delightful," "dangerous" and "delicious". Denim Alert: newly svelte Chanel designer Karl Lagerfeld has designed a limited-edition collection—cut on the skinny side!   www.diesel.com

NoHo (flagship)   **646-336-8552**
1 Union Square West   at 14th St.
NYC 10003   Mon-Fri 11-9, Sat 10-9, Sun 11-8

Upper East Side M/W/C   **212-308-0055**
770 Lexington Avenue   at 60th St.
NYC 10022   Mon-Sat 10-8, Sun 12-6

SoHo (Denim Gallery)   **212-966-5593**
68 Greene Street   bet. Prince/Spring
NYC 10012   Mon-Sat 11-7, Sun 12-6

DieselStyleLab

"The name 'StyleLab' originates from the desire to research and experiment with style, cuts, materials and ideas," says Diesel founder Renzo Rosso of this collection of high-end, avant-garde sportswear. Pants, jackets, shirts, sweaters, outerwear and accessories have been given the high-tech fabric treatment—and a little bit of Diesel-style controversy: "Let's Party" reads a T-shirt with a gun logo.   www.dieselstylelab.com

SoHo   **212-343-3863**
416 West Broadway   bet. Prince/Spring
NYC 10012   Mon-Sat 11-8, Sun 11-7

Dinosaur Designs

This Australian jewelry label launched in the motherland in the late Eighties and quickly developed a cult following for

DKNY

its chunky resin jewelry—rings, bracelets and knock-out strands of beads. Since then they have expanded into strong silver pieces as well as homewares, offering brilliantly colored vases and other home accoutrements. Confident, colorful and cool. www.dinosaurdesigns.com.au

NoLiTa **212-680-3523**
250 Mott Street bet. Houston/Prince
NYC 10012 Mon-Sat 11-7, Sun 12-6

DKNY

Donna Karan has always known what women want, New York women especially. Cue her DKNY line of high performance, affordable sportswear. The hip, color-coordinated collection of pants, tops, shirts, sweaters, knits, jackets, vintage pieces, jeans and eveningwear is easy to coordinate and wonderfully fresh—she even makes lemon yellow look good. Accessories include handbags and shoes. Check out DKNY's home collection as well as Blanche's Organic Café for the health-conscious crowd. www.dkny.com

Upper East Side **212-223-3569**
655 Madison Avenue at 60th St.
NYC 10021 Mon-Sat 10-8, Thur 10-9, Sun 10-7

SoHo **646-613-1100**
420 West Broadway bet. Prince/Spring
NYC 10012 Mon-Sat 11-8, Sun 12-7

D/L Cerney

Being trendy can be so exhausting—and no-one understands that better than husband-and-wife team Duane Cerney and Linda St. John. Their antidote: a collection of classic retro-inspired clothing featuring everything from simple gabardine shirts and straight skirts to fitted shift dresses and stretch pants. It's all in natural fabrics and hand-finished right down to the last button and stitch.

East Village **212-673-7033**
13 East 7th Street bet. 2/3rd Ave.
NYC 10003 Mon-Sun 12-7

Do Kham

Treasures from the Himalayas are beautifully displayed in this elegant SoHo shop, where you can choose from traditional Tibetan styled dresses, skirts and tops plus a collection of richly brocaded, fur-trimmed silk hats. Check out the fabulous selection of ever-versatile pashmina shawls ($125 to $195) as well as plain or embroidered scarves, boas and handbags in a myriad of colors and fabrics.

SoHo **212-966-2404**
51 Prince Street bet. Mulberry/Lafayette
NYC 10012 Mon-Sun 10-8

East Village **212-358-1010**
304 East 5th Street bet. 1/2nd Ave.
NYC 10003 Mon-Sun 11-8

Dolce & Gabbana 👨👩

Agent provocateurs Domenico Dolce and Stefano Gabbana get sex. They really get it—and their saucy vision rules everywhere from the streets of Milan to the Hollywood red carpet. They are so in synch with what the stars want to wear that they have designed stage costumes for everyone from Madonna to Kylie Minogue, while their signature curvy, bra-strapped dresses have brought out the babe in Isabella Rossellini, Gwyneth Paltrow...every celebrity worth their Vogue cover. This flagship store, their largest in the world, serves up a gorgeously rich collection of men's and women's ready-to-wear as well as some couture pieces from pinstriped suits (another Dolce classic) to seductive leopard dresses. Not to mention their to-die-for accessories like silk ribbon belts and denim stilettos. www.dolcegabbana.com

Upper East Side   **212-249-4100**
825 Madison Avenue   bet. 68/69th St.
NYC 10021   Mon-Sat 10-6, Thur 10-7

Domenico Spano 👨👩

Domenico Spano is quite simply the byword for bespoke tailoring in New York. Calabrian born tailor Domenico "Mimo" Spano has been creating extraordinary suits for tasteful gents for "longer than he'd like to admit!" laughs a staffer. Such experience yields treasures, and pieces that will last a lifetime. The former director of custom tailoring at Bergdorf Goodman designs many of his fabrics, and also provides a small tailoring service for women—think Katharine Hepburn's inimitable Thirties style and you've got it. If you want to indulge, this is one of the best places in the city for a wedding tuxedo, a bespoke wool version starting at $3,500 and prices escalating, depending on threads per square inch, from there.

Midtown East   **212-940-2792**
611 Fifth Avenue   at 50th St.
NYC 10022   Mon-Sat 10-7, Thur 10-8

☆ Domenico Vacca 👨👩

"The first authentic Italian boutique in the United States," promises owner Domenico Vacca, the man behind Borrelli, of this chic slice of Milano in the heart of Midtown. It's movie-star chic all the way with the collections of master tailor Cesare Attolini, whose father Vincenzo tailored suits for Clark Gable and the Duke of Windsor, next to fine shirting by Finamore and handmade belts and shoes by Stefano Bi and Andrea D'Amico. Then there's the house's signature collection of refined classic separates and suiting, all perfect for a sophisticated lunch at Harry Cipriani right next door.

Midtown East   **212-759-6333**
781 Fifth Avenue   bet. 59/60th St.
NYC 10022   Mon-Sat 10-7, Sun 12-6

Donna Karan Collection

Donna Karan is on a journey. She has carved out a bit of Zen on Madison Avenue with a calmly chic space complete with a serene bamboo garden in the rear. Karan has always designed what she herself wants to wear—distinctive yet comfortable clothes—and that's the secret of her success. This immense flagship boasts three floors of men's and women's suits, great black jackets (great black everything, actually), cozy sweaters, smart khaki trenchcoats, leathers and outerwear, as well as modern eveningwear like her sensuous jersey dress with Karan's signature off-the-shoulder styling. Also on offer are accessories and her curvy, African-inspired homewares.

Upper East Side 212-861-1001
819 Madison Avenue bet. 68/69th St.
NYC 10021 Mon-Sat 10-6, Thur 10-7

Dooney and Bourke

Dooney and Bourke's flagship offers its extensive collection of handbags, leathergoods and luggage crafted in durable wide-grained cowhide. These all-weather classics come in an abundance of colors and feature signature leather trim and saddle stitching. An alternative is its lightweight collection of stain-resistant, maintenance-free canvas bags. Don't miss their clothing: a sleek line of suede jackets and cashmere sweaters.   800-347-5000 www.dooney.com

Upper East Side 212-223-7444
28 East 60th Street bet. Madison/Park Ave.
NYC 10022 Mon-Sat 10-6

Dosa

LA-based Dosa designer Christina Kim makes a lot of women very, very happy with clothes that have a chicly bohemian vibe. The loose, girlish pieces come in the most delicious colors imaginable—best, the silks in rainbow colors and the covetable cashmeres. Kim's Asian heritage is in evidence in Tibetan-inspired tops and long, wrap skirts.

SoHo 212-431-1733
107 Thompson Street bet. Spring/Prince
NYC 10012 Mon-Sat 12-7, Sun 12-6

Double RL

This is the downtown outpost of the Ralph Lauren empire, where a more casual range of his easy American pieces mixes it up with select vintage items and a load of retro memorabilia, from old bikes to record players. It's a great place to get your Ralph jeans without heading uptown, or into the department store frenzy. Also available: a full range of accessories, including his fabulous chunky brown belts.

NoLiTa 212-343-0841
271 Mulberry Street bet. Jersey/Prince
NYC 10012 Mon-Sat 12-7, Sun 12-6

☆ Doyle and Doyle

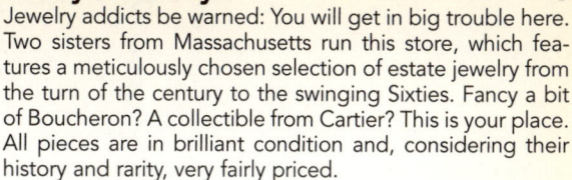

Jewelry addicts be warned: You will get in big trouble here. Two sisters from Massachusetts run this store, which features a meticulously chosen selection of estate jewelry from the turn of the century to the swinging Sixties. Fancy a bit of Boucheron? A collectible from Cartier? This is your place. All pieces are in brilliant condition and, considering their history and rarity, very fairly priced.

Lower East Side   **212-677-9991**
189 Orchard Street   bet. Houston/Stanton
NYC 10002   Tues-Fri 1-7, Thur 1-8, Sat & Sun 12-7

D. Porthault & Co.

Long recognized for luxurious bed and bath linens, D. Porthault is also the happy home of a small, enticing sleepwear department. Nighties, as they should be, are feminine and romantic, while nightshirts and robes are available in all the Porthault prints.   www.dporthault.fr

Upper East Side   **212-688-1660**
18 East 69th Street   bet. Madison/5th Ave.
NYC 10021   Mon-Sat 10-5:30

Earl Jean

Earl Jean was the first of the hip, micro-jeans brands that now include Lucky and Seven. They took on the Levi's and Diesels of the world. Devotees like Jennifer Aniston and Cameron Diaz swear by Earl designer Suzanne Costas Freiwald's super-flattering, leg-lengthening cuts and her fans grow daily. The look is ultra-sexy, low-slung jeans in dark denim, slim silhouettes and boot-leg cuts. Ask for Style 55—it guarantees a slender, long-legged look best worn with super-sexy heels. There's a world of other jean styles in fabrics like corduroy, chambray, leather and velvet, as well a collection of jean jackets, skirts and tops. Also check out Earl's accessory line of shoes, boots and belts. And there's good news for guys: Earl has just reintroduced its men's line, and it flatters in the same way as the women's.   www.earljean.com

SoHo   **212-226-8709**
160 Mercer Street   bet. Houston/Prince
NYC 10012   Mon-Sat 11-7, Sun 12-6

East Side Kids

An uptown neighborhood children's shop featuring back-to-school basics, party shoes, weekend casual wear and groovy duds from such brands as Sam & Libby, Enzo, Jumping Jack, Nike, Aster, Keds and Sonnets. From newborn to size 9/10.

Upper East Side   **212-360-5000**
1298 Madison Avenue   bet. 91/92nd St.
NYC 10128   Mon-Fri 9:30-6, Sat 9-6

Eastern Mountain Sports

EMS is a specialist in clothing and equipment for the outdoor sports of mountaineering, backpacking, hiking, ski-

Easy Spirit

ing and camping. Brand names include Columbia, North Face, Patagonia and its own label. 888-463-6367
www.emsonline.com

SoHo 212-966-8730
591 Broadway bet. Houston/Prince
NYC 10012 Mon-Fri 10-9, Sat 10-8, Sun 12-6

Upper West Side 212-397-4860
20 West 61st Street bet. B'way/9th Ave.
NYC 10023 Mon-Fri 10-9, Sat 10-6, Sun 12-6

Easy Spirit
This footwear company's patented, multi-layer cushioning support system guarantees a comfortable fit. Styles range from career and fitness to fun and casual. It's footwear that protects your feet from shock—and your wallet, too. www.easyspirit.com

Upper East Side 212-828-9593
1518 Third Avenue bet. 85/86th St.
NYC 10028 Mon-Fri 10-8, Sat 11-7, Sun 12-6

Upper West Side 212-875-8146
2251 Broadway bet. 80/81st St.
NYC 10024 Mon-Sat 10-7:30, Sun 11-6

Midtown East 212-715-0152
555 Madison Avenue at 56th St.
NYC 10022 Mon-Fri 9-7, Sat 10-6, Sun 12-5

Midtown West 212-398-2761
1166 Sixth Avenue at 46th St.
NYC 10036 Mon-Fri 9-7, Sat 10-5:30, Sun 12-5:30

Eclipse
In seven years, Dollhouse has become one of the most popular labels in junior fashions. Its secret: trendy clothes that won't burn a hole in your wallet. Cool silhouettes and techno-fabrics define its jeans, T-shirts, mini-skirts, dresses, tube tops, leathers, suedes and capri pants. It's perfect for trend-craving teens—just ask such devotees as teen-queen Britney Spears and eternal teen Drew Barrymore.

NoHo 212-539-1800
400 Lafayette Street at E. 4th St.
NYC 10003 Mon-Sat 11-8, Sun 12-7

Eddie Bauer
Eddie Bauer is a true American success story: expanding from a single store in Seattle to 600 stores nationwide. It's a top purveyor of classic, sporty, all-American lifestyle clothing that sticks to—and goes far beyond—its traditions as a rugged outdoor brand. Well-organized displays of merchandise and a friendly sales staff make shopping here a pleasure. Look for A/K/A, a dress/casual line of office clothing, as well as wrinkle-resistant khakis, polo shirts, jeans, sweaters, outerwear, underwear and eyewear. Buy up big and pack it all into one of their sport duffels. Terrific value. 800-426-6253 www.eddiebauer.com

Eileen Fisher

Upper East Side — 212-737-0002
1172 Third Avenue
NYC 10021
bet. 68/69th St.
Mon-Sat 10-8, Sun 11-6

Upper West Side — 212-877-7629
1960 Broadway
NYC 10023
at 67th St.
Mon-Thur 10-9
Fri & Sat 10-10, Sun 11-9

Midtown East — 212-808-0820
711 Third Avenue
NYC 10017
bet. 44/45th St.
Mon-Fri 11-8, Sat 11-6, Sun 12-5

SoHo — 212-925-2179
578 Broadway
NYC 10012
bet. Houston/Prince
Mon-Thur 10-8, Fri & Sat 10-9, Sun 11-7

Edmundo Castillo

Edmundo Castillo, winner of the Council of Fashion Designers of America's Best Accessories Designer award in 2001, recently opened what he calls "the ultimate shoe closet" in NoLita. The store, inspired by his own living room, lovingly showcases Castillo's super-sexy shoes, like spangly gladiator sandals that weave seductively around the ankles or bold and bright espadrilles. Expect the fashion flock to, um, flock here. Prices range from $345 to a heady $1,200.

NoLiTa — 212-431-5320
219 Mott Street
10012
bet Houston/Prince
Mon-Sat 11-7, Sun 12-6

Eileen Fisher

Fisher's claim to fame: casual, maintenance-free clothing that travels anywhere. There are jackets, skirts, pants with elastic waistlines and T-shirts designed in a relaxed fit. A solid, pretty color palette makes mixing and matching a cinch.   800-345-3362   www.eileenfisher.com

Upper East Side — 212-879-7799
1039 Madison Avenue
NYC 10021
bet. 79/80th St.
Mon-Sat 10-7, Sun 12-5

Upper West Side — 212-362-3000
341 Columbus Avenue
NYC 10024
bet. 76/77th St.
Mon-Sat 10-7, Sun 12-6

Midtown East — 212-759-9888
521 Madison Avenue
NYC 10022
bet. 53/54th St.
Mon-Sat 10-7, Sun 12-6

Flatiron — 212-924-4777
103 Fifth Avenue
NYC 10003
bet. 17/18th St.
Mon-Sat 10-8, Sun 12-6

SoHo — 212-431-4567
395 West Broadway
NYC 10012
bet. Broome/Spring
Mon-Thur 11-7, Fri & Sat 11-8
Sun 12-6

East Village (outlet) — 212-529-5715
314 East 9th Street
NYC 10003
bet. 1/2nd Ave.
Mon-Sat 12-8, Sun 12-7

Eisenberg and Eisenberg

For over a century, this shop has been one of New York's sources for inexpensive formalwear. Don't let the unglamorous façade deter you from venturing inside, where you'll find suits, slacks, sportcoats, blazers, shirts, men's furnishings and a full range of tuxedos. Pay an average price of $375 for suits and from $190 to $650 for tuxedos. Extra for alterations.

Chelsea
16 West 17th Street
NYC 10011
212-627-1290
bet. 5/6th Ave.
Mon-Fri 9-5:45, Thur 9-6:45, Sat 9-5

Elaine Arsenault

This jaunty accessories store recalls the equally jaunty aesthetic of Kate Spade in a range of clever totes with wooden-looking leather handles, each efficiently displayed like art on the wall. Perfect for taking to Sunday brunch, they come in neutral colors or sporty stripes. Also available: simple purses and wallets. www.elainearsenault.com

East Village
305 East 9th Street
NYC 10003
212-228-3251
bet 1st/2nd Ave.
Mon-Sat 12-7, Sun 12-6

Eleven

If Sofia Coppola and Spike Jonze are your style heroes, and the Beastie Boys are your favorite rockers, check out Eleven for downtown-cool vintage clothes, amongst them a collection of striped polo shirts, old baseball shirts, slouchy denim, kitsch shoes and expensive retro logo'd handbags. Best is their rocking collection of sneakers—from old-school Converse Chuck Taylors to Pumas.

NoLiTa
11 Prince Street
NYC 10012
212-219-1033
at Elizabeth
Mon-Sun 1-8

Emanuel Ungaro

Ungaro is every girl's guilty pleasure. "Pink is the institutional color for Ungaro," designer Emanuel Ungaro says, and it's more than obvious when you walk into this brilliantly rose-toned store. Ungaro gave up the ready-to-wear reins at his house two seasons ago to his former design assistant Giambattista Valli and while Valli's first season was a bit of a stumble, he hit his stride for fall by sticking to what Ungaro does best. This store is the perfect showcase for the company's deliciously feminine pieces; flirty dresses in chiffon or with floral prints that are regularly sported by seductive celebs like Elizabeth Hurley and Sarah Jessica Parker as well as the model set, who often dress the romantic pieces down by wearing them over jeans. Accessories include fabulously flirty shoes (some in, yes, pink), belts, bags and evening shawls.

Upper East Side
792 Madison Avenue
NYC 10021
212-249-4090
at 67th St.
Mon-Sat 10-6

Emporio Armani

Giorgio Armani redux: the look of the Italian classic without the high prices—think 50% cheaper, and a more youthful attitude. The palette: black, white, red and Armani's classic beige. Suits, sportswear, knockout sequined eveningwear, coats, jeans, knits, T-shirts, shoes and accessories are all here. A great entrée to the Armani world.   www.emporioarmani.com

Midtown East 212-317-0800
601 Madison Avenue bet. 57/58th St.
NYC 10022 Mon-Wed 10-7, Thur & Fri 10-8
Sat 10-7, Sun 12-6

Flatiron 212-727-3240
110 Fifth Avenue at 16th St.
NYC 10011 Mon-Sat 11-7, Thur 11-8, Sun 12-6

SoHo 646-613-8099
410 West Broadway at Spring
NYC 10012 Mon-Sat 11-7, Thur 11-8, Sun 12-6

Encore

One of the best consignment stores in New York, selling high-end designer labels in mint condition. Unlike the "rummage-sale" environment found in most resale shops, Encore's collection is well-edited and best known for its Chanel suits, Manolo Blahnik shoes and covetable Yves Saint Laurent blouses. Other luxe labels include Celine, Yohji Yamamoto, Prada, Chloé and Fendi—all at least a third off original prices.

Upper East Side 212-879-2850
1132 Madison Avenue, 2nd Fl. bet. 84/85th St.
NYC 10028 Mon-Fri 10:30-6:30, Thur 10:30-7,
Sat 10:30-6, Sun 12-6

Enerla Lingerie

For 22 years this East Village shop has been keeping the girls happy with its collection of sexy, romantic lingerie and great basics. The range includes sleepwear, robes, foundations, bustiers, swimwear and hosiery from labels like Lou, La Mystere, Claire Pettibone, Chiarigi, Orablu, Eberjey, Mary Green and the ubiquitous Cosabella.

East Village 212-473-2454
48 1/2 East 7th Street bet. 1/2nd Ave.
NYC 10003 Mon-Sat 12-9, Sun 12-8

Entre Nous

Just between us—or as the French say, *entre nous*—this shop is one of New York's best kept secrets. It's a sophisticated showcase of luxury European labels—Luciano Barbera's complete collection of pants, classic blazers, cashmeres and tailored, chic shirting; jeans by Cambio; evening dresses and gowns by Sylvia Heisel.

Upper East Side 212-249-2225
1124 Third Avenue bet. 65/66th St.
NYC 10021 Mon-Fri 10-6, Sat 11-6

Enzo Angiolini

Enzo Angiolini is Nine West's better footwear division. Find up-to-the-minute styles that include basic comfort flats, man-tailored loafers, trendy sandals, platforms, boots and more. It's about fashion-forward shoes that look expensive but aren't.

Midtown East   **212-339-8921**
551 Madison Avenue   at 55th St.
NYC 10022   Mon-Fri 9:30-7:30, Sat 10-6, Sun 12-5

Midtown East   **212-286-8726**
331 Madison Avenue   at 43rd St.
NYC 10017   Mon-Fri 8-8, Sat 10-6, Sun 12-5

Midtown West   **212-695-8903**
901 Sixth Avenue   in Manhattan Mall bet. B'way/33rd St.
NYC 10001   Mon-Sat 10-8, Sun 11-6

Epperson Studio

Singers Erykah Badu and Lauren Hill are devoted followers of husband-wife team Epperson and Lisha, the talents behind this trans-cultural clothing collection inspired by China, India and Africa. Deconstructed shapes, patchwork, raw edges and plenty of color are keys to the Epperson line of long dresses, capes, shirts, hats and head wraps.

SoHo   **212-226-3181**
25 Thompson Street   bet. Watts/Grand
NYC 10013   Tues-Sat 1-7

☆ Eres

With boutiques in Paris, Palm Beach and Manhattan, Eres' luxury lingerie draws its sleek-chic clientele (Vogue loves it) with its high-quality everyday basics and fabulous, perfect-fitting bra styles. Manufactured in trademark skin tones and featherweight fabrics (trying "le souffle" is a must), Eres' natural silhouettes can easily pass for custom lingerie, but at lower prices—panties are $65-$90 and bras $140-$190. Their swimwear is second-to-none: bikinis, thankfully, are sold as separates with racy styles like deep V-necks and low-cut backs, and sexy, boy-leg shorts paired with string tops. Pareos and cover-up dresses are also on show, not to mention a racy line of garter belts, bustiers, pantyhose and tights.   www.eresparis.com

Midtown East   **212-223-3550**
621 Madison Avenue   bet. 58/59th St.
NYC 10022   Mon-Sat 10-6

SoHo   **212-431-7300**
98 Wooster Street   at Spring
NYC 10012   Mon-Sun 11-7

Eric Shoes

This popular Upper East Side shoe shop features casual basics, career and evening shoes with edgy heel and toe treatments from such brands as Stuart Weitzman, Nicole Miller, Cynthia Rowley and Anne Klein, as well as its own private label.

Etro

Upper East Side   **212-289-5762**
1222 Madison Avenue   at 88th St.
NYC 10128   Mon-Fri 10-7, Sat 10-6, Sun 12-6

Upper East Side   **212-288-8250**
1333 Third Avenue   at 76th St.
NYC 10021   Mon-Fri 10-7, Thur 11-8
Sat 10-6, Sun 12-6

Erica Tanov

This large, clean space is the perfect backdrop for Erica Tanov's collection of sophisticated women's wear, bed linens, baby clothes, lingerie and accessories defined by elegant fabrics, classic styling and careful attention to detail. Her pieces are complemented by knitwear from John Smedley and Brooklyn Handknits, dresses by Megan Park and lingerie by La Cosa. Children can be turned out in Erica Tanov and I Golfini della Nonna's collection of cheerful printed rompers, bloomers and smocks.   www.ericatanov.com

NoLiTa   **212-334-8020**
204 Elizabeth Street   bet. Spring/Prince
NYC 10012   Mon-Sat 11-7, Sun 12-6

Ermenegildo Zegna

Zegna is, simply, the byword for luxury menswear. Their classic suits range from high-powered tailored styles to deconstructed modern versions at an average price of $1,840 (and much more for custom). Shirts, ties, sportswear, outerwear, shoes and accessories are also available.   www.ezegna.com

Fifth Avenue   **212-421-4488**
743 Fifth Avenue   bet. 57/58th St.
NYC 10022   Mon-Fri 10-6:30, Sat 10-6, Sun 12-6

Escada

Color me happy! That's what German fashion house Escada will do for you. Opulent fabrics, vibrant prints and lots of embroidery are the trademarks of their three collections Escada Couture, Escada Ready-to-Wear and Escada Sport, which are best for a more "mature" woman. This is the place to find that lime green skirt suit you've always dreamed of. Looks range from dressy wool suits and casual stretch denim to sequined, glitzy eveningwear. Accessories include handbags, scarves and shoes.

Fifth Avenue   **212-755-2200**
715 Fifth Avenue   at 56th St.
NYC 10022   Mon-Sat 10-6, Thur 10-7, Sun 12-5

Etro

A luxe Italian label that's perfect for seasoning your wardrobe with color, pattern and texture. This six-floor shop features ready-to-wear, weekend wear, home furnishings, shoes, accessories, luggage and fragrances, all in exclusive materials, modern designs and expert craftsmanship. Men can shop English tailored suits, shirts, paisley ties galore, sportswear and outerwear, while women can select from skirts, trousers, shirts, cashmeres, classic riding-styled jackets, outerwear and more. A great place to go to bring out the eccentric dresser in all of us.

Upper East Side 212-317-9096
720 Madison Avenue bet. 63/64th St.
NYC 10021 Mon-Sat 10-6

☆ Eugenia Kim

Walk into milliner Eugenia Kim's Rubik's Cube-colored shop to see firsthand her collectible, cool hats that are flaunted at awards shows everywhere by "look at me!" celebrities like Jennifer Lopez and Lil' Kim, not to mention the requisite socialites and downtown hipsters. Standouts include simple-chic leather and newsboy caps, floppy hippy hats with gold chain bands, felt cloches, shearling trooper hats and fur numbers from rabbit fur berets to the ultimate fox fur hat complete with head, tail and paws. Only for the brave! Prices run from $120 to $400. You'd be well-advised to make an appointment. www.eugeniakim.com

East Village 212-673-9787
203 East 4th Street bet. Ave. A/B
NYC 10009 Mon-Sat 12-8, Sun 1-7

Eva

A sleek one-stop-shop for everything from a languid evening dress to Hamptons weekend attire. There are collections from up-and-coming designers, local designers and everyone in between—Sky, Jill Stuart Jeans, the flirty Rubinchapelle and Uniform. Accessories include cool jewelry, handbags by Sold and Matt Murphy, and shoes by Sky.

NoLiTa 212-925-3208
227 Mulberry Street bet. Prince/Spring
NYC 10012 Mon-Sat 12-8, Sun 12-7

Express

This division of the giant fashion conglomerate The Limited is great for younger shoppers who are making the transition from school to the workplace—and who aren't exactly loaded. Basic dresses, pants, skirts, T-shirts, leggings and quick-hit accessories like leopard totes all match the latest color forecasts and trends—from hippy to clubby. Here's a tip: more than one glam actress-about-town swears by their thongs. Also keep your eyes peeled for their new unisex denim area, where you can bring the boys too. 877-657-2292

Upper West Side 212-580-5833
321 Columbus Avenue bet. 75/76th St.
NYC 10023 Mon-Sat 10-8, Sun 11-7

Midtown East 212-421-7246
722-28 Lexington Avenue bet. 58/59th St.
NYC 10022 Mon-Sat 10-8, Sun 11-6

Midtown East 212-644-4453
477 Madison Avenue bet. 51/52nd St.
NYC 10021 Mon-Sat 10-8, Sun 11-7

Façonnable

Midtown East 212-949-9784
733 Third Avenue at 46th St.
NYC 10017 Mon-Sat 10-8, Sun 12-7

Midtown West 212-629-6838
7 West 34th Street bet. 5/6th Ave.
NYC 10001 Mon-Sat 10-8, Sun 12-7

Midtown West 212-971-3280
901 Sixth Avenue bet. B'way/33rd St.
NYC 10001 Mon-Sat 10-8, Sun 11-6

Flatiron 212-633-9414
130 Fifth Avenue at 18th St.
NYC 10011 Mon-Fri 10-8, Sat 10-7, Sun 12-6

☆ Eye Candy

Eye Candy is a shining jewel of a store—literally; the cute, retro baubles in here may hurt your eyes. It's one of the best destinations in town for primo vintage accessories, from diamante and beaded jewelry, as well as sunglasses, a great-condition selection of shoes and a huge number of bags (everything from Sixties Gucci to colorful Mexican straw) that line the shop walls. Owner Ron Caldwell can often be found trying on groovy sunglasses and asking customers for their opinion. The wares aren't cheap, but they're distinctive enough to be worth it.

NoHo 212-343-4275
329 Lafayette Street bet. Bleecker/Houston
NYC 10012 Mon-Sun 12-8

Fabulous Fanny's

"If you have to wear them, make it fun" is the slogan of this antique eyewear store, which carries New York's largest selection of vintage glasses—some from as far back as the 1700s (we wouldn't advise you to wear those to the office!). They have a fantastic range of spectacles and sunglasses and welcome you to rummage through the drawers of optical oddities, each labeled by era and style. Also available are earrings and a collection of men's clothes from nearby retro emporium Amarcord. www.fabulousfannys.com

East Village 212-533-0637
335 East 9th Street bet 1st/2nd Ave.
NYC 10003 Mon-Sun 12-8

Façonnable

The perfect shop for the well-dressed man. No wardrobe is complete without a Façonnable tie or spread-collar shirt. Suits come in classic silhouettes, the sportswear is perfect for weekends and outerwear is a must, particularly the fab micro-fiber bomber jackets in spring and winter weights. It's a stylish French version of Ralph Lauren. One thing, however: the Façonnable logo is everywhere you look. And for the true fan, get ready for Façonnable heaven when the store moves to Sephora's former flagship in Rockefeller Center next year. There will be 24,000-square-feet of Façonnable, including its women's wear and more of its accessories.

Fame

Midtown East   **212-319-0111**
689 Fifth Avenue   at 54th St.
NYC 10022   Mon-Sat 10-7, Thur 10-8, Sun 12-6
(moving to Rockefeller Center, Fifth Avenue in 2003)

Fame

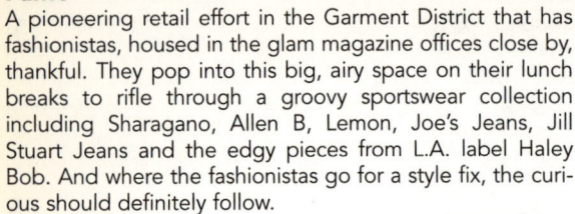

A pioneering retail effort in the Garment District that has fashionistas, housed in the glam magazine offices close by, thankful. They pop into this big, airy space on their lunch breaks to rifle through a groovy sportswear collection including Sharagano, Allen B, Lemon, Joe's Jeans, Jill Stuart Jeans and the edgy pieces from L.A. label Haley Bob. And where the fashionistas go for a style fix, the curious should definitely follow.

Midtown West   **212-730-4806**
512 Seventh Avenue   bet. 37/38th St.
NYC 10018   Mon-Thur 9-8, Fri 9-6, Sun 11-6

Fan Club

Veteran TV host Gene London and his partner John Thomas' fascination with glamorama movie stars led them to acquire one of the most extensive collections of showbiz wardrobes and memorabilia and inspired them to open this consignment shop. It's filled with sequined evening gowns, super-spangly couture by Bob Mackie (bring out the Cher inside you!), wedding gowns and other glittery show-stoppers.

Chelsea   **212-929-3349**
22 West 19th Street   bet. 5/6th Ave.
NYC 10011   Tues-Sat 12-5

February Eleventh

Women who like their fashion on the arty side will appreciate the tricksy handwork on display here in crocheted dresses, separates and shawls, as well as embroidered, lace and hand-dyed pieces. Equally detailed handbags and jewelry are also available. So what's with the store's name? It's the owner's birthday.

East Village   **212-529-1175**
315 East 9th Street   bet. 1/2nd Ave.
NYC 10003   Mon-Sun 1-8

Fendi

Karl Lagerfeld is a busy man: One minute he's turning out polished collections for Chanel and the next he's creating the darkly glamorous flash that is Fendi. Fendinistas flock here for tooled or bejeweled handbags, shoes, accessories and fabulous furs. The "baguette," ubiquitous a few years ago, is still going strong with styles from denim to crocodile trimmed with jeweled fasteners. Prices start at $450 and run to $6,000. In fur, Lagerfeld fancies mink, often in graphic, eye-popping patterns that will leave a lasting impression. So if you love logos, accessories and foxy dressing, congratulations—you're a Fendi lady.   800-336-3469   www.fendi.it

Fine & Klein

Fifth Avenue | **212-767-0100**
720 Fifth Avenue | at 56th St.
NYC 10019 | Mon-Fri 10-6, Sat 10-7, Sun 12-6

Filene's Basement 👫

A Boston institution that stocks reasonably priced designer overruns in career wear, sportswear, shoes, luggage, accessories and fragrances. If you're lucky you might even come across an outfit by Valentino, Donna Karan, Arnold Scassi or Liz Claiborne. But, like all discounters, it can be hit and miss. www.filenesbasement.com

Upper West Side | **212-873-8000**
2222 Broadway | at 79th St.
NYC 10024 | Mon-Sat 9:30-9, Sun 11-7

Chelsea | **212-620-3100**
620 Sixth Avenue | bet. 18/19th St.
NYC 10011 | Mon-Sat 9:30-9, Sun 11-6

Filth Mart 👫

Don't hold the name against it, because there isn't anything filthy about this vintage clothing store, owned by fashion-forward Sopranos actress Drea de Matteo. It carries a notable collection of kitsch, cool band T-shirts, baseball shirts, all manner of retro looks and, if you venture to the back of the narrow store, there are great straw handbags and sassy Seventies shoes—all at nice, clean prices.

East Village | **212-387-0650**
531 East 13th Street | bet. Ave. A/B
NYC 10003 | Sun-Tues 1-7, Wed-Sat 1-8

Find Outlet 👤

Just blocks from Chelsea's art galleries, this store features racks of one-of-a-kind designer samples and over-stocks. It's a brilliant destination for edgy clothing from such labels as D&G, Christian Louboutin, Helmut Lang, Chloé, Alice Roi, Earl Jeans, Mint and Tracy Feith, all at 50% to 80% off retail. Customers can receive e-mails about weekly arrivals, so get added to their list, quick! www.findoutlet.com

Chelsea | **212-243-3177**
361 West 17th Street | bet. 8/9th Ave.
NYC 10011 | Thur-Sun 12-7

NoLiTa | **212-243-3177**
229 Mott Street | bet. Prince/Spring
NYC 10012 | Mon-Sun 12-7

Fine & Klein 👤

The allure of Fine & Klein isn't its ambience but its well-priced selection of over 1,000 designer handbag styles. New Yorkers on limited budgets flock here for mass-designer brand names like Pierre Cardin and Sharif. Enjoy the great prices but watch out for crowds on Sundays and holidays.

Fiona Walker

Lower East Side 212-674-6720
119 Orchard Street at Delancey
NYC 10002 Mon-Thur 8:30-4:30, Fri 8:30-4
Sun 8:30-4:30

Fiona Walker
When department stores told Fiona Walker her clothes were too expensive to put into the young designer section, she opened her own digs in Hell's Kitchen. Having grown up studying textile and fabrics in Ireland, Walker is a knitter extraordinaire. Best are yarn-fringed tops, popcorn-stitched turtlenecks and tweedy sweaters. Custom is also available.

Midtown West 212-664-9699
451 West 46th Street bet. 9/10th Ave.
NYC 10036 Mon-Fri 1-7:30, Sat 12-7

Fiorucci
As any Seventies scenester will tell you, the name Fiorucci is synonymous with the disco era's racy style. Fiorucci's trademark winged logo is still drawing the 18-to-25-year-old crowd, who buy up a cool collection of sportswear and casual basics. Find jeans, printed T-shirts, mohair sweaters, swimwear, accessories, shoes and knick-knacks like salt and pepper shakers and bath toys. Price ranges from $45 to $380. Other amenities include a café and hair salon. www.fiorucci.com

NoHo 212-982-8844
622 Broadway bet. Houston/Bleecker
NYC 10012 Mon-Sat 11-8, Sun 11-7

Fisch for the Hip
Anyone in search of a vintage Hermès handbag in perfect condition (and that would be, like, everyone) should hurry down to Fisch for the Hip, a "luxe" consignment shop. In addition to stocking three display cases with said posh handbags and Louis Vuitton luggage, owners Pamela and Terin Fisch bring in the "best of the best" from labels like Gucci, Celine, Helmut Lang, Prada and Dolce & Gabbana. The merchandise is in mint condition and half the price of retail. Also find shoes by Manolo Blahnik, Prada and Chanel. Great sample sales.

Chelsea 212-633-9053
153 West 18th Street bet. 6/7th Ave.
NYC 10011 Mon-Sat 12-7, Sun 12-6

☆ Flight 001
This must be the coolest travel store in New York; hell, anywhere. It's all very wallpaper*, with snappy travel gear in cool colors that take their design straight from the mid-century style celebrated in that interior/travel magazine. It's very hard to go wrong here—from digital watches (with the all-important multiple time zones) to perfectly proportioned nylon carry-ons to cute bits and pieces like pens, stationery and the absolutely must-have aromatherapy "de-stress"

kits. The coolest thing? Each purchase is sealed with a sticker that looks like a boarding pass. Book that flight to Berlin immediately! www.flight001.com

West Village	**212-691-1001**
96 Greenwich Avenue	at 12th St
NYC 10014	Mon-Sat 11-8.30, Sun 12-6

Flood

When a costume designer, a photographer and a stylist open a store, you're pretty much guaranteed that it's going to score high on the cool scale. And Flood does. If you're a fan of the sartorial delights of the Eighties, you'll be spoilt for choice here. It's been well-reported that designer Michael Kors once came in and bought out their entire shoe, belt and boot collection. Rest assured they've re-stocked!

East Village	**212-260-2269**
26 First Avenue	bet. 1st/2nd St.
NYC 10003	Tues-Sat 11-8, Sun 12-7

Flying A

A new addition to the SoHo retail scene, Flying A provides a cool collection of sportswear from labels like Fred Perry, brashly colorful T-shirts from Custo Barcelona, girly shirts and skirts from Imperio, folksy tops and jeans from Ella Moss and easy-wearing accessories from Sequoia and Loop. They also sell a range of vintage clothes (as does every store worth its fashion cred these days). Coolest is their collection of original, crisp Green Flash sneakers from Dunlop—and if you like a more worn-in look, they also make a Dirty Flash (pre-stained with tea to look more fashionably beat up).

SoHo	**212-965-9090**
169 Spring Street	bet. West Broadway/Thompson
NYC 10012	Mon-Sat 11-8, Sun 12-7

☆ Foley & Corinna

Liv Tyler, Gwyneth Paltrow, Cameron Diaz, style queen Shiva Rose McDermott (wife of Dylan), Jennifer Connelly—what more proof is needed that this shop is hot with celeb fashionistas? All make the pilgrimage to snap up sparkly, ethnic-flavored designs by former playwright Dana Foley who, with her partner, Anna Corinna, runs the cult boutique. Foley's designs line the racks next to one-off vintage pieces that Corinna sources from around the world. Pick up anything from a pair of cowboy boots to cool hipster denim pants at prices around $75 to $200.

Lower East Side	**212-529-2338**
108 Stanton Street	bet. Ludlow/Essex
NYC 10002	Mon-Fri 1-8, Sat-Sun 12-8

Fogal

You can never have enough saucy stockings—so head to one of the best labels around (alongside Wolford), Fogal.

It's famous for its fabulous color selection—at last count, over 85 tempting shades—from sophisticated to downright saucy. They have everything from sheer and opaque hose at $25, patterned and textured styles like the "Duplice," a fishnet layered over an opaque, or the "Reticella," a sexy lace hose at $35. If you really want to indulge yourself, there are always Fogal's fabulous cashmere-silk tights, which will set you back a mere $370. But think of the joy they'll give you! Other items include luxurious bodysuits in cashmere/silk blends and lingerie. Good personalized service. www.fogal.com

Upper East Side
988 Madison Avenue
NYC 10021
212-717-7958
bet. 76/77th St.
Mon-Fri 10-6, Thur 10-8, Sat 10-5

Midtown East
510 Madison Avenue
NYC 10022
212-355-3254
at 53rd St.
Mon-Fri 10-6, Thur 10-8, Sat 10-5

Foot Locker

Foot Locker sells athletic wear and footwear for the entire family. There are workout clothes for fitness and basketball and a range of shoes suitable for running, tennis, basketball or cross training from such brands as Nike, Reebok, Adidas, Fila and New Balance. 800-991-6681 www.footlocker.com

Upper East Side
159 East 86th Street
NYC 10028
212-348-8652
bet. Lex./3rd Ave.
Mon-Sat 9-8, Sun 11-6

Upper East Side
1504 Second Avenue
NYC 10021
212-396-4567
bet. 78/79th St.
Mon-Sat 10-7, Sun 11-6

Midtown West
120 West 34th Street
NYC 10001
212-629-4419
bet. 6/7th Ave.
Mon-Fri 8-9, Sat 9-9, Sun 11-7

Midtown West
901 Sixth Avenue
NYC 10001
212-268-7146
at Manhattan Mall at 33rd St.
Mon-Sat 10-8, Sun 11-6

Midtown West
43 West 34th Street
NYC 10001
212-971-9449
bet. 5/6th Ave.
Mon-Fri 8-9, Sat 9-9, Sun 11-7

Flatiron
853 Broadway
NYC 10001
212-673-9749
at 14th St.
Mon-Sat 9-9, Sun 11-6

East Village
252 First Avenue
NYC 10009
212-254-9187
at 15th St.
Mon-Sat 10-8, Sun 11-7

Lower East Side
94 Delancey Street
NYC 10002
212-533-8608
bet. Ludlow/Orchard
Mon-Sun 10-7

NoHo
734 Broadway
NYC 10003
212-995-0381
at 8th St.
Mon-Sat 9-9, Sun 11-7

Forreal Basics

Lower Manhattan   212-608-3640
89 South Street Seaport   Pier 17
NYC 10038   Mon-Sat 10-9, Sun 11-8

Forman's

This is the place for designer sportswear, separates and outerwear at terrific discounted prices. Forman's also offers an extensive petite and plus-size department, and the merchandise changes constantly. Labels include Jones New York, Evan Picone, Ralph Lauren, Kasper and Liz Claiborne. Take an additional 40% off during end-of-season sales.

Midtown East   212-681-9800
145 East 42nd Street   bet. Lex./3rd Ave.
NYC 10017   Mon-Fri 8-8
    Sun 10-6

Lower East Side   212-228-2500
82 Orchard Street   bet. Broome/Grand
NYC 10002   Mon-Wed 9-6, Thur 9-8
    Fri 9-2, Sun 9-7

Fifth Avenue   212-719-1000
560 Fifth Avenue   at 46th St.
NYC 10017   Mon-Thur 8-9, Fri 8-2
    Sun 10-6

Lower Manhattan   212-791-4100
59 John Street   at Williams
NYC 10039   Mon-Wed 7:30-7, Thur 7:30-8
    Fri 7:30-2, Sun 11-5:30

Forreal

While Forreal Basics targets twentysomethings, Forreal appeals to women in search of dressier looks with a selection of slim-fitted pants, sexy knits, jackets, sweaters and T-shirts from such labels as Juicy Couture, Fred Sun, Vertigo, Michael Stars and Petit Bateau.

Upper East Side   212-396-0563
1369 Third Avenue   bet. 78/79th St.
NYC 10021   Mon-Sat 11-7, Sun 12-6

Upper East Side   212-717-0493
1200 Lexington Avenue   bet. 81/82nd St.
NYC 10028   Mon-Sat 11-7, Sun 12-6

Forreal Basics

Mothers bring their teenage daughters here for the hip assortment of jeans and casual basics, but get sucked in to the vortex and end up buying something for themselves as well. Jeans are from labels like Diesel, Miss Sixty, Mavi and Fred Perry and there also is an abundance of fitted tees and T-shirts from makers like Michael Stars, 3 Dot and Petit Bateau. Cutest are the terry running shorts by Puma.

Upper East Side   212-734-2105
1335 Third Avenue   bet. 76/77th St.
NYC 10021   Mon-Sat 11-7, Sun 12-6

☆ Forward

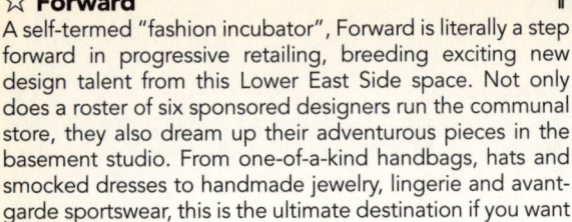

A self-termed "fashion incubator", Forward is literally a step forward in progressive retailing, breeding exciting new design talent from this Lower East Side space. Not only does a roster of six sponsored designers run the communal store, they also dream up their adventurous pieces in the basement studio. From one-of-a-kind handbags, hats and smocked dresses to handmade jewelry, lingerie and avant-garde sportswear, this is the ultimate destination if you want to be—pardon the pun—fashion forward...

Lower East Side 646-264-3233
72 Orchard Street bet. Broome/Grand
NYC 10002 Mon-Sun 12-7

Fossil

"The American classic, original and genuine" the nearly 50-year-old Fossil trumpets from the window of this huge, colorful store, the first to sell clothing and accessories from this company, which is best known for its funky watches. As far as Fossil gear is concerned, think Quiksilver with a Fifties retro edge: There is a huge range of activewear, including walls of Hawaiian shirts; cheeky tees for the chicks that read "Fast Girls," and a signature jeans collection. Great for gifts are, of course, the watches, which each come in a Fifties tin that the customer can choose.

SoHo 212-274-9579
541 Broadway at Prince
NYC 10036 Mon-Sat 10-9, Sun 11-7

Francis Hendy

This is Trinidad-born designer Hendy's (who started as a menswear designer) first New York outpost. The 1,700-square-foot space houses his men's and women's collections, including luxury sportswear, bridge and denim lines. The décor is equally slick: featuring steel and glass fixtures, abstract mirrors and muted lighting. Hendy has a love-in with musicians—having dressed Wyclef Jean, Missy Elliot, Britney Spears, DMX, Whitney Houston, R. Kelly, L.L. Cool J, the Backstreet Boys and Sean "Puffy" Combs in his slick, distinctive sportswear.

SoHo 212-354-4764
65 Thompson Street bet Spring/Broome
NYC 10011 Mon-Fri 9-6:30, Sat 10:30-5

Frank Shattuck

Frank Shattuck has taken over where his mentor Henry Stewart, one of New York's most distinguished Old World tailors, left off. Each suit is handmade from start to finish, from construction and drafting to the final three-hour pressing process. Pay $4,000 for one of his luxurious suits and expect to wear it for a lifetime.

Midtown East 212-636-9120
18 East 53rd Street, Room 8W bet. Madison/5th Ave.
NYC 10022 by appointment

French Corner

Frank Stella
The husband-and-wife team of Frank and Stella delivers a no-nonsense selection of menswear. Find suits by DKNY and Jack Victor, dress shirts, ties, sportcoats, corduroys, khakis, sweaters and outerwear.

Upper West Side   212-877-5566
440 Columbus Avenue   at 81st St.
NYC 10024   Mon-Fri 11-8, Sat 11-6, Sun 12-6

Midtown West   212-957-1600
921 Seventh Avenue   at 58th St.
NYC 10019   Mon-Fri 10-7, Sat 10-6, Sun 12-5

Fratelli Rossetti
Italian icon Fratelli Rossetti began making shoes for cyclists and skaters in the 1950s and later introduced the first brown loafer to the fashion world. Their design mission statement: Quality, elegance, comfort and practicality. The classic loafers and lace-ups are best suited for daytime wear. Prices run from $185 to $575 (for leather boots).

Midtown East   212-888-5107
625 Madison Avenue   at 58th St.
NYC 10022   Mon-Fri 10-6:30, Thur 10-7
    Sat 10-6, Sun 12-5

French Connection
A British company known for their sportswear geared toward an under-30 crowd—and their controversial 'FCUK' advertising campaign. Think Banana Republic or Express with a British edge—suits, jeans, logo'd T-shirts, cut summer dresses, casualwear, plus accessories and its burgeoning beauty line. Colors lean towards the discreet rather than the adventurous.   www.frenchconnection.com

Upper West Side   212-496-1470
304 Columbus Avenue   bet. 74/75th St.
NYC 10023   Mon-Sat 11-8, Sun 11-7

Midtown West   212-262-6623
1270 Sixth Avenue   at 51st St.
NYC 10020   Mon-Fri 9-9, Sat 10-8, Sun 11-7

NoHo   212-473-4699
700 Broadway   bet. Astor Pl./4th St.
NYC 10003   Mon-Sat 11-9, Sun 11-8

SoHo   212-219-1197
435 West Broadway   bet. Prince/Spring
NYC 10012   Mon-Sat 10-9, Sun 11-8

French Corner
We're not sure what's so French about this store, and it isn't on a corner, but anyway, head here for European designer casualwear on the flashy side. Labels include Roberto Cavalli jeans, Lacroix jeans, D&G jeans and Moschino jeans as well as a range of flirty tops and Paul & Emile ultrasuede dresses. If you like the sort of denims that lace up the thigh, then this is the place for you.

French Sole

SoHo
466 West Broadway
NYC 10012
212-219-3340
bet. Prince/Houston
Mon-Sat 11-7, Sun 12-6

French Sole
French Sole has the city's best selection of ballet flats in every color under the sun. They come quilted or plain, in leather or suede and feature an adjustable lace to ensure a comfortable fit. If you're looking for a dressier style, select from their "Frankie & Baby" collection featuring Chinese slippers and beaded mules. www.frenchsole.com

Upper East Side
985 Lexington Avenue
NYC 10021
212-737-2859
bet. 71/72nd St.
Mon-Fri 10-7, Sat 11-6

Furla
Furla provides non-designer accessories that look as slick as anything Prada could deliver. Crisp, structured lines and minimal hardware define their collection of great-looking Italian handbags and other accessories like sleek-chic belts. Also find key chains, coin purses and wallets that make fantastic gifts or stocking stuffers. They get top marks for quality, originality and good prices. 888-FURLA-US www.furla.it

Upper East Side
727 Madison Avenue
NYC 10021
212-755-8986
bet. 63/64th St.
Mon-Sat 10-6, Thur 10-6:30

SoHo
430 West Broadway
NYC 10012
212-343-0048
bet. Spring/Prince
Mon-Sat 10-7, Sun 12-6

Gabbriel Ichak
Gabbriel Ichak spirits up one-of-a-kind handbags from quirky recycled materials. Fifties magazine covers, CD jackets and product packaging (like Goya Rice and El Paso Taco boxes) serve as amusing fronts and backs for these super plastic pieces. Prices range from $25 up.

East Village
430 East 9th Street
NYC 10009
212-673-0673
bet. 1st/Ave. A
Mon-Sat 12-8

Gallery of Wearable Art
The term "wearable art" normally strikes fear into fashionistas, who envision necklaces made from lumps of clay and caftans made from hemp. But it's not all that bad. As its name suggests, this shop features one-of-a-kind clothing items from unusual daywear and limited-edition evening gowns to non-traditional bridalwear, furs and accessories. An adventure worth taking.

Upper East Side
34 East 67th Street
NYC 10021
212-425-5379
bet. Madison/Park Ave.
Tues-Sat 10-6

Galo
A veteran of Madison Avenue, established shoe label Galo offers a collection of loafers, flats, pumps, sandals and

Gap

boots. For children, there are styles from casual and contemporary basics to dress up. From toddler to size 5. Prices range from moderate to expensive. The handbag selection includes leather clutches, straw totes and shoulder bags.

Upper East Side 212-832-3922
825 Lexington Avenue at 63rd St.
NYC 10021 Mon-Fri 9:30-7, Sat 9:30-6, Sun 12:30-5:30

Upper East Side 212-688-6276
692 Madison Avenue bet. 62/63rd St.
NYC 10021 Mon-Fri 10-7, Sat 10-6, Sun 12:30-5:30

Gamine

Walk into this jewel box of a boutique and be darn near over-stimulated by its ultra-feminine collection with an ethnic edge, from flirty daytime dresses to informal eveningwear made up of sari prints, beading and embroidery. Fabulous handbags and colored stone jewelry complete the collection.

Upper East Side 212-472-6918
1322 Third Avenue bet. 75/76th St.
NYC 10021 Mon-Fri 11-8, Sat 11-7, Sun 12-6

Gant

Gant specializes in men's and boy's classic American sportswear. Three floors are devoted to casual basics—jeans, khakis, fleece outfits, rugby shirts, sweatpants, knits, outerwear and polo shirts in all colors. Fleece outerwear is their best bet. Good prices.

Fifth Avenue 212-813-9170
645 Fifth Avenue bet. 51/52nd St.
NYC 10022 Mon-Sat 10-7, Thur 10-8, Sun 11-7

SoHo 212-431-9610
77 Wooster Street at Spring
NYC 10012 Mon-Sat 11-7, Sun 12-6

☆ Gap

Gap is great! While its fashion has been hit-and-miss in the last few years, Gap remains the source of super staples for everyone—casual weekend wear like khakis for the professional, cool denims and cute T-shirts for twentysomething hipsters and a complete uniform for teenagers. Choose from racks and racks of jeans—from dark to dirty denim—shirts, sweaters, T-shirts, belts and accessories, all at some of the best prices in town. Their cute handbags, often for as low as $9, are a winner. Unbelievable sales ($4 T-shirt, anyone?). Gap's Body Collection features intimates (the best: seamless vests and underwear), sleepwear and bath and body products. 800-427-7895 www.gap.com

Upper East Side 212-794-5781
1511 Third Avenue at 85th St.
NYC 10028 Mon-Fri 9-9, Sat 10-9, Sun 11-7

Upper East Side 212-879-9144
1066 Lexington Avenue at 75th St.
NYC 10021 Mon-Fri 10-8, Sat 10-7:30, Sun 11-6

Gap

Upper East Side 212-472-4555
1131-49 Third Avenue at 66th St.
NYC 10021 Mon-Sat 10-8, Sun 11-7

Upper West Side 212-873-1244
2373 Broadway at 86th St.
NYC 10024 Mon-Fri 10-9, Sat & Sun 10-8

Upper West Side (W) 212-873-9272
335 Columbus Avenue at 76th St.
NYC 10023 Mon-Sat 9-8, Sun 10-7

Upper West Side 212-721-5304
1988 Broadway at 67th St.
NYC 10023 Mon-Sat 10-9, Sun 11-9

Midtown East 212-751-1543
734 Lexington Avenue bet. 58/59th St.
NYC 10022 Mon-Sat 9-8:30, Sun 10-7

Midtown East 212-223-5140
757 Third Avenue at 47th St.
NYC 10017 Mon-Fri 8-8, Sat 10-7, Sun 11-6

Midtown East 212-697-3590
657-659 Third Avenue at 42nd St.
NYC 10017 Mon-Fri 8-9, Sat & Sun 10-8

Midtown East 212-754-2290
900 Third Avenue at 54th St.
NYC 10022 Mon-Fri 9-8, Sat 10-6, Sun 12-5

Midtown East 212-688-1260
572 Madison Avenue at 54th St.
NYC 10022 Mon-Fri 9-8, Sat 10-8, Sun 11-6

Midtown West 212-956-3142
250 West 57th Street bet. B'way/8th Ave.
NYC 10019 Mon-Fri 8:30-8:30, Sat 10-8, Sun 11-6

Midtown West 212-764-0285
1212 Sixth Avenue bet. 47/48th St.
NYC 10036 Mon-Fri 8-9, Sat 10-8, Sun 11-6

Midtown West 212-768-2987
1466 Broadway at 42nd St.
NYC 10036 Mon-Fri 8-9, Sat 10-8, Sun 11-6

Midtown West 212-643-8960
60 West 34th Street at B'way
NYC 10001 Mon-Fri 9-9:30, Sat 10-9:30, Sun 11-8

Fifth Avenue 212-977-7023
680 Fifth Avenue at 54th St.
NYC 10019 Mon-Fri 10-8, Sat 9-8, Sun 11-7

Flatiron 917 408- 5580
122 Fifth Avenue bet. 17/18th St.
NYC 10011 Mon-Fri 10-9, Sat 10-8, Sun 11-7

East Village (M) 212-674-1877
750 Broadway at 8th St.
NYC 10003 Mon-Sat 10-9, Sun 11-8

East Village (W) 212-253-0145
1 Astor Place at B'way
NYC 10003 Mon-Sat 10-9, Sun 11-8

Gap Kids and Baby Gap

West Village
345 Sixth Avenue
NYC 10014
212-727-2210
at 4th St.
Mon-Sat 10-9, Sun 11-8

Gap Kids and Baby Gap

The ultimate destination for moderately priced—and just trendy enough—children's jeans, T-shirts, overalls, shirts, pants, sweatshirts, sweaters, dresses, pajamas, shoes and accessories. From outdoor play gear to back-to-school basics, Gap has it all, with great prices and some of the cutest designs around. From newborn to 13 years.

www.babygap.com

Upper East Side
1535 Third Avenue
NYC 10028
212-423-0033
bet. 86/87th St.
Mon-Sat 9-9, Sun 10-8

Upper East Side
1164 Madison Avenue
NYC 10028
212-517-5763
at 86th St.
Mon-Fri 10-8, Sat 10-7, Sun 11-7

Upper East Side
1037 Lexington Avenue
NYC 10021
212-327-2614
at 74th St.
Mon-Fri 10-8, Sat 10-7:30, Sun 11-6

Upper East Side
1131-49 Third Avenue
NYC 10021
212-472-4555
at 66th St.
Mon-Sat 10-8, Sun 11-7

Upper West Side
2300 Broadway
NYC 10024
212-873-2044
at 83rd St.
Mon-Fri 10-9, Sat &Sun 10-8

Upper West Side
1988 Broadway
NYC 10023
212-721-5119
at 67th St.
Mon-Sat 10-9, Sun 11-9

Upper West Side
341 Columbus Avenue
NYC 10023
212-875-9196
bet. 76/77th St.
Mon-Sat 10-8, Sun 11-6

Midtown East
545 Madison Avenue
NYC 10022
212-980-2570
at 55th St.
Mon-Fri 9-8, Sat 10-8, Sun 11-6

Midtown East
757 Third Avenue
NYC 10017
212-223-5140
at 47th St.
Mon-Fri 8-9, Sat 10-8, Sun 11-6

Midtown East
657-659 Third Avenue
NYC 10017
212-697-3590
at 42nd St.
Mon-Fri 8-9, Sat & Sun 10-8

Midtown West
250 West 57th Street
NYC 10019
212-315-2250
bet. B'way/8th Ave.
Mon-Fri 8:30-8:30, Sat 10-8, Sun 11-6

Midtown West
1466 Broadway
NYC 10036
212-302-1266
at 42nd St.
Mon-Fri 8-9, Sat 10-8, Sun 11-6

Midtown West
1212 Sixth Avenue
NYC 10036
212-764-0285
bet. 47/48th St.
Mon-Fri 8-9, Sat 10-8, Sun 11-6

Gas

Midtown West 212-643-8995
60 West 34th Street at B'way
NYC 10001 Mon-Fri 9-9:30, Sat 10-9:30, Sun 11-8

Fifth Avenue 212-977-7023
680 Fifth Avenue at 54th St.
NYC 10019 Mon-Fri 10-8, Sat 9-8, Sun 11-7

Flatiron 917-408-5580
122 Fifth Avenue bet. 17/18th St.
NYC 10011 Mon-Fri 10-9, Sat 10-8, Sun 11-7

West Village 212-777-2420
354 Sixth Avenue at Washington Pl.
NYC 10011 Mon-Sat 10-9, Sun 11-8

Lower Manhattan 212-786-1707
89 South Street South Street Seaport Pier 17
NYC 10038 Mon-Fri 9-9, Sat 10-9, Sun 9-8

☆ Gas

Fashion girls have been known to make cooing noises while looking at the window of this divine jewelry store in NoLiTa. The handmade pieces from Paris perfectly mix bohemia with cool—check out how the sales staff dress down their intricately beaded earrings with slouchy jeans and a T-shirt. Too-chic-to-speak, and not ridiculously expensive either.

NoLiTa 212-334-7290
238 Mott St bet. Prince/Spring
NYC 10012 Mon-Sun 12-7

Geiger

This established Austrian label is famous for its "boiled wool" outerwear. The jackets and coats are in traditional Alpine colors with embossed silver buttons and there's also a classic sportswear collection. No Austrian burgher's wardrobe is complete without a Geiger jacket.

www.geiger-fashion.com

Midtown East 212-644-3435
505 Park Avenue at 59th St.
NYC 10022 Mon-Sat 10-6

Geoffrey Beene

The low-key Geoffrey Beene is an iconic American designer for very good reason: his impeccable, architectural tailoring and timeless edge. Although Beene can create perfect suits for Ladies Who Lunch, he is most admired for his sharp evening looks, ranging from slim, cut-out gowns (where no curve of the body is ignored) to beautiful evening skirts paired with hand-knit, roll-neck sweaters. It's classic elegance at its best. Great personalized service.

www.geoffreybeene.com

Midtown West 212-371-5570
37 West 57th Street, 2nd Floor bet. 5/6th Ave.
NYC 10019 Mon-Fri 9-5 by appointment only

Geraldine

This tiny shoe store gives new meaning to the word exclusive. Geraldine's range is small and ruthlessly edited, but nothing short of fabulous. They stock unusual-cool looks from some of the world's edgiest (and hardest to find) designers but never forget that a girl needs a good pair of party shoes, too. Designer labels including Christian Louboutin, Chloé, Olivia Morris, Pierre Hardy and Veronique Branquinho sit alongside shiny, strappy numbers from Gina and Alessandro Dell'Acqua. Oh, they also stock Marc Jacobs, so if his store has sold out, rush on over here. Prices run from $180 to $1,200.

NoLiTa	**212-219-1620**
246 Mott Street	bet. Houston/Prince
NYC 10012	Mon-Sat 11:30-7:30, Sun 12-6

Gerry's

An easy access clothing store nestled in between the restaurants of the West Village, Gerry's carries a hip collection of menswear from American and European designers. A variety of Brit-style checked shirts by Ted Baker dominates the racks, while you can also find baseball shirts by Blue Marlin, sweaters by Nicole Farhi, jeans by Armani, and other clothing by Ben Sherman, Henry Cotton's and Masons. Retro-style sneakers by Puma and Camper. Check out the Fred Perry track suits.

West Village	**212-691-0636**
353 Bleecker Street	bet. 10th/Charles
NYC 10014	Mon-Sat 11-8, Sun 12-6

Gerry Cosby & Co.

A great source for pro sports equipment and clothing for basketball, football, baseball and hockey. Shop here for an NFL, NBA or NHL jersey or souvenir from your favorite team.

Midtown West	**212-563-6464**
3 Penn Plaza	at Madison Square Garden
NYC 10001	Mon-Fri 9:30-7:30, Sat 9:30-6, Sun 12-5

Ghost

Float away into British designer Tanya Sarne's world. Ghost is best known for soft, loosely feminine designs in vibrant colors and manufactured in special crinkly rayons, which are wrinkle-resistant and machine washable. The range, which some devotees buy in bulk every season, includes wash-and-wear girlish dresses, peasant tops, sweaters and drawstring pants.

NoHo	**646-602-2891**
28 Bond Street	bet. Bowery/Lafayette
NYC 10012	Mon-Sat 11-7, Sun 12-6

Ghurka

Classic, expertly handcrafted handbags, luggage and accessories perfect for an African safari. Choose from the exotic Savanna collection of bags in alligator, zebra print or water buffalo, all trimmed with sterling silver accents, or their durable leather-trimmed twill travel bags and handbags. A selection of Trafalgar suspenders exclusive to Ghurka is also available. 800-587-1584 www.ghurka.com

Midtown East	**212-826-8300**
41 East 57th Street	bet. Madison/Park Ave.
NYC 10022	Mon-Sat 10-6, Thur 10-7

Gianfranco Ferré

Season after season this Italian designer celebrates his über-glam—and high-drama—muse. This is a confident woman, unafraid to wear Ferré's deliberately sharp, structured pieces that walk a line between fashion and architecture. Ferré is a master at mixing extremes: hard with soft, tough with feminine. He loves a corset, fur and angular jackets. He is best for sleek pinstriped suits, beautifully detailed blouses, leather pants, fur-lined biker jackets and coats. For evening, Ferré's siren (think Sharon Stone in full diva-mode) will conquer all in a clingy cut-out jersey dress. For men, find a slick collection of suits and sportswear. www.gianfrancoferre.com

Upper East Side	**212-717-5430**
845 Madison Avenue	bet. 70/71st St.
NYC 10021	Mon-Sat 10-6

Gi Gi

Gi Gi is girlie with a capital…Gi. Its collection of sportswear pieces has a deliberately feminine edge, just like the pistachio colored walls. There are lots of pretty prints, ruffles and flowy chiffons in dresses, blouses and skirts from such labels as Rebecca Beeson, Blue Colt and its own Gi Gi line.

NoLiTa	**212-274-1570**
217 Mulberry Street	bet. Prince/Spring
NYC 10012	Mon-Sat 12-7, Sun 12-6

Giordano's

Anyone with tiny feet will lay down in gratitude before Giordano's great selection of casual and dressy shoes in sizes 4 to 5 1/2. Labels include Charles Jourdan, Martinez Valero, Stuart Weitzman and Via Spiga.

Upper East Side	**212-688-7195**
1150 Second Avenue	bet. 60/61st St.
NYC 10021	Mon-Fri 11-7, Sat 11-6

Giorgio Armani

What else can you say about fashion maestro Giorgio Armani, who for 25 years has defined understated elegance—dressing everyone who matters in Hollywood from Richard Gere in "American Gigolo" to Michelle Pfeiffer and Jodie Foster, well, for everything. Armani's pioneering approach to design is a synthesis of opposites: feminine/masculine, simple/complex and refined/sporty. Women can entrust their femininity to his well-tailored suits and sculpted jackets. Eveningwear includes backless dresses, beautiful beaded numbers and stunning jackets. Armani's menswear collection of sleek suits, relaxed jackets, shirts and knee-length coats is the epitome of urban modernism. If you're playing dress up, indulge in one of his tuxedos as megawatt celebrities do on Oscar night. www.giorgioarmani.com

Upper East Side   **212-988-9191**
760 Madison Avenue   at 65th St.
NYC 10021   Mon-Sat 10-6, Thur 10-7

Giraudon

Giraudon's footwear is fit for everyone who digs a chunky rubber sole. Two lines designed by Alain-Guy Giraudon feature everything from rugged boots and sporty loafers with lug soles to leather-soled dressy lace-ups and slip-ons.   800-278-1552   www.giraudonnewyork.com

Chelsea   **212-633-0999**
152 Eighth Avenue   bet. 17/18th St.
NYC 10011   Mon-Sat 11:30-11, Sun 1-7

Girlprops.com

Although this shop is below street level, its zebra-striped interior sucks you right into this "inexpensive"—we never say "cheap"—(the motto on the canopy entrance) accessory shop. It's packed to the rafters with an over-stimulating collection of camouflage belts, rhinestone jewelry, leather spiked bracelets, handbags, tiaras, sunglasses, beaded bracelets, turquoise and coral jewelry, dangly earrings, purple wigs and boas, all fabulously affordable and disposable   www.girlprops.com

SoHo   **212-505-7615**
153 Prince Street   at West Broadway
NYC 10013   Mon-Sun 10-11

Giselle

Please adjust your chronometers, ladies, you are now entering a time warp...Giselle caters to a mature, conservative customer in search of no-nonsense work suits, blouses, sportswear and coordinating accessories, all at 20% below retail. Labels include Bianca, Miss V (Valentino) and Ferré Studio in sizes 4-20. Free shipping.

Lower East Side   **212-673-1900**
143 Orchard Street   bet. Delancey/Rivington
NYC 10002   Sun-Thur 9-6, Fri 9-4

Giuseppe Zanotti Design

Giuseppe Zanotti is best known for his jewel-encrusted, high heeled sandals and stilettos that often feature embroidery, jewel and stone embellishments—which, all up, equal very sexy shoes. Looks include closed-toe pumps with mother-of-pearl heels, thigh-high, super pointy stiletto boots in embroidered leather and encrusted rubies, two and three band open-toed flirty sandals and classic croco-

Givenchy

dile pumps and slingbacks. Check out the ad campaign boot, a closed toe pump with suede laces up to your knees. Prices run from $285 to $1,300.

Upper East Side	212-650-0455
806 Madison Avenue	bet. 67/68th St.
NYC 10021	Mon-Sat 10-6

Givenchy

According to designer Julien Macdonald, today's Givenchy woman "wants an outfit that won't be hostile, but sexy and glamorous in a Givenchy style." Macdonald, who made his name with spangly, barely-there dresses, stays true to the Givenchy signatures of clean, simple lines and feminine styling. He has reinvented such classics as the Bettina blouse and the little black dress (you can never have too many) and works them big time in gorgeous Roman-inspired whites. Signature logo'd handbags and shoes also available. www.givenchy.com

Upper East Side	212-688-4338
710 Madison Avenue	at 63rd St.
NYC 10021	Mon-Sat 10-6, Thur 10-7, Sun 12-6

Goffredo Fantini

Goffredo Fantini is a fresco painter turned cobbler (no, we didn't make this up—he's a multi-tasker) and has invented the "Fressura," a space-age shoe with a permanent (read: indestructible) sole and changeable, elastic tops. You need to see it to believe it. Also, a small collection of urban, chunky heeled shoes. Good for teens.

NoLiTa	212-219-1501
248 Elizabeth Street	bet. Prince/Houston
NYC 10012	Mon-Sat 11-7, Sun 12-7

The Good, The Bad and The Ugly

Skateboarding, music, graffiti, hip-hop, art, the can-can… all are inspirations for designer Judi Rosen, the owner of this fun, East Village-cute shop. As with all the cool stores these days, Rosen is vintage inspired; her quirky pieces cover the gamut from bright-colored corduroy jackets (she's a brights fanatic) to sweatshirts to adjustable garters. Basically, the downtown girl can find it all here! That and the rainbow striped legwarmers she always wanted…

East Village	212-473-3769
437 East 9th Street	bet. 1st/Ave. A
NYC 10002	Mon-Sun 1-9

The Gown Company

Every blushing bride's dream of wearing a couture gown on her wedding day can become reality at The Gown Company, which offers huge savings on samples and excess inventory of current season bridal gowns by top designers. Dresses by Angel Sanchez, Helen Morley, Peter Langner, Lazaro, Youlin, Mariana Harwick and many more that would retail uptown for $1,500 to $6,000 can be

Gucci

found here for $800 to $1,500. Apart from the savings, they offer such services as custom tailoring and alterations, headpieces and veils and full service specialty dry cleaning. They also do custom-made gowns from $1,300-$4,500. www.thegowncompany.com

East Village 212-979-9000
326 East 9th Street bet. 1st/2nd Ave.
NYC 10003 Tues-Sat 12-7

Granny-Made
This shop specializes in hand knits from Italy, England and the U.S. Mothers can choose from a cute-as-pie collection of children's novelty sweaters featuring appliques, sweet embroideries, cute animals and floral motifs. For adults, a similar selection by labels like Christine Foley, Roni Rabl, Sigrid Olsen, weaver Lynn Yarington and English Weather. Accessories include socks and novelty pillows.
www.grannymade.com

Upper West Side 212-496-1222
381 Amsterdam Avenue bet. 78/79th St.
NYC 10024 Mon-Fri 10:30-7, Sat 10-6, Sun 12-5

Great Feet
Simply the best children's footwear selection in New York. If you can't find it here, you won't find it anywhere. Brand names include Stride-Rite, Keds, Nike, Sam & Libby, Kenneth Cole and Polo. Styles range from casual weekend wear to back-to-school classics and party shoes. They also carry the very latest in skateboard shoes (sadly, no knee pads!) as well as socks, tights and slippers. From newborn to size 6.

Upper East Side 212-249-0551
1241 Lexington Avenue at 84th St.
NYC 10028 Mon-Wed 9:30-6, Thur & Fri 9:30-8
Sat 9:30-6, Sun 11-5

Greenstones & Cie
Greenstones & Cie has been dressing fashion-forward kids in a variety of looks for 20 years, from posh imported European clothing to practical American-made togs, with brands like Jean Bourget, Kenzo (girls), Deux par Deux, Pampolina, Mini Man and Catimini. All perfect for school-time, play-time or party-time. And their hats are an absolute must. From newborn to 12 years.

Upper East Side 212-427-1665
1184 Madison Avenue bet. 86/87th St.
NYC 10028 Mon-Sat 10:30-6:30, Sun 12:30-5

Upper West Side 212-580-4322
442 Columbus Avenue bet. 81/82nd St.
NYC 10024 Mon-Sat 10-7, Sun 12-6

☆ Gucci
Ah, to be the Gucci woman! Designer Tom Ford's muse is sexy, strong and powerful—oh, and she's a complete babe.

Dripping with rosewood and travertine and open balconies overlooking each floor, this five-floor emporium is as modern, lean and sexy as the clothes. Shop ready-to-wear with slim cuts and a predominantly black and white color palette that delivers sex appeal in one knockout punch. Not to mention the Gucci classic handbags, jewelry, accessories and terrifyingly high, super-chic shoes. Tip: make sure you can actually walk in them before you hand over your credit card. 800-234-8224 www.gucci.com

Fifth Avenue 212-826-2600
685 Fifth Avenue at 54th St.
NYC 10022 Mon-Fri 10-6:30, Sat 10-7, Sun 12-6
(Moving to 69th & Madison in Autumn 2003)

Guess?

Remember those sexy-as-hell Guess? ads that made Claudia Schiffer famous? Well, that free and easy feeling remains in their flirty casual clothes: fashion jeans, khakis, shirts, T-shirts, outerwear and shoes, all keeping with the latest trends. Accessories include wallets, watches and sunglasses trademarked with the visible Guess? logo. Some dressier styles for women, if you want to bring out the Claudia inside you. www.guess.com

SoHo 212-226-9545
537 Broadway bet. Prince/Spring
NYC 10012 Mon-Sat 10-9, Sun 11-7

Lower Manhattan 212-385-0533
23-25 Water Street at South Street Seaport
NYC 10038 Mon-Sat 10-9, Sun 11-8

Gymboree

A children's shop featuring four lines of coordinating play clothes that are fun, colorful and easy-to-wear. The casual styles are popular with kids and the prices will please Mom and Dad—which helps when they grow out of them so quickly! From newborn to size 7/8. 800-222-7758
www.gymboree.com

Upper East Side 212-717-6702
1120 Madison Avenue bet. 83/84th St.
NYC 10028 Mon-Fri 10-7, Sat 10-6, Sun 12-5

Upper East Side 212-517-5548
1332 Third Avenue at 76th St.
NYC 10021 Mon-Sat 10-7, Sun 11-6

Upper East Side 212-688-4044
1049 Third Avenue at 62nd St.
NYC 10021 Mon-Sat 10-7, Sun 10-6

Upper West Side 212-595-9071
2271 Broadway at 82nd St.
NYC 10024 Mon-Fri 10-9, Sat 10-8, Sun 11-6

Upper West Side 212- 595-7662
2015 Broadway bet. 68/69th St.
NYC 10023 Mon-Fri 10-8, Sat 10-7, Sun 11-6

H. Herzfeld

Tailored looks with that particularly English styling is the name of the game at H. Herzfeld, especially in their fabulous haberdashery department which carries shirts, neckwear, sweaters, sportswear, underwear, pajamas and accessories, as well as shoes by Alden. Although suits are generally custom-made, you will find a good selection of off-the-rack. Hickey-Freeman suits priced from $875 to $1,600. Custom starts at $2,500.

Midtown East   **212-753-6756**
507 Madison Avenue   at 52/53rd St.
NYC 10022   Mon-Fri 9-6, Sat 9-5:30

Hable Construction

This jaunty textile company is named after sisters Katharine and Susan Hable's grandfather's road construction business, and their accessories are indeed more than roadworthy! Aiming to "fuse fabric, art and utlility," their collection of signature print fabrics is turned into colorful canvas totes and baskets, while exaggerated floral designs appear on indispensable wool felt shoe bags and cute shoe inserts—perfect for keeping your Jimmy Choos in tip-top order. A great gift stop.

NoLiTa   **212-343-8504**
230 Elizabeth Street   bet. Prince/Houston
NYC 10012   Tues-Sat 11-7, Sun 12-6

Haneza

A deliberately stark space in SoHo that mixes art by Nam June Paik with clothing by Haneza, who is one of South Korea's most celebrated designers. Like the space itself, Haneza's designs take their cues from the marriage of geometric forms and art. It's cutting edge with couture detailing.

SoHo   **212-343-9373**
93 Grand Street   bet. Greene/Mercer
NYC 10013   Mon-Sat 11-7, Sun 12-6

Hans Koch

Koch's passion for color drives all his designs in handcrafted, one-of-a-kind belts, handbags and jewelry. Belts are simple and versatile, while his clever handbag styles range from soft to constructed.

SoHo   **212-226-5385**
174 Prince Street   bet. Sullivan/Thompson
NYC 10012   Mon-Thur 12-8, Fri & Sat 12-9, Sun 1-8

Harriet Love

Formerly a vintage shop, Harriet Love now sells retro-look casualwear that can be dressed up or down. This small boutique is a leader in antique-inspired clothing with such labels as Ghost, Lilith, Germany's Drozdzik, Italy's quirky Fuzzi and Kristal Larson.

Harry Rothman's

SoHo   212-966-2280
126 Prince Street   bet. Wooster/Greene
NYC 10012   Mon-Sun 11-7

Harry Rothman's

A great source for well-priced men's clothing, Rothman's offers discounts of up to 40% on brand names like Hickey-Freeman, Canali, Joseph Abboud and Hugo Boss. Also find a selection of shirts, ties, underwear, sport jackets, outerwear and shoes.

Flatiron   212-777-7400
200 Park Avenue South   at 17th St.
NYC 10003   Mon-Fri 10-7, Thur 10-8
  Sat 9:30-6, Sun 12-5:30

The Hat Shop

Enter this tiny milliner and check out nearly 50 talented New York designers, including Deborah Harper, Brenda Lynn, Eric Javits, Jennifer Hoertz and Jennifer Ouellette. This whimsical world of toppers guarantees the perfect fit for every head and is pretty much a one-stop-shop for styles from classic straw boaters to wide-brimmed showstoppers.

SoHo   212-219-1445
120 Thompson Street   bet. Prince/Spring
NYC 10012   Mon-Sat 12-7, Sun 1-6

Hatitude

Despite the name, thankfully there isn't a whole lot of attitude in this store. Hats themselves take a back seat to the selection of dolls, vintage jewelry and fabulous fans, but it's fun to browse this eclectic store, which has the decadent feeling of a boudoir. When you do finally spot the hats, you'll find them in all shapes, sizes and fabrics with an emphasis on vintage.

TriBeCa   212-571-4558
93 Reade Street   bet. W. B'way/Church
NYC 10013   Mon-Fri 12-7, Sat 12-5

Hedra Prue

An independent showcase for up-and-coming designers, owners Anna Kim and Tracy Mayer do a bang-up job of culling the hottest items from each collection—and their prices aren't freakishly expensive. You'll find original pieces from hipster darlings like Lauren Moffat, Martin, L.A.'s Anja Flint, Development—even Bazar by Christian Lacroix. Choose from quirky skirts, sexy tops, suits, pants, cashmere sweaters, cool screen-printed sweatshirts and the ubiquitous super-low-cut jeans. Their accessories are equally carefully selected—and work perfectly with the clothes.

NoLiTa   212-343-9205
281 Mott Street   bet. Houston/Prince
NYC 10012   Mon-Sat 11:30-7:30, Sun 12-6:30

Helen Mariën

This store wins the award for the coolest names for its signature accessories—like the "Sunday Brunch" tote or the "Saturday on the Subway" shopper. Then there's the "Remember that couch in Brazil?" clutch, which conjures up visions of...who knows? The specialty here is chic, simple bags made from grosgrain and cotton, designed by this husband-and-wife team. Also available: chunky beaded jewelry.

NoLiTa   212-680-1911
250 Mott Street   bet. Prince/Houston
NYC 10012   Mon-Sun 11:30-7:30

Helen Yarmak

After wrapping Russians in sable and chinchilla, this theoretical mathematician-turned-fur designer now dresses celebrity clients like Melanie Griffith and Goldie Hawn. Yarmak's trademarks are her unique pelt processing, which leaves her furs virtually weightless, and her modern designs. Find over 350 different styles, including a line of reversibles, a one-size-fits-all collection (there's regular sizing, too) and a kneaded line for the softest feel. You'll find mink, fox, rabbit, chinchilla, and, of course, sable available for a bargain $49,000. Accessories include knit fox scarves, decadent fur-lined handbags and jewelry.   www.helenyarmak.com

Midtown West   212-245-0777
730 Fifth Avenue, 18th Fl.   bet. 56/57th St.
NYC 10019   by appointment only

Helene Arpels

For 45 years, Helene Arpels has been keeping her loyal, and well-heeled, customers happy with her unique footwear collection. Her clientele includes royalty and socialites from all over the world, who come for her pumps, loafers, slippers, ornate evening shoes, custom jewelry and caftans. But the prices are over-the-top—a pair of loafers sells for $575.

Midtown East   212-755-1623
470 Park Avenue   bet. 57/58th St.
NYC 10022   Mon-Sat 10-6

Hello Sari

This tiny shop is strictly devoted to authentic Indian and Pakistani merchandise, including beaded and embroidered dresses, cashmere shawls, scarves, saris, mirrored sandals and embroidered shoes. Sizes run from small to X-large. Best bet: the "Kameez," a Pakistani, open-front dress with side slits worn over pants (recently popularized by Jemima Khan). The perfect place to shop for an unusual ethnic piece to spice up your wardrobe—and every fashionable girl needs one of those...

Lower East Side   212-274-0791
261 Broome Street   bet. Allen/Orchard
NYC 10002   Mon-Sun 12-5

Helmut Lang 👤👤

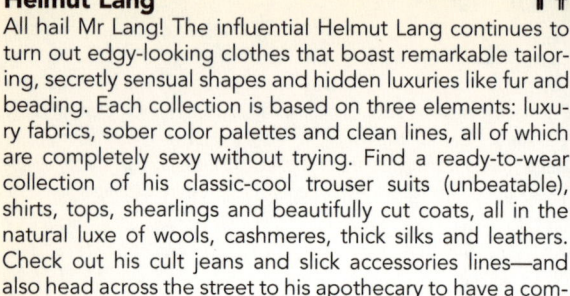

All hail Mr Lang! The influential Helmut Lang continues to turn out edgy-looking clothes that boast remarkable tailoring, secretly sensual shapes and hidden luxuries like fur and beading. Each collection is based on three elements: luxury fabrics, sober color palettes and clean lines, all of which are completely sexy without trying. Find a ready-to-wear collection of his classic-cool trouser suits (unbeatable), shirts, tops, shearlings and beautifully cut coats, all in the natural luxe of wools, cashmeres, thick silks and leathers. Check out his cult jeans and slick accessories lines—and also head across the street to his apothecary to have a complete Helmut Lang conversion.   www.helmutlang.com

SoHo
80 Greene Street
NYC 10012

212-925-7214
bet. Spring/Broome
Mon-Sat 11-7, Sun 12-6

H&M (Hennes & Mauritz) 👤👤

First thing's first: H&M rules! This rapidly expanding Swedish retailer continues to break land-speed records by turning out trendy, streetwear clothes (many taking influence literally straight from the catwalk) at incredibly low prices. Shop their 35,000 sq. ft. store on Fifth Avenue featuring 20 lines of hip clothing like sexy leather pants at $95, jeans trimmed in sequins at $35, embroidered tank tops for as little as $5.50, swimwear, accessories and cosmetics, as well as plus sizes. Keep an eye on their coat selection—on the right day you can pick up a chic black, fully-lined trench for $40. The clothes aren't built to last, but at these prices, who cares?   www.hm.com

Fifth Avenue
640 Fifth Avenue
NYC 10019

212-489-0390
at 51st St.
Mon-Sat 10-9, Sun 11-8

Midtown West
1328 Broadway
NYC 10001

646-473-1164
at 34th St.
Mon-Sat 10-9, Sun 11-8

SoHo
588 Broadway
NYC 10012

212-343-8702
bet. Prince/Spring
Mon-Sat 10-9, Sun 11-8

Henri Bendel 👤

Bendel's, as shopping pros call it, is prized by fashion fans for its coolly eclectic assortment. One of the best things is its relatively small size—you can be in and out in a flash. Cosmetics and accessories areas are compact and easy to get around, while clothing departments are small, well-organized and well-staffed. Bendel's continues to showcase some of the brightest new designers, including Amy Chan, Luella Bartley and Nanette Lepore, along with such favorites as Kors, Vivienne Tam and Anna Molinari. The sweater collection is so phenomenal it has warranted additional floor space. They also boast exclusive in-store shops for Diane von Furstenberg, Catherine Malandrino,

D&G and, most recently, cult Seventies designer Stephen Burrows, Patricia Field of "Sex and the City" fame and Ana Abdul of the downtown store Language. Hats, hosiery, casual wear and outerwear departments round out the assortment—while their activewear section (featuring Christy Turlington's Nuala label) is a hit with stylish, sporty types. Top hair stylist Garren is located on the 3rd floor. 800-423-6335 www.henribendel.com

Fifth Avenue   **212-247-1100**
712 Fifth Avenue   bet. 55/56th St.
NYC 10019   Mon-Sat 10-7, Thur 10-8, Sun 12-6

Henry Lehr

Henry Lehr carries a fabulous denim selection by the hottest labels in town. We're talking Juicy, Paper Denim and Cloth, Seven and AG Jeans. Prices run from $97 to $123. Buy them all, because you can never have too many, can you? Other items include jean jackets, button-down shirts and hip belts.

NoLiTa   **212-274-9921**
232 Elizabeth Street   bet. Prince/Houston
NYC 10012   Mon-Sun 11-7

Henry Lehr

Henry Lehr's second SoHo shop showcases T-shirts in an abundance of styles by Juicy Couture, Jet, 3 Dot, Michael Stars, Great Wall of China, In The Now and others. A good source for basic, casual tops at reasonable prices.

NoLiTa   **212-343-0567**
268 Elizabeth Street   bet. Prince/Houston
NYC 10012   Mon-Sun 11-7

Hermès

After a major renovation, this renowned French leather house boasts its five-floor 20,000 sq. ft. digs. Affluent types flock here for the distinctive neckties, scarves, handbags and leathergoods. Collecting Hermès scarves is a religion for some women—even at $250 a pop—and their classic Kelly and Birkin bags are clutched by the hands of the ultrachic. Even though you have to add your name to a waiting list and be prepared to part with over $5,000, the bag will last forever and never go out of style. The clothing collection, designed by the deliberately obscure Martin Margiela, is a world of luxury basics from chic shirts to unbelievably luxe cashmere sweaters. You'll drop a bundle for a slice of thoroughbred luxury, but it's still a better bet than a punt at the races.   800-441-4488

Upper East Side   **212-751-3181**
691 Madison Avenue   bet. 62/63rd St.
NYC 10022   Mon-Sat 10-6, Thur 10-7

Heun

Heun is a bigger version of its sister store Juno, which is located directly across the street. There is a full range of footwear, from classic shapes to super trendy street-smart styles in pumps, boots, slides and sandals for women and Prada-esque sneaker/dress shoes, boots and sandals for men. Labels include Juno and lots of imported Italians like Gianna Meliani and Bologna. Great children's shoes.

SoHo   **212-625-2560**
543 Broadway   bet. Prince/Spring
NYC 10012   Mon-Sun 10:30-8

Hickey-Freeman

One of America's premier names in men's tailored clothing, Hickey-Freeman and its brother label Oxxford have been clothing the great and good for decades—from American presidents to chief executives. This is its first flagship and, fittingly, it's just beside that other American icon Brooks Brothers. Suits, jackets and pants in luxurious fabrics and classic cuts are the Hickey-Freeman trademark. Also find their Bobby Jones sportswear collection featuring golf togs, as well as shirts, ties, and other accessories.   1-888-603-8968   www.hickeyfreeman.com

Fifth Avenue   **212-585-6481**
666 Fifth Avenue   bet. 52/53rd St.
NYC 10103   Mon-Sat 10-6, Sun 12-5

Himaya

The designer Gigi Ferrante is the talent behind Himaya, which means "sublime." Find a sophisticated ready-to-wear collection manufactured in advanced wools, silks and leathers with stretch capability for comfort and wrinkle resistance. Himaya's customer layers her looks, mixing tailored and deconstructed jackets, dresses, suits and separates as well as couture evening gowns.   www.himaya.com

Fifth Avenue   **212-973-9107**
551 Fifth Avenue, Suite 1620   at 45th St.
NYC 10176   Mon-Sat 10-6

Hiponica

Hiponica accessorizes downtown hipsters and uptown girls with everything from fabulous handbags to a small clothing line. Japanese owner Jem Filippi is a design perfectionist with a handbag line that is fun, functional and notable for its out-there colors. There are simple shapes in calfskin leathers, nylons and fabrics with playful details, such as vintage fabrics for linings and leather trimmings. Other items include glass-trimmed leather wallets, amusing change purses, fancy fabric briefcases and her cute apparel line of skirts and shirts.

NoLiTa   **212-966-4388**
238 Mott Street   bet. Prince/Spring
NYC 10012   Mon-Sun 12-7

Hogan

Tired of trudging around town in your battered Nikes? Head for Hogan, a sister store to the chic Tod's and the purveyor of a new breed of walking/comfort shoes. Equipped with rubber soles and designed in fabulous solid colors, these are hip, edgy sneakers. Check out Hogan's sporty, structured handbags in richly hued leather, canvas and suede. Shoe prices start at $295.

SoHo   **212-343-7905**
134 Spring Street   bet. Greene/Wooster
NYC 10012   Mon-Sat 11-7, Sun 12-6

Holland & Holland

What Hermès is to the equestrian world, Holland & Holland is to the hunting world. Originally a purveyor of hunting rifles, the company—a subsidiary of Chanel—now specializes in refined, luxurious sportswear. There are jackets in tweeds and suedes, shirts, pants, sweaters, outerwear and accessories with bucolic looks. A note of caution: even the mega-rich have been known to blink twice at the price tags. Their impressive gun room and fine art and book department are worth a look.   www.hollandandholland.com

Midtown East   **212-752-7755**
50 East 57th Street   bet. Madison/Park Ave.
NYC 10022   Mon-Fri 10-6:30, Sat 10-6

Hollywould

This shop channels a 1950's Hollywood cabana with its periwinkle striped fabric and wicker poolside stools with striped cushions. There's a fab collection of coordinating shoes and handbags with looks like glamorous pumps in chocolate brown with matching suede "shopper's" totes; red metallic evening sandals paired with extra long (16 inches) cigarette clutches and gorgeous ballet slippers in every color from bronze to electric blue. Very Bardot at the beach. Prices run from $200 to $500.

NoLiTa   **212-343-8344**
284 Mulberry Street   bet. Prince/Houston
NYC 10012   Mon-Sat 11:30-7:30

Hoofbeats, Ltd

This tiny children's and babywear store is drowning in both stock and good intentions. They clearly love kids here, because they sell everything for the little ones from monogrammed robes, shirts, handkerchiefs (all of which they do on-site) to tiny tots clothing to cheeky cushions inscribed with slogans like "Computer geek lives here." Small and sweet.

Upper East Side   **212-517-2633**
232 East 78th Street   bet. 2nd/3rd Ave.
NYC 10021   Mon-Fri 11-6, Thur 1-7

Hotel Venus

Owned by cult stylist Patricia Field of "Sex and the City" fame, Hotel Venus takes the same deliberately faddish approach as her downtown store Patricia Field's. Shop a daring and colorful selection of vinyl bustiers, sheer fitted shirts, leather halter tops, micro-minis, hard-core rubberized patent leather outfits, funky clubwear, boas, lingerie, shoes and accessories from labels like Clutch, Lip Service and Hysteric Glamour plus, of course, Patricia Field. It's worth a trip just to experience the amusing sales staff. For the camp and fearless.

SoHo   **212-966-4066**
382 West Broadway   bet. Broome/Spring
NYC 10012   Mon-Sun 11-8, Sat 11-9

Hugo Boss

This German company, already dressing stylish men world-over, landed in New York with a massive store that features clean, modern classics for him and her. The four floors are devoted to menswear, accessories, a new line of women's clothing and their young brand label "Hugo." The Boss man will find a full selection of tailored suits, jackets, pants, shirts, classic trenches, ties, shoes and grooming products. He can also get casual in "Boss Sport" or play the game in "Boss Golf." Women will find ultra-tailored looks in blazers and coats—perfect for the office, but never stodgy.   www.hugo.com

Fifth Avenue   **212-485-1800**
717 Fifth Avenue   at 56th St.
NYC 10022   Mon-Fri 10-7, Thur 10-8, Sat 10-6, Sun 12-6

Hugo Hugo Boss

Young, style-conscious men and women shop here for unusual and unconventional clothes that won't stretch the wallet. Clothes range from trendy suits and separates in quality fabrics to bubble skirts and reversible kangaroo jackets. Think of the hipsters bouncing around in the fragrance ads and you've pretty much got it. www.hugo.com

SoHo   **212-965-1300**
132 Greene Street   bet. Houston/Prince
NYC 10012   Mon-Sat 11-7, Sun 12-6

Huminska New York

A milliner who tired of making hats, Miss Huminska now designs a line of clothing with cuts and patterns that hardly ever vary, allowing her to pursue her love affair with fabrics. Limited-edition pieces include her signature laminated leather jackets with pressed peacock feathers, embroidered organza tops paired with shantung pants and silk blouses that double as jackets. Gingham is clearly a favorite. Accessories include hats (clearly old habits are hard to break) and a sprinkling of bags.

East Village   **212-677-3458**
315 East 9th Street   bet. 1/2nd Ave.
NYC 10003   Tues-Sun 1-7

Hunting World

If you're headed to Africa for a safari, a stop at Hunting World is a must. Outfit yourself in the latest bush gear of safari jackets, pants, vests, silk scarves, hats and shoes, then pack it all into their signature travel bags. Fishing gear and apparel for the complete angler are also available.   **800-833-1251**

Midtown East　　　　　　　　　　**212-755-3400**
16 East 53rd Street　　　　　　bet. Madison/5th Ave.
NYC 10022　　　　　　　　　　Mon-Sat 11-7, Sun 12-6

If

A SoHo purveyor of avant-garde clothing and accessories, with ready-to-wear from such directional designers as Commes des Garçons, Ivan Grundahl, Marc Le Bihan, Martin Margiela, Junya Watanabe, Dries Van Noten and hot Belgian name Veronique Braquinho. Shoes, hats, handbags and accessories also available.

SoHo　　　　　　　　　　　　**212-334-4964**
94 Grand Street　　　　　　　bet. Mercer/Greene
NYC 10013　　　　　　　　　Mon-Sat 11-7, Sun 12-6:30

Il Bisonte

Durable, handcrafted leather goods embossed with a bison logo and perfect for weekends. Undyed leather and brass hardware define Bisonte designs, with a complete line of handbags, small leathergoods, briefcases and luggage. Styles are functional and good for travel.

SoHo　　　　　　　　　　　　**212-966-8773**
120 Sullivan Street　　　　　　bet. Prince/Spring
NYC 10012　　　　　　Tues-Sat 12-6:30, Sun & Mon 12-6

☆ Ina

Ina's mission: "To select only what's in fashion from those who are in fashion, for those who want to be in fashion." This is a truly amazing consignment shop where the fashion cognoscenti part with their designer clothes—including such brands as Prada, Gucci, Marni, Armani, Calvin Klein and Versace—and the rest of the fashion cognoscenti scoop them up. A Helmut Lang dress for $90? You betcha. Handbags, scarves and shoes by Blahnik, Gucci, Chanel and Hermès round out the brilliantly edited assortment. Ina's secret recipe: her wares are in pristine condition, and her prices can't be beat.

SoHo　　　　　　　　　　　　**212-941-4757**
101 Thompson Street　　　　　bet. Spring/Prince
NYC 10012　　　　　　　　　　　Mon-Sun 12-7

NoLiTa　　　　　　　　　　　**212-334-9048**
21 Prince Street　　　　　　　bet. Mott/Elizabeth
NYC 10012　　　　　　　Sun-Thur 12-7, Fri & Sat 12-8

NoLiTa (M)　　　　　　　　　**212-334-2210**
262 Mott Street　　　　　　　bet. Houston/Prince
NYC 10012　　　　　　　Sun-Thur 12-7, Fri & Sat 12-8

Infinity

Despite its slightly chaotic atmosphere, Infinity is the answer for your "hard-to-shop-for" pre-teen. Looks run from formal skirt-and-jacket suits to trendy jeans and funky T-shirts. For special occasions, Infinity also offers off-the-rack or custom-order gowns and dresses. Dressy frocks, activewear, sportswear and casual duds from labels that include Ikkes, Sermoneta and David Charles.

Institut

Upper East Side   212-517-4232
1116 Madison Avenue   at 83rd St.
NYC 10028   Mon-Sat 10-6

Institut 👚

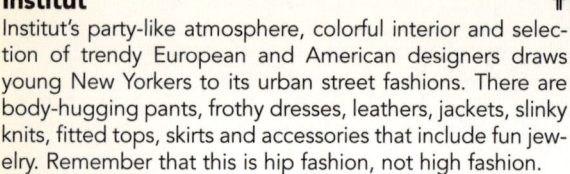

Institut's party-like atmosphere, colorful interior and selection of trendy European and American designers draws young New Yorkers to its urban street fashions. There are body-hugging pants, frothy dresses, leathers, jackets, slinky knits, fitted tops, skirts and accessories that include fun jewelry. Remember that this is hip fashion, not high fashion.

SoHo   212-431-5521
97 Spring Street   bet. Mercer/B'way
NYC 10012   Mon-Sun 11-8

SoHo   212-431-1970
99 Spring Street   bet. Mercer/B'way
NYC 10012   Mon-Sun 11-8

☆ Intermix 👚

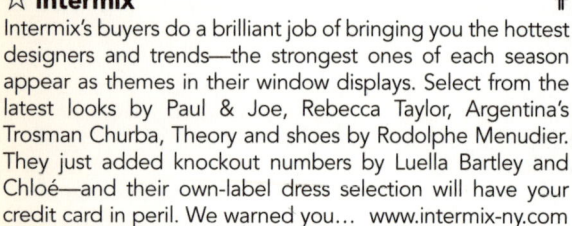

Intermix's buyers do a brilliant job of bringing you the hottest designers and trends—the strongest ones of each season appear as themes in their window displays. Select from the latest looks by Paul & Joe, Rebecca Taylor, Argentina's Trosman Churba, Theory and shoes by Rodolphe Menudier. They just added knockout numbers by Luella Bartley and Chloé—and their own-label dress selection will have your credit card in peril. We warned you… www.intermix-ny.com

Upper East Side   212-249-7858
1003 Madison Avenue   bet. 77/78th St.
NYC 10021   Mon-Sat 10-7, Sun 12-6

Upper West Side   212-769-9116
210 Columbus Avenue   at 69th St.
NYC 10023   Mon-Wed 11-7, Thur-Sat 11-7:30, Sun 12-6

Flatiron   212-533-9720
125 Fifth Avenue   bet. 19/20th St.
NYC 10003   Mon-Sat 11-8, Sun 12-6

Iramo 👕👚

Here's an innovative concept in retailing: when you want to open another hip-hop shoe store in the same neighborhood with exactly the same merchandise but want to stay "original," simply spell the name of your first store backwards and, voila, you've created a totally "new" store. If this makes no sense to you, go to Omari and read all about Iramo. That, and check out the street-cool shoes.

SoHo   212-334-9159
89 Spring Street   bet. Mercer/W. B'way
NYC 10012   Mon-Sat 11-8, Sun 11-7:30

Issey Miyake 👕👚

A landmark cast iron building, an interior of undulating titanium forms that curve throughout, and the sheer strength of Miyake's aesthetic make for a unique shopping experience. The Japanese designer's flagship is a magnet for devotees in search of creative and striking pieces. Unusually shaped, sculpture-like designs, synthetic materials and lots of color (oh, and did we mention pleats?) are Miyake's trademarks. Many of the looks are revealingly sheer and require serious underpinnings. Fabulous bags and accessories in interesting colors and patterns include designs like heavy cotton beach bags with brilliant color stitching and mirroring. www.isseymiyake.com

TriBeCa 212-226-0100
119 Hudson Street at N. Moore
NYC 10013 Mon-Sat 11-7, Sun 12-6

Upper East Side 212-439-7822
992 Madison Avenue at 77th St.
NYC 10021 Mon-Fri 10-6, Sat 11-6

Jane
This petite boutique has been dressing stylish East Side ladies in sophisticated European separates for the past 15 years. Designs range from casual to evening with an emphasis on luxurious fabrics and chic styling. Clements Ribeiro, BluMarine, Philosophy di Alberta Ferretti, United Bamboo and Les Copains are just some of their eclectic collection. Super friendly staff will assist you in searching through the overstuffed racks.

Upper East Side 212-772-7710
1025 Lexington Avenue bet. 73/74th St.
NYC 10021 Mon-Sat 10-6

J. Crew
J. Crew is where you shop for work-week basics and weekend staples. There are three dressing options: casual Friday clothes, dressy looks with classic styling and weekend wear. Shop for chinos, dress pants, cashmeres, button-down shirts, relaxed jeans, T-shirts, dresses, swimsuits, sleepwear and underwear, accessories and shoes. The J. Crew image epitomizes an active "all-American" lifestyle, even if you don't have one, and every now and then they'll hit the jackpot with a cute striped sweater, say, that looks designer. Great bang for the buck. 800-562-0258 www.jcrew.com

Fifth Avenue 212-765-4227
30 Rockefeller Center at 50th Street bet. 5/6th Ave.
NYC 10022 Mon-Sat 10-8, Sun 11-7

Flatiron 212-255-4848
91 Fifth Avenue bet. 16/17th St.
NYC 10003 Mon-Sat 10-8, Sun 11-7

SoHo 212-966-2739
99 Prince Street at Mercer
NYC 10012 Mon-Sat 10-8, Sun 11-7

Lower Manhattan 212-385-3500
203 Front Street at South Street Seaport
NYC 10038 Mon-Fri 10-8, Sat 10-9, Sun 10-8

J. Lindeberg

The uncommon combination of fashion and golf are what make Swedish designer Lindeberg tick and his passions coalesce into a contemporary sportswear collection showcased here, his first U.S. store. This 2,200 sq. ft. bi-level space, equipped with marigold Formica fixtures, showcases fashion-forward men's clothing from leathers, three-piece pinstriped suits to staples like black and khaki pants and button-down shirts. Lindeberg's ultra hip "On Course" golf collection is appropriate for on and off the links. Women's fashions are sexy and form-fitted, while golf attire for the fellows is preppy chic. www.jlindeberg.com

SoHo 212-625-9403
126 Spring Street at Greene
NYC 10012 Mon-Sat 11-7, Sun 12-6

J. McLaughlin

For over 22 years, J. McLaughlin has been putting its mark on classic, American sportswear. Men and women shop here for a casual, comfortable wardrobe that's appropriate for a relaxed work atmosphere or weekend living. The clothes combine tradition and preppy cool in looks like khakis, corduroys, polo shirts, cable sweaters, button-down shirts and quilted jackets. Accessories include handbags, scarves, socks and cufflinks.

Upper East Side 212-369-4830
1311 Madison Avenue bet. 92/93rd St.
NYC 10028 Mon & Fri 10-6, Tues-Thur 10-7
Sat & Sun 10-6

Upper East Side 212-879-9565
1343 Third Avenue at 77th St.
NYC 10021 Mon-Fri 10:30-8, Sat 11-6, Sun 11:30-6

☆ J. Mendel

A luxury fur store selling both contemporary and traditional coats, running from sporty chic to glam evening. Shop the finest quality furs including mink, chinchilla, sable, fisher and fox, as well as cashmere overcoats and rainwear lined or trimmed in one of these coveted pelts. Mendel's delivers European styling (think Valentino) with simple, often lacy, elegance. Expect to pay top dollar; however, at the end of the season, prices are negotiable.

Upper East Side 212-832-5830
723 Madison Avenue bet. 63/64th St.
NYC 10021 Mon-Sat 10-6

J.M. Weston

An expensive French footwear retailer renowned for handmade, classic shoes. Conservative styles in loafers, lace-ups and boots are all hand-stitched to endure a lifetime of wear. For a slice of this luxury, you'll have to pay anywhere from $400 to $600. The company also offers a collection of shoes designed by fashion footwear darling Michel

Perry. More good news, you can also return your worn shoes and, for a nominal fee, have them resoled and rebuilt. Classic loafers and lace-up split-toe shoes for women. 877-4-Weston www.jmweston.com

Upper East Side   **212-535-2100**
812 Madison Avenue   at 68th St.
NYC 10021   Mon-Fri 9:30-6, Sat 10-6

J. Press

One of the oldest menswear shops in New York, J. Press prides itself on its selection of traditional suits, furnishings, sportswear, formalwear, outerwear and accessories, all in good taste at reasonable prices. A great shop for young career guys. Suit prices start at $475.
www.jpressonline.com

Midtown East   **212-687-7642**
7 East 44th Street   bet. Madison/5th Ave.
NYC 10017   Mon-Sat 9-6

J.S. Suarez

For nearly 50 years, the Suarez family has been selling more than decent copies of such handbag brands as Gucci, Hermès and Chanel. Quality workmanship go into bags that generally cost 30% to 50% below retail. Belts, scarves and small leathergoods are also available.

Midtown East   **212-753-3758**
450 Park Avenue   bet. 56/57th St.
NYC 10022   Mon-Fri 10-6, Sat 10-5

Jacadi

A successful French company that makes shopping for your children a pleasure. Clothing is neatly displayed according to size, color and style and includes back-to-school basics, casual play clothes, shoes and accessories. Looks range from adorable smocked dresses to embroidered and appliqued overalls. A great sweater and blouse selection as well as a layette department selling everything from bumpers to towels. Newborn to age 12. Great sales.   www.jacadiusa.com

Upper East Side   **212-369-1616**
1281 Madison Avenue   bet. 91/92nd St.
NYC 10128   Mon-Wed, Fri, Sat, 10-6, Thur 10-7, Sun 12-5

Upper East Side   **212-535-3200**
787 Madison Avenue   bet. 66/67th St.
NYC 10021   Mon-Wed, Fri, Sat 10-6, Thur 10-7, Sun 12-5

Jack Silver Formal Wear

Looking for a tuxedo for your wedding or a gala event? Rent or buy from Jack Silver, which offers such labels as Oscar de la Renta, Pierre Cardin, After Six and Ralph Lauren. Tuxedos for purchase must be ordered; rentals are in stock. Shirts, bow ties, cummerbunds, suspenders and shoes also available.   www.jacksilverformalwear.com

Jack Spade

Midtown West   212-582-0202
1780 Broadway, 3rd Fl.   bet. 57/58th St.
NYC 10019   Mon-Fri 9-6, Sat 10-3

Jack Spade

For the past five years, female fashionistas have bought up handbags by accessories diva Kate Spade. Good news, gentlemen, it's your turn. Husband Andy Spade has created a collection of snappy, efficient travel bags, day bags, informal briefcases, totes, messenger bags, computer bags, banker's envelopes and wallets. They fall under the semi-eponymous Jack Spade label and in fabrications like canvas, nylon, worsted wools and water-repellent, waxed cotton canvas. Lots of extra amenities like pockets for cellphones and pens. Bags start at $150. Macintosh rainwear, and a new classic, American clothing line also available.

SoHo   212-625-1820
56 Greene Street   bet. Spring/Broome
NYC 10012   Mon-Sat 11-7, Sun 12-6

Jaeger

Jaeger is the latest establishment British label to enter the makeover cycle: the main line has been rejuvenated by a new creative director, who has produced modern classics with an urban edge. Meanwhile, quirky British designer Bella Freud (painter Lucien's daughter) has developed a capsule collection under her name that combines her arch wit with updated styles from the Jaeger archives. It all adds up to a contemporary selection of sportswear and work wear with looks like pinstriped pant suits in masculine cuts, navy, pale blue and heather Donegal tweed slim-fitting coats, zip-front jackets, logo'd cashmere knits, pencil skirts, belted minis and Jaeger's signature camel coat and cashmere knitwear.

Upper East Side   212-628-3350
818 Madison Avenue   bet. 68/69th St.
NYC 10021   Mon-Sat 10-6

Jamin Puech

A sophisticated, bohemian handbag shop catering to sophisticated, bohemian handbag addicts from the owner of Calypso St. Barths. Intricate beading, exotic feathers and soft, slouchy shapes give these handbags a vintage appeal. Find leather and straw bags, delicate knits, organza floral bags and peacock trimmed and beaded purses. Each handbag is beautifully made and detailed to perfection.

NoLiTa   212-334-9730
252 Mott Street   bet. Houston/Prince
NYC 10012   Mon-Sat 11-7, Sun 12-6

Janet Russo

Janet Russo's passion is for collecting unusual fabrics and each year she travels far and wide in search of everything from Indian saris and Chinese silks to Liberty of London prints. She then turns them into a collection of feminine dresses, tops, sweater sets and eveningwear in styles best suited to the curvaceous woman after a romantic look. A selection of cardigans and camisoles by Mary Beth's Design is also available, as are antique purses, earrings and everyday bags.

NoLiTa   **212-625-3297**
262 Mott Street   bet. Houston/Prince
NYC 10012   Mon-Sat 11:30-7, Sun 12-6:30

Jay Kos

Shopping at Jay Kos is like shopping at your own personal club. An intimate atmosphere of beautifully displayed merchandise makes you want to buy it all—classic Italian suits (ready-made or custom), tweed shooting jackets, all-weather coats (including Macintosh jackets and Austrian Loden coats), Scottish silk-lined cashmere sweaters, hand-cut shirts from one of the oldest workshops in Switzerland, neckwear and English corduroys. In addition, find furnishings and accessories that include fabulous English cufflinks, Swain Adeney & Brigg umbrellas and Borsalino and Lock hats. Kos's appeal is based on traditional styling, luxury fabrics and pure elegance. Expensive—but worth it.

Upper East Side   **212-327-2382**
986 Lexington Avenue   bet. 71/72nd St.
NYC 10021   Mon-Thur 10-7, Fri & Sat 10-6

Jean Paul Gaultier

Welcome to the Gaultier universe, a surprisingly recent addition to swanky Madison Avenue. The iconoclastic French designer has for years managed to marry chic and camp like no other: where else could you find his typically ethnic-printed layered pieces alongside snowglobes filled with JPG fragrance? His classic sailor striped T-shirts next to camouflage gym boots? Also, in this surprisingly minimal store, find sunglasses, boxer shorts and cheeky ties emblazoned with the designer's name. Buy up big and make like Cate Blanchett, a high-profile fan of Gaultier's divine couture.

Upper East Side   **212-249-0235**
759 Madison Avenue   bet. 65/66th St
NYC 10021   Mon-Wed 10-6, Thur & Sat 11-7, Fri 10-6

☆ Jeffrey New York

The Meatpacking District is now fashion central thanks largely to the pioneering efforts of Jeffrey Kalinsky, the impresario of this 18,000 sq. ft. multi-designer emporium. Kalinsky's unique ability to cull the highlights from each designer's collection sets this mini-department store apart from the rest—and the meat plants on every corner. He has chosen the best pieces from luxe labels like Jil Sander, Helmut Lang, Narciso Rodriguez and Dior plus Hedi Slimane's cult Dior menswear—that women covet as much as men. The best thing about Jeffrey is his fabulous—and dangerous—shoe selection: Gucci, Christian Louboutin, Versace, Robert Clergerie, Celine, Yves Saint Laurent,

Manolo Blahnik and Prada...Order a pair of shoes over the phone and have them delivered the same day. Now, that is service.

Chelsea	**212-206-1272**
449 West 14th Street	bet. 9/10th Ave.
NYC 10014	Mon-Fri 10-8, Thur 10-9
	Sat 10-7, Sun 12:30-6

Jenne Maag

Texan designer Jenne Maag has been making her signature hip-hugging stretch pants since the 70's, way before they were the "thing." Her boutique carries her line, which comes in matching groups (pants, jackets, halter-tops and shirt-dresses). Manufactured in her trademark "Tarrello" fabric, a polyester/Lycra blend (similar to what Prada uses), Maag's designs feature classic cuts, form-fitted shapes and always have a bit of stretch. "I try to make clothes that fit any shape, from skinny minis to fuller figures, and that make women feel and look great," she says. Sizes run P, S, M and L.

NoLiTa	**212-625-1700**
29 Spring Street	at Mott
NYC 10012	Mon-Sat 11-7, Sun 12-6

Jennifer Tyler

A designer cashmere line of multiple sweater styles, coats, pants, shawls, capes, blankets and accessories, all available in a range of weights and colors and all made in Italy and Scotland. Customers return season after season for Tyler's classic twinsets and roundneck sweaters in 100% cashmere and cashmere/silk blends—perfect for Palm Beach. Prices run from $295 to approx. $1,000.   www.jennifer-tyler.com

Upper East Side	**212-772-8350**
986 Madison Avenue	bet. 76/77th St.
NYC 10021	Mon-Sat 10-6, Sun 12-5

Jenny B.

Jenny B.'s ever-changing selection of merchandise keeps her customers coming back for more. Feminine ballet flats, hipster boots and sexy in-your-face stilettos are under the Jenny B. and Varda labels. For men, styles run from classic and dressy to hip and funky.

SoHo	**212-343-9575**
118 Spring Street	bet. Mercer/Greene
NYC 10012	Mon-Sun 11-7

Jill Anderson

A North Dakota-born designer who's a whiz at turning out comfortable clothes with offbeat detailing. Design is a kind of yoga, says Anderson, "where the space of calm contentment feeds my imagination." Clean lines and unusual, up-to-the-minute fabrics give a modern sensibility to her feminine dresses, including her signature widow dress (loose fitting, long sleeved and below-the-knee), skirts, jackets, easy-wearing lace tops and coats.

Jimmy Choo

East Village   212-253-1747
331 East 9th Street   bet. 1/2nd Ave.
NYC 10003   Mon-Sun 12-8

Jill Stuart

Jill Stuart gets what New York women want to wear: a combination of tasteful and approachable clothes with a deft mix of femininity and urban edge (her perfect-fit jeans are a must). This philosophy permeates her collection of dresses, skirts, jackets, cashmeres and tops—although she has recently moved into more decorative arenas of embellishment and patchwork. New and fabulous is Stuart's basement vintage boutique, a decadent setting housing armoires filled with floral print dresses and dramatic bias-cut evening gowns. Gorgeous.

SoHo   212-343-2300
100 Greene Street   bet. Prince/Spring
NYC 10012   Mon-Sat 11-7, Sun 12-6

Jil Sander

Jil Sander, the German mistress of minimalism, is no longer designing her cult collections, after a serious tiff with new company owners Prada. The task of continuing her tradition of luxurious edge has fallen to designer Milan Vukmirovic, a former buyer for cult Paris store, Colette. Sander loyalists say the label just isn't the same, but fans of simple, monochromatic chic are still buying up big time. This new, three-level flagship store aims for the "spirit of modern refinement and casual elegance," carrying both women's and men's collections and low-key luxe accessories. The perfect store to get back in black.

Midtown East   212-447-9200
11 East 57th Street   bet. 5th/Madison
NYC 10022   Mon-Sat 10-6, Thur 10-7, Sun 12-6

Jimmy Choo

When Madonna searched for the perfect shoes for her wedding and when President Bush's twin nieces Laura and Barbara twinkle-toed their way to the inaugural ball, which brand did they choo-se? Jimmy Choo, whose shoes have graced the feet of London and New York It girls (not to mention a movie star or two) for more than a decade. A rival to Manolo Blahnik, Choo causes women to throw logic to the winds and pay up to $1,200 for his creations. Narrow toes, high heels and serious femininity define the collection of delicate pumps, slingbacks, demure gingham kitten heels, reptile skin boots, fanciful stilettos (adorned with mink or seashells), slinky sandals with crystal embroidered straps and towering gold-ankle wrap stilettos.   www.jimmychoo.com

Fifth Avenue   212-593-0800
645 Fifth Avenue   at 51st St.
NYC 10022   Mon-Sat 10-6

John Anthony

Strictly couture! For grand occasions that require an elegant ballgown or dressy suit, John Anthony is at your service. Choose from his ready-made collection or custom order your own. Cosmically high prices; expect to pay $10,000 and up for a gown.

Midtown East   212-245-6069
130 West 57th Street, Suite 11 B   bet. 6/7th Ave.
NYC 10021   by appointment

John Fluevog Shoes

Fluevog's shoes may be the wildest footgear in Gotham. With their 6-inch platform heels, they "will keep you above the urban trash," says Fluevog. Serious clubhoppers and teen types will find everything from platforms to pedal-pushers. Although the shoes are well-made, it may require both youth and guts to strut the streets in these chunky numbers.   800-381-3338   www.fluevog.com

NoLiTa   212-431-4484
250 Mulberry Street   at Prince
NYC 10012   Mon-Sat 12-8, Sun 12-6

John Lobb

Since 1850, John Lobb's handmade shoes have been caressing the feet of distinguished gentlemen and reassuring them with their motto "Some things are forever." Now Britain's venerable shoemaker has crossed the pond and is open for business with a selection of straight-cap oxfords, loafers, buckle shoes, jodhpur boots, evening slip-ons and classic moccasins. Beautiful craftsmanship and traditional styling define the Lobb label. Pay an average price of $800, while custom-made starts at $3,800.

Upper East Side   212-888-9797
680 Madison Avenue   bet. 61/62nd St.
NYC 10021   Mon-Sat 10-6, Thur 10-7

Johnson

Designer Kim Johnson creates stylish dresses with a vintage edge. Other items include brown denim jeans with red stitching down the legs, snappy coats, simply-styled skirts and sporty shirts. She also carries assorted pieces by Lina Tsai. Good for a retail fix are her "wrist bags" in cute, pop prints.

Lower East Side   646-602-8668
179 Orchard   bet. Houston/Stanton
NYC 10002   Mon-Fri 1-7, Sat 12:30-7:30, Sun 12-6

John Varvatos

After tours of duty with fashion titans Calvin Klein and Ralph Lauren, John Varvatos stepped out on his own (with the help of sportswear group Nautica) with his exclusive men's shop. Who is his customer? According to the designer, "There's the modern guy who shops at Prada and Gucci, the classic

Armani customer and then the guy in the middle—the Varvatos customer, a modern man who wants to look elegant but with a relaxed feel." Choose from a selection of sophisticated wool suits, luxurious cashmeres, bulky knits, wide-legged pants, shearlings and peacoats. For a sneak preview, catch The Practice's Dylan McDermott wearing Varvatos in court. Very cool is his collaboration with Converse on designer sneakers, sported by more than one employee of cutting edge magazine Vogue Hommes. Expensive.

SoHo   **212-965-0700**
149 Mercer Street   bet. Houston/Prince
NYC 10012   Mon-Sat 11-7, Sun 12-6

Johnston & Murphy
This American men's footwear retailer has satisfied its customers since 1850 with a full range of shoe styles, from dress and formal shoes to casual basics and weekend wear. Prices range from $150 to $400.   800-424-2854
www.johnstonandmurphy.com

Midtown East   **212-527-2343**
520 Madison Avenue   at 54th St.
NYC 10022   Mon-Fri 9-7, Sat 10-7, Sun 12-5

Midtown East   **212-697-9375**
345 Madison Avenue   bet. 44/45th St.
NYC 10017   Mon-Fri 9-7, Sat 10-6, Sun 12-5

Joovay
A small lingerie boutique stocked with top-of-the-line American and European labels, including Lise Charmel, Marvel, Leigh Bantivoglio, Cosabella, LeJaby and La Perla. Looks run from dainty and sweet to sexy and hot in bras, panties, teddies, nightwear, camisoles and slips. Hosiery by Oroblu and Falke also available.

SoHo   **212-431-6386**
436 West Broadway   at Prince
NYC 10012   Mon-Sun 12-7, Sat 11-7

Jos. A. Banks
A Baltimore retailer featuring tailored career clothing for the conservative dresser. In keeping with their solid origins, Banks offers a comforting shopping environment for a complete selection of suits, sportswear, shirts, ties and underwear, as well as a Cole Haan shoe department. Every fall Banks invites you to trade in an old suit and get up to a $200 credit toward a new one—now, if only Prada did that...   800-285-2265

Midtown East   **212-370-0600**
366 Madison Avenue   bet. 46/47th St.
NYC 10017   Mon-Sat 9-7, Thur 9-8, Sun 12-5

Joseph
Chic London retailer Joseph Ettedgui has his customers coming back for more by sticking to what it knows best:

keeping the same basic styles, especially their cult pants, running every season, but updating them with the fabrics, colors and textures of the moment. It's all about modern separates in easy-to-wear shapes, including pants, shirts, jackets, leathers, knitwear and shearlings, as well as that one drop-dead, high-end piece that's introduced into each collection.

SoHo M/W   **212-343-7071**
106 Greene Street   bet. Spring/Prince
NYC 10012   Mon-Sat 11-6, Sun 12-6

Midtown East   **212-570-0077**
816 Madison Avenue   bet. 68/69th St.
NYC 10021   Mon-Sat 10-6:30, Sun 12-6

Judith Leiber

Accessories legend Judith Leiber features over 500 bags for evening and daytime wear, from a classic alligator style to an elaborately detailed design for fancy nights out. But true Leiber aficionados shop here for her rhinestone evening bags and tiny jewel-encrusted minaudières. These bags are often seen in the clutches of society types, including Nancy Reagan, oh, and avant-garde darlings like Bjork. See? Versatile.

Upper East Side   **212-327-4003**
987 Madison Avenue   bet. 76/77th St.
NYC 10021   Mon-Sat 10-6

Julian and Sara

A shop stocked with children's clothing lines from France and Italy. Find back-to-school basics, play clothes and accessories hand-picked from top labels like Lili Gaufrette, Arthur, Mona Lisa, Kenzo, Petit Bateau, Clayeux, Mini Man and Elsy. Newborn through age 12.

SoHo   **212-226-1989**
103 Mercer Street   bet. Prince/Spring
NYC 10012   Mon-Fri 11-7, Sat & Sun 11:30-6

Julie Artisan's Gallery

Since 1973 this artisan's gallery has showcased techniques like weaving, hand-painting, stitching, quilting and knitting. Each piece is a lovingly handcrafted work of art, either one-of-a-kind or sold in limited editions. Women shop here for intricate evening kimonos, loomed knitted jackets, colorful sweaters, hand-dyed shirts and more from such labels as Tim Harding and Linda Mendelson. For a mature customer who's into arty dressing, this is your spiritual home.

Upper East Side   **212-717-5959**
762 Madison Avenue   bet. 65/66th St.
NYC 10021   Mon-Sat 11-6

Jungle Planet

Find a "jungle" of merchandise spanning the world from Nepal to little ol' Gotham. There is a selection of Mandarin dresses, shirts, jeans, T-shirts, sarongs, scarves, beaded handbags and jewelry, as well as a few vintage pieces.

West Village   **212-989-5447**
175 West 4th Street   bet. 6/7th Ave.
NYC 10014   Mon-Thur 12:30-9, Fri 12:30-10
Sat 12:30-11, Sun 12:30-8

Juno
For shoe addicts who absolutely must have the very latest in footwear, from casual, sporty shoes to evening. Looks for women include sexy pumps, boots (a fantastic, well-priced selection—especially in winter), slides and sandals, while men can choose from Prada-esque sneaker/dress shoes, boots and sandals. Great children's shoes.

SoHo   **212-219-8002**
444 Broadway   bet. Grand/Howard
NYC 10012   Mon-Fri 10:30-8, Sat 10:30-8:30, Sun 11-8

SoHo   **212-625-2560**
543 Broadway   bet. Prince/Spring
NYC 10012   Mon-Sat 10:30-8, Sun 11-8

☆ Jussara Lee
Brazilian expat Jussara Lee recently opened a new signature store in this hipper-than-hip shopping district, a sleek white space that showcases her interactive approach to design. Customers are encouraged to open the sliding doors and play with the colorful fabrics, trimmings and linings on display, while Lee designs individual pieces from their choices. "I think that people want to feel a connection to things now, for their possessions to be more personal, so I ask women to become part of the process and discover their own creativity," she says. And we can't argue with that.

Chelsea   **212-242-4128**
11 Little West 12th Street   bet. 9th Ave./Washington
NYC 10014   Mon-Sat 11-7, Sun 12-7

Just for Tykes
As the name suggests, Just for Tykes sells all the practical essentials and little goodies you'll need for your little 'un, including clothing, cribs, furnishings, bedding, baby gear, painted trunks, gifts, accessories and a sprinkling of toys. So if you're shopping "for your new family" or looking for the perfect nursery gift, Just for Tykes will make your life a little easier.

SoHo   **212-274-9121**
83 Mercer Street   bet. Spring/Broome
NYC 10012   Mon-Fri 10-6, Sat 11-7, Sun 12-6

Jutta Neumann
Looking for one-of-a-kind, handcrafted sandals? Jutta Neumann is your weumann! Choose from virtually any kind of skin (cowhide, calf, suede, snake, stingray, python, alligator), as well as a surfeit of colors (turquoise, bright yellow,

orange and traditional browns and blacks). Then Jutta traces your feet and cuts a pattern. While you're there, she'll also design a handbag to match, with or without pockets and as wide or deep as you want, or make a coordinating belt or wristband. Custom sandals range from $180 to $250 with a three week delivery.   www.juttaneumann.com

Lower East Side 212-982-7048
158 Allen Street bet. Stanton/Rivington
NYC 10002 Mon-Sat 12-8

Katayone Adeli

Low-key designer Katayone Adeli has always had a loyal following, especially for her perfectly-cut pants that are worn by off-duty models everywhere from Paris to New York. Her secret: simple, monochromatic pieces that go from one year to the next. Now in her eighth season, Adeli turns out essential mix-and-match pieces that every cool New York woman wants in her wardrobe, including great dresses, skirts, sweaters, coats and those cult pants (if there are any left—Gwyneth Paltrow once said she scoops up every pair in sight).

NoHo 212-260-3500
35 Bond Street bet. Lafayette/Bowery
NYC 10013 Mon-Sat 11-7, Sun 12-6

Kate Spade

Fashionistas call her the "Purse Queen" and former accessories editor Spade lives up to the name with her Fifties-inspired handbags in bold, jaunty colors. Each season she reinvents her signature pieces in fashionable fabrics like glossy satin nylons, silks, bouclé wools and leathers. Looks run from practical shoulder and tote bags to jelly bean-bright silk and satin evening bags. As for her shoe designs: picture Sophia Loren on the Amalfi Coast, wearing a polka-dot mule during the day and a rhinestone slide at night. Small leathergoods, raincoats, pajamas, umbrellas, and Spade's line of sunglasses are also available.   www.katespade.com

SoHo 212-274-1991
454 Broome Street at Mercer
NYC 10013 Mon-Sat 11-7, Sun 12-6

SoHo (travel store) 212-965-8654
59 Thompson Street bet. Broome/Spring
NYC 10012 Mon-Sat 11-7, Sun 12-6

Kavanagh's Designer Resale Shop

Owner Mary Kavanagh, former director of personal shopping at Bergdorf Goodman, sells pre-owned but pristine, high-end designer clothing. Her specialty is Chanel suits priced at approx $900 but you also can find Armani, Ungaro, Jil Sander and Prada. Handbag and shoe labels include Fendi, Hermès, Gucci, Chanel, Tod's and Manolo Blahnik.

Midtown East　　　　　　　　　　　212-702-0152
146 East 49th Street　　　　　　　bet. Lex./3rd Ave.
NYC 10017　　　　　　　　　　Tues-Fri 11-6, Sat 11-4

Kazuyo Nakano
Head here for fun looks in handbags in colors from bold solids to combinations like luscious berry and botanical greens. A cornucopia of styles includes constructed leathers, geometric patchwork bags, python and embossed crocodile, calfskin embellished with fake fur, sleek python and evening bags covered in pastel paillettes. Other items include suede and leather pieces and a sprinkling of skirts and dresses. Also, lots and lots of corsages.　　www.kazuyonakano.com

NoLiTa　　　　　　　　　　　　　212-941-7093
223 Mott Street　　　　　　　　bet. Spring/Prince
NYC 10012　　　　　　　　　　　Wed-Mon 12:30-7

KC Thompson
Jewels, glorious jewels, and a fab store in which to buy them. Designer Kristen Thompson dreamed up a space (in a former nail salon) that she sees as a "pampered women's dressing room". Think large vanity mirrors where indulgent customers can try on such pieces as large, vintage-inspired flower earrings, or chunky-chic semi-precious necklaces featuring stones like cornelian, turquoise and coin pearls. Each piece has an 18-karat gold butterfly clasp. Expect to pay from $800 to $1,895 for her jewels—and spend hours more at the mirror at home admiring them.

Upper East Side　　　　　　　　　212-396-0974
22 East 72nd Street　　　　　　bet. 5th /Madison Ave.
NYC 10021　　　　　　　　　　　　　Mon-Fri 10-5

KD Dance
KD (we think) stands for Knitwear and Dance and that's exactly what you'll find here. Their specialty is dance, fitness and fashion knitwear that goes from yoga and Pilates straight to the streets. Find great-looking wrap dresses, tops, cardigans, yoga pants, legwarmers and stretch cotton/Lycra workout clothes in an abundance of colors. Better yet, it's all machine washable. Stylish clothes at great value.　　　　　　　　　　www.kddance.com

NoHo　　　　　　　　　　　　　　212-533-1037
339 Lafayette Street　　　　　　　　　at Bleecker
NYC 10012　　　　　　　　　Mon-Sat 12-8, Sun 1-5

Keiko
Have you ever wondered where those sexy swimsuits featured in fashion magazines come from? And how do they get such a perfect fit? Well, the answer to both questions is Keiko's, which offers a collection of bathing attire in mouth-watering colors. Prices start at $110 and they charge extra for alterations. Its tour de force, however, is a custom-designed suit (for men, women, and children) that will minimize the negatives and maximize the positives. Prices start at $250 with a four- to six-week delivery.

Kelly Christy

SoHo   **212-226-6051**
62 Greene Street   bet. Spring/Broome
NYC 10012   Mon-Fri 11-6, Sat 12-6, Sun 1-6

Kelly Christy

This eponymous boutique sells chic toppers that have a flair for the dramatic: Christy recently collaborated with Isaac Mizrahi on the costumes for hit Broadway play, The Women. Her forte is specialty hats, which she describes as "classic with a twist." Each design highlights her unique use of trim, including fedoras, boleros, cloches, berets and boaters. Choose from off-the-rack or indulge in a made-to-measure.

NoLiTa   **212-965-0686**
235 Elizabeth Street   bet. Houston/Prince
NYC 10012   Tues-Sat 12-7, Sun 12-6

☆ Keni Valenti

Located in the heart of the garment district, this four-floor showroom boasts one of the foremost collections of vintage fashions from the Twenties to the Eighties, including beautiful designer dresses, couture eveningwear, shoes, handbags and jewelry. From choice pieces by American sportswear legends like John Kloss and Clovis Ruffin to heavy-hitters like Yves Saint Laurent, Halston, Geoffrey Beene, Alaia and Courrèges, it's all in impeccable condition. Former Fiorucci designer Valenti has also designed his own line, called KV, featuring bias-cut silk jersey, evening dresses and luncheon-bound gabardine suits, that the model crew and downtown hipster Chloe Sevigny have been buying up bigtime. Expect to pay high couture designer prices for a little slice of vintage luxury. Also expect to look amazing.   www.kenivalenti.com

Midtown West   **212-967-7147**
247 West 30th Street, 5th Floor   bet. 7/8th Ave.
NYC 10001   Mon-Fri 10-6 by appointment only

Kenneth Cole

Designer-with-soul Kenneth Cole is on his way to becoming fashion's next super brand. He started by selling shoes out of a trailer and created a $300 million footwear empire, but is now becoming a major force in men's and women's wear, too. His hallmark: clean, urban functionality at incredible value. Both sexes can shop for fashionable sportswear like shiny jeans, embracing knits, sleek shirts and leather and shearling coats. In footwear, find a broad range of shoe styles from career and dress shoes to trendy and casual basics. Accessories include handbags, scarves and sunglasses. Smart goods at smart prices.   800-487-4389
www.kencole.com

Upper West Side   **212-873-2061**
353 Columbus Avenue   at 77th St.
NYC 10024   Mon-Sat 10-8, Sun 11-7

Midtown East (in Grand Central Station)   212-949-8079
107 East 42nd Street   at Park Ave.
NYC 10017   Mon-Fri 8-9, Sat 10-9, Sun 11-7

Midtown East   80-KEN-COLE
130 East 57th Street   at Lex. Ave.
NYC 10017   call for hours

Fifth Avenue   212-373-5800
610 Fifth Avenue   at Rockefeller Center
NYC 10020   Mon-Sat 10-8, Sun 12-6

Flatiron   212-675-2550
95 Fifth Avenue   at 17th St.
NYC 10003   Mon-Sat 10-8, Sun 11-7

SoHo   212-965-0283
597 Broadway   bet. Prince/Houston
NYC 10012   Mon-Sat 10-8, Sun 12-7

Kenzo

Experience the Kenzo spirit—an ethnic flavor inspired by every corner of the world from Africa to Asia. Find looks that run from classic and tailored to loose and relaxed in suits and separates; their bridge line "Jungle," offering fun, functional sportswear; and "Kenzo Jeans," a selection of denim, T-shirts and casual wear. Kenzo designs are colorful, versatile and ideal for mixing and matching. Accessories include shoes, handbags, belts and colorful print scarves.   www.kenzo.com

SoHo   212-966-4142
80 Wooster Street   bet. Spring/Broome
NYC 10012   Mon-Sat 11-7, Sun 12-6

Kerquelen

Named after the Kerquelen Islands in the southern Indian Ocean near Antarctica, this recently downsized store stocks avant-garde footwear by up-and-coming designers from Europe. Check out high-fashion heels, flats and casual shoes from two exclusive names only: Spain's Mascaro and France's Thierry Labotin.   www.kerquelen.com

SoHo   212-925-9115
430 West Broadway   bet. Spring/Prince
NYC 10012   Mon-Sat 10:30-8, Sun 11-6

Kids Foot Locker

Kids Foot Locker has a large selection of children's athletic wear, from baseball jerseys and tennis outfits to top-of-the-line sneakers. Brand names include Adidas, Nike and Reebok. From infants to size 6.   www.kidsfootlocker.com

Upper East Side   212-396-4567
1504 Second Avenue   bet. 78/79th St.
NYC 10021   Mon-Sat 10-8, Sun 11-6

Kinnu

Enter a world of Indian color, fabric and design. Hand-woven, iridescent silks and cross-dyed cottons made up in kurta-styled tunics, dresses, asymmetrical wraps and drawstring pants define the collection. Gold brocade trim on hems and cuffs, intricate embroidery, mirror-work and hand-dyeing reflect the elaborate workmanship that goes into each design. Decorative items like quilted bedspreads, wall-hangings and art work also available.

NoLiTa 212-334-4775
43 Spring Street bet. Mott/Mulberry
NYC 10012 Mon-Sun 11:30-7

Kirna Zabête

Owners Sarah Hailes (nicknamed Kirna) and Beth Shepherd (nicknamed Zabête) have created a 5,000 sq. ft. two-level mini fashion department store dedicated to Goth, glam, girly but, most importantly, high fashion. The savvy duo buy an eclectic mix of the hottest designers from London, Paris, Belgium and New York, including Bruce, Martine Sitbon, A.F. Vandevorst, Jurgi Persoons, Cacharel, Alice Roi, lots of Chloé, Wink and Balenciaga. The lower level is home to funky-chic and sporty looks featuring lots of knits, T-shirts with ironic messages, lingerie, shoes, hats and handbags. Other goodies include lotions and potions, a candy section and a pet section. Accessories include a huge handbag selection, hats, lingerie and pretty shoes.

SoHo 212-941-9656
96 Greene Street bet. Spring/Prince
NYC 10012 Mon-Sat 11-7, Sun 12-6

Klee

A cool downstore store boasting cool downtown clothes! Klee's in-house label, Doori is a hot mix of slick black separates and knockout party pieces that are coquettish without being twee. Best are their coolly sexy matte jersey dresses ($380-$410), a must for every city girl's wardrobe. Also check out kinky leather accessories like rock-chic chokers and a fab collection of stockings and other little somethings for the hip chick's wardrobe arsenal. www.doori-nyc.com

SoHo 212-334-9169
79 Sullivan Street bet. Spring/Broome
NYC 10012 Tues-Sat 12-8, Sun 12-7

Kleinfeld

The barons of designer bridal wear! It may be a trek to Kleinfeld's, but the savings alone make it worth the trip. Find over 1,000 gowns in stock at all times from labels including Carolina Herrera, Scassi, Givenchy and Dior.

www.kleinfeldbridal.com

Brooklyn 718-765-8500
8202 Fifth Avenue at 82nd St.
Brooklyn 11209 Mon 9-6, Tues & Thur 11-9
Wed, Fri & Sat 11-6 by appointment

Klein's

An Orchard Street institution for over 20 years, Klein's is where savvy shoppers go for luxury European clothing at prices 25% less than anywhere else. "It's a Parisian, Left Bank type of feeling," owner Eddie Klein says of the store that is as comfortable as your living room. Suits, jackets, pants, cashmere sweaters, blouses and outerwear are from designers like Luciano Barbera, MaxMara, Les Copains, Malo, René Lezard, Gunext and Clara Cottman. Accessories include belts, hats and scarves.

Lower East Side   212-966-1453
105 Orchard Street   at Delancey
NYC 10002   Sun-Fri 10-5

Klurk

Klurk's owner is a former desk clerk-turned-designer whose line of casual menswear is best for the young and adventurous. The collection combines cool urban streetwear with ironic collegiate styles—high-necked sweaters, knits with inside-out seams, funky patterned golf-like pants, dress pants with nylon waistbands and button-down cashmere shirts.

NoLiTa   212-966-3617
360 Broome Street   bet. Mott/Elizabeth
NYC 10012   Mon-Fri 1-7, closed Tues, Sat & Sun 12-7

Koh's Kids

A children's shop selling a unique clothing selection from European and American labels like Confetti, Flapdoodles, Cherry Tree, Zutano and Petit Bateau, as well as shoes by Elephanten. The hand-knit sweaters are standouts. Toys and accessories also available. From newborn to size 10.

TriBeCa   212-791-6915
311 Greenwich Street   bet. Duane/Reade
NYC 10013   Mon-Fri 11-7, Sat 10-6, Sun 11-5

Kors

Designer Michael Kors brings his classic American sportswear and accessories downtown to his new Kors store. This bright, modern space punctuated by a red lacquered floor is home to luxurious cashmere sweaters (in colors from camel to red), perfectly tailored pants, and coats from classic trenches to bold wool herringbone coats for winter. Aviator glasses, oversized totes, cashmere scarves and stacked stilettos fill the accessories wall. These clothes are simple, sleek and ever-chic.   www.michaelkors.com

SoHo   212-966-5880
153 Mercer Street   bet. Houston/Prince
NYC 10012   Mon-Sat 11-7, Sun 12-6

Krizia

Krizia designer Mariuccia Mandelli believes clothing is our second skin so her ready-to-wear designs are body-conscious and comfortable. The collection runs the gamut from a glam $8,000 dress to a simple T-shirt. Other items include sculpted black crepe suits, pants, stretch cashmere twinsets, separates and coats. Her best offering, though, is lux-

La Galleria La Rue

ury knitwear, from cling-to-the-body dresses to form-fitted sweaters. Eveningwear includes glamorous beaded chiffon gowns and slinky, black jersey dresses. Felinistas will purr with delight when they see her signature "cat" sweaters. Men's fashions border on avant-garde.

Upper East Side   212-879-1211
769 Madison Avenue   bet. 65/66th St.
NYC 10021   Mon-Sat 10-6

La Galleria La Rue

Personalized, attentive service is the watchword at La Galleria La Rue, a boutique that celebrates the beauty of all ages with a collection of lifestyle-friendly separates in tactile, techno fabrics that are appropriate for work, cocktails or dinner.

Flatiron   212-807-1708
12 West 23rd Street   bet. 5/6th Ave.
NYC 10010   Mon-Fri 12-8, Sat & Sun 12-6

La Layette

Attention all doting grandmothers! La Layette will meet all your exacting standards with a line of luxury European clothing and, of course, a complete layette selection. From hand-embroidered outfits and beautiful christening gowns to linens and hand-painted furniture, each item is prettier than the next. Expensive. Newborn to size 2.

Upper East Side   212-688-7072
170 East 61st Street   bet. Lex./3rd Ave.
NYC 10021   Mon-Fri 11-6, Sat 11-5

La Perla

Totally gorgeous, fiendishly expensive—the caviar of lingerie, basically! A legendary label of feminine intimates that run from tasteful and elegant to seductive and sexy. La Perla also features a fashion line of bustiers and bodysuits with built-in bra cups, as well as swimwear and sleepwear. Be prepared to pay up to a few hundred dollars for a single item.   www.laperla.com

Upper East Side   212-570-0050
777 Madison Avenue   bet. 66/67th St.
NYC 10021   Mon-Sat 10-6

SoHo   1-800 LA-PERLA
93 Greene Street   bet. Spring/Prince
NYC 10012   Mon-Sat 11-7, Sun 12-6

☆ La Petite Coquette

In business for 20 years, La Petite Coquette remains the in-place for high-end sexy lingerie. Just ask regulars like model Cindy Crawford and Sex and the City style legend Sarah Jessica Parker. Once you've seen the storefront windows, it's impossible to resist stepping into a space that feels more like a boudoir than a shop. There's an incredible selection of silk intimates in a multitude of colors and looks that run from alluring corsets and garters to flirty nighties and feminine basics. Labels include La Perla, Lise Charmel, Ravage, Elle of Italy, Andre Sarda, Natori, Cosabella and Aubade. One of the best lingerie shops in the city. www.lapetitecoquette.com

NoHo   **212-473-2478**
51 University Place   bet. 9/10th St.
NYC 10003   Mon-Sat 11-7, Thur 11-8, Sun 12-6

La Petite Etoile

Mothers shop here for designer children's wear, including casual play clothes, back-to-school basics and dressy ensembles, from European labels like Florianne, Sonia Rykiel, Babar, Lili Gaufrette, I Pinco Pallino, Petit Bateau and La Perla. From newborn to 12 years.

Upper East Side   **212-744-0975**
746 Madison Avenue   bet. 64/65th St.
NYC 10021   Mon-Sat 10-6, Thur 10-7, Sun 12-5

☆ Lacoste

The originator of the piqué polo shirt, Lacoste is in full swing again with its classic crocodile-bedecked sportswear collection suitable for golf, tennis and weekend relaxation. Hint: all the coolsters are picking up the limited edition polos with silver alligator. Accessories include golf bags, belts, hats, socks and sunglasses.   800-4-LACOSTE www.lacoste.com

Midtown East   **212-750-8115**
543 Madison Avenue   bet. 54/55th St.
NYC 10022   Mon-Sat 10-5, Thur 10-8, Sun 12-5

LaCrasia Gloves

Jay Ruckel is New York's master glovemaker, working above a souvenir shop cutting gloves for the rich and famous through the years —Jackie O, Mary J and other luminaries so fabulous their last names have been compressed to a single letter. LaCrasia Gloves sells everything from lacy fingerless styles, white debutante gloves, snakeskin numbers, leather driving gloves and much more.   www.wegloveyou.com

Fifth Avenue   **212-695-0347**
304 Fifth Avenue   at 32nd St. in the Empire State Bld.
NYC 10001   call for hours

Lady Foot Locker

Athletic wear and footwear strictly for women. Find workout clothes for fitness and basketball as well as footwear for running, tennis, basketball or cross training from such brands as Nike, Reebok, Adidas, Fila and New Balance.   800-877-5239 www.ladyfootlocker.com

Upper East Side   **212-396-4567**
1504 Second Avenue   bet. 78/79th St.
NYC 10021   Mon-Sat 10-8:30, Sun 11-6:30

Midtown West   **212-629-4626**
120 West 34th Street   at 6th Ave.
NYC 10120   Mon-Sat 10-9, Sun 11-6

Laina Jane Lingerie

Midtown West   **212-967-1239**
901 Sixth Avenue   bet. B'way/33rd St. at Manhattan Mall
NYC 10001   Mon-Sat 10-8, Sun 11-6

Lower Manhattan   **212-732-7240**
89 South Street   at South Street Seaport
NYC 10038   Mon-Sat 10-9, Sun 11-8

Laina Jane Lingerie

Slipping into a sound—and sexy—slumber is made easy in Laina Jane's great selection of nighties and pajamas from labels like Cherry Pie, Hanky Panky, and Only Hearts. They're also a great West Village destination for some of the top makers of bras and panties such as Eberjay, LeMystere, Cosabella and Gemma. Hosiery and a small selection of swimwear also available.

Upper West Side   **212-875-9168**
416 Amsterdam Avenue   at 80th St.
NYC 10024   Mon-Sun 11:30-7:30

West Village   **212-727-7032**
35 Christopher Street   bet. Waverly Pl./7th Ave.
NYC 10014   Sun-Wed 11:30-7:30, Thur-Sat 11:30-8

Lana Marks

Handbag aficionados shop here for Lana Marks' exotic skins like alligator, ostrich and lizard. Designs are classic and fashionable and the color assortment runs from black to vivid pink. Trying one on your shoulder, though, is almost impossible, as a tangle of chains and locks secures each bag to the display. They also offer slick skin belts.

Midtown East   **212-355-6135**
645 Madison Avenue   bet. 59/60th St.
NYC 10022   Mon-Fri 10-6:30, Thur 10-7, Sat 10-6

Lancel

Nicknamed "The French Coach," Lancel, one of France's leading leathergoods manufacturers, carries a variety of products with smart looks at affordable prices. Handbags come in a myriad of colors (aubergine, bordeaux, taupe, grey, violet and red) featuring looks like shoulder totes in sleek, brushed calfskin. Other items include hunting bags, backpacks, suitcases and travel bags. Handbags retail for $200-$550 and luggage averages $397-$595.   www.lancel.com

SoHo   **212-353-2430**
135 Prince Street   bet. Wooster/W. B'way
NYC 10012   Mon-Sat 11-7, Sun 12-6

Lane Bryant

A name synonymous with plus-sizes, but this does not mean that Lane Bryant ain't sexy. Absolutely not—it's getting positively racy: think a curvier Victoria's Secret and you've got it. Size 14-28's will find everything from a fabulous assortment of jeans to sexy intimate apparel, all moderately priced. Although it's a quite a trek to visit their only Manhattan store, located in Harlem, it's well worth the trip. www.lanebryant.com

Harlem 212-678-0546
222 West 125th Street bet. 7/8th Ave.
NYC 10027 Mon-Sat 10-7, Sun 12-5

☆ Language
The mellow-chic Language is one of the most desirable stores in NoLiTa. It carries a meticulously edited selection of high fashion clothing, accessories, homewares, even books. You'll be sucked in from the moment you see the graphic, sexy, and slightly boho Stella McCartney, Chloé or Matthew Williamson designs hanging just-so in the window. Inside, your credit card will quake when confronted by other luxe, edgy labels like London's Sofia Kokosalaki, Pucci, Marc by Marc Jacobs and Language's femme-friendly own line. Pair your new clothing with killer heels by Alexandra Neel (formerly of Balenciaga) that all the fashion pack are buying, and try to escape without lingering over the handmade jewelry collection or limited edition fashion publications like Visionaire. Staff are friendly, helpful and damn well dressed. Must be the discounts… www.language-nyc.com

NoLiTa 212-431-5566
238 Mulberry Street bet. Prince/Spring
NYC 10012 Mon-Sat 11-7, Thur 11-8, Sun 12-6

Lara Nabulsi
A haven for cool designer clothes in the mostly grungy environs of the Lower East Side, Jordanian-born designer Lara Nabulsi's store carries her signature floaty, chic pieces in delicious silks, many fabrics sourced from the same supplier as Katayone Adeli—some quirkier materials including vintage Bill Blass silk. Her sexy pieces have an Oriental edge, many dresses draping seductively around the shoulder and tops cut low in the back. Grown-up clothes for grown-up girls.

Lower East Side 212-260-0022
101 Stanton Street at Ludlow
NYC 10002 Mon-Sat 12-7, Sun 1-6

Laundry by Shelli Segal
Although she continues to supply major department stores, Segal also has her own store for her collection of softly shaped, reasonably priced pieces, from ruffled dresses, floral shirts to cashmere tops and drawstring pants. A Segal design is feminine, elegantly understated and easy-to-wear.

SoHo 212-334-9433
97 Wooster Street bet. Prince/Spring
NYC 10012 Mon-Sat 11-7, Sun 12-6

Laura Ashley
The Laura Ashley girl is a very good girl indeed. Famous for their home furnishings and their trademark floral fabrics,

Laura Ashley also features well-behaved clothing for women and girls. Customers with a traditional sensibility shop here for dress-down work attire and weekend wear, including long dresses, man-tailored shirts, pants, knits, T-shirts and accessories, all color coordinated. Mothers also can dress their daughters in a cheerful selection of smocked dresses, knits, sweaters and more. Children's sizes from size 2 to size 9. www.lauraashley.com

Upper West Side   **212-496-5110**
398 Columbus Avenue   at 79th St.
NYC 10024   Mon-Wed, Sat 10-7
Thur & Fri 10-8, Sun 12-6

Laura Beth's Baby Collection

Previously a buyer for Barneys' baby department, Laura Beth decided to go solo and open her own showroom offering one-stop-shopping for expectant mothers in search of perfect nursery accoutrements. Find crib linens, pillows, bumpers, gliders, bedskirts and decorative accessories like bookends, mirrors, mobiles and lamps. She even does birth announcements.

Upper East Side   **212-717-2559**
300 East 75th Street, Suite 24E   at 2nd Ave.
NYC 10021   by appointment only

Laura Biagiotti

Biagiotti has been crowned "The Queen of Cashmere" by the fashion set because her luxurious, featherweight knitwear is second-to-none. Biagiotti's designs are versatile and comfortable, boasting soft tailoring, intricate stitching and a focus on white, from pure to creamy. Every collection includes a series of comfortable baby doll dresses and pants with elasticated waists. Other looks include soft sweaters paired with chiffon skirts, suits, dresses, separates and coats in cashmere, silk and linen. www.laurabiagiotti.it

Midtown West   **212-399-2533**
4 West 57th Street   bet. 5/6th Ave.
NYC 10019   Mon-Sat 10-6

The Leather and Suede Workshop

Owner/tailor Ron Shahar's moniker is "The Leather Man." Choose from skins like suede, cowhide, leather and snakeskin in a multitude of colors and such styles as pants, jackets, long and short skirts, dresses, shirts, coats and even hats. Pants start at $300 while jackets start at $400. Shahar will custom tailor a micromini or a pair of black leather pants that fit like a glove.

Midtown East   **212-688-1946**
107 East 59th Street   bet. Lex./Park Ave.
NYC 10022   Mon-Fri 10-7, Sat 11-7, Sun 11:30-6:30

Leather Corner

A non-glam location for good value leather pieces: short and long leather coats, biker and bomber jackets and casual weekend wear from Kenneth Cole, Nine West, Andrew Marc and Tibor. Expect to pay $120 for plain leather and up to $800 for a full-length coat trimmed in fur.

Lower East Side   212-475-7231
144 Orchard Street   at Rivington
NYC 10002   Mon-Sun 9-6:30

The Leather Man

Okay, so bondage, handcuffs and Crispo masks aren't your thing. How about a pair of five-pocket jeans in motorcycle-weight leather to shake things up a bit? Well, The Leather Man is there for you. Prices for pants start at $395.

West Village   212-243-5339
111 Christopher Street   bet. Bleecker/Hudson
NYC 10014   Mon-Sat 12-10, Sun 12-8

Leather Rose

South African-born Aldo Kleyn will custom-make leather pants in any style, skin and color. Pick from swatches of lambskin, alligator, deer hide, black mamba snakeskin or plain, buttery leather. Expect a two month wait for delivery but it's worth it: his pieces will last a lifetime. Prices start at $800.

East Village   212-529-6790
412 East 9th Street   bet. 1st/Ave. A
NYC 10009   Tues-Sun 2-8

Le Corset

Ah, le corset! The seductive tool for breathless ladies that has the same (if slightly more forgiving) allure now as it did centuries ago. Owner Selima Salaun is a master at spotting new trends in lingerie and provides a fabulously alluring selection of new and vintage lingerie that runs from flirty to retro to unabashedly sexy. There are satin and silk bustiers, feminine camisoles, demi-cup bras that accentuate cleavage, bodysuits, lacy panties, chemises, garter belts and more from labels that include Le Corset, Leigh Bantivoglio, Aubade, Lise Charmel and the aptly named Passionbait.

SoHo   212-334-4936
80 Thompson Street   bet. Spring/Broome
NYC 10012   Mon-Sat 11-7, Sun 12-7

Lederer

For over a century, clever shoppers have been heading to Lederer for an alternative to high-price designer handbags. Its prices are terrific and the quality and workmanship are impressive. Shop for classics like handwoven leathers, bamboo-handled structured bags and their exclusive Angelica bag. Briefcases, luggage, small leathergoods and desk accessories, as well as hunting clothes, Wellington boots and Barbour outerwear are also available. There is also a repair shop located on the premises.   www.ledererdeparis.com

Midtown East   212-355-5515
457 Madison Avenue   at 51st St.
NYC 10022   Mon-Sat 9.30-6, Thur 9:30-6.30

Lee Anderson

Lee Anderson is a destination for New York matrons who order her couture collection of classic suits, pants, blouses, jackets and coats, as well as after-five and special occasion dress. Choose from off-the-rack or order custom. An Anderson design is not for uptown girls, think uptown women.

Upper East Side — 212-772-2463
23 East 67th Street — bet. Madison/5th Ave.
NYC 10021 — Mon-Sat 11-6 or by appointment

Legacy

"Vintage inspired" clothing without the musty smell or wear and tear of the real thing. Dresses, skirts, blouses, pants and more by a number of underground European designers all have a retro feel and a distinctive look.

SoHo — 212-966-4827
109 Thompson Street — bet. Prince/Spring
NYC 10012 — Mon-Sun 12-7

Leggiadro

Heading to sun yourself in Palm Beach or Miami? Then hit this shop for resort wear that will work it almost anywhere, including clothing and swimwear by Sugar, Lilly Pulitzer and Leggiadro, all in lots of preppy prints and bright colors. Accessorize with a wrap, skirt, sarong or shirt. Luxurious cashmere sweaters and Jackie Roger sandals also available.

Upper East Side — 212-753-5050
700 Madison Avenue — bet. 62/63rd St.
NYC 10021 — Mon-Sat 10:30-6

Legs Beautiful

Pretty much what it says—lots of legwear to make the most of your gams. The fabulous hosiery selection includes brand names like DKNY, CK, Hue and Hanes, but there is also sexy lingerie, bodysuits, stretch tops, amusing socks and tights. If only there were one on every street corner!

Upper East Side — 212-750-3730
1025 Third Avenue — bet. 60/61st St.
NYC 10022 — Mon-Fri 10-8, Sat 9:30-7, Sun 12-7

Midtown East — 212-688-9599
CitiCorp Center, 153 East 53rd Street — at Lex. Ave.
NYC 10022 — Mon-Fri 8-8, Sat 11-6, Sun 12-5

Midtown East — 212-949-2270
Metlife Bldg., 200 Park Avenue — bet. 44/45th St.
NYC 10166 — Mon-Fri 7:30-8

Leonard Logsdail

Once a Savile Row tailor, Leonard Logsdail now provides New York bankers, diplomats and high-powered lawyers with his bespoke tailoring. He takes your measurements, cuts his paper pattern and then ships your order to London to be hand-stitched. Made-to-measure suits of the best pedigree start at $2,500, while custom suits start at $3,800. Expect to wait 2½ months for delivery.

Midtown East   **212-752-5030**
9 East 53rd Street, 4th Fl.   bet. Madison/5th Ave.
NYC 10022   by appointment

Les Copains
A winning mix of the classic with the avant-garde in tailored suits, wool jackets, tweed pieces, sweaters and great coats. Highlights include knitwear, lightweight wool trousers, and cotton stretch pants. Its "Trend" label is just that, trendy, and meant for the young, while look for its "Blue E" line if you're after a casual, sporty look.   www.lescopains.it

Upper East Side   **212-327-3014**
807 Madison Avenue   bet. 67/68th St.
NYC 10021   Mon-Sat 10-6

☆ LeSportSac
LeSportSac is having a fashion moment. The accessories label features a range of cute, functional bags perfect for traveling, including totes, weekend duffels, cosmetic clutches and handbags. They're manufactured in 100% nylon, double stitched on the insides and, best of all, machine washable. The color assortment includes metallics, prints, solids, pastels and brights. Best are the red and beige logo'd totes emblazoned with quirky words like LeTotally, LeTasty, and LeCharm. Not to mention New York fashion queen Diane von Furstenberg's chicly spirited collection of handbags, totes, and cosmetic bags featuring geometric prints of interlocking letter Ys. Prices start at $11 (for a key chain) up to $148 (for a tennis bag).   800-486-BAGS   www.lesportsac.com

Upper East Side   **212-988-6200**
1065 Madison Avenue   bet. 80/81th St.
NYC 10028   Mon-Sat 10-7, Sun 11-6

SoHo   **212-625-2626**
176 Spring Street   bet. W. B'way/Thompson
NYC 10012   Mon-Sat 10-7, Sun 12-6

Lester's
A nondescript store that features a good selection of back-to-school basics, casual play clothes and trendy sportswear for hard-to-please juniors from brand names like Juicy, Hard Tail and Quiksilver. There also are full-service layette and shoe departments, as well as accessories. From newborn to size 16 and juniors.

Upper East Side   **212-734-9292**
1534 Second Avenue   at 80th St.
NYC 10021   Mon-Fri 10-7, Thur 10-8
    Sat 10-6, Sun 12-5

Levi Strauss
The king of the jeans business, Levi's is rising to the challenge of hip brands like Earl and Seven with limited edition ranges

like the twisty "Engineered" jeans, and the "Superlow" jeans, for girls who still think belly button flashing is vital. Of course, there is a huge range of 501s and other classic jeans styles. For the ultimate fit, have your jeans custom-made by Levi's Original Spin program. Choose a style, pick your color and wash, get yourself measured and, two weeks later—your personal jeans are delivered. Casual basics and accessories also available. 800-872-5384 www.levi.com

Midtown East   **212-826-5957**
750 Lexington Avenue   bet. 59/60th St.
NYC 10021   Mon-Sat 10-8, Sun 12-6

Midtown East   **212-838-2188**
3 East 57th Street   bet. Madison/5th Ave.
NYC 10022   Mon-Sat 10-8, Sun 11-6

Lexington Formalwear

Located in a 3,000 sq. ft. converted library, this midtown men's formalwear store offers an enormous selection of tuxedos, dinner jackets, white tie and tails, as well as morning suits, shirts, shoes and accessories. Tailoring is included in the price. Tuxedo rentals by Perry Ellis, Givenchy and Chaps run from $100 to $149.

Midtown East   **212-867-4420**
12 East 46th Street, 2nd Fl.   bet. Madison/5th Ave.
NYC 10017   Mon-Wed 9-5:30, Thur & Fri 9-6:30, Sat 10-4

Liana

One of the Upper West Side's best-kept secrets, this stylish store nods to the trends with a sizeable selection of casual basics to dresses, suits and eveningwear (there is a truly epic selection of Little Black Dresses). It's packed with names like Shin Choi, Tahari, Nanette Lepore, Theory, Emma Black, Trina Turk and Chaiken. Inside the front door, find a chic selection of Calvin Klein hose—and don't forget their jewelry, one of the best selections around.

Upper West Side   **212-873-8746**
324 Columbus Avenue   bet. 75/76th St.
NYC 10023   Mon-Sat 11-7, Sun 1-6

Lilliput/SoHo Kids

Inspired by the Lilliputians in Gulliver's Travels, this store carries a soup-to-nuts collection of children's clothing ideal for play, school and dress-up. For boys, choose from jeans, khakis, dress shirts, sweaters, T-shirts and windbreakers, while girls will find looks running from adorable print dresses and Madeline T-shirts to cool, fashionable leather jeans paired with a hip top. And for babies, they've got it all, from onezies in washable silks and cashmeres to a basic Petit Bateau undershirt. Labels include Lili Gaufrette, Honore, Baby Go-Go, I Golfini della Nonna, Baby Gordon and Diesel. Shoes, hats, pajamas, bags and toys round out the assortment. From newborn to 18 years old.   www.lilliputsoho.com

Little Eric Shoes

SoHo   212-965-9567
265 Lafayette Street   bet. Spring/Prince
NYC 10012   Tues-Sat 11-7, Sun 12-6

SoHo   212-965-9201
240 Lafayette Street   bet. Spring/Prince
NYC 10012   Tues-Sat 11-7, Sun 12-6

Linda Dresner

Linda Dresner is a legend in fashion-forward retailing, and she continues to lead the pack with her elite collection of cutting-edge designers like John Galliano, Yohji Yamamoto, Marni, Martin Margiela, Dries Van Noten, Chloé and Jil Sander. High-end shopping for drop-dead chic designer pieces, from knockout evening gowns to urban suits. There is also a limited selection of shoes and accessories.

Midtown East   212-308-3177
484 Park Avenue   bet. 58/59th St.
NYC 10022   Mon-Sat 10-6

Lingerie on Lex

An intimate apparel shop that features European lingerie, sleepwear, loungewear, hosiery and children's robes. Brand names include Hanro, Lise Charmel, Cosabella, La Perla, and LeJaby.

Upper East Side   212-755-3312
831 Lexington Avenue   bet. 63/64th St.
NYC 10021   Mon-Fri 10-7, Sat 11-6

Lisa Shaub

This quaint millinery is known for more than just hats. Lisa Shaub's collection of classic pieces features jewel-toned felts in Twenties and Thirties shapes, fedoras, cloches, boaters, wide-brimmed panamas, berets and newborn cotton baby hats. Other items include one-of-a-kind evening bags, floral scarves, hand-dyed sarongs, straw beach bags and feather headpieces. Custom also available.

NoLiTa   212-965-9176
232 Mulberry Street   bet. Prince/Spring
NYC 10012   Mon-Wed 12-5, Thur-Sat 12-7, Sun 1-6

Little Eric Shoes

Fancy some fancy footwear for your kids? Check out this exclusive collection of Italian footwear: casual basics, back-to-school essentials, formal dress shoes and high fashion styles for teenagers. The sales staff claim these shoes will out-wear your child. A good source for all ages, especially for your baby's first walking shoes. Expensive. From infants to size 10.

Upper East Side   212-717-1513
1118 Madison Avenue   bet. 83/84th St.
NYC 10028   Mon-Sat 10-6, Sun 12-5

Upper East Side   212-288-8987
1331 Third Avenue   at 76th St.
NYC 10021   Mon-Fri 10-7, Sat 10-6, Sun 12-6

Liz Claiborne

A brand synonymous with practical, professional clothing, Liz Claiborne continues to be a mainstay for career women. This spacious Fifth Avenue flagship store carries its various lines, from relaxed sportswear and casual basics to career wear. An extensive petite section, intimate apparel, sleepwear, swimwear and accessories also available. www.lizclaiborne.com

Fifth Avenue 212-956-6505
650 Fifth Avenue at 52nd St.
NYC 10019 Mon-Fri 10-8, Sat 10-7, Sun 12-6

☆ Liz Lange Maternity

A former Vogue editor, Liz Lange is the reigning queen of maternity chic (no longer an oxymoron) and her stylish store offers one-stop-shopping for sportswear, eveningwear and activewear. Her secret: easy, chic clothing you would wear even if you weren't pregnant. Looks include capri pants, cashmere twin sets, sexy halter tops, A-line dresses, shifts, tunics, denim and spaghetti strap evening dresses. Model mothers like Cindy Crawford and Elle Macpherson have compared Lange's designs to Michael Kors and Calvin Klein. 888-616-5777 www.lizlange.com

Upper East Side 212-879-2191
958 Madison Avenue bet. 75/76th St.
NYC 10021 Mon-Sat 10-7, Sun 12-5

☆ Loehmann's

Canny shoppers make this discounting legend their first stop when looking for top brand names at knockout prices. The selection includes men's and women's apparel, a petites section, accessories and shoes but the main attraction is without a doubt the "Back Room," a department stocked with designer labels like Calvin Klein, Donna Karan and Armani. A chic Moschino trench for $100? Yes, it is possible here! By the way, if you're not satisfied, Loehmann's has a 14 day, get-your-money-back return policy.

Chelsea 212-352-0856
101 Seventh Avenue bet. 16/17th St.
NYC 10011 Mon-Sat 9-9, Sun 11-7

Longchamp

This venerable French leathergoods company sells a classic collection of handbags, briefcases, luggage and small leathergoods. Structured handbags in leather, suede and nylon exemplify Longchamp's tradition of understated elegance. Not to be missed is their "Pliages" collection of nylon fold-up travel totes in a rainbow of colors and a matching nylon raincoat which folds up into a five-by-six inch case with a chic leather handle. Belts, scarves and gloves also available. www.longchamp.com

Upper East Side 212-223-1500
713 Madison Avenue bet. 63/64th St.
NYC 10021 Mon-Sat 9.30-6.30

Lost Art

Lord & Taylor 👤👩👤
While most New York department stores have aggressively upped the fashion ante of late, Lord & Taylor has remained true to its original mission of merchandising the "American Look": conservative and affordable clothing for sensible people. And its regular customers are very grateful. The selection is a melting pot of classic fashion designers like Ralph Lauren, Donna Karan and Calvin Klein. Known for its collection of special occasion formalwear and hard-to-find shoe styles, Lord & Taylor also boasts extensive petite, career and sportswear sections. Other departments include cosmetics, accessories, children's, men's, lingerie, outerwear and large sizes. 800-223-7440

Fifth Avenue   **212-391-3344**
424 Fifth Avenue   bet. 38/39th St.
NYC 10018   Mon-Fri 10-8:30, Sat 10-7, Sun 11-7

Lord of the Fleas 👩👤
Ah, to have a clever store name! This one is a winner, although there are definitely no flea market looks in here, more like trendy, tight-fitting, hip clothing for juniors and pre-teens, including T-shirts galore, tops, pants, jackets, knits and accessories.

Upper West Side   **212-875-8815**
2142 Broadway   bet. 75/76th St.
NYC 10023   Mon-Sun 11-8:30

East Village   **212-260-9130**
305 East 9th Street   bet. 1/2nd Ave.
NYC 10009   Mon-Sun 12-8:30

Loro Piana 👤👩
Apparently the higher a goat climbs, the finer its cashmere (impress your friends with this fact). Which means that Loro Piana's goats must have been climbing Everest. The collection features elegant knitwear, outerwear, pants, shirts and jackets in sumptuous fabrics like cashmere, silk and superfine wool. In addition, there is a luxurious assortment of cashmere shawls, scarves, stoles and capes in mouthwatering shades. Prices are sky high, but then again, those goats were too...

Upper East Side   **212-980-7961**
821 Madison Avenue   bet. 68/69th St.
NYC 10021   Mon-Sat 10-6, Thur 10-7

Lost Art 👤👩
Have a rock star inside you just screaming to get out? Well, follow the lead of Britney Spears, Aerosmith's Steven Tyler and designer Anna Sui and turn to Lost Art's Jordan Betten for rock'n'roll leather looks in cow, deer, elk, snakeskin, croc and alligator. Intricate handcrafted detailing includes antique beading, unique closures, stones, feathers and fur. Each creation is a one-of-a-kind artwork. Pay from $1,800 for pants and $3,500 for jackets. Best bet: his whip-stitched lace-up leather pants. Kinky.

Chelsea   **212-594-5450**
515 West 29th Street   bet. 10/11th Ave.
NYC 10001   Mon-Fri 10-5 by appointment only

Louie

In the new SoHo sea of Chanel, Louis Vuitton and Prada, Louie's owner Laura Pedone aims to "preserve those one-of-a-kind looks that you won't find anywhere else." Find skirts, pants, dresses, separates and accessories from underground, unique design talents like Julien Segura, Lauren Moffatt and Booty Wear by Judy B. The look is refreshingly feminine without being girly. Great looking handbags.

SoHo   **212-274-1599**
68 Thompson Street   bet. Spring/Broome
NYC 10012   Tues-Sat 12-7, Sun 12-6

Louis Féraud

The Louis Féraud label is a scion of the French fashion establishment, ever since the young Louis Féraud dressed Brigitte Bardot in a classic white sundress in the Fifties. Today, it is better known for classic designs for an older customer: ladies-who-lunch dresses and beautifully cut suits. Customers can expect a full-bodied cut, tailored looks and sizing that runs from 4 to 16. Their sportswear collection "Contraire" features versatile, classic basics. Accessories also available.

Midtown West   **212-956-7010**
3 West 56th Street   bet. 5/6th Ave.
NYC 10019   Mon-Sat 10-6, Thur 10-7

Louis Vuitton

Louis Vuitton is the last and most luxurious word in international chic. Who wouldn't love a complete set of LV luggage to make like a movie star/supermodel at the airport? Or one of influential designer Marc Jacobs' luxe coats or customized accessories that mix the classic logo with collaborations with cult artists like Stephen Sprouse? This flagship features Vuitton's luggage, handbags, travel accessories and Jacobs' complete ready-to-wear collection. Get a mini Vuitton hit with some hair bobbles or a Palm Pilot holder or pick up a classic investment like the logo'd tote. It will last you forever.   800-847-2956 www.vuitton.com

Fifth Avenue   **212-758-8877**
703 Fifth Avenue   at 55th St.
NYC 10022   Mon-Sat 10-7, Thur 10-7, Sun 12-6

SoHo   **212-274-9090**
116 Greene Street   bet. Spring/Prince
NYC 10012   Mon-Sat 11-7, Sun 12-5

Luca Luca

Designer Luca Orlandi is a brave man—he's long been known for his bold approach to fashion, involving a strong use of color and bright, eye-popping patterns. But because he is nothing if not diverse, he recently tamed his palette and refined his silhouettes in dress suits, bias-cut pleated leather jackets and dresses, cashmeres, suede shirtdresses, strapless eveningwear and beaded coats with fur collars. Perfect polished outfits for the lunching set.

Upper East Side   **212-288-9285**
1011 Madison Avenue   at 78th St.
NYC 10021   Mon-Sat 10-6:30, Thur 10-8, Sun 12-5

Upper East Side   **212-755-2444**
690 Madison Avenue   at 62nd St.
NYC 10021   Mon-Sat 10-6:30, Thur 10-8, Sun 12-5

Lucky Brand Dungarees

In the beginning there was Levi's; now there's Lucky Brand, a California-based company that features a floor-to-ceiling selection of jeans, loungewear and everything in between. Pay an average of $70 for a pair of jeans. "Lucky You" and a four-leaf clover logo marks the lining of each pair. Will they bring you good luck? Who knows…

www.luckybrandjeans.com

Upper West Side   **212-579-1760**
216 Columbus Avenue   at 70th St.
NYC 10023   Mon-Sat 11-8, Sun 12-7

Flatiron   **917-606-1418**
172 Fifth Avenue   at 22nd St.
NYC 10010   Mon-Fri 10-8, Sat 10-7, Sun 11-6

SoHo   **212-625-0707**
38 Greene Street   at Grand
NYC 10013   Mon-Sun 11-7

Lucy Barnes

Located in the heart of the ever-hip meat-packing district, this shop showcases Lucy Barnes's unique hand-work—crocheting, beading, patchwork and knitting. The collection includes intricately embroidered and beaded leathers, sharply tailored "pearly king" pants with vintage buttons, wispy lace tops, twinkly chiffon bias skirts, corsets and well-priced basics like A-line skirts, silk-lined wool pants, denim skirts and quality cashmeres. Visit Lucy's spacious atelier nearby for custom orders, including bridal, evening couture and maternity. Accessories include hats, scarves and jewelry.

Chelsea   **212-647-0149**
117 Perry Street   bet. Hudson/Greenwich
NYC 10011   Tues-Sat 11-7
Sun & Mon by appointment only

Luichiny

This footwear retailer is for the fearless, funky—and very well-balanced. Luichiny only does platforms, and darn bright platforms they are too—sandals, maryjanes, wedges and even stilettos mounted on the highest of bases, all manufactured in Spain.   www.luichiny.com

West Village   **212-477-3445**
21 West 8th Street   bet. 5/6th Ave.
NYC 10011   Mon-Sat 11-9, Sun 12-8

Lulu Guinness

Lulu Guinness is the fairy godmother of handbags, and her whimsical, girly accessories are coveted from London (her home) to New York. Flowers are an obsession: her best known bags are named "The Rose Florist Basket," and "Violet Hanging Basket." Other looks include flirty ginghams, houndstooth, and candy striped patterns—girly alert!—perfect for the Riviera (prices run $85 to $1,700). Look out for her retro Forties and Fifties footwear too—complete with witty names like "Twinkle Toes," Goody Two Shoes," and the profound "We suffer to be Beautiful." Then there's the new legwear range; stockings embellished with cameos and other Guinness whimsy. www.luluguinness.com

West Village	**212-367-2120**
394 Bleecker Street	bet. 11th/Perry
NYC 10014	Mon-Sat 12-8, Sun 12-7

Lynn Park NY

Downtown darling designer Lynn Park runs this eponymous boutique, specialising in cutting-edge fashion from herself and a great edit of young designers. She offers a complete collection of individual clothes; roughed up denim; pop colored dresses embellished with paillettes and roses, cute frilly mini skirts and ruched, customized tops and shirts. Alongside her own funky label, she also stocks coats by Chan Paul, and hip tops from My Salad Days by Amy Liu and Ouise by Chris Manthey. The menswear follows this hip aesthetic, but focuses on slouchy-cool denim by Park and designer Andrew Buckler. A line of fearless accessories completes the cooler-than-cool collection.

SoHo	**212-965-5133**
51 Wooster Street	at Broome
NYC 10012	Mon-Sat 11-7, Sun 12-6

Macy's

Macy's has just about everything under the sun—which pretty much makes it a parallel universe. There are extensive men's, women's and children's departments, home furnishings and cosmetics, as well as places to grab a bite to eat. The end result: the world's largest (and at times messiest) department store, packed to the rafters with aggressive, bargain-hunting shoppers. While designer labels are scarce, you'll find a decent selection of labels like Jones New York, Polo Ralph Lauren and Tommy Hilfiger, and there's a great range of jeans from classic labels like Calvin Klein. Extensive shoe departments for men, women and children have everything from sneakers to dress-up shoes. Another bonus is the vast array of services Macy's provides, such as an International Visitors Center, hair salons, restaurants, post office and jewelry appraising. 800-431-9644 www.macys.com

Midtown West	**212-695-4400**
Broadway at Herald Square	bet. B'way/34th St.
NYC 10001	Mon-Sat 10-8:30, Sun 11-7

Maggie Norris Couture

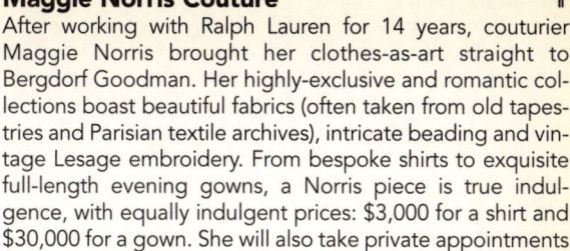

After working with Ralph Lauren for 14 years, couturier Maggie Norris brought her clothes-as-art straight to Bergdorf Goodman. Her highly-exclusive and romantic collections boast beautiful fabrics (often taken from old tapestries and Parisian textile archives), intricate beading and vintage Lesage embroidery. From bespoke shirts to exquisite full-length evening gowns, a Norris piece is true indulgence, with equally indulgent prices: $3,000 for a shirt and $30,000 for a gown. She will also take private appointments at her midtown studio.

Fifth Avenue 212-872-8957
754 Fifth Avenue at Bergdorf Goodman
NYC 10019 by appointment

Midtown West 212-768-1133
24 West 40th Street, 8th Fl. bet. 5/6th Ave.
NYC 10018 by appointment

Magic Windows

A full-service shop that gets top marks for putting the magic back into children's clothing. The assortment is vast, ranging from an incredible layette and baby selection to back-to-school essentials, casual basics, party clothes and special occasion dress (bridesmaid's dresses and christening gowns). The Teen Shop bridges the generation gap with cool casual wear that teens will love. Other items include personalized blankets, pillows and robes. Labels include Le Top, Kenzo, Sophie Dess, Petit Bateau, Petit Faune and Florence Eiseman. Newborns to pre-teen.

Upper East Side 212-289-0028
1186 Madison Avenue bet. 86/87th St.
NYC 10028 Mon-Sat 10-6, Sun 12-5

Make 10

Make 10 is a mainstream, funky collection of footwear that keeps in step with the trends. Brand names include Enzo, Dakota, Steve Madden, Nine West and Franco Sarte.

Upper East Side 212-472-2775
1227 Third Avenue bet. 70/71st St.
NYC 10021 Mon-Fri 11-7:30, Sat & Sun 12-6

Midtown West 212-956-4739
1386 Sixth Avenue bet. 56/57th St.
NYC 10019 Mon-Fri 10-7, Sat 11-6, Sun 12-6

Fifth Avenue 212-868-1202
366 Fifth Avenue bet. 34/35th St.
NYC 10001 Mon-Fri 10-7, Sat 11-7, Sun 12-6

NoHo 212-460-8144
680 Broadway bet. Bond/W. 3rd St.
NYC 10012 Mon-Sat 11-8, Sun 12-6

West Village 212-254-1132
49 West 8th Street bet. 5/6th Ave.
NYC 10011 Mon-Sat 11-8, Sun 12-6

Makie

There is nothing like the joy of a great pair of pajamas. So head to this tiny SoHo store for your happy hit: it's packed with nightwear, including classic-styled pajamas, nightshirts and unisex bathrobes manufactured in France by Bains-Plus. Solid colored looks are embellished with contrasting piping, or jacquards, checks, stripes and florals in top quality cottons with the vital elasticized waists. Prices start at $140. Buy kiddie pj's (from 2 to 12 yrs for $70), as well as rompers and cute handmade dresses. Also look out for canvas totes, vintage buttons and other goodies.

SoHo — **212-625-3930**
109 Thompson Street — bet. Prince/Spring
NYC 10012 — Mon-Sat 12-7, Sun 11-6

Makola

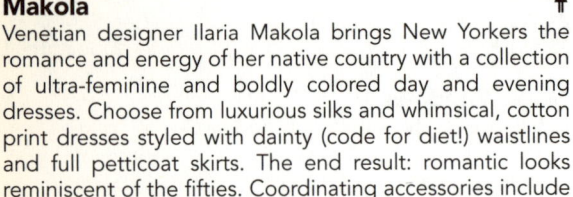

Venetian designer Ilaria Makola brings New Yorkers the romance and energy of her native country with a collection of ultra-feminine and boldly colored day and evening dresses. Choose from luxurious silks and whimsical, cotton print dresses styled with dainty (code for diet!) waistlines and full petticoat skirts. The end result: romantic looks reminiscent of the fifties. Coordinating accessories include shoes, handbags, jackets and hats. Very Doris Day.

Upper East Side — **212-772-2272**
1045 Madison Avenue — bet. 79/80th St.
NYC 10021 — Mon-Sat 10-6, Sun 12-5

Malatesta

Italian designer Cristina Gitti was so inspired by the jewel-like clothing she saw on a trip to India that she decided to launch a line of clothing built around one simple piece: a shawl/sarong packaged in an exotic floral, embroidered sack. Her one-stop shop contains her signature designs alongside shoes, bags, kurtas (classic Indian shirt dresses) and a line of Indian inspired swimwear by Delfina. No trip to the beach—or India for that matter—is complete without one of her gorgeous sarongs.

SoHo — **212-343-9399**
115 Grand Street — bet. B'way/Mercer
NYC 10012 — Mon-Sat 12-6:30, Sun 1-6

Malia Mills

Ah, swimsuit shopping terror—we know you well. Well, Malia Mills is there for you: her bathing suits fit like lingerie. Her collection contains beautiful and wearable suits in florals, prints and solid colors in sizes for most body types. All her suits are cleverly sold as separates (tops in bra cup sizes and bottoms in sizes 0-10) and come with cute names like "Skinny Dipper," "D-Mure", "Lolita," and "Naughty." Accessories include bags, sarongs, sunglasses, scarves, flip-flops, sandals and hair ornaments. You have to love a store that has a sign in front reading, "Love Thy Differences"… www.maliamills.com

NoLiTa
199 Mulberry Street
NYC 10012

212-625-2311
bet. Spring/Kenmare
Mon-Sun 12-7

Malo

Malo is the king of cashmere—theirs coming from the rugged Mongolian goat, which apparently has the best cashmere in the world. This is a New York staple for luxury knitwear: crewnecks, cardigans, v-necks, turtlenecks, twin sets and cablestitch pullovers. A cashmere ready-to-wear line of coats, jackets and pants complements the knitwear, while Malo's home collection includes pajamas, robes, slippers, pillows and blankets.

Upper East Side
814 Madison Avenue
NYC 10021

212-396-4721
at 68th St.
Mon-Sat 10-6, Thur 10-7

SoHo
125 Wooster Street
NYC 10012

212-941-7444
bet. Prince/Spring
Mon-Sat 11-7, Sun 12-6

Manhattan Portage

Hard-wearing nylon messenger bags are what made this groovy brand's name, and this store carries a full selection of the cult carry-alls in a rainbow of bright, urban colors (from $18 to $105). The line also includes one-strap backpacks, DJ bags for records and the odd-sounding (but very functional) "urban support system" which is basically a handy laptop bag-style tote.

East Village
333 East 9th Street
NYC 10003

212-995-5490
bet. 1st/2nd Ave.
Wed-Sat 12-8, Sun-Tues 12-7

☆ Manolo Blahnik

Forced to choose between their husbands or their Blahniks, many women might well choose the latter: fans include Faye Dunaway, Madonna, Donatella Versace, Diane von Furstenberg and every fashion magazine editor in the business. The Sultan of the stiletto, Blahnik designs the ultimate in sexy footwear. Each style is feminine, seductive and fabulously comfortable—and achieving this in a pair of sky-high heels is no mean feat. There are more demure offerings, from mules, glittery evening slippers, strappy spring sandals and chic loafers. And your wedding day will be sadly incomplete without a knockout pair of Blahnik bridal shoes. Prices typically run from $445 to approx $1,000.

Midtown West
31 West 54th Street
NYC 10019

212-582-3007
bet. 5/6th Ave.
Mon-Fri 10:30-6, Sat 10:30-5:30

Manrico Cascimir

Manrico's sweaters are deliciously pure, soft and warm. Styles include polos, zip fronts, cardigans, twin sets, crews, 16-ply cable stitch pullovers and vests in 100% cashmere or silk and cashmere blends. Visit this minimal store during their winter and summer sales when prices are 30% to 50% off.

Upper East Side   212-794-4200
802 Madison Avenue   bet. 67/68th St.
NYC 10021   Mon-Sat 10-6, Sun 12-5

Maraolo

An Italian company that manufactures shoes for Giorgio Armani, as well as their own collection. Its loafers, lace-ups, pumps, boots, sandals and casual weekend shoes are all in the requisite high-quality leathers and suedes (only the best for Mr Armani, after all). Best to shop during their sales when prices can be as low as cost.

Upper East Side   212-535-6225
1321 Third Avenue   bet. 75/76th St.
NYC 10021   Mon-Sat 11-8, Sun 1-6

Upper East Side   212-628-5080
835 Madison Avenue   bet. 69/70th St.
NYC 10021   Mon-Sat 9:30-7, Sun 12:30-5:30

Upper East Side   212-832-8182
782 Lexington Avenue   bet. 60/61st St.
NYC 10021   Mon-Sat 10-8, Sun 12:30-6

Upper West Side (Outlet)   212-787-6550
131 West 72nd Street   bet. Amsterdam/Columbus Ave.
NYC 10023   Mon-Fri 10:30-8, Sat 10-7, Sun 12-6

Midtown East   212-308-8793
551 Madison Avenue   at 55th St.
NYC 10022   Mon-Fri 9:30-7, Sat 11-7, Sun 12-6

☆ Marc Jacobs

Marc Jacobs is the king of New York fashion right now, as well as one of the world's most influential designers. From his infamous "Grunge" collection 10 years ago to his retro-luxe collections favored by sophisticated downtowners (and every model worth her Vogue cover) he can do no fashion wrong. He was the first big-name designer to hit Bleecker St in the West Village and now everyone else has followed. Visit Jacobs for luxe cashmere sweaters, swingy party dresses and cartoon-cute shoes, that all the Hollywood girls like Sofia Coppola wear. His Marc by Marc Jacobs line, a cheaper version of his luxe label has been a phenomenal success—hip fashionistas everywhere confess an addiction to his faded, creased jeans, Edwardian style jackets and rainbow shoes. The "Marc" store is regularly cleaned out by fashion locusts, so timing is everything… Accessories include his now classic handbags (average $900), leathergoods and shoes (from $250 to $580).

SoHo   212-343-1490
163 Mercer Street   bet. Prince/Houston
NYC 10012   Mon-Sat 11-7, Sun 12-6

West Village (Marc by Marc Jacobs)   212-924-0026
405 Bleecker Street   bet. W. 11th/Hudson
NYC 10012   Mon-Sat 12-8, Sun 12-7

West Village (Accessories) 212-924-6126
387 Bleecker Street bet. Perry/W. 11th St.
NYC 10012 Mon-Sat 12-8, Sun 12-7

Marc Jacobs 👤

Marc's menswear store is the destination for slouchy-cool downtown boys who wear their cashmere like an old sweatshirt—and for uptown boys who want to look cool. Jacobs offers a hip selection of sweaters, shirts and flat-front pants, and gorgeous accessories like ties, scarves, hats, small leathergoods, bags, underwear and orthopedic-chic shoes. Outerwear designs run from peacoats and fitted parkas to military-styled coats. Versace fans—stay away!

West Village 212-924-0026
403 Bleecker Street bet. W. 11th/Hudson
NYC 10012 Mon-Sat 11-7, Sun 12-6

MarcoArt 👤👤

Best known for designing and painting watch faces for mega-company Swatch, the multi-tasking Marco has also designed a collection of hand-printed (often with a cute slogan) T-shirts, halter tops, dresses and bags. Not for the shy and retiring...

Lower East Side 212-253-1070
181 Orchard Street bet. Houston/Stanton
NYC 10002 Mon-Sat 10-6

Mare 👤👤

This uncluttered, neat shop carries sleek Italian shoes under the Mare label in looks from classic to trendy. Good price points.

SoHo 212-343-1110
426 West Broadway bet. Prince/Spring
NYC 10012 Mon-Fri 11-8, Sat 11-7, Sun 12-7

Margie Tsai 👤

Tsai did time with Donna Karan and Vivienne Tam before breaking out on her own with clothes she calls "functional art"—telling a story with fabric. This translates into classically designed pieces spiced up with novelty textiles, the Karan influence visible in Tsai's fondness for draping. Styles range from gossamer-thin butterfly lace dresses to heavy rubber coats, or bias-cut knit tanks paired with iridescent capri pants. www.margietsai.com

NoLiTa 212-334-2540
4 Prince Street bet. Elizabeth/Bowery
NYC 10012 Mon-Sun 12-7

Marianne Novobatzky 👤

Has your wardrobe been attacked by black? Check out this colorful SoHo showroom packed with designs perfect for day, evening and special occasions. The daytime looks include girly floral dresses, structured silk/wool jackets, pants and Pucci-esque chiffon blouses, while women will love Novobatzky's raw silk ballgown skirts, bustiers, fancy-dress suits and taffeta gowns for evening—she'll even design your own.

SoHo	**212-431-4120**
65 Mercer Street	bet. Spring/Broome
NYC 10012	Mon-Fri 12-7, Sat 12-5

Mariko

Fancy a bit of glitz? Some costume jewelry to leave the other girls in the dust? Head to this boutique, where the walls drip with beads and baubles… and more beads. Paste diamonds and turquoise are popular here, but look out also for a range of chic silk shirts in jewel-like colors. A tip: put on your sunglasses before entering.

Upper East Side	**212-472-1176**
998 Madison Avenue	bet. 77th/78th St.
NYC 10021	Mon-Sat 10-6

Marina Rinaldi

This division of the chic Italian company MaxMara targets the plus-sized woman with dresses, suits, pants, blouses, sweaters and outerwear. The focus here is on neutral fabrics, classic designs and expert tailoring that nod just enough to the trends and are guaranteed to flatter even the fullest figure. Sizes range from 10 to 22. Customer service is exceptional. A limited selection of shoes.

Upper East Side	**212-734-4333**
800 Madison Avenue	bet. 67/68th St.
NYC 10021	Mon-Sat 10-6, Thur 10-7

Mark Montano

Fashion's fun-loving, downtown designer Mark Montano always draws a curious crowd to his bustling East Village boutique. Known for his vibrant, often trippy colors and campy "dress-me-up" style, Montano caters to club hoppers and party-goers with everything from flirty, lace-trimmed corsets and loud, pink suits to large washable totes and fun jewelry. Not for the shy and retiring. www.markmontano.com

East Village	**212-505-0325**
434 East 9th Street	bet. 1st/Ave. A
NYC 10009	Tues-Fri 1-7, Sat 12-8, Sun 1-6

Mark Schwartz

Not surprisingly, designer Mark Schwartz believes "a woman should begin [her wardrobe] with her shoes and build from there." Ideally, with his unusual, colorful shoes, of course! Find pony-skin mules, suede flats, strappy python pumps, sexy evening shoes, suede and leather round-toe boots, wooden-bottom sandals and bridal shoes.   www.markschwartzshoes.com

NoLiTa   212-343-9292
45 Spring Street   bet. Mott/Mulberry
NYC 10012   Mon-Sat 11-7, Sun 12-6

Marmalade

Marmalade is all about what the cool downtown girls (especially Stevie Nicks fans) want to wear: epic lacy dresses, denim stilettos, slouchy blouson tops, studded Eighties-style scrunchy boots and quirky handbags. Not to mention the odd pair of Peter Pan boots—and did we say lace? It's a lace festival. All up, Eighties trash-glam girl meets downtown fashionista.

Lower East Side   212-473-8070
172 Ludlow Street   bet. Houston/Stanton
NYC 10002   Mon-Sun 1-9

Marni

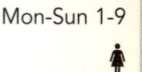

Marni is a favorite amongst fashion editors for its optimistic chic with an Italian flavor, happily provided by designer Consuela Castiglione. Her collections are big on prints and simple whites, all with a girly edge. Lately, Castiglione has translated the peasant look to a more "grungy" aesthetic, but of course, in Marni world, grunge isn't grungy at all—more a jaunty range of stripey separates and scarves. In this clean, chirpy space in SoHo, you can also shop a colorful accessories collection and Marni's distinctive shoes. All made with love from Italy…

SoHo   212-343-3912
161 Mercer Street   bet. Houston/Prince
NYC 10012   Mon-Sat 11-7, Sun 12-6

Marsha D.D.

This store is the hottest ticket in town for trendy tween-age fashions with an enormous selection of jeans, cool T-shirts, sweatshirts, minis and party dresses for special occasions by labels like Miss Sixty, Hollywood, Hard Tail, Juicy Couture, Roxy and Riley. And there are clothes for the boys too—cargo pants, collared shirts, sweaters, T-shirts, swimsuits, jeans, polar fleeces, sweatshirts and outerwear from sporty-streety labels like Quiksilver, Rusty, Metropolitan Prairie and Diesel. Great accessories. From 7 years to 16.

Upper East Side   212-831-2422
1574 Third Avenue   bet. 88/89th St.
NYC 10028   Mon-Sat 10-6

Upper East Side   212-534-8700
1324 Lexington Avenue (clearance store)   bet. 88/89th St.
NYC 10028   Mon-Sat 10-6

Martier

At Martier, you get two shops rolled into one: upstairs is filled with fashion-forward clothing, while downstairs boasts an abundance of sexy lingerie plus some swimwear. Typical fare includes sexy leather pants, body-hugging tops and print dresses by labels like Anti-Flirt, Exte, Vertigo, Gili,

Mandalay and Ferre. Downstairs is home to a colorful selection of saucy intimates by La Perla, Lise Charmel, Malizia, Ritratti and Aubade. Helpful sales staff.

Upper East Side   **212-758-5370**
1010 Third Avenue   at 60th St.
NYC 10022   Mon-Sat 10-8, Sun 12-6:30

☆ Martin

Harper's Bazaar once named Martin "the fashion insiders' closet addiction." And they'd be right on the money. Designer Anne Johnston Albert spins fabulously cool clothes that defy the seasons. Her muses? Jane Birkin, Charlotte Rampling and Brigitte Bardot, whose photos line the wall of her store. Her signature piece is her hip-hugging, boot-cut jeans with a distinctive back pocket double M stitching. What to wear with them? Try fitted soft jersey tops, low-slung skirts, delicate silk chiffon blouses, saucy-chic halter dresses, and moleskin military jackets. Pay $165 for jeans, $180 for tops, and $500 for jackets.

East Village   **212-358-0011**
206 East 6th Street   bet. 2/3rd Ave.
NYC 10003   Tues-Sun 1-7

Martinez Valero

A convenient neighborhood shoe shop featuring trendy styles at attractive prices. Shop a selection from classic to trendy and looks that will complement any outfit, whether it's satin evening pumps, boots or summer sandals. Prices run from $125 to $265 for boots.

Upper East Side   **212-753-1822**
1029 Third Avenue   at 61st St.
NYC 10021   Mon-Fri 10-8, Sat 11-7, Sun 12-6

Martino Midali

Martino Midali is known for its fabrics and textures and its signature knits play a predominant role in monochromatic coats, pants, tops and some great long skirts. Midali has daytime and eveningwear with contemporary looks, roomy cuts and fabrics like wool, viscose, suede, faux fur and leather.

Upper East Side   **212-879-2563**
1015 Madison Avenue   bet. 78/79th St.
NYC 10021   Mon-Sat 10-6, Thur 10-7, Sun 12-5

Mary Adams

Because you can-can-can! Yep, think Moulin Rouge and you've captured the essence of Mary Adams' creations. Her Victorian-inspired designs are festooned with lace, peplums and ruffles and include elaborate corsets, feminine skirts with full petticoats, iridescent silk ballgowns and unconventional wedding dresses. Custom order also available.

Lower East Side   **212-473-0237**
138 Ludlow Street   bet. Stanton/Rivington
NYC 10002   Wed-Sat 1-6, Sun 1-5 or by appointment

Mary Efron

A selection of "fine and rare antique wearables" from the turn of the century to the 1950s including silk and embroidered Chinese jackets, dresses from the 1920s, evening and special occasion wear and beaded, jeweled and painted handbags. A mini-museum of antique clothing.

SoHo   **212-219-3099**
68 Thompson Street   bet. Broome/Spring
NYC 10012   Tues-Sun 1-7

Mason's Tennis Mart

Mason's is the oldest, most respected tennis retailer in the city. Athletic apparel, including cute tennis dresses, warm-ups, sweaters and shirts, comes from top-of-the-line labels like Ellesse, Polo, Fila, LBH, 0/40, Nike, Adidas and Lacoste. Equipment brands include Babalot, Gamma, Wilson, Volkl, Head and Prince. Great children's department. Same day stringing for rackets.

Midtown East   **212-755-5805**
56 East 53rd Street   bet. Madison/Park Ave.
NYC 10022   Mon-Fri 10-7, Sat 10-5

Maternity Work

This is the outlet store for Mimi Maternity, A Pea in the Pod and Motherhood Maternity, featuring on-sale items in career wear and casual basics.

Midtown West   **212-399-9840**
16 West 57th Street, 3rd Fl.   bet. 5/6th Ave.
NYC 10019   Mon-Wed 10-7, Thur 10-8
    Fri & Sat 10-6, Sun 12-6

Maud Frizon

"Elle est Maud" reads this French footwear icon's elegant cards, and they are right. She is Maud, one of the grand dames of designer footwear, with a nearly 50 year history of dressing the feet of France's "très elegante". After an eight year absence from Manhattan, the label has returned to a lilac, sweet-smelling boutique on the Upper East Side. Inside you will find a small, chic selection of Frizon classics, from black stilettos to floral mules. A limited selection of bridal shoes is also available.

Upper East Side   **212-517-8522**
1023 Lexington Avenue   bet. 73rd/74th St.
NYC 10021   Mon-Sat 10-6

Mavi

Denim addicts, especially sexy denim addicts, head to Mavi for low-rise, form-fitted, lightweight, stretch or non-stretch, sexy and cut to fit jeans. Moderately priced, you can expect to pay anything from $50 to $74 and expect a veritable denim buffet of sizes and lengths. Remember, girls, jeans are your friend...   www.mavi.com

MaxMara

SoHo
510 Broome
NYC 10013

212-625-9458
bet. Thompson/W. B'way
Mon-Sun 11-8

MaxMara

MaxMara is a low-key Italian classic, perfect for sophisticated women who prefer simplicity and ease over of-the-moment trendiness (no fashion victims here). The three floors of luxury basics include beautifully tailored suits, dresses, subtle printed shirts, separates and outerwear. The designs are clean, crisp and classic. Best are the too-chic-to-speak overcoats (check out the ever-classic beige which you will wear forever). Shoes and accessories also available.

Upper East Side
813 Madison Avenue
NYC 10021

212-879-6100
at 68th St.
Mon-Sat 10-6, Thur 10-7

SoHo
450 West Broadway
NYC 10012

212-674-1817
bet. Prince/Houston
Mon-Sat 11-7, Sun 12-6

Max Studio

Designer Leon Max made his name from turning out classic pieces in clean, simple lines that defy the seasons. Find finely spun cashmeres, soft leathers, white shirts, bias-cut skirts, embroidered eveningwear, bootleg pants, knits and some slick ultra suede pieces. Accessories include handbags and belts.
www.maxstudio.com

SoHo
415 West Broadway
NYC 10012

212-941-1141
bet. Prince/Spring
Mon-Thur 11-7
Fri & Sat 11-8, Sun 12-6

Mayle

Jane Mayle's boutique was one of the first to happen in Nolita, and it's a magnet for the Nolita Girl™—think a lacy top and jeans wearing lass, an ex-model preferably. Her flirty tops (around $200) draw in hipsters who love their clothes girly without being precious, and she cuts a lean and mean pair of pants too. Mayle world is a seductive (and fragrant—she burns beautiful scented candles) place to be. As are her sales!

NoLiTa
252 Elizabeth Street
NYC 10012

212-625-0406
bet. Prince/Houston
Mon-Sat 12-7, Sun 12-6

☆ Me & Ro

The hip jewelry line founded by Michele Quan and Robin Renzi is having a major fashion moment. The duo first made it big when they designed a hoop earring with dangling garnet or eyelet beads, which since appeared on "Friends" and "Will and Grace". The biggie, though, was when Julia Roberts wore their specially designed Indian rose-cut diamond drop earrings the night she won the Oscar for "Erin Brockovich". This new, minimalist space on Broadway showcases their divine, Eastern-inspired pieces, often hand-carved with symbolic Sanskrit and Tibetan calligraphy. Gorgeous.

SoHo 917-237-9215
239 Elizabeth Street bet. Houston/Prince
NYC 10012 Mon-Sat 12-7, Sun 12-6

Medici

A world of accessories on the Upper West Side, where techno music plays backdrop to a collection of trendy shoes on the Medici label, the youthful CJ Bis by Charles Jourdan... and everything else besides, from fringed bags, hats for the races, belts, even birthday cards. Best for men's shoes and summer sandals.

Upper West Side 212-712-9342
620 Columbus Avenue bet. 80th/81st St.
NYC 10023 Mon-Sun 10-8

Meg

If you're tired of paying posh uptown prices, then get down to Meghan Kinney's East Village store, which specializes in polished, multi-purpose sportswear that can be custom-fitted. Separates are key: match pants with a double-knit wool jersey and work it with a jacket or coat. Each season Kinney introduces a new blend of fabric and texture combinations into her dominantly neutral color palette.

East Village 212-260-6329
312 East 9th Street bet. 1st/2nd Ave.
NYC 10003 Mon-Fri 1-8, Sat 12-8, Sun 1-6

Mêmes

This flava-ful shop sells "fresh baked gear" to men seeking cool, urban streetwear. Yep, it's a hip-hop kinda deal. The core of their collection is straight-legged fatigue pants but they also peddle track and nylon pants, lots of denim (hip-hop fabric of choice), sweaters, coats, jackets and funky footwear like spacey sneakers. A sprinkling of collectibles, sunglasses and (you guessed it, hip-hop) CDs are also available.

NoHo 212-420-9955
3 Great Jones Street bet. Lafayette/B'way
NYC 10012 Mon-Sun 12-8

Men's Wearhouse

When is a department store not a department store? When it's Men's Wearhouse, which has the same merchandise but at prices 25% cheaper on average. There are reliable suits by Hugo Boss, Canali, DKNY, Chaps Ralph Lauren and Gianfranco Ferré, men's furnishings, dress shirts, tuxedos, casual sportswear, outerwear, socks, and underwear. A complete shoe department with labels by Principe, Bostonian and Florsheim. Courteous sales staff. 800-776-7848 www.menswearhouse.com

Me Too

Midtown East   212-856-9008
380 Madison Avenue   at 46th St.
NYC 10017   Mon-Fri 8:30-7:30, Sat 10-6, Sun 12-6

Chelsea   212-243-3517
655 Sixth Avenue   at 20th St.
NYC 10010   Mon-Fri 10-9, Sat 10-7, Sun 11-6

☆ Me Too

Cute, groovy shoes and bags under the slick Me Too label. Check out this clean, airy store with a selection of tempting accessories. The bags are best: confident printed carry-alls, chicly simple leather totes and some great black handbags with white stitching that look perfectly Marc Jacobs-esque, for only $149. Classics that pack a punch (and, if you like, your lunch).

SoHo   212-431-9855
500 Broome Street   at West Broadway
NYC 10012   Mon-Fri 12-7, Sat 11-7, Sun 12-6

Metro Bicycle

Metro Bicycle puts service first. Bikes come with a three-year warranty that includes gear and brake adjustments as well as replacement of defective parts. The mountain, road and suspension bikes are from makers such as Trek, Raleigh and Gary Fisher and are all at competitive prices. Bicycles are available for rent by the hour or the day.

Upper East Side   212-427-4450
1311 Lexington Avenue   at 88th St.
NYC 10128   Mon-Sun 9:30-6:30
    Wed & Thur 9:30-7:30

Midtown West   212-581-4500
360 West 47th Street   at 9th Ave.
NYC 10036   Mon-Fri 9-7, Sat 10-6, Sun 10-5

Chelsea   212-255-5100
546 Sixth Avenue   at 15th St.
NYC 10011   Mon-Sun 9:30-6:30

East Village   212-228-4344
332 East 14th Street   bet. 1st/2nd Ave.
NYC 10003   Mon-Sun 9:30-6

TriBeCa   212-334-8000
417 Canal Street   at 6th Ave.
NYC 10013   Mon-Sun 9:30-6:30

Metropolis

A skip away from NYU, Metropolis is a late-night destination for student hipsters seeking to forget that dull lecture with a shopping hit. It's all quick-fix fashion, with sparkly T-shirts, retro overcoats, multipocketed cargos (for your lecture notes, see) and cool denims. Owner Christine Colligan plans on opening 24/7, so if you need a pair of fuchsia platform maryjanes at 2am, you know where to go…

East Village   212-358-0795
43 Third Avenue   bet. 9/10th St.
NYC 10003   Mon-Thur 12-11
Fri-Sat 12-midnight, Sun 1-11

Michael Kors

Michael Kors exemplifies what American designers do best: chic, soigné sportswear. His designs "meld the anything-goes attitude of Greenwich Village and the mannered glamour of Fifth Avenue." This translates into both sleek urban clothes and country posh classics like his famous knits, his boldly chic patterns of plaids and tweeds, cozy cashmeres, and fabulous shearlings, as well as eveningwear and a healthy dose of fur. His menswear line is the epitome of sporty luxury with its boot-cut pants, slick blazers, suits in cashmeres and merino wool, cashmeres and knits, and outerwear. Accessories include handbags, shoes, and eyewear.   www.michaelkors.com

Upper East Side   212-452-4685
974 Madison Avenue   at 76th St.
NYC 10021   Mon-Sat 10-6

Michael's, The Consignment Shop for Women

For 45 years, Michael's has set the pace in the consignment industry by stocking the ultimate in pre-owned couture clothing and bridal wear. Brides-to-be can select from magnificent dresses by Vera Wang, Arnold Scassi or Dior while non-brides (or bride wannabes) can select from designer frocks and accessories by fashion powerhouses like Prada, Gucci, Manolo Blahnik, Galliano and Hermès. You'll love the great prices, not to mention the thrill of the hunt.

Upper East Side   212-737-7273
1041 Madison Avenue, 2nd Fl.   bet. 79/80th St.
NYC 10021   Mon-Sat 9:30-6, Thur 9:30-8

Michel Perry

Need a little sexual heeling? Then head straight to Michel Perry, France's glamarama shoemaker who sees his fabulous footwear as lingerie for the feet. His heels are sculpted, his colors daring, his prices high and he's a major fan of "toe cleavage". We're talking lean, mean, super-sexy, pointy-toed stilettos that will have you strutting the streets. Because Michel Perry women don't just walk…

Midtown East   212-688-4968
320 Park Avenue   at 51st St.
NYC 10022   Mon-Sat 10:30-7

Michele Saint-Laurent

Finally, it is possible to be pregnant and stylish at the same time. This upscale maternity shop is perfect for women who appreciate good fabrics and classic styles and don't want to relinquish them just because they're pregnant. In addition

Michelle Roth & Co.

to basics such as skirts, sweaters, tops and even swimwear, Michele also offers custom eveningwear. Bring in a photo of a non-maternity evening dress you like, and she will make a stretch version which accommodates your growing tummy. Sizes run 1-4 (petite to large.) Extra clever is her "six-easy-pieces" maternity kit, which includes a little black dress, jacket, straight skirt, cigarette pant, white cotton Lycra tee and a bandeau belt all made from a high-quality, woven stretch French fabric.

Upper East Side   **212-452-4200**
1028 Lexington Avenue   bet. 73/74th St.
NYC 10021   Mon-Fri 10-7, Sat 10-6, Sun 12-5

Michelle Roth & Co.

A specialist in European couture wedding dresses. Roth's trademarks: a perfect fit, an adventurous use of color (from Wedgwood blue and celadon to maize yellow), a dramatic silhouette and, most importantly, a sexy, fashionable look. There are exclusive collections by Elizabeth Emanuel (the designer of Princess Diana's wedding dress), Peter Langner, Domo Adami and Max Chaoul at prices that run from $3,000 to $18,000. Take your mom—there are elegant mother-of-the-bride outfits too. Also check out Roth's unconstructed eveningwear collection for soft, simple style.   www.michelleroth.com

Midtown West   **212-245-3390**
24 West 57th Street, Suite 203   bet. 5/6th Ave.
NYC 10019   by appointment only

Mika Inatome

For the non-traditional bride, this TriBeCa store run by Japanese designer Mika Inatome specializes in slim, form-fitted gowns rather than a romantic—dare we say puffy?—dress. Styles include fashionable column dresses, either plain or embroidered, and decorative gowns trimmed in pearl, lace and sterling silver beading. Best to custom order your own. Prices start at $1,700.   www.mikainatome.com

TriBeCa   **212-966-7777**
11 Worth Street, Suite 4B   bet. W. B'way/Hudson
NYC 10013   by appointment only

Milen Shoes

This Eighth Street neighborhood shoe store features European brands and styles that range from work shoes and evening to casual and relaxed. The fairer sex will find mules, sandals, boots and evening shoes. For men, there are leather and suede loafers, boots and sandals. Brand names include Dibrara, Andrea Pfister, Sebastiano Migliore and Shade. Prices run from $150 to $500.

West Village   **212-254-5132**
23 West 8th Street   bet. 5/6th Ave.
NYC 10011   Mon-Sat 11-9, Sun 12-9

Minette by Blue Bag

Miller Harness Company 👨👩
New York's oldest saddlery shop. Since 1912 Miller Harness has catered to the English rider from children size 4 to adults. There is a complete selection of riding attire and equipment perfect for you and your favorite equine, fitted or custom riding boots, accessories, gifts and toys, as well as top of the line saddles by Crosby, Hermès, Excel and Pessier. www.millerharness.com

Flatiron 212-673-1400
117 East 24th Street bet. Park/Lex. Ave.
NYC 10010 Mon-Sat 10-6, Thur 10-7

Mimi Maternity 👩
Don't fall into a fashion rut just because you're pregnant. Thankfully, there are now great sources for stylish maternity wear and Mimi Maternity is one of them with a selection of clothing that delivers comfort and fashion at the same time.

Upper East Side 212-737-3784
1125 Madison Avenue at 84th St.
NYC 10028 Mon-Fri 10-7, Sat 10-6, Sun 12-6

Upper East Side 212-832-2667
1021 Third Avenue bet. 60/61st St
NYC 10021 Mon-Fri 10-7, Thur 10-8
Sat 10-6, Sun 11-6

Upper West Side 212-721-1999
2005 Broadway bet. 68/69th St.
NYC 10023 Mon-Thur 10-8, Fri & Sat 10-7, Sun 12-5

Mina Mann 👩
If you are looking high and low for that just-right shawl, wrap or stole, a visit to Mina Mann, which carries one of the most exceptional ranges in the city, is a must. The shop's eponymous label is a fusion of natural patterns, luscious colors, and exotic fabrics. An attentive sales staff will happily assist you with custom designs. A small selection of handbags, as well as hats by Christine A. Moore also available. Remarkably affordable.

West Village 212-633-9908
13 Christopher Street bet. Greenwich/7th Ave.
NYC 10014 Mon 3-8, Tues-Sun 12-8

Minette by Blue Bag 👩
Minette is a treasure trove stocked with wonderfully girly accessories from France. High-turnover merchandise that arrives every 15 days makes shopping here a truly excellent adventure. Find fabulous jewelry, great belts, scarves, wallets, hand-crocheted make-up bags that double as evening clutches, a few hats and hair accessories, as well as bathing suits, sandals and sarongs during the summer months. Prices range from $75 to $350.

NoLiTa 212-334-7290
238 Mott Street bet. Prince/Spring
NYC 10012 Mon-Sun 11-7

Minium New York

This store is cute, and small: it's no larger than a dressing room, but what it lacks in size it makes up for in stock. There is a quirky collection of pieces by yet-to-be-known designers making their debut with flirty, dressy tops, jeans, T-shirts, witty sweaters, underwear, shoes, scarves and handbags. On one rack you will find cleverly edited vintage pieces in great condition. And the prices aren't bad either.

NoLiTa   **212-226-7840**
49 Prince Street   bet. Lafayette/Mulberry
NYC 10012   Mon-Sat 1-7, Sun 1-6

Min Lee

Japanese designers have been with us for years, and we are no strangers to the fashions of India, China and Southeast Asia. Now it's Korea's turn to take the stage. This sweet boutique is home to Korean designer Min Lee's collection of feminine bias-cut dresses, low-cut pinstriped pants, chiffon peasant styled tops, drop-waist Twenties-style slip dresses, A-line skirts and silk organza roll-top blouses. Many pieces are one-offs, made even more unique with a subtle vintage twist. Select accessories include scarves, belts, polka dot bags and hats.

NoLiTa   **212-334-6978**
7 Prince Street   bet. Elizabeth/Bowery
NYC 10012   Mon-Sat 12-7, Sun 12-6

Miracle

It might not be truly miraculous, but despite its funky location, Miracle's owner and designer Vanessa Lundborg delivers a colorful yet understated collection of dresses, pants, tops and sweaters in quality fabrics. Bridesmaid and special occasion dresses can be custom ordered in a rainbow of available silks.

East Village   **212-614-7262**
100 St. Mark's Place   bet. 1st/Ave. A
NYC 10009   Wed-Sat 12-8, Sun 2-6

Miss Sixty

Since their comeback, the Sixties seem here to stay and Miss Sixty rides that long, long wave. Think velour trenches or miniskirts, ribbed turtlenecks, corduroy shirts and, of course, the cuts that make the chubbiest of legs model-thin. The Miss Sixty girl is not to be ignored. She's a cheeky, cheeky minx. Probably lacking in hips. Which is, of course, perfect to slither into the label's tight, flared, boot-cut low-waisted jeans in vintage washes and special rinses. Find a world of flirty jean styles with pin-tuck detailing down the front, studded legs, tie front closures, and the perfect amount of stretch. Team them with a cute striped halter, tight'n'bright sweater or cropped jacket. Not to mention swimwear pieces, accessories, and shoes.   www.misssixty.com

NoLiTa | **212-431-6040**
246 Mulberry Street | bet. Prince/Spring
NYC 10012 | Mon-Wed 10-7, Thur & Fri 10-8
 | Sat 11-8, Sun 12-7

SoHo | **212-334-9772**
386 West Broadway | bet. Spring/Broome
NYC 10012 | Mon-Wed 10-7, Thur & Fri 10-8
 | Sat 11-8, Sun 12-7

Missoni

For years, the Missoni family has ruled the fashion world with their distinctive sexy, slinky, stripey knitwear. Designer Angela Missoni is mad for wild, geometric patterns and sharp-edged graphics in bold color combinations. In short, you will not find basic black here! Missoni has turned knitwear into a complete line of women's ready-to-wear that includes pants, halter dresses, skirts, sweaters and swimwear. The style crowd are mad for the super-long, boho fringed scarves (approx $260), a great investment and a true fashion classic. www.missoni.it

Upper East Side | **212-517-9339**
1009 Madison Avenue | at 78th St.
NYC 10021 | Mon-Sat 10-6

Miss Pym

Have you noticed how beautiful kids' clothes are becoming, how designers on both coasts and all over Europe are turning out enchanting stuff for little ones? Seems the dungarees and suspenders that did for Huck Finn won't cut it any more. So, if it's couture for kids you're after, Miss Pim is the atelier for you. Owners Lisa Hall and Julia Roshkow are very particular about what they will and won't create. "We don't do primary colors, lace, Peter Pan collars, puffy sleeves or smocking." Expensive, sophisticated clothing for mothers who want their children on the best-dressed list. www.misspym.com

Upper East Side | **212-879-9530**
1025 Fifth Avenue | bet. 83/84th St.
NYC 10028 | by appointment

Miu Miu

Miu Miu is Prada's cute, playful and slightly mad little sister—a girl who wears floral platform shoes, ragged mini dresses and handbags that look like a prop from Sesame Street. Uptown girls and downtown hipsters (who can afford the label—this second line sadly comes with first line costs) come here for a dose of fashion fun. Miu Miu's shoes and fashionable handbags will have you one step ahead of the fashion meter—witness the ever present crowd of hipper-than-hip Japanese tourists snapping up multiple pairs of girly, cartoon shoes. www.miumiu.com

Mixona

Upper East Side   **212-249-9660**
831 Madison Avenue   bet. 69th/70th St.
NYC 10021   Mon-Sat 10-6, Thur 10-7

SoHo   **212-334-5156**
100 Prince Street   bet. Greene/Mercer
NYC 10012   Mon-Sat 11-7, Sun 12-6

Mixona

This cool NoLiTa lingerie shop's name is a composite of Korean symbols: mi–beauty, xo–play of opposites and na–me. Which basically just means gorgeous lingerie with a chic kick. Unlike Victoria's Secret on nearby Broadway, there's nothing pink or prissy about this shop. Dressing rooms are draped in chic, crimson red silk and are spacious enough for husbands/boyfriends to get a private viewing—ooh, saucy. The lingerie is fun, playful, sexy—labels include Passionbait, La Perla, Hanky Panky, Christina Stott, Fifi Chachnil, Ravage and Malitzia. Everyday basics by legends like Hanro and La Cosa, silk sleepwear and daywear also available. Great sales.

NoLiTa   **646-613-0100**
262 Mott Street   bet. Houston/Prince
NYC 10012   Mon-Sun 11:30-8:30

Modell's

One of America's oldest sporting goods chains, Modell's is the city's largest resource for gear and apparel for fishing, camping, fitness, baseball, swimming and more. Also a large selection of brand-name sneakers at low prices.

800-275-6633   www.modells.com

Upper East Side   **212-996-3800**
1535 Third Avenue   bet. 86/87th St.
NYC 10028   Mon-Sat 8:30-9, Sun 10-6:30

Midtown East   **212-661-4242**
51 East 42nd Street   bet. Vanderbilt/Madison Ave.
NYC 10017   Mon-Fri 8-8, Sat & Sun 9:30-6

Midtown West   **212-594-1830**
901 Sixth Avenue   at 32nd St.
NYC 10001   Mon-Sat 10-8, Sun 11-6

Lower Manhattan   **212-964-4007**
200 Broadway   bet. Fulton/John
NYC 10038   Mon-Fri 8:30-6, Sat 10-5, Sun 11-4

Mommy Chic

Pregnant with her first child, Angela Chew had trouble finding fashionable maternity clothes and ended up settling for leggings and her husband's sweaters. Her clever solution: Mommy Chic. Her chic (yes, they are what she says) designs run the gamut from casual wear and business attire to evening and holiday wear. She favors silks, cashmeres, and stretch fabrics with hand crochet, beading and embroidery detailing. Find stretch bootleg jeans, cashmere twin sets, suits, and evening looks like sequined dresses and tops. Check out her children's line, as well as the Marie-Chantal label. From newborn to size 6.   877-973-2864

www.mommychic.com

Moschino

NoLiTa   **646-613-1825**
235 Mulberry Street   bet. Prince/Spring
NYC 10012   Mon-Wed 11-7, Thur-Sat 11-8, Sun 11-7

Mom's Night Out / One Night Out

Mom's Night Out and One Night Out are separate stores located across a hall. The former caters to expectant mothers while the latter is for women who, well, aren't. Both stores offer an intimate shopping environment filled with glamorous eveningwear and allow you to rent, buy or custom-order—for all the repressed designers out there. Cocktail dresses, ballgowns and suits come with designer labels like Vera Wang, Halston and their own signature line. Looks run from fashion forward to downright sexy. Yummy Mummies—this is your store... www.momsnightout.com

Upper East Side   **212-744-6667**
147 East 72nd Street, 3rd Floor   bet. Lex./3rd Ave.
NYC 10021   Mon-Fri 10:30-6, Thur 10:30-8

Montmartre

A style stalwart of Columbus Avenue that offers easy-wearing, fashionable clothes that run from casual and contemporary to career and eveningwear. Find hip pieces by Paul & Joe, Rebecca Taylor, Joie, Alvin Valley, Trina Turk and Theory. Also, a good range of Juicy jeans. Accessories include shoes, handbags, belts and fun jewelry.

Upper West Side   **212-875-8430**
2212 Broadway   bet. 78/79th St.
NYC 10024   Mon-Sat 11-8, Sun 12-7

Upper West Side   **212-721-7760**
247 Columbus Avenue   bet. 71/72nd St.
NYC 10023   Mon-Sat 11-8, Sun 12-7

Morgane Le Fay

Argentinian designer Liliana Casabal expertly translates fantasy into wearable reality with her softly feminine, clean designs in fabrics from silk charmeuse to "dreamy" chiffon and organza. The collection includes elegant dresses, slacks, coats, cashmeres and the creamiest ecru wedding gowns. This is the perfect place to shop for refined romantic clothing.

Upper East Side   **212-879-9700**
746 Madison Avenue   bet. 64/65th St.
NYC 10021   Mon-Sat 10-6, Sun 1-6

SoHo   **212-219-7672**
67 Wooster Street   bet. Spring/Broome
NYC 10012   Mon-Sun 11-7

Moschino

This clever-chic Italian luxury label never takes fashion too seriously. The whimsical interior of this store is dominated by a spiral staircase adorned with wrought iron question marks and heart and peace signs are scattered throughout—feel the love! The clothing, meanwhile, manages to marry chic with just the right degree of novelty—strong classics with clever detailing, suits with hand-stitched lapels, fur-trimmed suede bomber jackets, eyelet trimmed gingham coats and miniskirts with tiers of ruffles. The store also sells the "Cheap & Chic" line and its "Diffusion" jeans collection. www.moschino.it

Upper East Side 212-639-9600
803 Madison Avenue bet. 67/68th St.
NYC 10021 Mon-Sat 10-6

Motherhood Maternity

A very affordable alternative to the pricier Manhattan maternity boutiques with suits, casual wear, knits, lingerie, intimate apparel, jeans and accessories. Fabrics tend to be synthetic. 800-4-MOM-2-BE www.motherhood.com

Upper East Side 212-734-5984
1449 Third Avenue at 82nd St.
NYC 10028 Mon-Fri 10-7, Thur 10-8
Sat 10-6, Sun 12-6

Midtown West 212-564-8170
901 Sixth Avenue at 33rd St. at Manhattan Mall
NYC 10001 Mon-Sat 10-8, Sun 11-6

Midtown West (outlet) 212-399-9840
16 West 57th Street bet. 5/6th Ave.
NYC 10019 Mon-Wed 10-7, Thur 10-8
Fri & Sat 10-6, Sun 12-6

Chelsea 212-741-3488
641 Sixth Avenue at 20th St.
NYC 10011 Mon-Sat 10-7, Sun 11-6

Mshop

Funky, flashy (and maybe a little trashy?) chicks come here to hit the racks of clothes and accessories by up-and-coming designers. Find sexy looks like cross-stitched, plastic coated corsets, halter dresses, hand-crocheted tops, bold geometric print dresses, hand-knitted bikinis and hand-crafted shoes from labels that include Troy Smith, Wanda Marie and Calin. www.mshopnyc.com

Lower East Side 212-505-9371
177 Orchard Street bet. Houston/Stanton
NYC 10002 Mon-Sat 11-7, Sun 12-6

MZ Wallace

A collection of tote and travel bags in durable materials like leather, Cordura nylon, burlap and printed, laminated cottons. These simply shaped weekend bags come in color combinations like fuchsia, orange, green and light blue. The creator's goal: "to create cool bags that have a chic and groovy look." Goodo. www.mzwallace.com

SoHo 212-431-8252
93 Crosby Street bet. Prince/Spring
NYC 10012 Tues 11-6, Wed-Sat 11-7, Sun 12-6

N. Peal

Ooh, cashmere. The ultimate purveyor of traditional, luxury cashmere, this 200-year-old private label company features a brilliant selection of Scottish knitwear in fabulous colors and textures. Styles include plain or cabled v-necks, round necks, cardigans, twin sets and turtlenecks from single-ply to six-ply. In addition, find skirts, robes, gloves and socks.

Midtown West	212-333-3500
5 West 56th Street	bet. 5/6th Ave.
NYC 10019	Mon-Sat 10-6

Nahbee

This chic downtown shoe store's unusual name is Korean for butterfly. So if butterflies (or dressing like them) do it for you, enter the large Zen-like space and discover a selection of classic, ultra-feminine shoes for day and evening from luxe European designers like Christian Lacroix, Vera Wang, Sebastian, Jacques Le Corre, Autre Chose and Monique. Styles include mules, delicate sandals, boots, ballet flats and beautiful pumps and prices run from $100 to $600.

NoLiTa	646-613-0860
262 Mott Street	bet. Houston/Prince
NYC 10012	Mon-Sun 12-7

Nancy & Co.

An Upper East Side shop packed with the latest looks for moms who want to look fashionable without being overly trendy. There is a massive selection of knits, pants, cashmeres, dresses and accessories, all designed to be mixed and matched, from such labels as Cambio, Michael Stars, Whistles, 3 Dots, Shin Choi, Ghost, Jenne Maag and Harari.

Upper East Side	212-427-0770
1242 Madison Avenue	at 89th St.
NYC 10128	Mon-Sat 10-6, Sun 12-6

Nancy Geist

Nancy Geist is one quirky lady—witness her signature shoes in a rainbow of wonderful colors and featuring unusual heels that possess an uncompromising femininity. Find leather boots, mules, denim espadrilles with appliques, strappy sandals, baby doll flats and evening shoes in looks from flirty to city. Prices run from $185 to $600.   www.nancygeist.com

SoHo	212-925-7192
107 Spring Street	at Mercer
NYC 10012	Mon-Fri 11-8, Sat 11-7, Sun 12-7

Nanette Lepore

Nanette Lepore's clothes have been known to inspire cat fights between rock stars. So there you have it—this is one party girl label. Her pieces are fabulously sexy and feminine and fearless in color and pattern—all up it's glam girl meets gypsy. Lepore's SoHo store carries lots of flirty dresses, corsets and hip suits in luxe fabrics. Accessories include her

Nautica

coveted handbags and select shoe designers. Great sales help. www.nanettelepore.com

SoHo | **212-219-8265**
423 Broome Street | bet. Lafayette/Crosby
NYC 10012 | Mon-Sat 12-8, Sun 12-6

Nautica

Known for great casual and outdoor wear—for casual and outdoorsy types—this flagship store features Nautica's huge collection of shirts, sweaters, jeans, shorts, khakis, swimwear and windbreakers in its trademark colors and quality fabrics. Also check out its sportswear collection of dressy pants, hooded cashmeres and smart wool coats. For comfortable workout gear, check out its "Nautica Competition" line. www.nautica.com

Fifth Avenue | **212-664-9594**
50 Rockefeller Center | bet. 49/50th St.
NYC 10023 | Mon-Sat 10-8, Sun 12-6

Nellie M.

A fashion oasis of hip designer labels like How & Wen, Rebecca Taylor, Nanette Lepore, Tibi, Theory and Chaiken. From eveningwear, sportswear and separates to coats and accessories, it's all about fashionably hip clothes at competitive prices. www.nelliemboutique.com

Upper East Side | **212-996-4410**
1309 Lexington Avenue | at 88th St.
NYC 10128 | Mon-Fri 10-8, Sat & Sun 11-8

Net-a-Porter

You won't find this shop on any high street—it's fashion's best virtual boutique, created by a gang of brilliant alumnae from that stylish and unique magazine Tatler. The original concept was to create an online magazine with fashion features just like the glossies, but which visitors could buy from (see Gisele in a stunning Missoni bikini, double-click and it's yours). The idea has since expanded into an online emporium of hot designer names, featuring gypsy tops by Marc Jacobs, Maharishi cargo pants, Jeans by Seven, and Cacharel eveningwear. Shoes by luminaries like Christian Louboutin and Jimmy Choo, and separate sections for beauty, jewelry and music, make this a chic one-stop-shop for those who prefer logging on to trekking about.

www.net-a-porter.com

New & Almost New (NAAN)

A SoHo consignment shop that features designer pieces that are—you guessed it—new and almost new. You may come across a Comme des Garçons jacket, a Tracy Feith dress, a pair of Miu Miu shoes, a Chanel handbag or even an Hermès scarf. Remember, it's all in the timing, as merchandise changes frequently.

SoHo | **212-226-6677**
65 Mercer Street | bet. Spring/Broome
NYC 10012 | Mon-Fri 12-6:30, Sat 1-6

The New York Look

New Balance New York
New Balance is the brand for athletic types who are into an impressive sneaker selection that covers running, cross-training, hiking, walking, tennis, golf and basketball. The NB apparel line runs from basic shorts and tank tops to microfiber jackets and pants that offer performance, fit and a little fashion too. Men's casual shoes and children's sneakers are also available. www.newbalancenewyork.com

Midtown East — 212-421-4444
821 Third Avenue
NYC 10022
bet. 50/51st St.
Mon-Fri 10-7, Thur 10-8
Sat & Sun 12-5

Midtown West — 212-997-9112
51 West 42nd Street
NYC 10036
bet. 5/6th Ave.
Mon-Fri 10-7, Sat 10-6, Sun 12-4.45

New Frontier
Great for fashionable wardrobe staples that don't try too hard. Find casual basics and work clothes with desk-to-dinner versatility, including suits, separates, jackets, dresses and sweaters.

Upper West Side — 212-873-7444
230 Columbus Avenue
NYC 10023
bet. 70/71st St.
Mon-Sat 11:30-7:30, Sun 12-7

New York City Custom Leather
For years designer Agate Blouse has dressed rock stars and supermodels in her signature custom leather designs; most famously, her Sixties-inspired, hip-hugging pants with a flared leg made in the best cowhides ("soft, but not wimpy"). She'll cut any pattern you desire, including vests, jackets, bras and hats. Prices run from $700 to $1,000. Delivery dates vary.

Lower East Side — 212-375-9593
168 Ludlow Street
NYC 10002
bet. Houston/Stanton
by appointment

New York Golf Center
The city's largest golf store carries the best equipment for novices and pros, including golf apparel for men and women and clubs from makers like Callaway, Taylor Made, Ping and Titleist. Rainwear, socks, shoes, golf bags, balls, books and accessories also available. Inquire about on-premise lessons.

Midtown West — 212-564-2255
131 West 35th Street
NYC 10001
bet. 7th Ave./B'way
Mon-Fri 10-8, Sat 10-7, Sun 11-5

The New York Look
A chain of stores selling contemporary career, casual and eveningwear for girls-on-the-go. Great buys from labels like Teen Flo, Tahari, Michael Stars, Plenty, Theory and Whistles. Accessories include shoes and handbags.

Nicole Farhi

Upper West Side   **212-765-4758**
30 Lincoln Plaza   bet. 62/63rd St.
NYC 10023   Mon-Thur 10-9, Fri 10-8
Sat 11-9, Sun 12-7

Upper West Side   **212-362-8650**
2030 Broadway   bet. 69/70th St.
NYC 10023   Mon-Fri 10-9, Sat 11-9, Sun 12-7

Midtown West   **212-382-2760**
570 Seventh Avenue   at 41st St.
NYC 10018   Mon-Fri 9-7, Sat 10:30-7

Fifth Avenue   **212-557-0909**
551 Fifth Avenue   at 45th St.
NYC 10176   Mon-Fri 9-8, Sat 10-8, Sun 10-6

SoHo   **212-598-9988**
468 West Broadway   bet. Houston/Prince
NYC 10012   Mon-Sat 11-8, Thur 11-9, Sun 12-8

Nicole Farhi

Chic British designer Nicole Farhi calls her clothes "constant friends", but you could also call them instant classics. This three-floor, 16,000 sq. ft. flagship offers just that featuring men's and women's ready-to-wear and a home collection. Find racks of pantsuits, embroidered skirts, brilliant chunky cashmeres and plenty of leather and suede, as well as classic (but never dull) shoes and accessories. Grab a bite downstairs at Nicole's, her modern and sleek-looking restaurant.

Upper East Side   **212-223-8811**
10 East 60th Street   bet. Madison/5th Ave.
NYC 10022   Mon-Fri 10-7, Sat 10-6, Sun 12-5

Nicole Miller

Fashion powerhouse Nicole Miller offers something for everyone, all with a clean, stylish—often colorful—edge. Each season she turns out a collection of bridal wear, cocktail dresses, sportswear and accessories, including chiffon blouses, embroidered bustiers, sweaters, skirts, denim and eveningwear. Her trademark is a perfect combination of youthful energy and urban sophistication. Also find an ever-changing line of men's ties, featuring her famously tongue-in-cheek prints. Bridal by appointment.   800-365-4721 www.nicolemiller.com

Upper East Side   **212-288-9779**
780 Madison Avenue   bet. 66/67th St.
NYC 10021   Mon-Fri 10-7, Sat 10-6, Sun 12-5

SoHo   **212-343-1362**
134 Prince Street   bet. Wooster/W. B'way
NYC 10012   Mon-Sat 11-7, Sun 12-6

Niketown

What can you say about Nike, apart from the fact that it rules the world? Niketown's exterior mimics the facade of a New York high school circa 1950, while its interior is a high-tech atrium. Enter through a set of turnstiles to find yourself in a five-floor, futuristic environment replete with video screens constantly plugging Nike products. While most of the merchandise is readily accessible, sneakers ascend at high speed from the basement via a series of five-story clear plastic air tubes. All up, 100% pure adrenaline… NB, look out for a smaller boutique store, rumored to be opening soon in NoLiTa. www.nike.com

Midtown East   **212-891-6453**
6 East 57th Street   bet. Madison/5th Ave.
NYC 10022   Mon-Sat 10-8, Sun 11-7

Nikki B

The owner and designer of this low key store and label, former model Nikki Butler, has hit on a winning recipe for effortless, low-key—dare we say modelly?—style. This out-of-the-way shop is well worth a visit to check out Butler's innovative accessories collection: think colored aviator sunglasses with pastel leather stems (cooler than Ray Ban!) and some gorgeously fine jewelry like delicate charm bracelets and dainty-cool earrings. She also carries a tight edit of ready-to-wear, of which the Jill Stuart jeans ($140) are a must. Also, cute make-up and bits from Bloom and Lola.

TriBeCa   **212-343-9731**
20 Harrison Street   bet. Greenwich/Hudson
NYC 10013   Mon-Sun 11-8

The 1909 Company

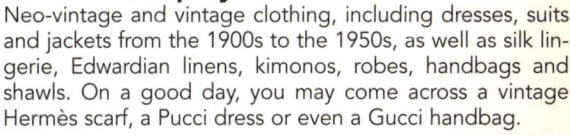

Neo-vintage and vintage clothing, including dresses, suits and jackets from the 1900s to the 1950s, as well as silk lingerie, Edwardian linens, kimonos, robes, handbags and shawls. On a good day, you may come across a vintage Hermès scarf, a Pucci dress or even a Gucci handbag.

SoHo   **212-343-1658**
63 Thompson Street   bet. Broome/Spring
NYC 10012   Mon-Sun 12-7

99X

Come here, you little punk! No, literally. This rockin' store carries predominantly English clothing with a retro feel, ranging from Sixties mod to Eighties skinhead. It's packed with kick-ass "vegetarian" (non-leather) footwear by Dr. Martens, Creepers and Vegetarian Shoe Co. in styles from hardcore steel-toed shoes to limited edition Vans sneakers. Also find shirts by Ben Sherman, Lonsdale and the city's best selection of Fred Perry.

East Village   **212-460-8599**
84 East 10th Street   bet. 3/4th Ave.
NYC 10003   Mon-Sat 12-8, Sun 12-7

Nine West

This footwear behemoth claims to "sell two pair of shoes per second." Nine West carries it all at the most affordable prices in town (even though the service can be downright terrible). Footwear styles run from classic flats and loafers to trendy platforms and boots. Keep an eye on the store, because every so often you'll find a pair of heels that looks like it came straight from Gucci (fool your friends!) Accessories include handbags, leathergoods, sunglasses and jewelry, as well as a slick outerwear collection in leathers, nylons and shearlings. 800-260-2227 www.ninewest.com

Upper East Side 212-987-9004
184 East 86th Street bet. Lex./3rd Ave.
NYC 10028 Mon-Fri 10-8, Sat 10-7, Sun 11-6

Upper East Side 212-472-8750
1195 Third Avenue bet. 69/70th St.
NYC 10021 Mon-Wed & Sat 10-7
Thur & Fri 10-8, Sun 12-6

Upper West Side 212-799-7610
2305 Broadway bet. 83/84th St.
NYC 10024 Mon-Fri 10-8, Sat 10-9, Sun 12-7

Midtown East 212-370-9107
341 Madison Avenue at 44th St.
NYC 10017 Mon-Fri 8-8, Sat 10-6, Sun 12-5

Midtown East 212-486-8094
750 Lexington Avenue bet. 58/59th St.
NYC 10022 Mon-Fri 10-8, Sat 10-7, Sun 12-5

Midtown East 212-371-4597
757 Third Avenue bet. 47/48th St.
NYC 10017 Mon-Fri 8-8, Sat 11-6, Sun 12-5

Midtown West 212-397-0710
1230 Sixth Avenue at 49th St.
NYC 10020 Mon-Fri 9-8, Sat & Sun 10-5

Midtown West 212-564-0063
901 Sixth Avenue bet. 32/33rd St. at Manhattan Mall
NYC 10001 Mon-Sat 10-8, Sun 11-6

Fifth Avenue 212-319-6893
675 Fifth Avenue at 53rd St.
NYC 10022 Mon-Sat 10-7, Sun 10-6

Flatiron 212-777-1752
115 Fifth Avenue at 19th St.
NYC 10003 Mon-Sat 10-8, Sun 11-7

SoHo 212-941-1597
577 Broadway at Prince
NYC 10012 Mon-Sat 10-8, Sun 11-7

Nisa

This romantic and intimate store gives swimwear and lingerie the attention it deserves. Check out specialty swimwear ranging from Lisa Curran Swim (which fits A–DD cup sizes) to chic lines by the Brazilian Rosa Cha and many more, all retro without being kitsch. Other items include lingerie stained with tea leaves and brushed with gold leaf by Khurana, beautiful lace pieces by Australian designer Collette Dinnigan, and cult basics from Cosabella and Gemma. The sales help is eager and helpful.

NoLiTa 212-925-4772
250 Elizabeth Street bet. Houston/Prince
NYC 10012 Mon-Wed, Fri & Sat 11:30-7
Thur 11:30-8, Sun 12-6

Nocturne

Dedicated solely to sleepwear, the elegantly named Nocturne offers a lovely selection of feminine nightgowns, pajamas and robes, plain or delicately embroidered with ladybugs, Chinese symbols, and flowers. Adorable children's slippers and cosmetic bags are also available.

Upper East Side	212-427-8282
1744 First Avenue	bet. 90/91st St.
NYC 10028	Mon-Sat 10-6

Noriko Maeda

Japanese designer Noriko Maeda is an authority in ultra-feminine clothing. Her superb tailoring skills and classic, ladylike styling in luxury fabrics cater to mature women in search of refined fashions reminiscent of style icon Audrey Hepburn. All you need is pearls. Sizes tend to run small.

Upper East Side	212-717-0330
985 Madison Avenue	bet. 76/77th St.
NYC 10021	Mon-Sat 10-6

Norma Kamali

New Yorker Norma Kamali—and her signature jersey pieces—are what fashion icons are made of. Kamali has been having a resurrection of late, now selling as many cult vintage pieces as new (singer Mandy Moore is a fan). Her coveted wrinkle-free jersey line remains a must for day, evening and even your yoga class. In addition, she offers multi-functional swimwear that goes from poolside straight to lunch and a mix of classic everyday pieces like reversible slip dresses, wide-legged or pencil pants and sleeveless Ts, as well as glamorous eveningwear and vintage bridal. One of the first designers to mix vintage with new—Kamali is completely of the moment. www.normakamali.com

Midtown West	212-957-9797
11 West 56th Street	bet. 5/6th Ave.
NYC 10019	Mon-Sat 10-6

North Beach Leather

Leather, leather and more leather is the message here in sexy, body-hugging designs including halter dresses, miniskirts with matching jackets, bustiers, pants, car coats and cropped jackets. The collection comes in colors from red and turquoise to black and winter white. Bootcut leather pants retail for $450, classic long coats for $895 and jackets for $695. www.northbeachleather.com

SoHo	212-625-8668
523 Broadway	at Spring
NYC 10012	Mon-Fri 10-8, Sat 10-9, Sun 12-6

No. 436

A real neighborhood jewel, No. 436 carries a quirky range of pieces from underground designers, all with a distinctively feminine edge. The colorful space houses a collection heavy on prints with childlike Elodie Blanchard tanks, sassy 'Eva' dresses (printed with cartoon foxy ladies), tube tops with pinwheel appliques, oriental tops from Samoy Lemko and individual Riz Sauvage bags. Novel and very cool is a vending machine from which you can dispense the accessory of your choice. Far better for you than chocolate!

East Village   **212-529-8231**
436 East 9th Street   bet. 1st/Ave. A
NYC 10009   Mon-Sat 1-8, Sun 12-6

Nursery Lines

Nursery Lines specializes in furnishings for the nursery, whether it's upholstered furniture, window treatments, custom bumpers, linens, monogrammed quilts or interior design for your child's bedroom. They also carry classic Italian clothing including dresses, rompers, sweaters and the Princess Marie Chantal baby collection. Best for pajamas and robes, either off-the-rack or custom-made. From newborn to size 4.

Upper East Side   **212-396-4445**
1034 Lexington Avenue   at 74th St.
NYC 10021   Mon-Fri 10-5, Sat 10-6

Oilily

Spice up your child's wardrobe with Oilily's bold approach to fashion. Prints, prints, PRINTS everywhere—even on their shoes! Find patterned dresses, shirts, pants, sweaters, jackets and accessories with plenty of cheer and lots of color. Newborn to 12 years old. 800-556-0585 www.oililyusa.com

Upper East Side   **212-628-0100**
870 Madison Avenue   bet. 70/71st St.
NYC 10021   Mon-Sat 10-6, Thur 10-7, Sun 12-5

Oilily for Women

These are the equivalent of play clothes for adults. Cheerful and fresh prints are the focus and they are ubiquitous on dresses, pants, overalls, jeans, sweaters, shoes and accessories. It's cute clothing with easy wearability.
800-850-9551 www.oililyusa.com

Upper East Side   **212-772-8686**
820 Madison Avenue   bet. 68/69th St.
NYC 10021   Mon-Sat 10-6, Thur 10-7, Sun 12-5

Old Navy Clothing Company

Old Navy is the best! Weighing in at 100,000 square feet per location, it is a retail behemoth that gives shoppers maximum buying power for casual clothing that pays homage to designer trends perfectly (put it this way—Marc Jacobs would freak out in here). Kids, teens, adults, mothers-to-be and the plus-size set love shopping here for reliable, hip and affordable basics. This superstore is packed with fun essentials like jeans, T-shirts, swimwear, shorts, sweatshirts, sweaters and jackets. Best buys: the ribbed tanks for about 10 bucks. 800-653-6289 www.oldnavy.com

Midtown West
150 West 34th Street
NYC 10001

212-594-0049
bet. 6/7th Ave.
Mon-Sat 9-9:30, Sun 11-8

Chelsea
610 Sixth Avenue
NYC 10011

212-645-0663
bet. 17/18th St.
Mon-Sat 9:30-9:30, Sun 11-8

SoHo
503 Broadway
NYC 10012

212-226-0865
bet. Spring/Broome
Mon-Sat 10-9, Sun 11-8

Olive & Bette's

It goes like this: two girls come to the Big Apple with a dollar and a dream, become best friends and decide to open a boutique packed with trendy designer labels similar to those you might find in Barneys' super-cool Co-op. And that they do: this is the shop for flirty females with labels like Alice and Olivia (for the coolest striped pants around) Theory, Vivienne Tam, Rebecca Taylor, Nanette Lepore, Trina Turk and Juicy. Best for cheeky tanks and, for the brave (and thin), rainbow trimmed terry shorts.

888-767-8475 www.oliveandbettes.com

Upper East Side
1070 Madison Avenue
NYC 10028

212-717-9655
bet. 80/81st St.
Mon-Sat 11-7, Sun 11-6

Upper West Side
252 Columbus Avenue
NYC 10023

212-579-2178
bet. 71/72nd St.
Mon-Sat 11-8, Sun 11-7

SoHo
158 Spring Street
NYC 10012

646-613-8772
bet. Wooster/W. B'way
Mon-Sat 11-7, Sun 12-6

Omari

Yet another funky SoHo shoe shop for the young and swinging with styles that include chunky heeled sandals, sneaker boots, stilettos, combat boots and two-toned leather cowboy boots. Best are the Helmut Lang-esque strap shoes. All come under the Omari label with prices ranging from $150 to $450.

SoHo
68 Spring Street
NYC 10012

212-219-0619
bet. Crosby/Lafayette
Mon-Sat 11-8, Sun 11-7:30

1 on G

Have a thing for whacked out Japanese streetwear, and simply will not look at an accessory unless it is on a conveyor belt suspended from the ceiling? Well, fortunately, 1 on G is there for you. Owned by a Japanese music stylist, these are clothes for the fearless and for those familiar with their underground Tokyo labels (plastic daisy covered tube top, anyone?). They also carry a smaller selection of conceptual designers like king-of-black Jean Colonna, Commes des Garçons and New York label Azure NYC. In the rear of the store, find a bizarre world of Astro Boy memorabilia and kitsch accessories like leopard print flip-flops. Only for the brave…

Only Hearts

NoHo 212-505-6610
55 Great Jones Street bet. Bowery/Broadway
NYC 10012 Mon-Wed 1-8, Thur-Fri 1-9
 Sat 12-9, Sun 12-7

Only Hearts

For the hopeless romantic, here is your home. It's a mecca for those who adore—what else?—hearts. It's packed with heart-shaped printed or packaged paraphernalia including everything from bath beads and paperweights to antiques and intimate apparel. Designer Helena Stuart brings intimate apparel out of the bedroom and into everyday wear with her selection of sweet and flirty lingerie and underpinnings, including camisoles, teddies, lace tanks, sexy underwear and a selection of sleepwear and robes. Bridal shower gift items, bags and a huge range of jewelry also available.

Upper West Side 212-724-5608
386 Columbus Avenue bet. 78/79th St.
NYC 10024 Mon-Sat 11-8, Sun 11-6

NoLiTa 212-431-3694
230 Mott Street bet. Prince/Spring
NYC 10012 Mon-Sat 11-7, Sun 12-6

Onward Soho

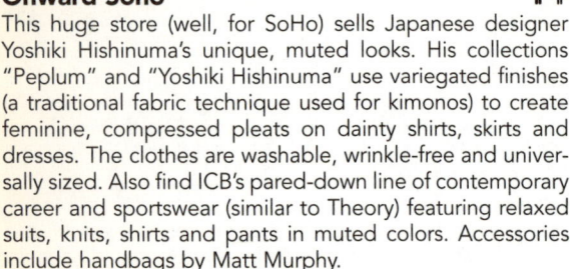

This huge store (well, for SoHo) sells Japanese designer Yoshiki Hishinuma's unique, muted looks. His collections "Peplum" and "Yoshiki Hishinuma" use variegated finishes (a traditional fabric technique used for kimonos) to create feminine, compressed pleats on dainty shirts, skirts and dresses. The clothes are washable, wrinkle-free and universally sized. Also find ICB's pared-down line of contemporary career and sportswear (similar to Theory) featuring relaxed suits, knits, shirts and pants in muted colors. Accessories include handbags by Matt Murphy.

SoHo 212-274-1255
172 Mercer Street at Houston
NYC 10012 Mon-Sat 11-7, Sun 12-6

The Open Door Gallery

Painter-turned-fashion designer Madani views her work as art. And it looks like it too: movement and color play a vital roles in her designs. She uses silks, linens, cottons and interesting prints and mixes them together to create individual pieces finished with raw, zig-zagged edges. Her styles often call for wrapping yourself in sarong-like ways. Feminine, flowy and festive.

East Village 212-777-3552
27 East 3rd Street bet. 2nd Ave./Bowery
NYC 10003 Mon-Sun 2-7

Original Leather

Sensibly priced clothing that is innovative in styling and clever in cut. The large selection of coats, jackets, pants (in every color, fit and style), skirts and accessories in durable leathers will convince you that if Original Leather doesn't have it, no one does.

Upper East Side   **212-585-4200**
1100 Madison Avenue   bet. 82/83rd St.
NYC 10028   Mon-Sat 10-7, Sun 12-6

Upper West Side   **212-595-7051**
256 Columbus Avenue   at 72nd St.
NYC 10023   Mon-Sat 11-8, Sun 11-7

Chelsea   **212-989-1120**
84 Seventh Avenue   bet. 15/16th St.
NYC 10011   Mon-Sat 11-8, Sun 12-7

West Village   **212-675-2303**
171 West 4th Street   bet. 6/7th Ave.
NYC 10014   Mon-Wed 11-9
    Thur-Sat 11-Midnight, Sun 12-9

West Village   **212-777-4362**
552 LaGuardia Place   bet. Bleecker/W. 3rd St.
NYC 10012   Mon-Sat 11-8, Sun 12-7

SoHo   **212-219-8210**
176 Spring Street   bet. Thompson/W. B'way
NYC 10012   Mon-Fri 11-8, Sat 10-8, Sun 12-8

Orva

A full-service department store for the price-conscious woman. You could arrive naked (not that we'd advise that) and leave fully dressed in its selection of designer and brand name sportswear, lingerie, activewear, juniors, hosiery, accessories and well-stocked shoe department. Labels like Nine West, Kenneth Cole, Calvin Klein, French Connection, Donna Karan and Anna Sui are 10% to 30% below retail prices.

Upper East Side   **212-369-3448**
155 East 86th Street   bet. Lex./3rd Ave.
NYC 10028   Mon-Sat 10-9, Sun 10-8

Orvis

A terrific assortment of equipment for hunting, fishing and bird watching. Outfit yourself for everything from a weekend outing to an African safari. Orvis also offers sporting trips and fishing and shooting lessons. A line of Barbour sportswear and outerwear is also available.   www.orvis.com

Fifth Avenue   **212-697-3133**
522 Fifth Avenue   at 44th St.
NYC 10017   Mon-Fri 9-6, Wed 9-7, Sat 10-5

OshKosh B'Gosh

Childrenswear icon OshKosh's claim to fame: the "bib overall," originally worn by farmers and railroad workers in the 1900's, today worn by every toddler and child worldwide—in smaller sizes, of course! Parents flock here for durable, well-styled clothes that scream pure Americana. It offers everyday essentials like jeans, overalls, corduroys, T-shirts, activewear, swimwear, shoes and accessories, all color-coordinated with the OshKosh B'Gosh logo. Newborn to size 16.   800-282-4674   www.oshkoshbgosh.com

Ottiva

Fifth Avenue   **212-827-0098**
586 Fifth Avenue   bet. 47/48th St.
NYC 10036   Mon-Fri 10-7, Sat 10-6, Sun 12-5

Ottiva 👨👩

Here's a genius concept in retailing: When you want to open another trendy shoe store in the same neighborhood with exactly the same merchandise but want to be "new", what should you do? Spell the name of your first store backwards. If this makes no sense to you, go to Avitto and read all about Ottiva…

SoHo   **212-625-0348**
192 Spring Street   bet. Thompson/Sullivan St.
NYC 10012   Mon-Sun 11-9

Otto Tootsi Plohound 👨👩

It's a strange name, no-one knows what it means, but when they see the shoes, no-one really cares. This is a fabulous footwear store that straddles the divide between downtown and designer perfectly. Alongside Helmut Lang, Miu Miu, Costume National and Prada Sport, you'll find their own label, Otto, that dilutes the trends into super-affordable and distinctive shoes. They have fantastic sales too.

Midtown East   **212-231-3199**
38 East 57th Street   bet. Park/Madison Ave.
NYC 10022   Mon-Wed 11:30-7:30
    Thur & Fri 11-8, Sat 11-7, Sun 12-6

Flatiron   **212-460-8650**
137 Fifth Avenue   bet. 20/21st St.
NYC 10010   Mon-Fri 11:30-7:30, Sat 11-8, Sun 12-7

SoHo   **212-925-8931**
413 West Broadway   bet. Prince/Spring
NYC 10012   Mon-Sat 11:30-7:30, Sat 11-8, Sun 12-7

SoHo   **212-431-7299**
273 Lafayette Street   bet. Houston/Prince
NYC 10012   Mon-Fri 11:30-7:30, Sat 11-8, Sun 12-7

Oxxford Clothes 👨

An American menswear institution that will spare men the headaches of department store shopping (oh, we know how you love it). There are classic off-the-rack suits (or custom-order one), navy blazers ($1,450 to $1,650), pants ($350 to $695), dress shirts, neckwear, casual sportswear and accessories, all in an American cut with conservative styling.

Midtown East   **212-593-0205**
36 East 57th Street   bet. Park/Madison Ave.
NYC 10022   Mon-Sat 10-6

Pan American Phoenix 👨👩👨

A cute little store stocking wares imported exclusively from Mexico. The sweetest little traditional dresses for girls mix it up with peasant blouses in bold colors for their fashion-forward mothers. The best—and brightest: woven shawls in gorgeous stripes (think a classic Missoni scarf, and cut the price in half). Also a great homewares collection that will save you a trip south over the border... www.panamphoenix.com

Upper East Side   212-570-0300
857 Lexington Avenue   bet. 64/65th St.
NYC 10021   Mon-Fri 10.30-6.30, Sat 11-7

Paragon Sporting Goods

This is truly a sporting goods store for the Noughties. Over 100,000 sq. ft. devoted to equipment and apparel for every sport imaginable, including everything from racket sports, water sports, skiing and hiking to golf, camping, fitness and fishing. The selection is enormous, but this well-organized store makes shopping easy and pleasurable.   800-443-9120   www.paragon.com

Chelsea   212-255-8036
867 Broadway   at 18th St.
NYC 10003   Mon-Sat 10-8, Sun 11-6:30

Parke & Ronen

Body conscious but forgiving—that's a winning combination, and one this design team works in streamlined sportswear geared toward a younger (and trimmish—they only forgive so much) customer. In addition to casual pants and shirts, look for knits, vests, scarves and hats as well as a selection of Frank and Daniel belts, bags and Dita sunglasses.   www.parkeandronen.com

Chelsea   212-989-4245
176 Ninth Avenue   bet. 20/21st St.
NYC 10011   Mon-Sat 12-8, Sun 1-6

Pat Areias

Upon entering this Madison Avenue belt store, face right and select from over 500 hanging belt straps in skins like calfskin, alligator, crocodile, lizard, ostrich and horsehair. Decide on a color from standard fare neutrals to bold brights and soft pastels. Then admire the sterling silver buckles in the glass display case. Match a belt strap with a buckle, and voila—you've just designed your own belt. Straps run from $50 to $450, while buckles go from $80 to $6,000 for an 18-karat gold and diamond number.

Upper East Side   212-717-7200
966 Madison Avenue   bet. 75/76th St.
NYC 10021   Mon-Sat 10-6, Sun 11-5

Patagonia

From its modest roots making climbing gear in a tin shed in Ventura, California, Patagonia has evolved into a company with worldwide distribution. It now makes functional and cool outdoor clothing for a variety of activities, from kayaking and surfing to climbing, hiking and skiing. The clothes are innovative, reliable and durable. Highlights include button-down A/C shirts, excellent polar fleeces and unsexy but vital "baggies," Patagonia's lightweight, quick-drying nylon shorts.   800-638-6464   www.patagonia.com

Patch NYC

Upper West Side   **917-441-0011**
426 Columbus Avenue   bet. 80/81st St.
NYC 10024   Mon-Sat 10-7, Sun 11-6

SoHo   **212-343-1776**
101 Wooster Street   bet. Prince/Spring
NYC 10012   Mon-Sat 11-7, Sun 12-6

Patch NYC

Fashionistas have embraced this quirky accessories label and flock to its store, home to the complete Patch NYC by Ross & Carney collection. Each piece is highly individual and looks like your nanna might have made it (but in a cool way). It's got handbags, jewelry, stripey hats, cute crochet scarves, tops, and home furnishings to boot. Best is their collection of one-of-a-kind handbags with unique detailing (leather flowers, hand-painted cameos, beading, appliques and vintage fabrics). Prices run from $240 to $400.   www.patchnyc.com

West Village   **212-807-1060**
17 Eighth Avenue   bet. 12th St./Jane
NYC 10014   Mon-Fri 11-7, Sat 11-6, Sun 12-6

Patina

A tiny SoHo boutique offering a wide selection of vintage clothing, handbags and other goodies like ceramics, decorative glass and period costume jewelry. There are beaded sweater sets, dresses, skirts and handbags from the '40s thru the '70s, all in good condition. But as with all vintage shops, timing is everything.

SoHo   **212-625-3375**
451 Broome Street   bet. B'way/Mercer
NYC 10012   Mon-Sat 12-7, Sun 1-6

Patricia Field

Downtown design legend Pat Field is having herself quite the fashion moment, the result of her role as costume designer on Sex and the City. Yep, she made Sarah Jessica Parker hip, and cool girls worldwide emulate her funky styling. Her eponymous store was around before all that, though, and it is a far campier proposition. It's a club crowd paradise, where you will find bright patent leather outfits to wigs from the 60's and 70's... and everything in between. Think of it as if Carrie took a trip—and we don't mean a holiday...   www.patriciafield.com

NoHo   **212-254-1699**
10 East 8th Street   bet. 5th/Univ. Pl.
NYC 10012   Mon-Sun 12-8

Paul & Joe

Isn't Paul and Joe French for chic? Well, no but this label is chic incarnate. French designer Sophie Albon (who named the label after her two sons) spirits up a well-tailored, eclectic collection of boldly wearable pieces with a vintage

Paul Smith

edge. Find a full ready-to-wear collection known amongst fashion watchers for its great pants and wonderful—often striped—shirts. Other looks include feminine, flirty blouses, hip-hugging pants, lovely cashmere sweaters, coats, and sparkly jeans. Look out for its newish menswear line and accessories too. Not cheap—but worth it.

NoHo	**212-505-0974**
2 Bond Street	bet. B'way/Lafayette
NYC 10012	Mon-Sat 11-7, Sun 12-7

Paul & Shark

This Italian retailer of yachting attire for, one suspects, the permanently landlocked fuses urban and nautical influences. Its two-level shop sells chic men's and women's sportswear including everything from sweaters, shirts and warm-up suits to swimwear, light-weight boating jackets, winter-weight coats and a line of polar fleece. It's all specifically fashioned for outdoor living and, best of all, is water-resistant. Golf apparel and canvas and leather boating shoes for men only. www.paulshark.it

Upper East Side	**212-452-9868**
772 Madison Avenue	bet. 66/67th St.
NYC 10021	Mon-Sat 10-6, Thur 10-7

Paul Frank

California designer Paul Frank is a cheeky monkey. Well, sort of. His cartoon chimpanzee Julius has become cult amongst equally cheeky fashion girls who like a bit of kitsch with their cool. Think the Hello Kitty of America. This downtown store carries the full Paul Frank range, from furniture to womens and menswear to handbags to wallets. He recently introduced eyewear too, so to be Franked, this is your place.

NoLiTa	**212-965-5079**
195 Mulberry Street	at Kenmare
NYC 10013	Sun-Wed 11-7, Thur-Sat, 11-8

Paul Smith

One of Britain's most successful designers and knighted by the Queen to boot, Sir Paul Smith keeps his male customers coming back for more. What distinguishes a Paul Smith design: a bold approach to fabric, pattern and color with traditional Old World styling. His classic pieces are never stuffy, more warm and clever—his striped shirts are a must for both sexes. Shop a collection of English tailored menswear that includes suits, at an average price of $1,200, dress and casual shirts, sport jackets, outerwear and men's furnishings. Accessories include watches, cufflinks and eyewear. www.paulsmith.co.uk

Flatiron	**212-627-9770**
108 Fifth Avenue	at 16th St.
NYC 10011	Mon-Sat 11-7, Thur 11-8, Sun 12-6

Paul Stuart

The label of choice for high-powered bankers, lawyers and stockbrokers with its no-nonsense collection of suits, furnishings, shirts, sportswear and outerwear, as well as English bench-made shoes and accessories. Find the same straightforward looks for the corporate woman. Paul Stuart is a great source for traditional clothing that says you mean business—but be prepared to drop a bundle. 800-678-8278

Midtown East — 212-682-0320
Madison Avenue — at 45th St.
NYC 10017 — Mon-Fri 8-6:30, Thur 8-7
Sat 9-6, Sun 12-5

Peacock NYC

A great destination for an East Village fashion fix: cute tie tops in bright colors and relentlessly form-fitted jeans, pants and skirts, mostly in stretch fabrics, make for a hot-to-trot look—perfect for peacocks, really. Labels include Sharagano and Diab'less. Also available: raffia and slouchy leather bags and a cool collection of beaded jewelry and heart pendants. www.peacocknyc.com

East Village — 212-260-1809
440 East 9th Street — bet. 1st/Ave. A
NYC 10009 — Mon-Sun 1-8

A Pea in the Pod

At this flagship store, women no longer have to fret about putting together the perfect pregnancy wardrobe. It's 3,300 sq. ft. of selling space offering A Pea in the Pod's private-label collection as well as designs from the maternity lines of Nicole Miller, La Perla, Tahari, Seven and 3 Dot. The clothes are attractive, comfortable and versatile. 800-4-Mom-2-Be www.apeainthepod.com

Upper East Side — 212- 988-8039
860 Madison Avenue — at 70th St.
NYC 10021 — Mon-Fri 10-7, Sat 10-6, Sun 12-6

Midtown East — 212-826-6468
625 Madison Avenue — bet. 58/59th St.
NYC 10022 — Mon-Fri 10-7, Sat 10-6, Sun 12-6

Peanutbutter and Jane

Anyone looking for cute and cool childrenswear should head for Peanutbutter and Jane, which carries baby and toddler clothes as well as teen sizes. Teens will get a kick from Chinese print dresses with matching jackets, stretchy lace skirts and pleated tops with capri pants. Labels include Le Tout Petits, Cherry Tree, Petit Faune, Cotton Caboodle, Petit Bateau, U Go Girl and Metropolitan Prairie. From newborn to size 14. Sadly, no peanut butter sandwich with purchase!

West Village — 212-620-7952
617 Hudson Street — bet. Jane/W.12th St.
NYC 10014 — Mon-Sat 10:30-7, Sun 12-6

Pearl River

A Chinese department store that lets you experience shopping Asian-style without leaving Manhattan. It's packed to the rafters with everything from A to Z—appliances, housewares, video rentals, wonderful teas, soaps, food and, yes, even clothing. Find Mandarin jackets, Cheongsam dresses, silk pajamas, kimonos, straw and embroidered slippers and much more at fabulous bargain prices. Best are the cool-kitsch floral handbags for ten bucks.   www.pearlriver.com

NoLiTa	**212-966-1010**
200 Grand Street	at Mott
NYC 10013	Mon-Sun 10-7:30
TriBeCa	**212-431-4770**
277 Canal Street	at B'way
NYC 10013	Mon-Sun 10-7:30

Pelle Via Roma

Owned by Max Fiorentino, this shop offers a similar selection of handbag and luggage pieces crafted a la Florentine. The classic styles are in supple and exotic skins like lamb, calf, alligator, lizard and deer and shapes like the Fendi baguette, the Hermès bucket bag and Tod's and Pradaesque designs. Prices run from $250 to $900. Also shop an enormous selection of pashmina shawls retailing at $155.

Upper East Side	**212-327-3553**
1322 Third Avenue	bet. 75/76th St.
NYC 10021	Mon-Fri 10-8, Sat 11-7, Sun 11-6

A Perfect Day In Paradise

If you want every day to be a Palm Beach day (and who doesn't, really) dive into store owner Denice Summers' collection of brightly colored, Lilly Pulitzer-esque print dresses, skirts, tops, pants, silk, corduroys, cashmeres and Mackintosh raincoats. Men will find corduroys, polos and oxford shirts in a rainbow of bold and pastel colors. Pay $140 for a pair of cords, $350 for a cashmere sweater and $1,500 for a custom-made evening frock.

Upper East Side	**212-639-1414**
153 East 70th Street	bet. Lex./3rd Ave.
NYC 10021	Mon-Fri 10-6, Sat 11-5

Peter Elliot

A great alternative to frenetic department store shopping and over-hyped designer boutiques, Peter Elliot boasts classic menswear. It carries high-end Italian and English designer merchandise by Kiton, Brioni and Luigi Borelli as well as classic polo shirts, casual knits, preppy ties, shirts, outerwear and accessories like embroidered belts with quirky motifs. Personal services include a 24-hour emergency hotline, a delivery service and free alterations.

Upper East Side	**212-570-2300**
1070 Madison Avenue	at 81st St.
NYC 10028	Mon-Fri 10:30-7, Sat 10:30-6, Sun 1-5

☆ Peter Elliot Kids

There's Peter Elliot for men, Peter Elliot for women and now Peter Elliot Kids, which sells classic children's clothing—i.e not trendy in the slightest, more like old fashioned, well-made clothes, including exquisite French, Italian, and English labels, as well as their own private line. Labels include Cacharel, Portofino, Chipie, Krizia and Corgii Cashmere of England. Special amenities include a play area for kids, a changing area for babies, and a photo gallery starring their youthful customers. From 2 to 12 years old.

Upper East Side   **212-570-5747**
1067 Madison Avenue   bet. 80/81st St.
NYC 10028   Mon-Sat 10-6, Sun 1-5

Peter Fox Shoes

A full-service shoe store that runs the gamut from casual to dressy styles with its Peter Fox line of classic designs. Brides-to-be can choose from an extensive selection of bridal shoes.

SoHo   **212-431-7426**
105 Thompson Street   bet. Spring/Prince
NYC 10012   Tues-Sat 11-7, Sun 12-5:45

Peter Hermann

A great assortment of briefcases, luggage, handbags, knapsacks, totes and wallets from labels like Mandarina Duck, Lamarthe, Orla Kiely, Desmo, the boho Jamin Puech and Strenesse. Also find eyewear by the English company of Cutler & Gross.

SoHo   **212-966-9050**
118 Thompson Street   bet. Spring/Prince
NYC 10012   Mon-Sat 12-7, Sun 1-6

Petit Bateau

Petit Bateau makes the best T-shirts in the world, many a fashionista will tell you. This French label is renowned for turning out simple, chic, affordable clothing bursting with joie de vivre. This 3,000 sq. ft. shop has three sections: "Les Bebes" for 0-24 months, "Les Petits" for 2-8 year olds, and "Les Grands" for tweens to adults. Find casual daywear, loungewear, sleepwear, underwear, and plenty of their classic tees in soft muted colors—each one coming in its own cute lemon-colored box. Prices run from $10 to $150. Petit Bateau's perfume and body products are also available.   www.lepetitbateau.com

Upper East Side   **212-219-9456**
1100 Madison Avenue   at 82nd St.
NYC 10028   Mon-Sat 10-6

Petit Peton

This upscale shoe store, nominated by Vogue and Elle magazines as one of the top three in the U.S., is a sexy shoe lover's dream come true. Find a collection of high fashion footwear from top designer labels like Gianfranco Ferré, Casadei, Roberto Cavalli and Giuseppi Zanotti.

NoHo
27 West 8th Street
NYC 10011

212-677-3730
bet. 5/6th Ave.
Mon-Sat 11-9, Sun 12-8.30

Phat Farm

Rap impresario Russell Simmons' "Classic American Flava" label Phat Farm lives the rap and hip-hop lifestyle full force. Find a denim-based collection, lots of knits and velour, T-shirts, sweatshirts and pants, and their signature argyle pieces. Not to mention Simmons' wife Kimora's hot collection for women, Baby Phat, which is a sassy, sexy mix of Oriental and hip-hop style. Alicia Keys, Britney Spears, and Destiny's Child are all famous fans.

SoHo
129 Prince Street
NYC 10012

212-533-7428
bet. W. B'way/Wooster
Mon-Sat 11-7, Sun 12-8

Philosophy Di Alberta Ferretti

Alberta Ferretti's women are beautiful creatures. Her silhouette is romantic without being cloying, wearable without being basic. Her ethereal dresses are perfection, often understated in design and color and distinguished by intricate, weightless folds, smocking and embroidery. Looks run from frothy chiffon skirts and pearly satin tops to velvet dresses and wool coats, all marked by a delicate femininity.   www.philosophy.it

SoHo
452 West Broadway
NYC 10012

212-460-5500
bet. Houston/Prince
Mon-Sat 11-7, Sun 12-6

Piccione

Is Italy the true home of custom tailoring? A visit to Signor Piccione's workshop will most likely convince you it is. He will graciously make a suit, sportcoat or pair of slacks for men, or a pant and jacket ensemble for women. Choose a fabric from the finest mills such as Zegna, Loro Piana, Holland & Sherry and Scabel. Suits prices start at $3,000 with delivery in five weeks. In addition, Piccione also sells ready-made shirts, cashmere knitwear and ties.

Midtown West
7 West 56th Street
NYC 10019

212-956-2102
bet. 5/6th Ave.
Mon-Sat 10-6

Pierre Garroudi

Do you need an evening gown, wedding dress or suit created in the next 24 hours? Pierre Garroudi is there to help with your fashion crisis. This designer will re-create any gown from the latest fashion magazines, the Oscars, you name it. Garroudi also sells off-the-rack designs that are long, clingy and sheer. A Garroudi original starts at $700 while a custom-made designer wedding dress will run you $1,100 and up. It's best to insist on reviewing the specifications and details when ordering your gown.   www.pierregarroudi.com

Pilar Rossi

SoHo   **212-475-2333**
139 Thompson Street   bet. Prince/Houston
NYC 10012   Mon-Fri 11-8, Sat & Sun 11-7

Pilar Rossi

An embellishment-addicted Spanish designer known for her collection of bridal wear, evening gowns and dressy suits for special occasions. Choose from off-the-rack styles or custom order your own. A sequined, beaded, frilly Rossi gown will run you at least $3,000, but you will be smartly, if a little ornately, decked out.

Upper East Side   **212-288-2469**
784 Madison Avenue   bet. 66/67th St.
NYC 10021   Mon-Sat 10-6:30

Pleats Please, Issey Miyake

Pleats Please? Yes, please. Pressed pleats? Yes, please. Mid-priced, nice-priced, feather-weight pleats? Yes, please. Wrinkle proof pleats? Yes, yes, yes, please! Slim fit? Yes, that's it. Rainbow bright? Yes, that's right, even for night. A mix of East and West? Yes, yes, that works best. What a treat these pleasing pleats! You probably get that Japanese designer Miyake's store is known for its pleats, by now, yes?   www.pleatsplease.com

SoHo   **212-226-3600**
128 Wooster Street   at Prince
NYC 10012   Mon-Sat 11-7, Sun 11-6

Plein Sud

Celebrities and fashionistas—of slim and sexy figures—come to Plein Sud for French designer Faycal Amor's slinky collection of beautiful knits, curvy leathers and suedes and lots of clingy fabrics. Styles include long dresses cut on the bias, square-shouldered jackets, form-fitted pants, head-turning skirts and a healthy dose of fur.

SoHo   **212-431-6500**
70 Greene Street   bet. Spring/Broome
NYC 10012   Mon-Sat 11-7, Sun 12-6

Plenda

A good store to take your mom, Plenda offers easy pieces for the conservative dresser—and for those with fuller figures. Loose lineny pieces by Flax sit next to pastel knits by Princess, all nestled in a collection of floral print dresses. They also stock a good range of beaded jewelry—very art school teacher chic.

West Village   **212-352-2161**
543 Hudson Street   bet. Perry/Charles
NYC 10014   Tues-Sat 12:30-6:30

☆ Pookie & Sebastian

A groovy little store in an unexpected location that sells a collection of girly (but not too girly) casual pieces. Pink roses welcome you into a world of paisley and print tops that sit oh-so-prettily next to Seven jeans, Cosabella lingerie, I Love NY T-shirts and an ingenious shelf filled with a rainbow of well-made tube tops for a great value $22. Staff are cheerful and friendly—must be the roses…

Upper East Side   **212-717-1076**
249 East 77th Street   bet. 2/3rd Ave.
NYC 10021   Mon-Sat 11-9, Sun 11-6

Powers Court Tennis Outlet

Tennis merchandise at some of the lowest prices in town, including clothing, footwear, rackets and accessories. Brand names include Prince, Wilson, Head and K-Swiss.

Chelsea   **212-691-3888**
132 1/2 West 24th Street   bet. 6/7th Ave.
NYC 10011   Mon-Fri 10-6, Thur 10-7:15, Sat 10-4

☆ Prada

Even if you can't afford anything in there, you have to check out Italian powerhouse Prada's monolithic, conceptual new super-store on Broadway. Designed by edgy architect Rem Koolhaas, Miuccia Prada's designer baby aims to transcend the basic store concept. That it does, from the esoteric murals on the walls to the shoe display area that turns into seating for lectures. She also provides a select range of vintage Prada pieces; remember the "geek chic" wallpaper jackets and "bourgeoise" chiffon blouses? You can buy them again here. Not to mention the latest beautiful, intelligent Prada clothes that have made this label king.   www.prada.com

SoHo   **212-334-8888**
575 Broadway   at Prince
NYC 10012   Mon-Sat 11-7, Sun 12-6

Upper East Side   **212-327-4200**
841 Madison Avenue   at 70th St.
NYC 10021   Mon-Sat 10-6, Thur 10-7

Midtown East (shoes only)   **212-308-2332**
45 East 57th Street   bet. Park/Madison Ave.
NYC 10022   Mon-Sat 10-6, Thur 10-7

Fifth Avenue   **212-664-0010**
724 Fifth Avenue   bet. 56/57th St.
NYC 10019   Mon-Sat 10-6, Thur 10-7, Sun 12-6

Precision

A neighborhood boutique packed with trendy American and European labels—and slightly rude staff. They boast a large collection of Tark pants, as well as labels like Earl, Jules, Theory, Poleci, Ticci Tonetto and Juicy Couture. Accessories include hats and girly handbags.

Upper East Side   **212-879-4272**
1310 Third Avenue   at 75th St.
NYC 10021   Mon-Sat 11-8, Sun 12-6:30

Princeton Ski Shop

Midtown East   212-683-8812
522 Third Avenue   at 35th St.
NYC 10016   Mon-Fri 11:30-8, Sat 11-7, Sun 12-6:30

Princeton Ski Shop
Avid skiers, snowboarders and skaters head here for their gear from labels like Bogner, Columbia, Obermayer and Burton. The ski and snowboard equipment is from equally top-of-the-line manufacturers.   www.princetonski.com

Flatiron   212-228-4400
21 East 22nd Street   bet. B'way/Park Ave. South
NYC 10010   Mon-Fri 10-10, Sat 10-7, Sun 12-6

Project
Billed as "the perpetual sample sale", this consignment store is for the persistent shopper who doesn't mind even more persistent sales staff. It's very much the luck of the draw here, but it's possible to find Armani suits for $250, and pants for a bargain $50. Also available is a range of La Perla lingerie and eveningwear, some Prada pieces, Replay sportswear and Diego Della Valle shoes.

Lower East Side   212-505-0500
175 Orchard Street   at Stanton
NYC 10002   Mon-Sun 10-7

Pucci
Pucci has a rich tradition—of movie stars on holiday, the luxe resort life—that it retains with its distinctive, knockout printed pieces. Now that designer Julio Espada has been replaced by color king Christian Lacroix, expect even more technicolor brilliance. Whoever is at the helm, Pucci's tradition is fabulous enough to make its clothes and accessories eternally desirable. Since 1949, Pucci has been designing clothes in their signature colorful, graphic prints derived from abstract drawings. Find a series of dresses, from mini shirtdresses to Sixties shifts, skirts, pants, swimsuits (some of the best) and accessories.   www.pucci.com

Upper East Side   212-752-4777
24 East 64th Street   bet. Madison/5th Ave.
NYC 10021   Mon-Sat 10-5

☆ The Puma Store
One of the world's hippest sneaker brands just got its own universe. Puma has stayed cool over the years, and never more so than in this huge two-storey shop where Fatboy Slim blasts and graffiti art lines the walls containing a full collection of sportswear—T-shirts with both the modern and retro logos ($22), and everything from World Cup soccer wear to sweats to groovy roller-skates (Roller Girl, eat your heart out). A great buy are their fab leather tote bags, a favorite of downtown fashionistas who have never played sport in their lives…   www.puma.com

SoHo   212-334-7861
521 Broadway   bet. Spring/Broome
NYC 10012   Mon-Sat 10-8, Sun 11-7

Ralph Lauren

Pumpkin Maternity

A colorful boutique that brightens up an otherwise gloomy neighborhood with its ultra-cool maternity clothes. Among its many offerings are pencil skirts, yokeless bootcut pants and jeans, cigarette pants, tank tops, blouses, dresses, coats and its trademark FreeBelly Skirt, which liberates the belly from all fabric. Pumpkin also carries sarongs, underwear, comfy flip-flops, cosmetics and other accoutrements to hide or flaunt your belly. While expectant customers may feel like pumpkins, Pumpkin is the owner's actual name, a sobriquet she earned at birth due to her gargantuan size! 800-460-0337 www.pumpkinmaternity.com

NoLiTa — **212-334-1809**
407 Broome Street — bet. Lafayette/Center
NYC 10013 — Mon-Sat 12-7, Sun 12-5

Quiksilver

Surf's up! Catch the best waves at Quiksilver, the hottest Boardrider's Club in town. This is a concept shop where Californ-i-aaay surf and fashion meet head on. Adults and kids can shop for the latest in board equipment as well as surfwear and snowboard apparel, swimwear, casual wear (including high-tech nylon pants), logo T-shirts, fleece, shirts, sweatshirts and a line of sneakers and accessories. 877-246-7257 www.quiksilver.com

SoHo — **212-334-4500**
109 Spring Street — bet. Mercer/Greene
NYC 10012 — Mon-Sat 11-7, Thur 11-8, Sun 12-7

Rafé New York

When the celebs are buying up your beauteous bags, you know you're on to a good thing. Cameron Diaz has snapped up a Rafé multi-colored wooden bead bag, Sandra Bullock, a lacquered straw tote, while model Helena Christensen bought up a denim/leather number. Rafé specializes in simple shapes in sleek leathers, studded lambskin, metallic leather and splatter-painted tulle clutches, equestrian-inspired drawstring shoulder bags, wool flannel totes, briefcases with pigskin trim and evening knockouts like ladylike elbow purses in a rainbow of fabrics.

NoHo — **212-780-9739**
1 Bleecker Street — at Bowery
NYC 10012 — Tues-Thur 11-7, Fri & Sat 11-8, Sun 12-7

☆ Ralph Lauren

"The romance, the beauty, the world of Ralph Lauren" say the fragrance advertisements, and don't we all want a piece of it. Ralph Lauren is the king of the American fashion establishment, one who has earned his title over the past 20 years by delivering a luxe interpretation of classic American sportswear. His clothes embody the "aspirational" American lifestyle, one of leisure, privilege…and polo. And Ralph is on form—following a highly-imitated

Ralph Lauren

prairie-themed collection last year, he segued effortlessly into Victoriana, all the while retaining the quintessential Lauren look. Think Penelope Cruz in an evening dress in the rain, and dream... As for men, Ralph is your man. He has cultivated the preppy look for years, and it works a charm. At this store, enter Lauren's Anglophile world, where you'll find everything from ready-to-wear and Oscar caliber eveningwear to sportswear and casual wear. Looks include tissue-thin leathers and suedes, luxurious cashmeres paired with tweed jackets, military styled shirtdresses, checked ponchos and strapless evening gowns. So for very incarnation of American style, just look for the little polo player. www.polo.com

Upper East Side   212-606-2100
867 Madison Avenue   at 72nd St.
NYC 10021   Mon-Sat 10-6, Thur 10-8

☆ Ralph Lauren

Dressier looks, especially for men, rule at the mansion, while Ralph Lauren Sport and Black Label take center stage at this location. Once again, you'll find the look for just about any lifestyle as well as sporty merchandise devoted to the worlds of running, cycling, aquatics and skiwear. "Polo Golf" features the ultimate in classic golfing attire, and "Polo Tennis" caters to both player and spectator with its selection of chic tennis duds. Interspersed is Ralph Lauren's all-American sportswear, including fabulous suedes and leathers, cashmere sweaters, shirts, jackets, chinos, resort, shoes and select vintage pieces.

Upper East Side   212-434-8000
888 Madison Avenue   at 72nd St.
NYC 10021   Mon-Sat 10-6, Thur 10-7, Sun 12-5

SoHo   212-625-1660
381 West Broadway   bet. Broome/Spring
NYC 10012   Mon-Wed 12-8
    Thur-Sat 11-8, Sun 12-6

Rampage Clothing Co.

A fun mix of fashion fix clothing for the under-30 crowd. Shop a constantly changing selection of merchandise like asymmetrical skirts, dresses, tight tops, pants, jeans and T-shirts, as well as racy, lacy lingerie. Coordinating accessories include handbags, scarves, feather chokers, hats and sunglasses. Find it at affordable prices, but remember this clothing is for one season only. www.rampage.com

SoHo   212-995-9569
127 Prince Street   at Wooster
NYC 10012   Mon-Sat 10-8, Sun 11-7

Rapax

A good neighborhood shoe store that carries a large selection of fashionable classics, including simply styled flats, mules, sandals and evening pumps by Rapax, Claudio Merazzi and Roberto Rinaldi. Prices run from $99 to $300.

Upper East Side
1100 Madison Avenue
NYC 10028

212-734-5171
bet. 82/83rd St.
Mon-Sat 10-7, Sun 11-5

R by 45rpm
This cool store filled with floor-to-ceiling columns made from Japanese chestnut trees is home to one of Japan's hottest jeans companies. It's the ultimate destination for denim fanatics who want their jeans aged 'just so', because each pair is worn-in by hand and then personally stamped on the inside pocket by the employee who 'distressed' them. Prices range from $150-$600. Other items include denim skirts, jackets, shirts and T-shirts.

SoHo
169 Mercer Street
NYC 10012

917-237-0045
at Houston
Mon-Sun 11-7

Really Great Things
Although the buzzer on the door is a bit intimidating, once you walk into this sophisticated store, you will indeed find… really great things. Owner Ryan Zentner says he is looking for "the next Tom Ford", but until then will settle for selling chic pieces from designers who aren't yet household names, like vintage fabric reinventor Claudette, Japanese name Nabo Nakana and the low-key Tara Jarmon. Also find Gerard Yosca jewelry, Michel Perry shoes, cute Spencer and Rutherford handbags and the obligatory Gucci sunglasses. The store provides a service for special event clothing, regularly used by celeb fans like Alison Janney, Gretchen Moll and Roberta Flack.

Upper West Side
284-A Columbus Avenue
NYC 10023

212-787-5354
bet. 73/74th St
Mon-Sun 11-7

Red Wong
Owner Suzy Wong never has a dull (retail) moment. Her Red Wong line is big on dresses—silk ones with plenty of color, her signature silk charmeuse cowl-neck and bateau-neck styled dresses, and her super-short, one-shouldered blouson dresses. The shop also sells items from other select designers like beautiful hand knits and chunky sweaters by Zoli and Olivia Eaton, unique legwarmers and great underwear basics for girls who live in low-rider pants.

NoLiTa
181 Mulberry Street
NYC 10012

212-625-1638
bet. Kenmare/Broome
Mon-Sat 12-8, Sun 12-6

Reebok
A large, futuristic showplace for Reebok's line of fitness, tennis, running and cycling gear. The clothes are practical, good looking and well priced. Reebok's sneaker selection is outstanding, even for kids. www.reebok.com

Upper West Side
160 Columbus Avenue
NYC 10023

212-595-1480
bet. 67/68th St.
Mon-Sat 10-8, Sun 12-6

☆ Reem Acra

This Lebanese-born bridal designer with not only make the brides blush, but also gush over her exquisite designs for that day-of-days. She is best known for her signature use of embroidery, which has influenced many other designers in the bridal industry. Think delicate Swarovski crystals to seed pearls, all woven into gowns that beautifully marry (pun intended) the modern and the traditional. Prices range from approx $2,900-$6,000.

Upper East Side 212-414-0980
10 East 60th Street bet. Madison/5th Ave.
NYC 10022 Mon-Fri 10-7, Sat 10-6, Sun 12-5

Reminiscence

A big draw for younger types who want a bit of retro grooviness in their wardrobe. Find fun and affordable Hawaiian T-shirts, baggy tie-string overalls, tube tops, halter tops, bike jackets, wrap skirts, vintage lingerie and boas, as well as military-styled clothing. Accessories include handbags, body glitter, bikini headbands and more. www.reminiscence.net

Chelsea 212-243-2292
50 West 23rd Street bet. 5/6th Ave.
NYC 10010 Mon-Sat 11-7:30, Sun 12-7

René Collections

Iconic designer handbags get knocked off in style at this shop, which carries all shapes, sizes and colors at great prices. From Hermès' Kelly bag to Gucci's Hobo, it's hard to tell the copy from the original. Costume jewelry and belts also available.

Upper East Side 212-987-4558
1325 Madison Avenue bet. 93/94th St.
NYC 10128 Mon-Sat 10-7, Sun 12-6

Upper East Side 212-327-3912
1007 Madison Avenue bet. 77/78th St.
NYC 10021 Mon-Sat 10-6:30, Sun 12-5

René Mancini

Refined, elegant shoes that are meticulously crafted in France. A signature Mancini design comes with perfect cap toes and delicate small heels, although they can get adventurous with clear plastic stilettos. Although expensive, they are worth it. It's best to stock up during their semi-annual sales.

Midtown East 212-308-7644
470 Park Avenue at 58th St.
NYC 10022 Mon-Sat 10-5:45

Replay Store

"Heavy duty, durable and dependable" is the tag line for this Italian line of casual, outdoor clothing, which follows just enough of the fashion trends. The Replay label is found on sportswear, jeans, underwear, shoes and even, um, china. Grab a bite at their in-store eatery called The Replay Café. www.replay.it.com

SoHo   **212-673-6300**
109 Prince Street   at Greene
NYC 10012   Mon-Sat 11-7, Sun 11-6

☆ Resurrection Vintage

In a city teeming with vintage clothing stores, Resurrection is one of the best. It's packed with well-chosen, mint condition clothing from the Sixties to the Eighties, edited to reflect the current movements in fashion (which, of course, often looks backward for inspiration). It's a retro designer universe from Sixties Courreges to Seventies Cacharel and Chloé, to Valentino, Yves St. Laurent, Pucci, Ferragamo, Gucci…you name it. This is the store where the designers shop—Chloé's Phoebe Philo has been known to pick up Chloé originals here…

NoLiTa   **212-625-1374**
217 Mott Street   bet. Prince/Spring
NYC 10012   Mon-Sat 11-7, Sun 11-7

East Village   **212-228-0063**
123 East 7th Street   bet. 1st/Ave. A
NYC 10009   Mon-Sat 2-10, Sun 2-9

Reva Mivasagar

A good destination for social butterflies whose schedules are booked solid with special occasions. This Australian designer specializes in eveningwear—from cocktail dresses to fancy gowns—and bridal wear that is modern and non-traditional. Choose from off-the-rack designs or custom order. Custom bridal ranges from $2,000-$5,000 with a six month delivery time; custom eveningwear ranges from $1,500-$4,000, two-month delivery time.

SoHo   **212-334-3860**
28 Wooster Street   at Grand
NYC 10013   Mon-Fri 11:30-7, Sat 11-7, Sun 12-6

Richard Metzger

This designer has made it his mission to dress plus-size women sumptuously with body conscious, sexy designs, and a lot of plus-size women are very grateful. By appointment only, he will show you his looks for the season (everything from tailored casual to drop-dead-entrance-making eveningwear) and tailor them just for your body. With curvaceous celebrity devotees such as Oprah Winfrey, Queen Latifah and Emme, Metzger is well on his way to being the couturier for plus-size women.

Chelsea   **1-877-METZGER**
140 Seventh Avenue   bet. 18/19th St.
NYC 10011   by appointment only

Richard Metz Golf Equipment

A golfer's paradise; it even has a practice cage and putting green for lessons. There's also men's apparel like wind shirts, vests, rain suits, socks, shoes and hats and the latest in top-quality golf equipment by makers like Callaway, Taylor Made, Hogan and Titleist. www.richardmetzgolf.com

Midtown East — **212-759-6940**
425 Madison Avenue, 3rd Fl. — at 49th St.
NYC 10017 — Mon-Fri 9-7, Sat 11-6, Sun 10-5

Ripplu

A firm bod without surgery—or a life in the gym? "Yeah right, whatever", you say. Well, speak to the folks at Ripplu, who will fit you with a series of custom bras and panties that will lift and reshape those critical anatomical parts. If you find this hard to believe, just look at the sales helps' hourglass figures (incidentally, the staff are also courteous and helpful). Bra sizes run from 30A to 40G. Custom fittings and free alterations.

Fifth Avenue — **212-599-2223**
575 Fifth Avenue, 2nd Fl. — bet. 46/47th St.
NYC 10017 — Mon-Sat 11-7

Ritz Furs

Foxy ladies come here for "gently" pre-owned furs. For years Ritz has been a destination for a fine selection of used mink, lynx, fox, sable and more, which it expertly restores into like-new condition. In addition, find shearlings, fur-trimmed and lined outerwear, fur hats and stoles. An attentive, polite sales staff and great prices are the key to Ritz's 70 successful years.

Midtown West — **212-265-4559**
107 West 57th Street — bet. 6/7th Ave.
NYC 10019 — Mon-Sat 9-6

Robert Clergerie

Footwear fashionistas crave Clergerie's chic, modern classics with styles ranging from trendy wedges and platforms to feminine heels. Styles include cute ballet pumps, boots, loafers, sandals and evening shoes in great colors and serious quality leathers. A Clergerie design is a foot-flattering statement to add to any outfit. A limited selection of men's oxfords, loafers, boots and sandals is also available. Expensive.

Upper East Side — **212-207-8600**
681 Madison Avenue — bet. 61/62nd St.
NYC 10021 — Mon-Sat 10-6, Sun 12-5

Robert Danes

What happens to a Yale graduate with a passion for history and architecture when his parents give him a sewing machine? In Robert Danes' case, you become a fashion designer. Find his ready-to-wear collection of day-to-evening dresses, jackets, and separate ensembles that are modern, colorful and feminine. His eveningwear line features beautiful bias-cut dresses and Oscar worthy gowns. Wedding bells in your future? Try Danes' bias-cut silk patchwork gowns, elegant column dresses, and modern alternative ballgowns. Pay $1,700 to $8,000 with a two-to-six month delivery.

SoHo	**212-941-5680**
62 Wooster Street	bet. Spring/Broome
NYC 10012	Tues-Sat 11-7 (appointments recommended for brides)

Roberta Freymann

Chic retailer (and former hand-knitter) Roberta Freymann sells a "little bit of everything". This translates to a fabulously eclectic range of ethnic-inspired women's and children's clothing and home accessories. Freymann travels the world to source both clothing and fabrics from India, Argentina, Bolivia, Vietnam, even Uzbekistan. She will take home furnishing fabric from Thailand, for example, and fashion it into an elegant ready-to-wear collection of separates. Her focus is on distinctive eveningwear in jewel-like colors. Go take a journey…

Upper East Side	**212-794-2031**
23 East 73rd Street, Apt 5F	bet. Madison/5th Ave.
NYC 10021	Mon-Fri 11-6, Sat 12-6

Roberto Cavalli

Ladeez, Roberto Cavalli thinks you are booty-licious. To wit, the sex-o-matic Italian designer offers high-energy, sultry fashions that will do something chronic to any helpless man in their path. From glam rock to glam chic, Cavalli has built his reputation around his larger-than-life approach to fashion: unusual prints, bright colors and luxuries like suede, leather and fur. Oh, and skin, skin, skin! There are lots of printed stretch denim, tapestry ensembles, sexy knits, sheer blouses, deer and eagle printed dresses, enormous shearlings, lush lynxes, sensuous chiffon evening dresses and va-va-voom lingerie. Shrinking violets, please stay home!   www.robertocavalli.com

Upper East Side	**212-755-7722**
711 Madison Avenue	at 63rd St.
NYC 10021	Mon-Sat 10-6, Thur 10-7, Sun 12-6

Robert Talbott

A fashionable California-based shirt shop where you can choose from 40 ready-made styles or custom order from its selection of over 200 fabric swatches. Dress shirts are tailored in a full cut and manufactured in top quality cottons and broadcloths. Ties, cufflinks, cummerbunds and pocket squares make perfect accessories. Shirt prices average $150.   800-747-8778   www.roberttalbott.com

Roberto Vascon

Upper East Side   **212-751-1200**
680 Madison Avenue   bet. 61/62nd St.
NYC 10021   Mon-Sat 10-6

Roberto Vascon

We're all familiar with custom suits, shoes, you know it. Now go for a custom handbag. Roberto Vascon works a myriad of shapes and styles in dozens of colors and fabrics, including leather, patent, faux-alligator, embossed crocodile, python, canvas and assorted prints. Pay anywhere from $125 to $500 and allow 20 days for delivery.   www.robertovascon.com

Upper West Side   **212-787-9050**
140 West 72nd Street   bet. B'way/Columbus Ave.
NYC 10023   Mon-Sun 11-7

Rochester Big & Tall

America's #1 source for the discriminating man in need of larger and lengthier sizes. A full-service shop running the gamut from underwear to designer suits with labels like Zegna, Canali, Donna Karan and Versace. Sportswear, casual and activewear and accessories complete the collection. Shoes are by Allen Edmonds, Cole Haan, Ferragamo and Bruno Magli.   800-282-8200

Midtown West   **212-247-7500**
1301 Sixth Avenue   at 52nd St.
NYC 10019   Mon-Fri 9:30-6:30, Thur 9:30-8, Sat 9:30-6

Lower Manhattan   **212-952-8500**
67 Wall Street   at Pearl
NYC 10005   Mon-Fri 9-6, Sat 9-5

Rockport

Rockport's mission statement is "to make the world more comfortable" and indeed they do. Choose from comfortable yet rugged hiking boots, sneakers, loafers, sandals, lace-ups, hearty pumps and nifty looking golf shoes as well as foot-soothing products like massagers and sprays. Rockport is the official footwear of the "Men in Black", if that does anything for you…   800-762-5767   www.rockport.com

Upper West Side   **212-579-1301**
160 Columbus Avenue   bet. 67/68th St.
NYC 10023   Mon-Sat 10-8, Sun 12-6

SoHo   **212-529-0209**
465 West Broadway   bet. Houston/Prince
NYC 10012   Mon-Sat 11-7, Sun 12-6

Rodier

Ultra-conservative, long-lasting knitwear is Rodier's specialty. There are coordinating suits, pants, sweaters and dresses manufactured in fabrics like linen, wool blends, polyester acrylic and cottons.

Upper East Side   **212-439-0104**
1310 Third Avenue   at 75th St.
NYC 10021   Mon-Sat 10-6, Sun 12-5

Rosa Custom Ties

Globe-trotting executives visit Rosa's while in New York to custom-order luxurious cravats. Choose from over 5,000 Italian silk prints, stripes, wovens and solids, then wait two weeks for your tie to be hand-stitched and interlined to perfection. Prices range from $95 to $125. No minimum order required.

Midtown West   **212-245-2191**
30 West 57th Street, 6th Fl.   bet. 5/6th Ave.
NYC 10019   Mon-Fri 9:30-5:30, Sat by appointment

Rosette Couturiere

Brenda Barmore now runs this women's custom tailor founded by Rosette Harris. She will duplicate a design, add her own interpretation or merely do alteration work. A 9-to-5 suit will run you $550 (fabric price not included), while dinner suits start at $650.

Upper West Side   **212-877-3372**
160 West 71st Street, 2nd Fl.   bet. Columbus/B'way
NYC 10023   Tues-Fri 10-6, Sat 10-5

Roslyn

Fashion-forward girls who frequent Steven Alan's SoHo shop also have somewhere to shop uptown: Roslyn, his accessories store on the Upper West Side run by—you guessed it—Roslyn, his mother. True to form, this is a fabulous outpost for the latest in jewelry, hats and killer handbags. The jewelry selection includes diamonds, semi-precious stones and antique pieces—best, the boho pieces from Me & Ro. Hat-wise, styles run from chic wide-brimmed hats and cloches to brightly colored rain caps by cool labels like Eugenia Kim, Misa Harada, Kelly Christy and Jacqueline Lamont. Not to mention the sporty handbag selection, featuring snappy nylon totes and everything in between by LeSportSac, Cammie Hill, Un Après Midi de Chien and Hervé Chapelier.

Upper West Side   **212-496-5050**
276 Columbus Avenue   at 73rd St.
NYC 10023   Tues-Sun 12-7

Ruco Line

A store specializing in chunky footwear, similar in style to Spain's cult, quirky Camper brand. Think solid sneakers in earthy colors, some covered with the company logo and a healthy selection of walking sandals. They also carry a small selection of "R" embossed shoulder bags.

Upper East Side   **212-861-3020**
794 Madison Avenue   at 67th St.
NYC 10021   Mon-Sat 10-6

☆ Rugby North America

This friendly, two-floor store does what the Canadians (see Club Monaco) do so well—chic basics for Americans. Leather is a focus here, from a huge range of coats and jackets (the mens' are a standout) to matching accessories like sleek handbags, briefcases and purses all stamped with the subtle Rugby logo. But look out for the brilliant selection of high-quality viscose T-shirts, polo shirts and simple cotton skirts, in a rainbow of colors and all at easy-access prices. www.rugby-na.com

SoHo 212-431-3069
115 Mercer Street bet. Prince/Spring
NYC 10012 Mon-Sat 11-7, Sun 12-6

Saada

Downtown goes uptown at this groovy Upper East Side boutique. Its eclectic collection of pieces from up-and-coming designers is well worth checking out. Cute dresses, pants, tops and accessories like fun hats and cool handbags from some of the hottest labels in town, including Tracey Reese, Nanette Lepore, Rene Bardo, Kablan, Paper, Denim and Cloth jeans and Kazuyo Nakano bags.

Upper East Side 212-223-3505
1159 Second Avenue bet. 60/61st St.
NYC 10021 Mon-Sat 11-8, Sun 12-6

Sacco

Sacco is a footwear chain that makes the girls happy—because there truly is something for everyone. There are mules, pumps, loafers, maryjanes, platforms, slingbacks, sandals, great boots and more from such labels as Cynthia Rowley, Audley, Lisa Nading and Sacco's own line. Pay an average price of $150—and their sales are great too. Also, check out a jaunty selection of handbags, from floral prints to basic black. 877-464-7771 www.sacco.com

Upper West Side 212-874-8362
2355 Broadway bet. 85/86th St.
NYC 10024 Mon-Fri 11-8, Sat & Sun 11-7

Upper West Side 212-799-5229
324 Columbus Avenue bet. 75/76th St.
NYC 10023 Mon-Fri 11-8, Sat 11-7, Sun 12-7

Chelsea 212-675-5180
94 Seventh Avenue bet. 15/16th St.
NYC 10011 Mon-Fri 11-8, Sat 11-7, Sun 12-7

SoHo 212-925-8010
111 Thompson Street bet. Spring/Prince
NYC 10012 Mon-Fri 11-8, Sat 11-7, Sun 12-7

Saint Laurie, Ltd.

A reliable supplier of traditional, made-to-measure suits, jackets and shirts for the man-about-town. Choose from its selection of fabrics and let Saint Laurie's tailors get to work with its exclusive 3D body-scanner, which ensures the accuracy of all measurements. Custom suit prices start at $1,000 and dress shirts from $200-$275. Off-the-rack suits, furnishings and tuxedos also available. For women, find made-to-measure only. The super-attentive sales staff make shopping here a pleasure. www.saintlaurie.com

Salvatore Ferragamo

Midtown East   **212-473-0100**
350 Park Avenue   bet. 51/52nd St.
NYC 10022   Mon-Fri 9:30-6:30, Sat 9:30-6

Saks Fifth Avenue 👤👩👤

This iconic New York City department store in a landmark building is in the midst of a five-year, $100 million renovation to improve floor space and beef up designer labels. By the scheduled completion date later this year, Saks will be one of the finest up-to-the-minute fashion emporiums in the city. Cosmetics, handbags, hosiery and accessories occupy the frenzied main floor, but women's fashions take center stage with four floors devoted to ready-to-wear, eveningwear and sportswear from the gamut of designers—from the glossy Celine, Gucci, Dolce & Gabbana and Michael Kors through downtown Marc Jacobs to the cutting-edge Alexander McQueen. Other departments include women's designer and contemporary shoes, bridal, furs, outerwear, lingerie and children's. Men will find two complete floors devoted to American and European designer labels, including suits by Hickey Freeman, Alan Flusser, Armani and Zegna. Also find men's furnishings, outerwear, formalwear and shoes. Finally, visit the Elizabeth Arden Spa salon or grab a bite to eat in the café.   800-345-3454   www.saksfifthavenue.com

Fifth Avenue   **212-753-4000**
611 Fifth Avenue   bet. 49/50th St.
NYC 10022   Mon-Sat 10-7, Sun 12-6

Salvatore Ferragamo 👩

The Ferragamo name has historically been associated with classic shoes—especially sparkly numbers for one Marilyn Monroe—with its stylish customers swearing by their superb comfort and fit. Find politely chic styles in luxury leathers with sizes that range from 5AAA to 11B. Semi-annual sales are the best time to stock up. Ferragamo's equally luxurious clothing exudes refinement, including tailored suits, jackets, skirts, separates and coats. Handbags, accessories and Ferragamo's signature printed scarves are in the same tradition.   800-628-8916   www.salvatoreferragamo.com

Fifth Avenue   **212-759-3822**
661 Fifth Avenue   bet. 52/53rd St.
NYC 10022   Mon-Sat 10-6, Thur 10-7, Sun 12-5

SoHo   **212- 226-4330**
124 Spring Street   at Greene
NYC 10012   Mon-Sat 11-7, Sun 12-6

Salvatore Ferragamo 👤

Ferragamo's men's collection—suits, sportswear, shirts and outerwear—promises equally tasteful styling. And, like the womenswear, its fashion influence is strongest in its rich, whimsical neckwear (buy up those ties!) and shoes. Footwear runs from business and formal to casual and sporty. The designers at Ferragamo continue to remain faithful to its classic standards while marrying them with the best of modern trends.   800-445-1874   www.salvatoreferragamo.com

Fifth Avenue **212-759-7990**
725 Fifth Avenue bet. 56/57th St.
NYC 10022 Mon-Sat 10-6, Thur 10-7, Sun 12-5

Sample
This tiny boutique carries a signature collection of knitwear in special yarns from Italy. There is a good color selection featuring silk/cotton blends in sensuous designs, including 1/2-turtlenecks, ruffle-edged cardigans, ribbed boat-neck sweaters, roll-neck tops and zipped-front cardigans perfect over a pair of Sample's slim-cut pants. Also available, great oversized printed totes, towels, bath products and semi-precious and precious jewelry.   www.samplestudio.com

NoLiTa **212-431-7866**
268 Elizabeth Street bet. Houston/Prince
NYC 10012 Mon-Sat 12-7, Sun 12-6

Samuel's Hats
Samuel's Hats specializes in high fashion pieces by American and European designers like Eric Javits, Kokin, Philip Treacy and Frederick Fox. Find a wide selection of designs, from handmade one-of-a-kinds and giant, posh-girl hats to sporty styles. Check out the great hat boxes for travelling and storage.   www.samuelshats.com

Lower Manhattan **212-513-7322**
74 Nassau Street bet. John/Fulton St.
NYC 10038 Mon-Fri 9-7, Sat 10-5

San Francisco Clothing
This long-established Lexington Avenue shop sells fad-free sportswear and understated eveningwear with a western edge. This translates into skirts, jackets, dresses, blouses and tailored shirts in natural fabrics and straightforward designs. In addition, shop a lively and refreshing children's collection featuring labels like Flap Happy, Yams and Le Top. Cute-as-pie looks from newborn to 6X.

Upper East Side **212-472-8740**
975 Lexington Avenue bet. 70/71st St.
NYC 10021 Mon-Sat 11-6

Santoni
An Italian purveyor of conservative, handmade shoes predominantly for men. Attention to style, shape, color and fit is the Santoni trademark in two collections that cover the gamut from casual to dressy or corporate. Prices range from $300 to $2,200. Women can choose from a small selection of driving shoes, mules and loafers.

Upper East Side **212-794-3820**
864 Madison Avenue bet. 70/71st St.
NYC 10021 Mon-Fri 10-7, Sat 10-6

Scandinavian Ski Shop 👨👩
A convenient Midtown source for ski and winter sports apparel and equipment with clothing and accessories by Bogner, Helly Hanson, Obeymeyer, RLX and Killy. When the snow melts, Scandinavian outfits its customers for tennis, hiking and competition swimming. 800-722-6754
www.scanskishop.com

Midtown West **212-757-8524**
40 West 57th Street bet. 5/6th Ave.
NYC 10019 Mon-Fri 10-6:30, Sat 10-6, Sun 11-5

Scoop 👨👩
At Scoop, there's a party going on, and everyone's invited. This progressive store was one of the first in town to stock the cult Marc by Marc Jacobs line, its huge, fun interior also housing flirty, colorful wrap dresses from Diane von Furstenberg, chic tops from Katayone Adeli, boho beauties from Matthew Williamson, slick pieces from Kors and Michael Kors, cult hoodies by Juicy Couture and one of the coolest—and most extensive jeans collections around, including Seven, Earl and Paper, Denim and Cloth. Not to mention the fab handbag selection that decorates the walls. And the belts. And the jewelry. AND the new men's selection at the uptown store: take a deep breath—Clements Ribeiro, Diesel, Helmut Lang, John Varvatos, Lacoste, Lucien Pellat-Finet, Miu Miu and Paul Smith. And that's just for starters... www.scoopnyc.com

Upper East Side **212-535-5577**
1275 Third Avenue bet. 73/74th St.
NYC 10021 Mon-Fri 11-8, Sat 11-7, Sun 12-6

SoHo **212-925-2886**
532 Broadway bet. Prince/Spring
NYC 10012 Mon-Sat 11-8, Sun 11-7

Screaming Mimi's 👨👩
Although this was already a cult store amongst downtown fashionistas, Sex and the City made it famous. Carrie and co are often decked out in this hip vintage garb dating from the Forties to the Eighties. Although the clothing is from past eras, the collection is surprisingly modern, due to the fact that the store's owners cleverly edit the pieces to reflect current fashion trends. There's men's clothing from the Sixties and Seventies, as well as girly looks in dresses, vintage bras and bustiers, skirts, tops and color-coded shoes. Accessories include new and vintage sunglasses, hats, jewelry and handbags.

NoHo **212-677-6464**
382 Lafayette Street bet. Great Jones/4th St.
NYC 10003 Mon-Sat 12-8, Sun 12-6

Seam 👩
Owners/designers Joanna Garza and Dori Adler are all about clothes that are cut to fit "real women" who actually have hips and curves in all the right places. Find dresses,

pants, jackets and shirt-dresses designed to be layered, mixed and matched and that best of all, defy the fickle fashion seasons. Check out their georgette sheer coat paired with a pair of pants. Also shop T-shirts, sweaters, sarongs, handbags and jewelry. Sizes run from 4 to 16.

TriBeCa   **212-732-9411**
117 West Broadway   bet. Duane/Reade
NYC 10013   Mon-Sat 11-7, Sun 1-6

Sean

The French connection to upper-crust menswear with a look that is Ralph Lauren meets agnès b. Find designer Emil Lafaurie's collection of well-made wool suits, silk ties, fabulous shirts in solid shades, cotton and corduroy pants, casual painter's jackets and Italian parkas. All up, just cool enough.

Upper West Side   **212-769-1489**
224 Columbus Avenue   bet. 70/71st St.
NYC 10023   Mon-Sat 11-8, Sun 12-6

SoHo   **212-598-5980**
132 Thompson Street   bet. Houston/Prince
NYC 10012   Mon-Sat 11-8, Sun 12-7

Searle

What happens when you start as a sportswear company, but then start making fantastic coats? You get pigeon-holed as an outerwear company. Well, that was then—Searle is finishing what it started. Although there's still plenty of outerwear (shearlings, microfiber reversibles, cashmeres, alpaca/wool blends, trenchcoats and the coveted Montcler puffer jackets), the real focus here is on contemporary sportswear. Find over 60 trendy labels like Lauren Moffat, Allen B., Alvin Valley (who makes some of the leanest, meanest pants around), and How & Wen, as well as shoes, Puma sneakers and stylish accessories. Great service.

Upper East Side (W)   **212-988-7318**
1124 Madison Avenue   at 84th St.
NYC 10028   Mon-Sat 10-6, Thur 10-7, Sun 12-5

Upper East Side (W)   **212-717-4022**
1035 Madison Avenue   at 79th St.
NYC 10021   Mon-Sat 10-6, Thur 10-7, Sun 12-5

Upper East Side   **212-628-6665**
805 Madison Avenue   bet. 67/68th St.
NYC 10021   Mon-Fri 10-7, Sat 10-6, Sun 12-6

Upper East Side   **212-717-5200**
1296 Third Avenue   at 74th Street
NYC 10021   Mon-Fri 10-7, Sat 10-6, Sun 12-6

Upper East Side (W)   **212-838-5990**
1051 Third Avenue   at 62nd St.
NYC 10021   Mon-Sat 10-6, Thur 10-7, Sun 12-5

Midtown East   **212-753-9021**
609 Madison Avenue   bet. 57/58th St.
NYC 10021   Mon-Fri 10-7, Sat 10-7

Seigo

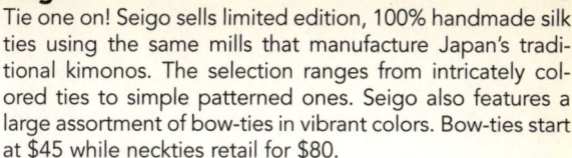

Tie one on! Seigo sells limited edition, 100% handmade silk ties using the same mills that manufacture Japan's traditional kimonos. The selection ranges from intricately colored ties to simple patterned ones. Seigo also features a large assortment of bow-ties in vibrant colors. Bow-ties start at $45 while neckties retail for $80.

Upper East Side   **212-987-0191**
1248 Madison Avenue   bet. 89/90th St.
NYC 10128   Mon-Sat 10-6:30, Sun 11:30-5:30

☆ Seize sur Vingt (16/20)

Luxury ready-to-wear and custom-made clothing for both sexes. Choose from their specialty, impeccably tailored Italian cotton shirts, cashmere sweaters, pants, jackets and suits, as well as handmade boxers—ooh, fancy!—and accessories. While Seize sur Vingt has given itself the French school grade of 16/20 (equivalent to an A-), we'll give 'em a 20/20. Great men's-styled collar shirts for women, too.   www.16sur20.com

NoLiTa   **212-343-0476**
243 Elizabeth Street   bet. Houston/Prince
NYC 10012   Mon-Sun 12-7

Selia Yang

A high-end boutique selling safely feminine fashions like dresses in simple hourglass silhouettes, skirts, shirts and knits that are perfect for cocktails. Her favorite fabrics are silk organza and beaded satin. Great coordinating accessories include handbags, tiaras and jewelry. Custom bridal also available.

East Village   **212-254-9073**
328 East 9th Street   bet. 1st/2nd Ave.
NYC 10003   Tues-Fri 1-8, Sat & Sun 12-6

Selvedge

Art meets cutting-edge fashion at this tiny Levi's-owned boutique. A graffiti covered wall is a hip backdrop for the deliberately elusive (they don't want just anyone to have it) Levi's Vintage and Red collections, many displayed like art on the walls. Most of the merchandise is limited edition and notable for its special wash or conceptual cut. Vintage sneakers also available.

NoLiTa   **212-219-0994**
250 Mulberry Street   bet. Prince/Spring
NYC 10012   Mon-Thur 12-7, Fri & Sat 11-7, Sun 12-6

Sergio Rossi

Ooh, Mr Rossi! You are very, very bad—but so, so good... Mr Rossi's designs are so fabulous that women have been known to buy an outfit just to match a pair of his shoes. Rossi's look-at-me numbers are for glamour girls who aren't afraid of pointy, needle high heels and who love anything metallic, beaded and knockout sexy. Find classic pointy-toe pumps with curved heels, beaded satin mules, platforms, wedges and more. An expanded line of men's casual and dressy shoes also available. www.sergiorossi.com

Upper East Side — **212-327-4288**
772 Madison Avenue — at 66th St.
NYC 10021 — Mon-Sat 10-6

Seven

Seven is one of the most progressive stores in New York, and is helping establish the Lower East Side as a vital fashion destination. Its mission statement is "a perfect combination of art and fashion where one foot is in retailing and the other in the art world." Cult circle bags from As Four are stocked next to Tess Giberson's handmade arty T-shirts and Bernard Willhelm sweaters, then there's French knitter Pierrot, and downtown up-and-comer, Benjamin Cho. Each piece is a complete original. They also hold art exhibitions and installations for their eclectic design talent.

Lower East Side — **646-654-0156**
180 Orchard Street — bet. Houston/Stanton
NYC 10002 — Mon-Wed 12-7, Thur-Sat 12-9, Sun 12-6

Shack Inc.

Of the shops that have migrated south from retail-choked SoHo to laid-back TriBeCa, Shack is a highlight. Designer J. Morgan Puett takes her inspiration from nature, history and daily events to create unisex clothing that women will "feel utterly at ease in." Most of her clothing is made in the shop and her fabrics of choice are silk, linen and cotton gauze in soft shades. On offer: coordinating separates like dresses, skirts, shirts, drawstring pants, tops and easy-wearing jackets.

TriBeCa — **212-267-8004**
137 West Broadway — bet. Duane/Thomas
NYC 10013 — Mon-Fri 11-6, Sat & Sun 12-6

Shanghai Tang

Despite its moody, mysterious decor, there is a blaze of brilliant color from Tang's Asian-inspired fashions and accessories. Everyone should experience this vibrant fusion of East meets West at least once. Shop a full range of Shanghai Tang's signature silky clothing, accessories and home products (great Oriental lamps), from traditional Mao jackets and long Cheongsam dresses to modern reproductions in lush velvets, silk, linens and printed cottons. Best bet: their silk "Coolie" and "Tang" jackets. Custom also available. www.shanghaitang.com

Upper East Side — **212-888-0111**
714 Madison Avenue — bet. 63/64th St.
NYC 10021 — Mon-Sat 10-6, Sun 12-6

Sharagano

Wondering where to get those hotpants you love so much? Well, fear not, the flashy Sharagano will have your booty—barely—covered. You may have guessed that this is a flaunt-it kind of store, for sassy girls who must have the very latest in clothing trends, from military to denim to peasant to prints (and probably ditch them tomorrow). Find dresses, frilly blouses, sweaters, pants and coats—but dominant is their range of super-tight jeans. Good prices. www.sharagano.com

SoHo **212-941-7086**
529 Broadway bet. Spring/Prince
NYC 10012 Mon-Sat 10-9, Sun 11-8

☆ Shelly Steffee

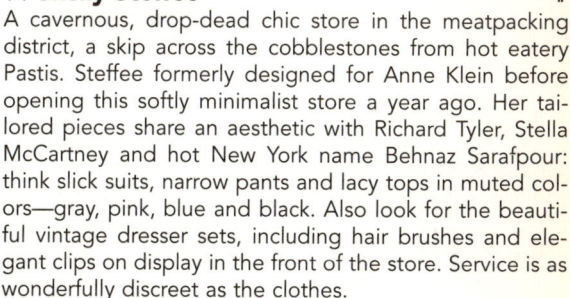

A cavernous, drop-dead chic store in the meatpacking district, a skip across the cobblestones from hot eatery Pastis. Steffee formerly designed for Anne Klein before opening this softly minimalist store a year ago. Her tailored pieces share an aesthetic with Richard Tyler, Stella McCartney and hot New York name Behnaz Sarafpour: think slick suits, narrow pants and lacy tops in muted colors—gray, pink, blue and black. Also look for the beautiful vintage dresser sets, including hair brushes and elegant clips on display in the front of the store. Service is as wonderfully discreet as the clothes.

Chelsea **917-408-0408**
34 Gainsvoort Street at 9th Avenue
NYC 10014 Tues-Sat 1-10, Sun 12-6

Shen

If you like a layer, or two, or three in your look, get yourself to Shen immediately! Sample their gossamer-weight chiffon pieces, stretch gabardine pants, jersey jackets with coordinating round neck tops, silk skirts, tunic tops, comfortable pants and sweaters. FYI: They make it a rule not to carry dresses. We don't know why.

Upper East Side **212-717-1185**
1005 Madison Avenue bet. 77/78th St.
NYC 10021 Mon-Fri 10-6:30, Sat 10-6

Shin Choi

Korean designer Shin Choi caters to women in search of chic basics at bridge prices with a simple and effective collection that includes sheath dresses, 3/4-length jackets, skirts, shirts and knits. Quality fabrics, clean lines and wearability define Choi's timeless and tasteful designs. Best are her white shirts.

SoHo **212-625-9202**
119 Mercer Street bet. Prince/Spring
NYC 10012 Mon-Sat 11-7

The Shirt Store

The stars of the Broadway hit Thoroughly Modern Millie got their stage shirts here, so why shouldn't you? At least you'll know it will last through a song-and-dance number (so

Shoe

important). Request off-the-rack, made-to-measure or custom. Each shirt is finely tailored in Sea Island cotton and reasonably priced from $50 to $250. Request any alteration, whether adding a pocket or shortening a sleeve. Custom shirts run from $125 to $240 with an eight-to-ten-week delivery. Ties, cufflinks and suspenders are also available. 1-800-buy-a-shirt www.shirtstore.com

Midtown East 212-557-8040
51 East 44th Street at Vanderbilt Ave.
NYC 10017 Mon-Fri 8-6:30, Sat 10-5

Lower Manhattan 212-797-8040
71 Broadway bet. Rector/Exchange
NYC 10006 Mon-Fri 7:30-6:30

Shoe

Men are particular fans of this store for LA designer Balouzin's "Cydwoq" collection, a line of deconstructed, handmade shoes that combine form, function and pure comfort. It also carries an assortment of select footwear labels with styles that include dainty mules, pumps, boots and sandals—for women, of course! Great Indian sandals also available. Complement your feet with Shoe's accessory collection of tote and fringed leather handbags, beaded evening purses and kidskin gloves in luscious colors.

NoLiTa 212-941-0205
197 Mulberry Street bet. Spring/Kenmare
NYC 10012 Mon-Sun 12-7

The Shoe Box

You'll find a great selection of popular shoe brands at this clean, unimposing shop. From mid-priced, unfussy, casual shoes by Via Spiga, Stuart Weitzman, Lilly Pulitzer and Giuseppe Zanotti to snappy dress-up numbers by Vera Wang, Casadei, D&G and Jimmy Choo, there is something for glam girls to…grandmothers.

Upper East Side 212-535-9615
1349 Third Avenue at 77th St.
NYC 10021 Mon-Fri 10-7:30, Sat 9:30-6, Sun 12-6

Shoofly

A stylish, well-priced footwear store for your small fry. Find styles with European labels like Aster, Mod 8, Minibel, Venetinni and Babybotte in sizes from newborn to size 9. Great accessories like wild-print tights, summer and winter hats, jewelry and cute beaded and faux-fur bags. www.shooflynyc.com

Upper West Side 212-580-4390
465 Amsterdam Avenue bet. 82/83rd St.
NYC 10024 Mon-Sat 11-7, Sun 12-6

TriBeCa 212-406-3270
42 Hudson Street bet. Duane/Thomas
NYC 10013 Mon-Sat 11-7, Sun 12-6

Silverado

Shop 👤
This tiny downtown boutique is too cool for school. Find flirty, unconventional looks like low-slung cords, hip-hugging jeans, cute skirts, T-shirts, separates and select vintage pieces. The bestselling labels include LA's Heza, Alice Roi, Mint, Jill Stuart, Milk Fed, Tracy Reese and Underglam underwear.

Lower East Side **212-375-0304**
105 Stanton at Ludlow
NYC 10002 Mon-Sun 12-7

Shop Noir 👤
Owner/designer Leeora Catalan sells spunky accessories that spell flamboyance. For six years famous fashionistas like Sarah Jessica Parker and Madonna have been sporting her lace-embossed fluorescent leather handbags, rhinestone-studded belts and edgy jewelry. Catalan's store has graffatti-esque and paparazzi-inspired portraits on leather bags, shoes, belts and T-shirts, as well as rhinestone brooches, pendants, cuff bracelets and crystal-studded items. Catalan will customize your mouse, cellphone or anything else with a rhinestone slogan or design.

NoLiTa **212-966-6868**
246 Mott Street bet. Prince/Houston
NYC 10012 Mon-Sat 11-7, Sun 12-6

Sigerson Morrison 👤
Sigerson Morrison sets the standard in downtown designer shoes with a sprightly range of heels and flats in a rainbow of colors (predominantly black and berry) that consistently have the fashion crowd in a dither. Although their shoes are highly fashionable, they are never seasonal (i.e they don't date—yes!). The phenomenal success of their shoe line inspired them to open a simple, chic accessories store just down the street.

NoLiTa **212-219-3893**
28 Prince Street bet. Mott/Elizabeth
NYC 10012 Mon-Sat 11-7, Sun 12-6

Sigerson Morrison 👤
...Down the street lies Sigerson Morrison's gorgeously fashionable and cunningly functional handbag store. Styles include ideal boxy day totes, retro make-up cases, triangular-shaped bags with metal handles, Seventies-style gym bags, large functional duffels, and weekender bags with removable compartments. Textures include leather, patent, suede, wool and corduroy. Prices run from $240 to $1,100. www.sigersonmorrison.com

NoLiTa **212-941-5404**
242 Mott Street bet. Prince/Houston
NYC 10012 Mon-Sat 11-7, Sun 12-6

Silverado 👤👤
Unsurprisingly, you'll find only leather here. Pants, jackets, shearling outerwear, Western boots, briefcases, handbags

and accessories are manufactured in lambskin, cowhide, leather and suede. Pay $500 for jackets and $550 for pants. Allow three to four weeks for custom made.

SoHo	**212-966-4470**
542 Broadway	bet. Spring/Prince
NYC 10012	Mon-Fri 11-8, Sat 11-9, Sun 11-8

Sisley

Benetton's top-of-the-line label, Sisley is packed with well-priced, up-to-date basics and fun pieces for a fashion fix. Find suits, dresses, pants, sweaters, tops and outerwear that give you a total look. Which, oddly, isn't nearly as saucy as their naughty advertising! Prices won't put a strain on your wallet. www.sisley.com

Upper West Side	**212-769-0121**
2308 Broadway	bet. 83/84th St.
NYC 10024	Mon-Sat 10-8, Sun 11-8
SoHo	**212-375-0538**
469 West Broadway	bet. Prince/Houston
NYC 10012	Mon-Sat 11-8, Sun 11-7

Skechers USA

This California-based company, born by the water in Manhattan Beach, sells easy, breezy footwear for the easy, breezy crowd. Choose from a selection of men's, women's and children's shoes loaded with hip-hop attitude, including utility rugged wear, casual basics, sport joggers and sneakers. 800-shoe-411 www.skechers.com

Upper West Side	**212-712-0539**
2169 Broadway	bet. 76/77th St.
NYC 10024	Mon-Sat 10-8, Sun 11-6
Midtown West	**646-473-0490**
140 West 34th Street	bet. 6/7th Ave.
NYC 10001	Mon-Sat 9-9, Sun 11-8
Flatiron	**212-627-9420**
150 Fifth Avenue	bet. 19/20th St.
NYC 10011	Mon-Sat 10-8, Sun 11-6
West Village	**212-253-5810**
55 West 8th Street	bet. 5/6th Ave.
NYC 10011	Mon-Thur 10-9, Fri & Sat 10-10
	Sun 11-7
SoHo	**212-431-8803**
530 Broadway	at Spring
NYC 10012	Mon-Fri 10:30-8:30, Sat 10:30-9
	Sun 10:30-8

Skella

This boutique sells feminine clothing for the 20-to-40 crowd, including gauzy separates and dresses, wedding dresses and custom order. And it's also the perfect destination for...bustle skirts. Check out Deborah Skella's modern take on the bustle, available in denim, linen, precious silk and cashmere. Prices start at $450 for a denim version and run to $2,000 for cashmere.

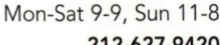

Lower East Side 212-505-0115
156 Orchard Street bet. Rivington/Stanton
NYC 10002 Tues-Sat 2-8, Sun 12-5

Sleek on Bleecker

One of the few West Village shops to sell trendy sportswear—such a relief for its hipster residents. There are pants, dresses, shirts, sweaters, T-shirts and jeans by hip domestic and imported labels like Seven, Paul & Joe, Urchin, See by Chloé, Kors, Milly, Vince and Rebecca Taylor. They also sell Sigerson Morrison shoes, right down the back of the store.

West Village 212-243-0284
361 Bleecker Street bet. W. 10th St./Charles
NYC 10014 Mon-Sat 12-8, Sun 12-6

Smaak

You need Smaak. Oh yes, you do. Smaak means good taste in Swedish and is also the name of this cool NoLiTa shop. Swedish-born owner Susannah Gaterud-Mack sells clothing by Scandinavian and Dutch designers making their premiere in New York. The list includes Filippa K—who is nicknamed the Scandinavian Calvin Klein due to her simple, clean lines. Also other items like chunky sweaters, quilted tops, classic bohemian long skirts and coats. Expect plenty of color and floral prints, great basics and clean, feminine lines. www.sma2k.com

NoLiTa 212-219-0504
219 Mulberry Street bet. Prince/Spring
NYC 10012 Tues & Wed 11-7, Thur-Sat 11-8, Sun 12-7

Small Change

A children's shop packed with casual basics, dress wear, outerwear and accessories from such labels as Cacharel, Sonia Rykiel, Lilli Gaufrette, Timberland, Chevignon and Petit Bateau. During the winter, shop their enormous outerwear selection for the perfect snowsuit, coat, hat or pair of gloves. Shoes by Start-Rite and Babybotte. From newborn to 14 years.

Upper East Side 212-772-6455
964 Lexington Avenue bet. 70/71st St.
NYC 10021 Mon-Fri 10-5:30, Sat 10-4:45

SoHo Baby

Dorothy Shu grew so frustrated buying clothes for her own baby, she decided to open her own store. SoHo Baby sells everything from layettes, casual clothing and special-occasion dress to flotation swimsuits, sleepwear, raincoats and accessories. Labels include Jean Bourget, Berlingot, Le Top, Kenzo, Baby Steps and Alphabets. Newborn to size 8. Reasonably priced.

NoLiTa 212-625-8538
247 Elizabeth Street bet. Houston/Prince
NYC 10012 Mon-Sat 11-7, Sun 12-6

SoHo Woman

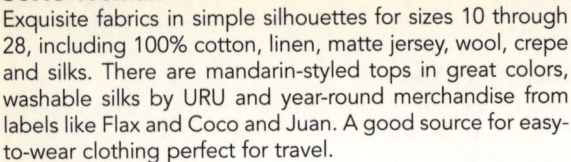

Exquisite fabrics in simple silhouettes for sizes 10 through 28, including 100% cotton, linen, matte jersey, wool, crepe and silks. There are mandarin-styled tops in great colors, washable silks by URU and year-round merchandise from labels like Flax and Coco and Juan. A good source for easy-to-wear clothing perfect for travel.

Midtown West 212-391-7263
32 West 40th Street bet. 5/6th Ave.
NYC 10018 Mon-Fri 11-7, Sat 12-5

Sonia Rykiel

French designer Sonia Rykiel's pieces will be chic until the end of time. Long known as the "Queen of Sweaters," the ultimate item from Rykiel would have to be her slinky black sweaters with colored stripes. Realizing the label's renewed appeal, Rykiel's daughter Natalie recently released a line called "Modern Vintage" which is reissued versions of Rykiel classics. Of course, the fashionistas went crazy. Swimwear and sarongs available in summer, but the primo accessory here are her handbags—a past hit, a leather shoulder bag covered in punky studs. www.soniarykiel.com

Upper East Side 212-396-3060
849 Madison Avenue bet. 70/71st St.
NYC 10021 Mon-Sat 10-6

Sorelle Firenze

This tiny yet charming neighborhood store is run by two Italian sisters, Barbara and Monica Abbatemaggio, and it's full of lace, sparkle and spirit. Mixing a collection of clothes from small, independent designers—like delicate satin slip tops by Lucy Barnes—with gorgeous cashmere sweaters imported from Italy and topping it off with delicate pieces that the sisters designed themselves, it's all about loving your clothes—and who could argue with that?

Tribeca 212-571-2720
139 1/2 Reade Street bet. Hudson/Greenwich
NYC 10013 Mon-Sat 1-7

Space Kiddets

Everything from soup to nuts in clothing for children from infants to teens. It's all about hip jeans, print lace dresses and Stevie's platform shoes from such labels as Naf Naf, Charlie Rocket, Diesel, Hollywood, Heart Tails and Fly Girls.

Flatiron 212-420-9878
46 East 21st Street bet. B'way/Park Ave. South
NYC 10010 Mon, Tues & Fri 10:30-6
Wed & Thur 10:30-7, Sat 10:30-5:30

Speedo Authentic Fitness

The official outfitter of the U.S. Olympic swim team also outfits the everyday sports enthusiast in its Authentic Fitness stores. Athletic apparel includes bike shorts, leggings, bra tops, sweatshirts, unitards, polar fleece outerwear and slick, functional one- and two-piece swimsuits. The quality is good and so are their prices. Swimwear runs from $19.99 to $39.99 for solids and $49.99 for prints. 800-577-3336 www.speedo.com

Upper West Side	**212-501-8140**
150 Columbus Avenue	bet. 66/67th St.
NYC 10023	Mon-Fri 9-9, Sat 10-9, Sun 11-7
Midtown East	**212-688-4595**
721 Lexington Avenue	at 58th St.
NYC 10022	Mon-Fri 9-9, Sat 10-8, Sun 10-6
Midtown East	**212-838-5988**
40 East 57th Street	bet. Park/Madison Ave.
NYC 10022	Mon-Fri 10-8, Sat 11-7, Sun 11-6
Midtown East	**212-682-3830**
90 Park Avenue (downstairs)	at 39th St.
NYC 10016	Mon-Fri 8-8, Sat 10-6, Sun 11-6
Fifth Avenue	**212-768-7737**
500 Fifth Avenue	at 42nd St.
NYC 10110	Mon-Fri 8-8, Sat 10-8, Sun 11-6
NoHo	**212-260-2151**
753 Broadway	at 8th St.
NYC 10003	Mon-Sat 10-9, Sun 11-6

Sports Authority

Sports Authority caters to everyone's sports needs with apparel and equipment for skiing, skating, rollerblading, biking, tennis and football. Pump yourself up big-time with state-of-the-art body-building equipment and fitness machines. www.sportsauthority.com

Midtown East	**212-355-9725**
845 Third Avenue	at 51st St.
NYC 10022	Mon-Fri 8:30-8, Sat 10-7, Sun 11-6
Midtown West	**212-355-6430**
57 West 57th Street	at 6th Ave.
NYC 10019	Mon-Fri 9-8, Sat 10-7, Sun 11-6
Chelsea	**212-929-8971**
636 Sixth Avenue	at 19th St.
NYC 10001	Mon-Fri 10-8, Sat 10-7, Sun 11-6

Spring Flowers

A good children's alternative to Bonpoint. Here you'll find both casual and fancy European clothing at attractive prices, including Cacharel print dresses, outfits by Petit Bateau and smocked dresses by Sophie Dess at a reasonable $100. From newborn to size 10. Imported shoes up to age 8.

Upper East Side	**212-717-8182**
905 Madison Avenue	bet. 72/73rd St.
NYC 10021	Mon-Sat 10-6, Sun 11-6
Upper East Side	**212-758-2669**
1050 Third Avenue	at 62nd St.
NYC 10021	Mon-Sat 10-6, Sun 11-6

Stackhouse

One of the better streetwear stores on this streetwear block of Lafayette Street, Stackhouse has an easy access selection of hip clothes for, er, hip-hoppers. A cool selection of 2K tees line the wall, while the racks are stuffed with Blue Marlin tops, Hummel hoodies and Ben Sherman shirts. There is also the requisite selection of bandannas (with Andy Warhol prints) and sneakers—also from Ben Sherman and Etnies, to boot. The coolest new addition, though are Howe jeans, from former Sean John accessory designer Jade Howe, "a mix between cowboy punk and English-country-gentleman rockstar." Got it?

SoHo
282 Lafayette Street
NYC 10012

212-925-6931
bet. Prince/Houston
Mon-Fri 12-7.30
Sat 11.30-7.30, Sun 12-6.30

Stanley

There are three types of women who shop at Stanley: downtown fashionistas after its signature edgy looks, uptown girls looking for a bit of the avant-garde... and dog lovers who pop in to play with owner Robin Brouillette's dog Simba. Stanley's in-house line (fab long halter dresses and pretty silk tops) sits alongside select pieces by high concept Los Angeles designers like Ina Cilaye and Edwardian-inspired pieces by stylist-turned-designer Magda Berliner. Accessories include Lola Ehrlich hats and jewelry. Also check out the cool collection of vintage Balenciaga scarves.

Lower East Side
169 Ludlow Street
NYC 10002

212-254-7055
bet. Houston/Stanton
Tues-Sat 12-8, Sun 12-7

Stella McCartney

Stella McCartney shot out of nowhere to helm French label Chloé five years ago, and quickly quintupled its sales with her cheeky rock'n'roll aesthetic—remember those naughty slogan T-shirts and diamante sunglasses? Following backing by the Gucci Group, Stella is going it alone with her signature label that focuses on her strengths in tailoring (Chloé suits were a hit), with a hint of knowing raunchiness. She still loves a slogan T-shirt, but has added more subtle pieces like knits and slouchy jackets. In keeping with the staunch vegetarian's principles, the store also sells a range of accessories made from non-leather materials—which may seem ironic when you consider the store lies in a neighborhood so closely associated with meat...

Chelsea
429 West 14th Street
NYC 10014

212-255-1556
bet. 9th/Washington
Mon-Sat 11-7, Sun 12-6

Stephane Kelian

An elite footwear designer who made his glossy reputation in the 80's, Stephane Kelian is the master of hand-woven leather shoes. His slick collection includes platforms, wedges, boots, open-toed slings, bi-colored woven pumps, sandals and loafers. Best bets: stretch leather knee-length boots, sandals and perfect black stilettos. His comfort line, a sneaker/loafer hybrid, is available in textured leathers and suedes. He has also expanded his men's line. Accessories include handbags.

Upper East Side	**212-980-1919**
717 Madison Avenue	bet. 63/64th St.
NYC 10021	Mon-Sat 10-6, Thur 10-7, Sun 12-5
SoHo	**212-925-3077**
158 Mercer	bet. Houston/Prince
NYC 10012	Mon-Sat 11-7, Sun 12-6

☆ Steven Alan

Steven Alan carries progressive fashion at its best—for women who love edgy, up'n'coming designers. The store carries the coolest labels around, like Katayone Adeli, Earl, Milk Fed, Rubinchapelle, Alice Roi, Lauren Moffat, A.P.C, United Bamboo, Paul & Joe, 6 by Martin Margiela and the Steven Alan house label. It's a serious fashion destination for serious fashion lovers—or not so serious: check out their naughty slogan tanks.

SoHo (W)	**212-334-6354**
60 Wooster Street	bet. Broome/Spring
NYC 10012	Mon-Sat 11-7, Sun 12-7
TriBeCa	**212-343-0692**
103 Franklin Street	bet. W. B'way/Church
NYC 10013	Mon-Sat 11-7, Thur 12-10, Sun 1-6

Steven Stolman

Designer Steven Stolman's signature is feminine, colorful and ever-so-preppy clothing made from fine decorative fabrics from design houses like Scalamandre and Clarence House. His collection includes piqué sundresses, toile pants, chinoiserie shifts and monochromatic luxury separates like cashmere twin sets that work perfectly with his evening looks like taffeta ball skirts, silk crêpe trousers and satin dance skirts. Perfect for the Palm Beach party circuit… www.stevenstolman.com

Upper East Side	**212-249-5050**
22 East 72nd Street, #4A	bet. Madison/5th Ave.
NYC 10021	Mon-Fri 10-6, Sat 11-5

Steve Madden

Over-the-top, right-price shoes for young hipsters in search of the latest trends. If Madden is going to feature, say, leopard one season, he'll do 10 times more of it than anyone else. The collection includes platform-based styles like open-backed mules, platform boots, bumped-toe mary-janes, high wooden-stacked sandals—a summer staple—and sneakers. 800-747-6233 www.stevemadden.com

St. John

Upper East Side   **212-426-0538**
150 East 86th Street   bet. Lex./3rd Ave.
NYC 10028   Mon-Fri 11-8,
Sat 11:30-8:30, Sun 11-7

Upper West Side   **212-799-4221**
2315 Broadway   at 84th St.
NYC 10024   Mon-Thur 11-8
Fri & Sat 11-8:30, Sun 11-7:30

Midtown West   **212-736-3283**
45 West 34th Street   bet. 5/6th Ave
NYC 10001   Mon-Fri 10-9, Sat 10-9:30, Sun 10-6

SoHo   **212-343-1800**
540 Broadway   bet. Prince/Spring
NYC 10012   Mon-Thur. 11-8
Fri & Sat 11-8:30, Sun 11-7:30

Chelsea   **212-989-1120**
84 Seventh Avenue   bet. 15/16th St.
NYC 10011   Mon-Sat 11-8, Sun 12-7

St. John

Power dressing lives on and on at St John. This knitwear company sells head-to-toe outfits perfect for executives, ladies-who-lunch, and more than a few politicians. It's not shy of color and other decorative touches like shiny buttons, silk flowers, paillettes and serious sequins. St. John's signature "Santana" fabric is wrinkle resistant and ideal for travel. Looks include suits and elegant chiffon evening pants, classic black jackets paired with colorful underpinnings, sporty leathers and long knit gowns dusted with crystals and sequins. Also accessories like shoes, handbags, belts, jewelry and fragrances. Sizes from 2 to 14. Suits start at $1,200 and evening couture $3,000.

Fifth Avenue   **212-755-5252**
665 Fifth Avenue   at 53rd St.
NYC 10022   Mon-Sat 10-7, Sun 11-6

The Stork Club

Shopping at this small store is like going back in time. It's complete with old pedal cars and antique toys and packed with whimsical children's clothing, including hand-loomed sweaters, dresses in vintage fabrics, hand-knit tops, T-shirts, hats and accessories. Wicker baskets, complete with three-piece baby sets (chenille blanket, hat, and toy), make wonderful baby shower gifts.

SoHo   **212-505-1927**
142 Sullivan Street   bet. Prince/Houston
NYC 10012   Mon-Sat 11-7, Sun 12-6

Stuart Weitzman

Women shop at this sensible store knowing that Weitzman has a shoe for every foot, small or large (size 2 to 12), narrow or wide (from AAAA to C). Styles run from casual slip-on mules, wood-stacked heel slides and sporty golf shoes to dress pumps, spindly boots (OK, not so sensible), crystal sandals and made-to-order rhinestone pumps. Choose from over 40 bridal shoes. Handbags also available. www.stuartweitzman.com

Midtown East 212-750-2555
625 Madison Avenue bet. 58/59th St.
NYC 10022 Mon-Fri 10-6:30, Sat 10-6, Sun 12-5

Stubbs & Wootton

Perhaps it's because so many of his clients are Manhattan, Palm Beach and Hamptons socialites that owner Percy Steinhart says his shoes "socialize—and they spectate, they dance and they lounge." His collection features slippers, mules and slides in patterned needlepoints, velvets and European fabrics, often with amusing imprints like sharks, golf balls... and the odd dancing devil. Custom order also available, as well as coordinating handbags and ribbon belts. 877-4-Stubbs www.stubbsandwootton.com

Upper East Side 212-249-5200
22 East 72nd Street, Suite 2A bet. Madison/5th Ave
NYC 10021 Mon-Thur 10-6, Fri 10-5, Sat 11-5

Studio 109

Rock'n'roll! That's the Studio 109 look, which has attracted big name fans like Keith Richards (and he knows his leathers) and Lauryn Hill. Designer Patricia Adams works with a variety of skins, so she's the woman to see whether you're in the market for a saucy leather bra top, a pair of elk or deerskin pants, a python jacket or a suede skirt. Choose from her book of swatches and expect a two-to-three-week delivery time. Custom leather pants start at $1,700, jackets at $1,200, and skirts at $750. www.studio109.com

East Village 212-420-0077
115 St. Mark's Place bet. 1st/Ave. A
NYC 10009 Mon-Sun 12-8

Stüssy

In 1980, Sean Stüssy was surfing California's Laguna Beach and selling his laidback T-shirts to his surf buddies. Over 20 years later he runs an empire that covers the globe, selling his streety, underground clothing like checked shirts, T-shirts, sweatshirts and caps, all covered with Stüssy's scrawling signature logo. Head to this coolly minimal store—complete with graffiti wall—and also check out Head Porter's line of industrial-strength nylon bags including backpacks, messenger bags, and briefcases. www.stussy.com

SoHo 212-995-8787
140 Wooster bet. Houston/Prince
NYC 10012 Mon-Wed 12-7, Thur.-Sat 11-7, Sun 12-6

Sunrise Ruby

Store owner Allison Furman Norris travels far and wide—from Hollywood film sets to Parisian flea markets—for her collection of secondhand clothing, including cutting-edge designers, great vintage items and select consignment pieces at bargain hunter prices. The selection covers such coveted luxe labels as Prada, Gaultier and Anna Sui. She also sells reliably hip ready-to-wear like Juicy Couture, Seven and the essential Cosabella thongs.

TriBeCa   **212-791-7735**
141 Reade Street   bet. Greenwich/Hudson
NYC 10013   Mon-Sat 12-7 by appointment

Super Runners Shop
The serious runner shops here for shoes, clothing and accessories from brand names like Nike, New Balance, Asics, Adidas, In Sport and Moving Comfort. The sales staff are all super runners, too, so you'll get firsthand advice during your selection.   www.super-runners.com

Upper East Side   **212-369-6010**
1337 Lexington Avenue   at 89th St.
NYC 10028   Mon-Fri 10-7, Thur 10-9
    Sat 10-6, Sun, 12-5

Upper East Side   **212-249-2133**
1244 Third Avenue   bet. 71/72nd St.
NYC 10021   Mon-Fri 10-7, Thur 10-9
    Sat 10-6, Sun 12-5

Upper West Side   **212-787-7665**
360 Amsterdam Avenue   bet. 77/78th St.
NYC 10024   Mon-Fri 10-7, Thur 10-9
    Sat 10-6, Sun 11-5

Supreme
Thumping hip-hop plays at this extremely edgy Japanese streetwear store, that carries skater-favorite slogan tees, the requisite baggy jeans (both under the Supreme label), and peculiar skateboards with images from "The Last Supper" printed on the bottom. Good for your younger brother—or your DJ friend…

NoLiTa   **212-966-7799**
274 Lafayette Street   bet. Prince/Houston
NYC 10012   Mon-Sat 12-7, Sun 12-6

Suzanne Couture Millinery
Squeeze into this tiny millinery shop stuffed with every hat imaginable. An excellent source for fancy dress or special occasion hats, like her natural straw "Cannes" hats. If you're off to the Saratoga races, visit Suzanne for a memorable topper. Her bridal range is also excellent.

Upper East Side   **212-593-3232**
27 East 61st Street   bet. Madison/Park Ave.
NYC 10021   Mon-Sat 11-6

Sylvia Heisel
One reason designer Sylvia Heisel's customers are so devoted is that they can custom order just about anything. Custom-made clothing comes in over 40 fabric samples and with a super speedy two-week delivery. Off-the rack

merchandise includes luxury sportswear, eveningwear and accessories that straddle the divide between classy and casual. Special occasion designs are Heisel's forte.

SoHo   **646-654-6768**
131 Thompson Street   bet. Houston/Prince
NYC 10012   Mon-Sat 11-7, Sun 12-6

Tani

Long an unassuming fixture on the Upper West Side, Tani had an interior facelift and the result is a clean, bright store that effectively showcases a great, colorful selection of shoes. There's everything from chunky and funky to sleek and feminine from such labels as Robert Clergerie, Cynthia Rowley, Via Spiga, BCBG, Freelance, Lisa Nading and more.

Upper West Side   **212-873-4361**
2020 Broadway   bet. 69/70th St.
NYC 10023   Mon-Sat 10-8, Sun 12-7

T. Anthony

In 1946 T. Anthony's collection of sophisticated luggage catered to the world's social elite, including the Duke and Duchess of Windsor. The tradition continues today with briefcases, handbags, small leathergoods, desk sets, photo albums, jewelry boxes, and, of course, its signature leather and canvas luggage. Up there in the prestige stakes with the estimable Louis Vuitton. 888-722-2406 www.tanthony.com

Midtown East   **212-750-9797**
445 Park Avenue   at 56th St.
NYC 10022   Mon-Fri 9:30-6, Sat 10-6

☆ Takashimaya

Takashimaya is a clean, minimalist piece of Tokyo on Fifth Avenue. The first floor is home to a floral boutique, as well as the Arena Gallery, a revolving showcase of art and design exhibitions. The next levels include a travel boutique selling everything from totes and carry-ons to rainwear and travel journals, Takashimaya's Home Collection of unique tabletop items and giftware, and accessories. The fifth level showcases sumptuous essentials for bed, bath and baby, while the sixth floor is home to an unrivalled beauty and skin care department featuring an array of treatments and essences from around the world. Hot news is the new department called Now, which carries a range of accessories and ready-to-wear from edgy European designers (recommended: the cool basics from Madame a Paris). Fashion fatigued? Head downstairs to the Tea Box, which features a light and delicious Japanese menu.

Fifth Avenue   **212-350-0100**
693 Fifth Avenue   bet. 54/55th St.
NYC 10022   Mon-Sat 10-7

Talbots

From their mail-order business to their nationwide chain of stores, Talbots is an affordable and reliable source for classic career and casual clothing. Discover the head-to-toe essentials you need to build a conservative and sensible wardrobe—but not a ballgown! Misses and petite sizes also available. Shoes and accessories complete the assortment. 800-992-9010 www.talbots.com

Upper East Side 212-988-8585
1251 Third Avenue at 72nd St.
NYC 10021 Mon-Fri 10-8, Sat 10-7, Sun 12-6

Upper West Side 212-875-8754
2289-2291 Broadway bet. 82/83rd St.
NYC 10024 Mon-Sat 10-9, Sun 12-6

Midtown East 212-838-8811
525 Madison Avenue bet. 53/54th St.
NYC 10022 Mon-Fri 10-7, Sat 10-6, Sun 12-5

Lower Manhattan 212-425-0166
189-191 Front Street at South Street Seaport
NYC 10038 Mon-Sat 10-9, Sun 11-8

Talbots Kids
Talbots Kids caters to your wee one's everyday needs. Unlike its conservative women's collection, children's looks are pure fun, including pants, dresses, blazers, ties, skirts, dress shirts, T-shirts, sweatshirts, sleepwear and even underwear. And their prices aren't too bad either... 800-992-9010 www.talbots.com

Upper East Side 212-570-1630
1523 Second Avenue at 79th St.
NYC 10021 Mon-Sat 9-7, Thur 9:30-8, Sun 12-5

Tanino Crisci
For the customer seeking conservative handmade shoes, from well-crafted riding boots and classic wing-tipped lace-ups to casual loafers. Each shoe is meticulously crafted in luxury leathers, including alligator pumps and loafers for women. Expect to pay anywhere from $430 to $2,200. Jackets, ties, belts and wallets also available.

Upper East Side 212-535-1014
795 Madison Avenue bet. 67/68th St.
NYC 10021 Mon-Sat 10-6

Tardini
For three generations, the Tardini family has been dedicated to manufacturing modern handbags, belts, shoes and small leathergoods in a variety of leathers, exotic skins and high-tech fabrics. The most striking characteristic of their first flagship is an alligator skin mosaic that slithers and weaves from floor to ceiling. Standouts in the women' collection are sexy, feminine, stiletto-heeled shoes and great oversized bags, while gentlemen with a spare $2,000 can slip into a great pair of alligator loafers. New to the store is a sexy collection of leather clothing by American designer Anton. www.tardini.com

SoHo 212-253-7692
142 Wooster Street bet. Houston/Prince
NYC 10012 Mon-Sat 11-7, Sun 12-6

Tartine et Chocolat

Designer Catherine Painvin does a brilliant job at turning out elegantly tailored children's clothing, that children actually want to wear. Mothers-to-be can shop Tartine et Chocolat's signature layette collection featuring adorable onezies, as well as linens, bedroom furniture and snugly upholstered strollers. Girls will be girls in Painvin's collection of smocked dresses, while boys will be boys in sporty basics like sturdy cords and tweedy checks. Pay $116 for dresses, $70 for boy's shirts and $80 for onezies. In addition, find shoes and accessories that will coordinate with all their outfits. From newborn to 10 years.

Upper East Side   212-717-2112
1047 Madison Avenue   at 80th St.
NYC 10021   Mon-Sat 10-7, Sun 12-5

Midtown East   212-508-0090
475 Park Avenue   bet. 57/58th St.
NYC 10022   Mon-Sat 10-7, Sun 12-5

Tatiana Resale Boutique

As the name suggests, Tatiana peddles new and slightly used designer clothing, accessories and shoes at rock-bottom prices. Search for an Armani pantsuit, a Dolce & Gabbana frock, a Fendi sweater, a pair of Prada flats or an Hermès handbag, all at fabulous prices. But timing, of course, is everything.

Upper East Side   212-717-7684
860 Lexington Avenue, 2nd Fl.   bet. 64/65th St.
NYC 10021   Mon-Fri 11-7, Sat 11-6, Sun 12-5

Ted Baker London

Ted Baker shirts are a favorite of youthful British guys everywhere who swear by their relaxed cut and cool colors. Some have been known to claim that donning a Ted Baker shirt is like "wearing lingerie" (um, not that they would know, we hope). Manufactured in high-tech fabrics, these silky, soft shirts come long and short-sleeved in adventurous shades like lavender, pink and yellow. Contemporary-styled suits, knitwear and pants are also available. Baker's "Endurance" line includes wrinkle-free wool suits ideal for travel, mosquito-repellant shirts, as well as sun-resistant and anti-stain shirts.

SoHo   212-343-8989
107 Grand Street   bet. Mercer/B'way
NYC 10012   Mon-Sat 11:30-7, Sun 12-6

Tehen

Owned by one of France's largest textile companies, Tehen's forte is gorgeous fabrics and textures, from fluid wovens to ethnic prints. This chic wooden-walled store features a color-coordinated collection in no-nonsense shapes, including easy-wearing pants, jackets, skirts, oversized sweaters and tops. Also look out for pretty shell necklaces and belts.

Terra Plana

SoHo
91 Greene Street
NYC 10012

212-925-4788
bet. Prince/Spring
Mon-Sat 11-7, Sun 12-6

Terra Plana
Choose from a selection of sporty, casual shoes including lace-up boots, oxfords and step-ins in standard black and brown leathers and suedes. Footwear with a modern edge. Best for men. www.terraplana.com

NoLiTa
260 Elizabeth Street
NYC 10012

212-274-9000
bet. Houston/Prince
Tues-Sat 12-7, Sun 12-6

TG-170
TG-170's owner Terri Gillis is a fashion pioneer, launching the careers of many extremely cool designers from this sweet-smelling boutique. Her cutting edge stock features labels like Built by Wendy, United Bamboo, Ulla Johnson, Lauren Moffat, Paul & Joe and Karen Walker. In short, everything for the hipster girl from low-rider pants, cute striped tops and funky dresses. Great for an instant fashion fix, in New York's grooviest new neighborhood. www.tg170.com

Lower East Side
170 Ludlow Street
NYC 10002

212-995-8660
bet. Houston/Stanton
Mon-Sun 12-8

☆ 37 = 1
Not since Agent Provocateur hit the lingerie scene in the Nineties has there been such a sexy, kill for it label that gets girls hot under the collar—and doubtless, their poor boyfriends too. Not that 37 = 1, the brainchild of designer Jean Yu, is just lingerie, it's more like a couture atelier in the Vionnet mold. And although Yu's chic made-to-measure pieces and garter belts are worth the trip alone (lingerie here has no elastic and is made from the most delicate fabrics, secured with subtle hooks), she also dreams up beautifully constructed silk dresses with a slightly decadent Twenties bent. In a word: extraordinary.

SoHo
37 Crosby Street
NYC 10012

212-226-0067
bet. Grand/Broome
Wed-Sun 1-7

Thomas Pink
Not every shirt is pink at Thomas Pink, thankfully! They are, however, very elegant indeed. This LVMH-owned company occupies a spacious store filled with its extraordinarily colorful selection of luxury shirts and ties. Find ready-made shirts in quality fabrics, traditional British tailoring and wonderful patterns, with prices starting at $125. Pay $10 for sleeve alterations and $12 for monogramming. Accessories include ties, cashmere sweaters, cufflinks, suspenders, pocket squares and scarves. 888-336-1192 www.thomaspink.co.uk

Timberland

Midtown East   **212-838-1928**
520 Madison Avenue   bet. 53/54th St.
NYC 10022   Mon-Fri 10-7, Thur 10-8
Sat 10-6, Sun 12-6

Midtown West   **212-840-9663**
1155 Sixth Avenue   at 44th St.
NYC 10036   Mon-Fri 10-7, Thur 10-8
Sat 10-6, Sun 12-5

Thread

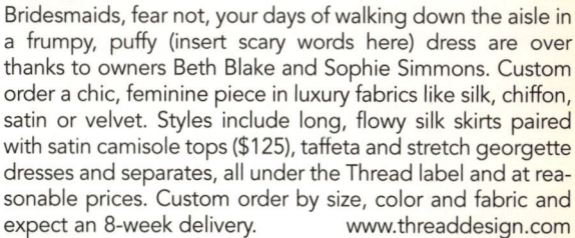

Bridesmaids, fear not, your days of walking down the aisle in a frumpy, puffy (insert scary words here) dress are over thanks to owners Beth Blake and Sophie Simmons. Custom order a chic, feminine piece in luxury fabrics like silk, chiffon, satin or velvet. Styles include long, flowy silk skirts paired with satin camisole tops ($125), taffeta and stretch georgette dresses and separates, all under the Thread label and at reasonable prices. Custom order by size, color and fabric and expect an 8-week delivery.   www.threaddesign.com

Chelsea   **212-414-8844**
408 West 15th Street, 4th Floor   bet. 9/10th Ave.
NYC 10011   Wed-Sat 10-7 by appointment only

Tibet Arts & Crafts

This tiny boutique encapsulates the distinctive charm of Tibetan style. Best pieces include raw silk shirts at $75 (a favorite of actress Cameron Diaz), reversible pashmina scarves and shawls in dazzling color assortments, antique patched and brocade bags at a mere $12, raw and patterned silk shawls, traditional ceremonial hats and jewelry. Best bet is the pashmina shawls—over-exposed in fashion but still fabulous for travelling.   www.tibetanstore.com

SoHo   **212-529-4344**
144 Sullivan Street   bet. Houston/Prince
NYC 10012   Mon-Sun 11-8

West Village   **212-260-5880**
197 Bleecker Street   bet. MacDougal/6th Ave.
NYC 10012   Mon-Fri 11-9, Sat & Sun 11-10

Tibet Bazaar

A heady whiff of incense leads you into this specialty boutique featuring clothing and accessories direct from the Himalayas. Select from traditional silk wrap skirts and mandarin-styled tops manufactured in shantung silks, brocade hats with fur trim, plain or beaded cashmere and wool shawls from India and a collection of pashmina wraps priced at $160.

Upper West Side   **212-595-8487**
473 Amsterdam Avenue   bet. 82/83rd St.
NYC 10024   Mon-Sun 11-7

Timberland

Timberland is a now-classic label in outdoor footwear, apparel and accessories that are all guaranteed to withstand the rigors of time while providing excellent comfort. Styles run from casual shoes to rugged boots and include hiking boots, driving moccasins, boating shoes and weatherbucks. Men's outdoor apparel also available. Children's from size 5 toddler and up.   800-445-5545   www.timberland.com

Upper East Side — 212-754-0434
709 Madison Avenue — at 63rd St.
NYC 10021 — Mon-Fri 10-7, Sat 10-6, Sun 12-6

Timtoum
Owner Erika Lively (and she is) carries everything from old records (at her Supersonic Record Market) to clothing made out of vintage fabrics, including her own label Go-Global, to real vintage pieces at this old-school-cool Lower East Side store. Check out her unusual bag designs made of Jeep-top fabric in fun shapes with handy side-pocket compartments—and buy a funk CD while you're at it.   www.timtoum.com

Lower East Side — 212-780-0456
179 Orchard Street — bet. Houston/Stanton
NYC 10002 — Mon-Sun 1-8

Tip Top Kids
This Upper West Side children's shoe store will have your kids in tip-top shape for summer camp and back-to-school. Find trendy looks, everyday casual shoes and sneakers by labels like Stevies, Ecco, Nike, Stride Rite and Skechers. From newborn to size 6.

Upper West Side — 212-874-1004
155 West 72nd Street — bet. B'way/Columbus Ave.
NYC 10023 — Mon-Sat 9:30-6:45, Sun 12-5

TJ Maxx
Off-price merchandise for the entire family, as well as a large selection of accessories for home, bed and bath. If you're lucky, you might find a designer name like Polo, DKNY or Yves Saint Laurent.   www.tjmaxx.com

Chelsea — 212-229-0875
620 Sixth Avenue — bet. 18/19th St.
NYC 10011 — Mon-Sat 9:30-9, Sun 11-7

Today's Man
A stop for value-priced menswear, including business attire, sportswear, casual wear, shoes and even underwear. Suit prices run from $199 to $400 and you may even come across styles from Hugo Boss, Canali or Missoni as well as the Today's Man private label.   800-950-7848
www.todaysman.com

Fifth Avenue — 212-557-3111
529 Fifth Avenue — at 44th St.
NYC 10017 — Mon-Fri 9-7, Sat 9-6, Sun 12-5

Chelsea — 212-924-0200
625 Sixth Avenue — bet. 18/19th St.
NYC 10011 — Mon-Sat 9:30-9, Sun 11-7

Tod's ♂♀

Tod's shoes are cult amongst glamorous Hollywood actresses and society types who swear by the signature "pebble" driving shoes—in a rainbow of colors—priced at $295. Other guaranteed chic styles include smart-looking mules, classic loafers, stylish pumps and sexy black boots with contrast heels. The status symbol in handbags continues to be Tod's structured leather D bag. Pay up to $1,500 for one of these calfskin beauties. Sportier looks include the Tod's "Miky," a deconstructed shoulder bag priced at $990.   800-457-TODS www.tods.com

Midtown East   **212-644-5945**
650 Madison Avenue   bet. 59/60th St.
NYC 10022   Mon-Sat 10-6, Thur 10-7, Sun 12-5

Toga Bike Shop ♂♀♂

Voted one of the top 100 bicycle shops in the country, Toga is the oldest and largest cycling retailer in New York with bikes by Cannondale, Bianchi, Specialized, Lite-speed and Santa Cruz as well as a good selection of accessories. Its specialty: designing men's and women's saddles for ultimate comfort and fit. Repair classes and bike rentals at $30 per day also available.

Upper West Side   **212-799-9625**
110 West End Avenue   at 64th St.
NYC 10023   Mon-Fri 11-7, Thur 11-8
                    Sat 10-6, Sun 11-6

Togs ♀

Urban streetwear and Euro chic are happily married in Togs' collection of imported Italian clothing. Contemporary separates, tops, knitwear, leather pants, and a large selection of jeans are all surprisingly affordable. Low key labels include Anima, Cristina Gavioli, Blu Sand and Esempio. Perfect for resort.

SoHo   **212-237-1882**
68 Spring Street   bet. Lafayette/Crosby
NYC 10012   Mon-Sat 11-8, Sun 11-7

Tokio 7 ♂♀

Don't let his consignment shop's dingy interior deter you, because here you will find a collection of labels priced according to designer popularity, style and, of course, condition. On a good day you might come across a $200 Yohji Yamamoto suit or a pair of $120 Helmut Lang pants, as well as items by Gaultier, Paul Smith or Betsey Johnson. It's hip, hand-me-down clothing in fair condition. www.tokio7.com

East Village   **212-353-8443**
64 East 7th Street   bet. 1st/2nd Ave.
NYC 10003   Mon-Sun 12-8:30

Tokyo Joe ♂♀

A cramped, overstocked consignment shop featuring hip designer labels at accessible prices. The merchandise changes each day so scoop something up when you see it, because it ain't gonna be there tomorrow. It offers designer clothing, shoes, bags and accessories by labels like Gucci, Marc Jacobs, Prada, Comme des Garçons, Miu Miu and Donna Karan. Items are generally in good condition and the prices can't be beat. Current season shoes from top designers have been known to turn up, worn only once...

East Village   212-473-0724
334 East 11th Street   bet. 1st/2nd Ave.
NYC 10003   Mon-Sun 12-9

Midtown East   212-532-3605
240 East 28th Street   bet. 2/3rd Ave.
NYC 10016   Mon-Sat 11-7:30

Tommy Hilfiger

Welcome to Tommy World, at this three floor, 11,000 sq. ft. specialty store catering to both sexes—from preppies to rappers. Known for his quintessential all-American designs, Hilfiger's strength is classic sportswear with a twist, including his signature red, white, and blue logo-a-go-go'd pieces. The store, catering to the SoHo hipster crowd, will also carry select vintage pieces and licensed products. "SoHo is the place where you get the real Tommy customer—it's youth, international, global," they say. See, Tommy World.   800-888-8802 ext.1180

SoHo   917-237-1902
372 West Broadway   bet. Spring/Broome
NYC 10012   Mon-Sat 11-7, Sun 12-6

Toto

It's a world of gorgeous Indian and ethnic shawls in this low-key neighborhood store, where wedding guests particularly can find that perfect embroidered pashmina to wear over their festive frock. The handwork in some of the pieces is stunning, while more low-key types will find a large selection of block colored wraps and simple knitwear.   www.totopashmina.com

Upper East Side   212-288-7171
870 Lexington Avenue   at 65th St.
NYC 10021   Mon-Sat 10-7

Tracey Tooker Hats

Tracey Tooker hats have crowned the heads of power-players like Senator Hillary Clinton. With stores in Manhattan, Southampton and Palm Beach, Tooker turns out chic toppers that go from a day at the beach to a day at the races. This tiny store is filled with handmade hats in fleece, fur, felt and straw—and accessorized with trimmings like feathers, silk flowers and beautiful ribbons.

Upper East Side   212-472-9603
1211 Lexington Avenue   at 82nd St.
NYC 10028   Mon-Sat 11-7, Sun 12-5

Triple Five Soul

Tracy Feith

Surf dude turned designer Tracy Feith is very, very smart. Not only does he know what the girls want to wear, he knows what their boyfriends want them to wear too. His jewel colored clothes are a riot of bold prints and feminine flounces—unbelievably gorgeous are his strapless patchwork floral dresses that are the ultimate in haute hippy-on-holiday chic.

NoLiTa 212-334-3097
209 Mulberry Street bet. Spring/Kenmare
NYC 10012 Mon-Sat 11-7, Sun 12-7

Training Camp

"Footwear is my addiction...the only thing I like more than footwear is my wife," owner Udi Avshalom says. Now that is love! Training Camp followers like P. Diddy shop here for the latest in brand name sneakers, including Nike Air Jordans and Bo Jacksons, and streety looks by Avirex, Phat Farm and the cool Aussie import Royal Elastics. Prices run from $30 to $160. www.trainingcamponline.com

Midtown West 212-840-7842
25 West 45th Street bet. 5/6th Ave.
NYC 10036 Mon-Sat 9-7:30, Sun 10-6:30

Midtown West 212-921-4430
1079 Sixth Avenue at 41st St.
NYC 10036 Mon-Sat 9-7:30, Sun 10-6:30

Transfer International

A consignment shop for clever girls in search of designer looks at reasonable prices. Labels include Gucci, Prada, Hermès, Miu Miu and Chanel. Some outfits have never even been worn—yes!

SoHo 212-355-4230
594 Broadway bet. Prince/Houston
NYC 10012 Tues-Sun 1-8 and by appointment

TriBeCa Luggage & Leather

There is, in fact, very little luggage here, just a fabulous selection of handbags that includes straw totes, leather everyday bags, crocheted and beaded pieces, knapsacks, messenger bags, briefcases, weekend and travel bags and carry-on luggage. Labels include Longchamp, Rafé, Francesco Biasia, Matt Murphy, Kazuyo Nakano and Diesel. Prices run from $100 to $440. Wallets, toilet kits, photo albums and umbrellas complete the assortment.

TriBeCa 212-343-8159
90 Hudson Street at Harrison
NYC 10013 Mon-Fri 10-7:30, Sat 11-6, Sun 12-5

Triple Five Soul

Streetier-than-street, Triple Five Soul dominates this block, that is home to a number of, you guessed it, streetwear stores. Dangling from cool metal hangers that extend from the ceiling, the casual clothing is heavy on logos—T-shirts, terry tank tops, jeans, "Brooklyn" embossed hoodies, flip flops, watches, even record cases (for wannabe DJs). This is hip-hop wear extraordinaire.

NoLiTa
290 Lafayette Street
NYC 10012

212-431-2404
bet. Houston/Prince
Mon-Sat 11-7.30, Sun 12-7

Tristan & America

A Canadian import that caters to the young professional in search of career and casual clothing at reasonable prices. Styles are simple, classic and sporty and include an ample selection of suits. Pay $140 to $200 for men's suits, while women's jackets run $100-$150 and skirts average $58.

Midtown West
1230 Sixth Avenue
NYC 10020

212-246-2354
at 49th St.
Mon-Sat 9-8, Sun 12-6

☆ Tse Cashmere

There's a revolution going on at Tse. The luxe label best known for its cashmere—and a brief design stint by London conceptualist Hussein Chalayan—is getting the Richard Chai treatment. Chai, who until September 2001 was Design Director at Marc Jacobs, is responsible for reinventing the Tse brand. This means more than just sweaters—Chai is designing a full collection of "thought provoking" clothes in muted colors, all possessing a cool, melancholy chic. Chai is the man to watch right now, so get down to the store and check out his master plan. Also, the younger line, Tsesay, a "mixed up" version of the main collection. Tse will still offer the standards: robes, blankets, mufflers and gloves are also available.

Upper East Side
827 Madison Avenue
NYC 10021

212-472-7790
at 69th St.
Mon-Sat 10-6, Thur 10-7

Tupli

A modern footwear store for the modern fellow—no gray shoes here! There are Italian-made suede and leather loafers, lace-ups, an updated Forties soccer shoe and Prada look-alikes from labels that include Hugo Boss, MOMA, Sky Wrek and GFF.

West Village
378 Bleecker Street
NYC 10014

212-620-0305
bet. Charles/Perry
Mon-Fri 11-7:30, Sat & Sun 12-6

Turnbull & Asser

Turnbull & Asser has dressed England's aristocrats, moguls and movie stars since 1855. This New York outpost of London's finest haberdasher offers traditional suits, men's furnishings, formalwear, sportswear, outerwear, sleepwear, shoes and accessories. But the best bet remains its bespoke shirt department, which boasts over

600 fabrics, from bold stripes to scores of checks and patterns. 877-887-6284 www.turnbullandasser.com

Midtown East   **212-319-8100**
42 East 57th Street   bet. Park/Madison Ave.
NYC 10022   Mon-Sat 9:30-6

Union

This closet-sized men's boutique is a launching pad for the latest looks by edgy designers, including button-down polos by the cult English label Duffer of St. George, simple sweaters, jackets, Adidas hoodies, lots of T-shirts by local artists, cool short-sleeved check shirts and jeans by Tenderloin.

SoHo   **212-226-8493**
172 Spring Street   bet. W. B'way/Thompson
NYC 10012   Mon-Sat 11-7, Sun 12-7

Unis

Cool minimalism rules at Unis, an American label with a distinctly casual European look (think the readers of wallpaper* magazine). This store is great for men's basics, from simple corduroy trousers, Samurai printed T-shirts, and button-down shirts in muted colors. They also, in fact, sell wallpaper (talk about knowing your customer…)

NoLiTa   **212-431-5533**
226 Elizabeth Street   bet. Houston/Prince
NYC 10012   Mon-Thur 12-7, Fri-Sat 12-8, Sun 12-7

Unisa

A well-stocked store of fashionable, fun and well-priced shoes, including mules, sandals, driving moccasins, pumps, boots and great wedges, all under the Unisa label. Finally, a hip shoe retailer on Madison Avenue that doesn't cost an arm and a foot… Fun handbags, too.   800-327-3619   www.unisa.com

Upper East Side   **212-753-7474**
701 Madison Avenue   bet. 62/63rd St.
NYC 10021   Mon-Sat 10-7, Thur 10-8, Sun 12-5

Untitled

A terrific selection of sexy clothing by fashion-forward designers like Roberto Cavalli, D&G, Moschino, Jean Paul Gaultier, Diab'less, Juicy and Margiela jeans. Styles run from casual street-smart to evening chic.

West Village   **212-505-9725**
26 West 8th Street   bet. 5/6th Ave.
NYC 10011   Mon-Sat 11.30-9, Sun 12-9

☆ Urban Outfitters

Urban Outfitters is the perfect location for a quick fashion fix. Its collegiate-cool clothing and cute pick-me-up accessories (let alone its funky home wares and CD collection) make it worth a pilgrimage. Fast becoming an American classic, the labels here include Bulldog, Lux, Bella Dahl,

Utility Canvas

Lee, Free People, Mooks and Urban Outfitters. Tip 1: if something you like is a little pricey, wait a week or so—it will go on sale for sure. Tip 2: buy, buy, buy the cool printed tank tops—often as low as $4.99.   www.urbn.com

Upper West Side — 212-579-3912
2081 Broadway — at 72nd St.
NYC 10023 — Mon-Sat 11-7, Sun 12-5

Chelsea — 646-638-1646
526 Sixth Avenue — at 14th St.
NYC 10011 — Mon-Fri 10-9, Sat 10-10, Sun 11-8

East Village — 212-375-1277
162 Second Avenue — bet. 10/11th Ave.
NYC 10002 — Mon-Wed 12-10
Thur-Sat 11-11, Sun 12-9

West Village — 212-677-9350
374 Sixth Avenue — bet. Waverly/Wash. Pl.
NYC 10011 — Mon-Sat 10-10, Sun 12-9

NoHo — 212-475-0009
628 Broadway — bet. Houston/Bleecker
NYC 10012 — Mon-Sat 10-10, Sun 12-8

Utility Canvas

Canvas-ianados will be beside themselves at this store's collection of practical, versatile all-American clothing manufactured in canvas, from heavy-duty industrial weights to light-as-air soft-brushed textures. There are canvas-lined wool jackets, shirts, pants and shorts, as well as a few non-canvas (controversial) pieces like anoraks and nylon jackets by the Artist in Orbit label. Best bet is its line of canvas bags, from a $98 bucket tote to a $60 binocular bag.   1-800-680-9290   www.utilitycanvas.com.

SoHo — 212-673-2203
146 Sullivan Street — bet. Houston/Prince
NYC 10012 — Mon-Fri 11-7, Sat 11-8, Sun 12-6

Valentino

Valentino is the master of old-school glamour that even the new girls want to wear (think super-modular Claudia Schiffer's wedding dress). He is king of meticulous detailing and beautiful embroidery that is never ostentatious yet fabulously luxurious. And his favorite color? Racy red. For day, Valentino ladies will find beautiful suits, ruffled and pleated silk shirts paired with simple black pants, mink-edged cashmere cardigans, delicate lace blouses worn with long tweed skirts and saucy leathers. Eveningwear is Oscar-caliber and ranges from black crêpe column dresses to taffeta ballgowns. Men will find smart-looking suits, shirts, casual wear and Oscar night tuxedos. Prices are over-the-top, but that's Valentino—and we wouldn't have him any other way…   877-360-0864   www.valentino.it

Upper East Side — 212-772-6969
747 Madison Avenue — at 65th St.
NYC 10021 — Mon-Sat 10-6

Vanessa Noel

"My shoes don't wear you, you wear them," is the mantra of ultra-feminine footwear designer Vanessa Noel (and a few other designers too, when you think about it). At this swank townhouse shop, there are three different collections featuring mules, sling-backs, pumps and boots in sumptuous leathers, lizards, suedes and crushed velvets, all finished with a range of heels from 1/4" heels to 4 1/2" stilettos. A large selection of bridal shoes is also available. www.vanessanoel.com

Upper East Side — **212-906-0054**
158 East 64th Street — bet. Lex./3rd Ave.
NYC 10021 — Mon-Sat 10-6

Varda

Italian handmade shoes in one-width sizing and classic designs that make the transition from day to evening as easy as one-two-three. Although the sales staff claims its neutral colored shoes will fit narrow or wide feet, you will have to be the judge. Prices run from $200 to $550.

Upper East Side — **212-472-7552**
786 Madison Avenue — bet. 66/67th St.
NYC 10021 — Mon-Sat 10-7

Upper West Side — **212-873-6910**
2080 Broadway — bet. 71st/72nd St.
NYC 10023 — Mon-Sat 10-7:30, Sun 12-7

SoHo — **212-941-4990**
9 Spring Street — bet. Wooster/W. B'way
NYC 10012 — Mon-Sun 10-7:30

Variazioni

An snappy Italian clothing chain for the yuppie set that features contemporary, easy clothing from business suits and eveningwear to sporty and casual wear. Labels include Diane von Furstenberg, Karen Robertson, Beautiful People, Anna Argiolera, Plenty, and Easel. Girly handbags, cases full of fun jewelry and, most importantly, the local stop for your very necessary Seven and Juicy jeans.

Upper West Side — **212-874-7474**
309 Columbus Avenue — bet. 74/75th St.
NYC 10023 — Mon-Sat 11-8, Sun 11-7

Midtown West — **212-980-4900**
37 West 57th Street — bet. 5/6th Ave.
NYC 10019 — Mon-Sat 10-7:30, Sun 12-6

Ventilo

The story began in 1972 with the design of an old-style shirt and has since blossomed into Ventilo boutiques worldwide. Designer Armand Ventilo fuses Asian and Indian influences with French sophistication. The three collections range from simple layered outfits in cool linens, silks and organzas to well-tailored suits in gabardine and tweed. The "Chemise Blanche" is a fundamental part of the Ventilo line; easy to wear, classic and feminine, it coordinates beautifully with everything. Also recommended are their fabulous candy-colored scarves. www.ventilo.fr

Upper East Side
810 Madison Avenue
NYC 10021

212-535-9362
bet. 67/68th St.
Mon-Sat 10-7

SoHo
69 Greene Street
NYC 10012

212-625-3660
bet. Spring/Broome
Mon-Sat 11-7, Sun 12-6

☆ Vera Wang Bridal House, Ltd.

Designer Vera Wang has revolutionized the wedding dress—and that has made her bridal collections world renowned. This heavenly bridal salon will have the bride even more luminous than usual—just ask glamorous customers like Sharon Stone and Karena Gore. Sheer elegance, sophisticated styling and beautiful craftsmanship define a Wang design, from the simple to the elaborate. Also find gorgeous eveningwear (favored by the Hollywood crowd) like long beaded column dresses, as well as a complete ready-to-wear collection. www.verawang.com

Upper East Side
991 Madison Avenue
NYC 10021

212-628-3400
at 77th St.
Mon-Sat 9-6 by appointment only

☆ Vera Wang Maids on Madison

Across the street from Wang's bridal salon is this store dedicated entirely to bridesmaids. "The entire bridal party should be as beautiful as the bride," Wang says. The whole wedding world is here, from dresses, skirts, separates, camisoles, to blouses and sweaters in wonderful shades of champagne, lilac, maize, soft pink and navy. By appointment only except on Tuesdays and Wednesdays.

Upper East Side
980 Madison Avenue, 3rd Fl.
NYC 10021

212-628-9898
bet. 76/77th St.
Tues-Sat 10-6, Thur 11-7
Sat 10-6, Sun 11-5

Veronique Maternity

Veronique's mission: "To design clothes like the ones you're used to wearing when you're not pregnant." Now there's an idea! The exclusive collections are imported from Paris and Milan and emphasize comfort, fit and fashionablity. Looks include flat-front pants and ultra suede jackets by labels like Amy Zoller and L'Atessa. Expensive, but worth it. www.veronique.com

Upper East Side
1321 Madison Avenue
NYC 10128

212-831-7800
at 93rd St.
Mon-Thur 10-7, Fri & Sat 10-6

Versace

Viva Versace! Flashy and fearless, the Milanese label—from Gianni to Donatella—takes sex by the horns (or was that the heels?). The powerhouse that is Versace continues to fuse the worlds of fashion, royalty and music, earning Donatella the sobriquet "rock 'n' roll designer." These clothes are for vixens (or Elizabeth Hurley) who want to feel young, sexy and be noticed—kinetic, kaleidoscope prints, biker leathers and skinny silhouettes. Find ready-to-wear, sportswear, glam-slam couture, racy eveningwear and a world of accessories (Medusa head bathrobe, anyone?). Sin is in. www.versace.com

Upper East Side   **212-744-6868**
815 Madison Avenue   bet. 68/69th St.
NYC 10021   Mon-Sat 10-6

Fifth Avenue   **212-317-0224**
647 Fifth Avenue   bet. 51/52nd St.
NYC 10022   Mon-Sat 10-6:30, Sun 12-6

Vertigo

This French retailer is for young professional women in search of slim-fitted European classics. The collection includes fashionable suits that go from desk to dinner, cashmere sweaters, shirts, handbags and belts.

Upper East Side   **212-439-9626**
755 Madison Avenue   bet. 65/66th St.
NYC 10021   Mon-Sat 10-7, Sun 12-6

Verve

A West Village accessories shop that includes optional extras from Cynthia Rowley, Kazuyo Nakano, Christopher Kon, Santi, Hollywould, Lola and Wendy Mink. There are over 125 different lines in this tiny shop, from handbag and hat styles to sunglasses, jewelry and watches. Handbags include leather day bags and beaded purses, while hats work it from the streets to the beach. Spotted: a more-than-respectable rip-off of the now-classic Balenciaga tasseled bag and the Statue of Liberty gloves that complete every wardrobe...

West Village   **212-691-6516**
353 Bleecker Street   bet. W. 10th St./Charles
NYC 10014   Mon-Sat 11-8, Sun 12-6

Verve Shoes

Located around the corner from its sister store, Verve Shoes peddles footwear by fun, fashion-forward designers like Cynthia Rowley, Jacques Le Corre, Fausto, Nancy Nancy and IXOS. It's the destination of choice for young professionals-about-town, with cool sneakers by Louis Norman and sandals by Exquisite J—all running the gamut from conservative to funky. Other items include handbags, briefcases and travel bags.

West Village   **646-336-1147**
105 Christopher Street   bet. Bleecker/Hudson
NYC 10014   Mon-Sat 11-8, Sun 12-6

Via Spiga

Three lines of moderately priced Italian footwear for all times of day, including wedges, slide mules, sling-backs,

Victoria's Secret

thongs, pumps and boots that come in everything from leopard print to tooled leather. Looks range from casual and classic to funky and trendy. It's fashionable, well-made footwear with something for everyone. A small selection of men's shoes.

Upper East Side
765 Madison Avenue
NYC 10021
212-988-4877
bet. 65/66th St.
Mon-Sat 10-6, Sun 12-5

SoHo
390 West Broadway
NYC 10013
212-431-7007
bet. Spring/Broome
Mon-Sat 11-7, Sun 12-6

Victoria's Secret

All you can see is curves, don't you know. Well, Gisele's curves mostly, but there's hope here for the rest of us mortals too! Kudos to this lingerie power brand, which markets romance and allure at totally reasonable prices. Find short, sexy, baby-doll teddies, racy black garters and stockings, bustiers, lots of bras (plain or lacy and embellished), the best seamless thongs and sleepwear and slinky accessories in bright colors and soft feminine prints. Look out for the sale tables too, where you can pick up pretty butterfly print thongs for five bucks. Get ready to visit the new mega-mega store on Herald Square and thank God Victoria shared her secret... 800-888-1500 www.victoriassecret.com

Upper East Side
1240 Third Avenue
NYC 10021
212-717-7035
bet. 71/72nd St.
Mon-Sat 10-8, Sun 12-6

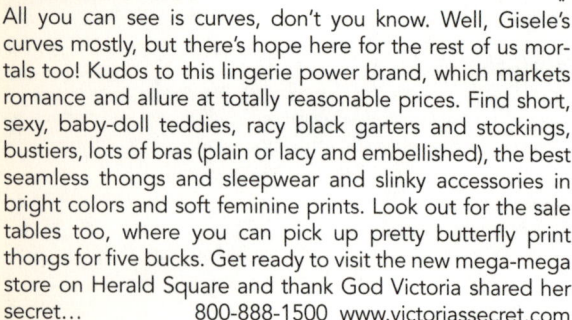

Upper West Side
1981 Broadway
NYC 10023
646-505-2280
at 67th St.
Mon-Sat 10-8, Sun 12-6

Midtown East
34 East 57th Street
NYC 10022
212-758-5592
bet. Park/Madison Ave.
Mon-Fri 10-8, Sat 10-7, Sun 12-6

Midtown West
901 Sixth Avenue
NYC 10001
646-473-0950
at 33rd St. at The Manhattan Mall
Mon-Sat 10-8, Sun 12-6

Flatiron
115 Fifth Avenue
NYC 10011
212-477-4118
bet. 18/19th St.
Mon-Sat 10-8, Sun 12-6

SoHo
565 Broadway
NYC 10012
212-274-9519
at Prince
Mon-Sat 10-9, Sun 12-7

Lower Manhattan
South Street Seaport
NYC 10038
212-962-8122
Pier 17
Mon-Sat 10-9, Sun 11-8

Vilebrequin

If your child has ever wanted to dress like you (and, well, vice versa) this is your place. Mothers and daughters have long worn matching outfits for fun and here, the boys can too. This French store sells cute father-son swim trunks in snappy prints—perfect for that Kodak moment. From classic drawstring styles to surfer trunks, you and your little buddy will own the beaches. Pay $100 -$135 for men's and $37-$58 for boys. From 2 years to adult.   www.vilebrequin.com

Upper East Side	**212-650-0353**
1070 Madison Avenue	at 81st St.
NYC 10028	Mon-Sat 10-6, Sun 11-5
SoHo	**212-431-0673**
436 West Broadway	bet. Spring/Prince
NYC 10012	Mon-Sun 11-7

The Village Scandal

Have Hedda Hopper rising? Perhaps not, but vintage addicts will love the selection of retro pieces at this cool East Village store. Boxes of vintage hats are artfully arranged along the top shelves—from a pink Jackie O pillbox to a plethora of turbans dripping with fake flowers. Also check out flirty dresses and coats from the 1920s through the 1960s, and a fab selection of look-at-me handbags trimmed with marabou feathers. The best bit? It's open until midnight. Scandalous.

East Village	**212-460-9358**
19 East 7th Street	bet. 2nd/3rd Ave.
NYC 10003	Mon-Fri 3-12, Sat 1-12, Sun 3-11.

Vincent and Edgar

There is Lobb, there is Cleverley—and then there is Vincent and Edgar. V & E is New York's finest custom-made shoe establishment. Shoemaker Roman Vaingauz can labor for 40 hours to produce a single pair of his bespoke shoes. Men's shoes start at $1,700 and women's at $1,300, with an additional $575 for a pair of wooden shoe lasts. Four-to-five months for delivery.

Upper East Side	**212-753-3461**
972 Lexington Avenue	at 71st St.
NYC 10021	by appointment

Vincent Nicolosi

A high-end tailor of classic suits for "chairman of the board" types. Expect six-to-eight-week delivery. Will not quote prices over the phone.

Midtown East	**212-486-6214**
510 Madison Avenue	at 53rd St.
NYC 10022	Mon-Sat 9-5

Vivaldi Boutique

An Upper East Side boutique for lovers of power glamour from French designers like Christian Lacroix, Sonia Rykiel and Thierry Mugler. There are cocktail and special occasion dresses, day and evening suits, and formal gowns. Vivaldi is ideal for women who need personalized attention when choosing their wardrobe. Accessories include jewelry, handbags, hats and scarves.

Vivienne Tam

Upper East Side 212-734-2805
1288 Third Avenue at 74th St.
NYC 10021 Mon-Sat 11-7, Thur 11-8, Sun 12-5

Vivienne Tam
New York style stalwart Vivienne Tam says her pieces take on a new feeling with each person. "Once I put an idea on cloth, that cloth becomes a garment," she says. "When somebody wears it, the garment comes to life." She applies her signature arty, crafty, East-meets-West style to her collection of sheer floral dresses, pinstriped suits, embroidered skirts, jackets, printed nylon mesh tops and separates, many with delicate beading and embroidery.

SoHo 212-966-2398
99 Greene Street bet. Spring/Prince
NYC 10012 Mon-Fri 11-7, Sat 11:30-7:30, Sun 12-7

Vivienne Westwood
Ah, the wacky, punky, kinda-sorta literary world of British fashion queen Vivienne Westwood. The co-founder of punk is still shaking it up—with clothes built for naughty girls and boys—and the odd Marie Antoinette for good measure. Her collections are colorful, scandalous and campy, filled with tarty minis and tiger-striped dresses (and great cardigans, by the way). Wild, non-conformist fashions from a wild, non-conformist woman.

SoHo 212-334-5200
71 Greene Street bet. Spring/Broome
NYC 10012 Mon-Sat 11-7, Sun 12-6

Vlada
Vlada has done stints at both Donna Karan and Chanel, but her own clothing passions have a vintage bent—from the Sixties to the Eighties especially. Check out deconstructed wool and cashmere sweaters, silk jersey dresses with vintage buckles and military-inspired jackets and coats. Other items include cool retro jewelry, belts and her own quick-hit cosmetics line. Reasonably priced.

Lower East Side 212-387-7767
101 Stanton Street at Ludlow St.
NYC 10002 Mon-Sun 1-8, Sat 12-8

Võ
Ngoc Võ's love of original and artful clothes is the inspiration behind her eponymous boutique, which carries collections by talented new designers and an interior fitted with a zen-like waterfall. Clothes are cut to measure, while fabrics like synthetic rubber, boiled wools and silks give an edgy—if not comfy!—feel. Find sexy frocks by Troy Smith and halter dresses and apron skirts by Hut Up.

Lower East Side 212-387-7760
169 Ludlow Street bet. Houston/Stanton St.
NYC 10002 Mon-Sun 1-8

Walter Steiger

Walter Steiger is one of the founding members of the shoe establishment: in a word, quality. Known for its unusual heel shapes, Steiger offers a range of feminine styles, including sexy stilettos, mid-heeled pumps, platforms, sandals, loafers and even a treaded walking shoe (best though are their cool two-toned golf shoes). Men's shoes feature pointy-toed loafers, boots, sleek sneakers and golf shoes. The spiritual home for the well-heeled. www.waltersteiger.com

Midtown East **212-826-7171**
417 Park Avenue at 55th St.
NYC 10022 Mon-Fri 10-6, Sat 10-5

Wang

The Wang sisters design practical, feminine fashions with desk-to-dinner versatility—coordinating skirts, dresses, jackets with tailored cuts and vintage, one-of-a-kind T-shirts, all at moderate price points.

NoLiTa **212-941-6134**
166 Elizabeth Street bet. Spring/Kenmare
NYC 10012 Mon-Sat 12-7, Sun 12-6

Warehouse

Another hugely popular British high street label to hop the pond, Warehouse is best for affordable hits of trendy, disposable (and club-friendly) clothing for the 18-to-35 crowd, including casual suits, skirts, jackets, tops, jeans and accessories. Moderate prices.

Flatiron **212-243-7333**
150 Fifth Avenue bet. 19/20th St.
NYC 10011 Mon-Thur 10-8, Fri & Sat 10-9, Sun 12-6

SoHo **212-941-0910**
581 Broadway bet. Houston/Prince
NYC 10012 Mon-Fri 11-8, Sat 10-9, Sun 12-8

Warren Edwards

Simply speaking, exotic and luxurious footwear. For women, Edwards' glamorous evening pumps, mules, animal print suede loafers, driving moccasins, sandals and boots. For the fellows, suede and crocodile loafers, dress shoes and styles for weekend wear. Prices run from $495 to $950.

Upper East Side **212-223-4374**
107 East 60th Street bet. Park/Lex. Ave.
NYC 10022 Mon-Sat 10-6

Western Spirit

"The largest western store in NYC" trumpets Western Spirit's business cards, and they'd be right—the place is bigger than Texas. Everything you could want to bring out the cowboy inside you can be found here—from hats to buckles to boots to shirts to children's clothing... to moccasins. Labels include Montana, Stetson, Akubra, Renegade and the best named Charlie 1 Horse. Saddle up... www.westernspirit2000.com

Wet Seal

SoHo | **212-343-1476**
486 Broadway | at Broome
NYC 10013 | Mon-Sun 10:30-8

Wet Seal 👨 👩
This California-based company markets ultra-hip clothing for the junior set—everything from jeans, T-shirts and clubwear to underwear, sleepwear and accessories. Sexy, tight-fitting little numbers for girls and street-smart looks for guys. Shoes also available.

Midtown West | **212-216-0622**
901 Sixth Avenue | at Manhattan Mall
2rd Floor | at 33rd St.
NYC 10001 | Mon-Sat 10-8, Sun 11-7

NoHo | **212-253-2470**
670 Broadway | at Bond
NYC 10012 | Mon-Sat 10-9, Sun 12-7

What Comes Around Goes Around 👨 👩
…And indeed it does—about every five years! This vintage boutique sells its recycled wares to stylists, celebs and fashionistas city-wide. The collection includes everything from Victorian tops to Thirties ballgowns, Sixties Pucci, Seventies Cacharel… you get the idea. Also head here for Hawaiian shirts, retro shoes and the must-have military jackets (rather hot right now). Sales staff are knowledgeable and eager to please. www.nyvintage.com

SoHo | **212-343-9303**
351 West Broadway | bet. Broome/Grand
NYC 10013 | Mon-Thur 11-8
 | Fri & Sat 11-midnight, Sun 12-7

Whiskey Dust 👨 👩 👨
Willie Nelson plays softly in this huge western wear emporium that sells just about everything apart from whiskey: bandanas, badges, barrels, belts, bolo ties, boots, buckles, bull whips—not to mention cowboy clothes not starting with B… "Go west without leaving New York" is the promise. And with this massive selection of everything from funny T-shirts to chaps to holsters, you'll be the John Wayne of the West Village… www.whiskeydust.com

West Village | **212-691-5576**
526 Hudson Street | bet. W. 10th St./Charles
NYC 10014 | Mon-Sat 12.30-7, Sun 1-6

The Wicker Garden 👨
A neighborhood shop offering everything your baby needs under one roof. New mothers and mothers-to-be can shop an enormous assortment of baby furniture, as well as a complete layette selection. Find wonderful cribs, changing tables, adorable, hand-painted chests, gliders and bedding. From 0-2 years.

Upper East Side | **212-410-7001**
1327 Madison Avenue | bet. 93/94th St.
NYC 10128 | Mon-Sat 10-6

William Fioravanti

Descended from a long line of Neopolitan tailors, Fioravanti sets the standard for custom made. He has a waiting list just to get an appointment but once you've got a foot in the door, you're in for a sartorial treat. Choose from luxurious English and Italian fabrics and customize a suit, shirt or topcoat. Suits start at $4,250. Expect a 10-to-12 week delivery.

Midtown West	**212-355-1540**
45 West 57th Street	bet. 5/6th Ave.
NYC 10019	Mon-Fri 9-5 by appointment

Wolford Boutique

Long considered the Rolls-Royce of hosiery (and with the sexiest image—check out those Helmut Newton campaigns), Wolford is the ultimate provider of novelty hose, sheers, thigh-highs, opaques and knee-highs in colors running from cute to kinky. For the silkiest sheers, ask for the "Aura 5 Collection" and for a great run-resistant, microfiber hose, ask for their best-selling "Individual 10." It's also the place for killer bodysuits, swimwear and…men's socks.

Upper East Side	**212-327-1000**
996 Madison Avenue	bet. 77/78th St.
NYC 10021	Mon-Sat 10-6
Midtown East	**212-688-4850**
619 Madison Avenue	bet. 58/59th St.
NYC 10021	Mon-Sat 10-6
NoHo	**212-358-1617**
52 University Place	bet. 9/10th St.
NYC 10003	Mon-Sat 11-7
SoHo	**212-343-0808**
122 Greene Street	at Prince
NYC 10012	Mon-Sat 11-7, Sun 12-6

Women by Peter Elliot

Fusing masculine tailoring with feminine styling, Women offers a great selection of high-end European labels including suits and handsome blazers by Isaia and Kiton, hacking jackets by Belvest, traditional men's shirts adapted for women, four-ply cashmere sweater sets from Scotland, double-faced cashmere coats with luxe chinchilla collars and chic alligator shoes. Prices are in the bridge to designer range and alterations are free.

Upper East Side	**212-570-1551**
1071 Madison Avenue	bet. 80/81st St.
NYC 10028	Mon-Sat 10-6, Sun 1-5

World of Golf

This small store sells an enormous volume of golf equipment, including brand names like Callaway, Top-Flite, Cobra, Ping, Mizuno and Taylor Made. A limited selection of clothing.

Y & Kei water the earth

Midtown East
147 East 47th Street
NYC 10017

212-755-9398
bet. 3rd/Lex. Ave.
Mon-Sat 9-7, Sun 11-5

Y & Kei water the earth
Yes, it is a spectacularly odd name, but these designers' intentions are pure; if not exactly watering the earth, they do a fine job of dressing its inhabitants. The husband and wife team of "Y"(Hanii Yoon) and "Kei" (Gene Kang) spirit up feminine pieces like ruffled shirts with tulle detail in all colors from lemon to black, also deconstructed denim jeans, shoes and boho belts. Best bets in this bright, airy store are the monochromatic suits—head to the back...

SoHo
125 Greene Street
NYC 10012

212-477-7778
bet. Prince/Spring St.
Mon-Sat 11-7, Sun 12-6

Yaso
Turkish owner Janan Tomko is very proactive, launching the careers of many undiscovered design talents from Europe and L.A. The large selection includes labels like Punch, Ines Raspoort, Claudette, Michael Stars, Lotta, Belgium's Just in Case and Yaso Pazo vintage private label. Also, handmade belts by Paolo Angeluc, hats by Eric Javits and Louise Green and the absolutely, positively vital dog carriers for your pooch by Emre NY.

SoHo
62 Grand Street
NYC 10012

212-941-8506
bet. Wooster/W. B'way
Mon-Sun 11-7

Yohji Yamamoto
Yohji Yamamoto is perhaps today's most influential designer precisely because he never succumbs to current trends. Although his collections are complex (he frequently uses tricky draping, ruching and folding), his clothes remain true classics—remember Carolyn Bessette-Kennedy's black-based style? His new fascination with sportswear concepts (even Adidas stripes and Yohji trainers) keeps him ahead of the cutting edge. And no one makes a better suit, especially his impeccably tailored gabardine suits, which are best paired with his signature white shirts.

SoHo
103 Grand Street
NYC 10013

212-966-9066
at Mercer
Mon-Sat 11-7, Sun 12-6

☆ Yona Lee
At last, a vintage clothing store in the East Village where you don't have to rummage through baskets of old shirts and scarves! Owner Yona Lee made sure her space was "shopping-friendly", the large shop housing a well-chosen collection of retro somethings, mostly from the Sixties and the Seventies, and a range of gently-used denim. Everything is arranged by color and nothing is over $100. She also stocks cool porcelain pendants from local designers, Sixties bangles and a few pieces of imported Indian jewelry.

East Village   212-253-2121
412 East 9th Street   bet. 1st/Ave. A
NYC 10003   Mon-Sat 1-9, Sun 1-7

Young's Hat Corner

Since 1890, Young's Hat Corner has catered to "gentlemen" (no "guys" here, thanks very much) in search of the appropriate hat style. Styles run from casual to dressy, including fancy toppers, English caps, baseball caps and straw hats for summer.

Lower Manhattan   212-964-5693
139 Nassau Street   at Beekman
NYC 10038   Mon-Fri 9-5:30, Sat 10-2:30

Yumi Katsura

An upscale bridal salon with an extensive selection of "marry me" gowns. Erisa, who designs for Yumi Katsura and The Erisa Collection, wants "to shatter the mold of traditional bridal dressing." That she does: from simple chic to elaborate embroideries, her pieces are never less than modern. Three to four months delivery time. Prices start at $3,200.   www.yumikatsura.com

Upper East Side   212-772-3760
907 Madison Avenue   bet. 72/73rd St.
NYC 10021   Mon-Fri 11-6, Sat 10-5 by appointment only

Yves Saint Laurent

This is the Yves Saint Laurent woman: "She never goes without what she wants. She drinks. She smokes. She has sex. She probably eats red meat. She wears fur. She lives." Fashion genius Tom Ford, fresh from reinventing Gucci, pulled off a second miracle with his dark vision for the iconic French fashion house—from his first show of classic tuxedos to gypsy-chic to safari to the recent Belle du Jour inspired collection, YSL is the very definition of louche French chic. Seemingly effortlessly, Ford has managed to give the fashion crowd an attack of gotta-have-it-itis bordering on a medical emergency, with clothing that marries burning passion with surface cool. This black orchid of a store carries the full women's collection (the classic Le Smoking suit sits amongst the seasonal pieces), while upstairs houses the cult accessories and deathly high shoes. Ford has also lured a new customer to his men's line, with a decadent collection of pieces in the traditional YSL palette of blacks, whites, gray flannels and pinstripes that pack a tough-chic punch. Close-cut suits are anchored by black ribbed T-shirts, velvet, corduroy and satin jeans paired with simple turtlenecks, narrow-cut trousers, hour-glass double breasted dinner coats and sexy leathers. YSL, once again, is the very incarnation of French fashion.   800-424-8600   www.yslonline.com

Upper East Side   212-988-3821
855 Madison Avenue   bet. 70/71st St.
NYC 10021   Mon-Sat 10-6

Yvone Christa

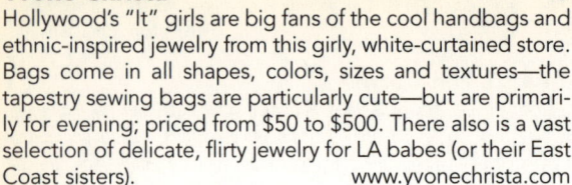

Hollywood's "It" girls are big fans of the cool handbags and ethnic-inspired jewelry from this girly, white-curtained store. Bags come in all shapes, colors, sizes and textures—the tapestry sewing bags are particularly cute—but are primarily for evening; priced from $50 to $500. There also is a vast selection of delicate, flirty jewelry for LA babes (or their East Coast sisters).   www.yvonechrista.com

SoHo 212-965-1001
107 Mercer Street   bet. Prince/Spring
NYC 10012   Mon-Fri 12-7, Sat 12-8. Sun 1-7

Zabari

Zabari will take a trend and run with it—translation, it's perfect for teenagers. This bright, cavernous store stocks all the latest looks, from capri pants and skimpy tops to slip dresses, jeans and jackets. Zabari's bright fabrics look great from a distance but feel a leetle flimsy up close. Best buys are their hip, colorful knickers and fun handbags. Labels include Alice & Trixie, Zabari, Plenty and Anna Kuan.

SoHo   212-431-7502
506 Broadway   bet. Spring/Broome
NYC 10012   Mon-Sun 11-8

☆ Zara International

This super-cool Spanish chain is taking over the globe with clothes that hit the fashion moment right on the head. Zara is so up to the minute, it's unbelievable (check out their Marc Jacobs-influenced suits and shoes, or YSL-themed lace-up dresses that are almost shocking in their resemblance to the luxe labels). Young professionals head here for smart suits, brilliantly basic shirts, sweaters and coats (for a bargain $160) for work, while clubber types can find spangly Lycra halters and super-tight jeans. Timing is everything here—make Zara a regular stop in your shopping schedule and just try to leave empty-handed.   www.zara.com

Midtown East (W)   212-754-1120
750 Lexington Avenue   at 59th St.
NYC 10022   Mon-Sat 10-8, Sun 12-6

Midtown West   212-868-6551
39 West 34th Street   bet. 5/6th Ave.
NYC 10001   Mon-Fri 10-9, Sat & Sun 10-8

Flatiron   212-741-0555
101 Fifth Avenue   bet. 17/18th St.
NYC 10003   Mon-Sat 10-8, Sun 12-7

SoHo   212-343-1725
580 Broadway   at Prince
NYC 10012   Mon-Sat 10-8, Sun 12-7

Z' Baby Company

A children's store packed with trendy domestic and imported clothing for cutting-edge kids from newborn to size 7. Find fun play clothes, pretty dresses, sweaters, T-shirts and underwear from designers like Cacharel, Kenzo, Missoni, Laura Lynn, Les Tout Petit and Petit Bateau. www.zbabycompany.com

Upper East Side   **212-472-2229**
996 Lexington Avenue   at 72nd St.
NYC 10021   Mon-Sat 10-7, Sun 11:30-5

Upper West Side   **212-579-2229**
100 West 72nd Street   at Columbus
NYC 10023   Mon-Sat 10:30-8, Sun 11-6:30

Zeller Tuxedo

Rent or purchase men's formalwear here from a good selection of designer names. Oscar de la Renta or Loro Piana are available for rentals while men can buy such lines as Calvin Klein, Joseph Abboud and Mani, as well as less-expensive brands. Rental prices start at $135 up to $165, while buying runs from $400 to $1,000. Shirts and black tie accessories available. www.zellertuxedo.com

Upper East Side   **212-688-0100**
1010 Third Avenue, 2nd Fl.   bet. 60/61st St.
NYC 10021   Mon-Fri 9-6:30, Sat 10-5:30, Sun 11-4:30

Zero

Actresses, models (lots of models), 20 year olds and, yes, 60 year olds are all among the women who shop here. Designer Maria Cornejo's strength is in subtle, geometric clothes: her signature piece is "the circle top," a circle of fabric that drapes over the shoulder with holes for the head and arms. Other looks include dresses cut in one piece without seams and shirts that twist provocatively around the body, wool jersey dresses and raw shearlings.

NoLiTa   **212-925-3849**
225 Mott Street   bet. Prince/Spring
NYC 10012   Mon-Fri 12:30-7:30, Sat & Sun 12:30-6:30

Z' Girl

With Z' Baby just down the block, Z' Girl is for the grown-ups—well, for hip juniors and women who love trends. It's all about sassy plain, studded and appliqued jeans, cool T-shirts, stretch tops, print dresses, sexy swimsuits and plenty of accessories, including rhinestone belts, jewelry, handbags and hair accessories. Labels include Amnesia, Hard Tail, Anti-Flirt, Seven, Rhinestone Cowboy and Diab'less. Think Britney and you've pretty much got it. www.z-girl.com

Upper East Side   **212-879-4990**
976 Lexington Avenue   bet. 71/72nd St.
NYC 10021   Mon-Sat 10-7, Sun 12-5

☆ Zitomer

A mini-department store—with crazy themed windows—boasting three floors of shopping for everything from beauty to toys. The main floor is home to every beauty, bath and health product imaginable, as well as pashminas, beach scarves, cashmere shawls, jewelry and a wide assortment of hair accessories. The second and third floors are dedicated to children's clothing and a toy department. Whether it's the latest in beauty and health products or the hottest new kid's toy, Zitomer will have it. If that's not enough, Zitomer will even cater to your pet's needs with its pet shop just two doors down. 888-219-2888 www.zitomer.com

Upper East Side   **212-737-4480**
969 Madison Avenue   bet. 75/76th St.
NYC 10021   Mon-Fri 9-8, Sat 9-7, Sun 10-6

Zora

Zora's owner Bushra Gill has been many things: a sculptor, a museum educator and, finally, a clothing designer. She now specializes in bridal clothing, her sculptural edge apparent in her elegant, non-conformist pieces. Her made-to-measure collection runs $900-$3,000 and for bridesmaids, $250-$400. Accessories include jewelry, handbags, and sandals.

Midtown West   **212-840-7040**
55 West 45th Street, 4th Fl   bet. 5th/6th
NYC 10001   by appointment only

Stores by Category

Women's

Men's

Unisex

Children's

Stores by Category

Women's Accessories

Add
Alexandre de Paris
Alexia Crawford
Amy Chan

Annika Inez
Anthropologie
Barneys New York
Bergdorf Goodman

Bloomingdale's
Boyd's Pharmacy
Calypso St. Barths
Catherine

Chanel
Clyde's on Madison
Decollage
Destination

Dinosaur Designs
Doyle & Doyle
En Soie

Eye Candy
Fabulous Fanny's
Flight 001

Gamine
Gas

Girlprops.com
Helen Marien
Henri Bendel
Hermès

Hiponica
Hollywould
LaCrasia Gloves
Language

Lord & Taylor
Macy's
Me & Ro
Me Too

Mina Mann
Orva
Pat Areias
Patch NYC

Pearl River
Precision
The Puma Store

Roslyn
Shop Noir
Toto

Yvone Christa
Zitomer

Women's Ballet/Dance & Work-Out Apparel

Adidas
Capezio
Champs

Crunch
Danskin

KD Dance
Lady Foot Locker
Niketown

The Puma Store

Women's Bridal

Amsale
Barneys New York
Bergdorf Goodman
Carolina Herrera

Cose Belle
The Gown Company
Kenneth Cole (shoes only)

Kleinfeld
Lucy Barnes
Manolo Blahnik (shoes only)

Michael's, The Consignment Shop for Women
Michelle Roth & Co.

Mika Inatome
Morgane Le Fay
Nicole Miller

Peter Fox (shoes only)
Pilar Rossi
Reem Acra
Reva Mivasagar

Robert Danes
Saks Fifth Avenue
Selia Yang

Stuart Weitzman (shoes only)
Thread (bridesmaid only)
Vanessa Noel (shoes only)

Vera Wang
Vera Wang Maids on Madison

Yumi Katsura
Zora

Women's Career

Anik
Ann Taylor
Barami
Barneys New York

Bergdorf Goodman
Bloomingdale's
Brooks Brothers

Dana Buchman
J. McLaughlin
Jaeger

Liz Claiborne
Lord & Taylor
The New York Look
Paul Stuart

St. John
Talbots
Tristan & America

Vertigo
Zara International

Women's Cashmere / Knitwear

Bergdorf Goodman
Berk
Best of Scotland
Bloomingdale's

Cashmere Cashmere
Cashmere New York
Jennifer Tyler
Laura Biagiotti

Loro Piana
Malo
Manrico Cascimir
N. Peal

Ralph Lauren
Saks Fifth Avenue
Sample
Tse Cashmere

Stores by Category

Women's Casual

Abercrombie & Fitch
American Colors
American Eagle Outfitters
Ann Taylor Loft

Anthropologie
A Perfect Day in Paradise
April Cornell
A/X Armani Exchange

Banana Republic
Barneys New York
Basic Basic
Benetton

Bloomingdale's
Canal Jean Co.
Diesel
Eddie Bauer

Express
Forreal Basics
Fossil
Gap

Granny-Made
Guess?
Henry Lehr
J. Crew

Lacoste
Leggiadro
Levi Strauss
Lord & Taylor

Lucky Brand Dungarees
Macy's
Old Navy Clothing Co.
Petit Bateau

Phat Farm
The Puma Store
Rugby North America
Quiksilver

Replay Store
Saks Fifth Avenue
Tommy Hilfiger
Utility Canvas

Women's Classic

Arleen Bowman
Beretta
Bottega Veneta
Brioni

Burberry
Cose Belle
Davide Cenci
Entre Nous

Etro
Geiger
Hermès
Holland & Holland

Hunting World
Jane
J. McLaughlin

Klein's
Laura Ashley
Loro Piana
Luca Luca

Noriko Maeda
Paul & Shark
Ralph Lauren
Saks Fifth Avenue

San Francisco Clothing
Shen
Steven Stolman
St. John

Sylvia Heisel
Ventilo
Women by Peter Elliot

Stores by Category

Women's Consignment

Alice Underground
Allan & Suzi
Bis
Encore

Fan Club
Fisch for the Hip

Ina
Kavanagh's Designer Resale

Michael's, The Consignment Shop for Women
New and Almost New (NAAN)

Project
Tatiana Resale Boutique

Tokio 7
Tokyo Joe
Transfer International

Women's Contemporary

A. Cheng
A Détacher
Afterlife
agnès b.

Alpana Bawa
Alskling
Amy Chan
Anik

Anna
Anthropologie
The Apartment
A.P.C.

Assets London
Atrium
Baby Blue Line
Bagutta

Barneys New York
Basiques
BCBG by Max Azria
Bebe

Bergdorf Goodman
Betsey Bunky Nini
Big Drop
Bisou Bisou

Bloomingdale's
Bond 07
Boudoir
Calypso St. Barths

Catherine
Central Park West
Christopher Totman
Claire Blaydon

Club Monaco
C. Ronson
C.P. Shades
Darryl's

Deborah Moorfield
Decollage
Detour
Diana & Jeffries

DieselStyleLab
DKNY
D/L Cerney
Dosa

Eileen Fisher
Emporio Armani
Epperson Studio
Erica Tanov

Fame
February Eleventh
Find Outlet
Fiona Walker

Fiorucci
Foley & Corinna
Forreal
French Connection

Gamine
Ghost
Gi Gi
Hedra Prue

Hennes & Mauritz
Henri Bendel
Himaya
Hiponica

Hugo Boss
Hugo Hugo Boss
Huminska New York
If

Institut
Intermix
J. Lindeberg
Jeffrey New York

Categories

243

Stores by Category

Women's Contemporary *(continued)*

Jenne Maag
Jill Anderson
Johnson
Joseph

Katayone Adeli
Kirna Zabête
La Galleria la Rue
Language

Laundry by Shelli Segal
Liana
Linda Dresner
Lucy Barnes

Lynn Park NY
Margie Tsai
Mark Montano
Marni

Martier
Martin
Martino Midali
Max Studio

Mayle
Meg
Minium New York
Min Lee

Miracle
Miss Sixty
Montmartre
Mshop

Nancy & Co.
Nanette Lepore
Nellie M.
No. 436

Oilily for Women
Olive & Bette's
1 on G
Onward Soho

The Open Door Gallery
The Otter Sleek on Bleecker
Parke & Ronen

Paul & Joe
Peacock NYC
Pleats Please

Plein Sud
Pookie & Sebastian
Precision
Rampage

Really Great Things
Red Wong
Robert Danes
Roberta Freymann

Saada
Saks Fifth Avenue
Scoop
Seam

Selia Yang
Shack Inc.
Shanghai Tang
Sharagano

Shin Choi
Shop
Shop Noir
Sisley

Skella
Smaak
Sorelle Firenze
Stanley

Steven Alan
Tehen
TG – 170
Togs

Tracy Feith
Untitled
Variazioni
Vertigo

Vlada
Võ
Wang
Warehouse

Yaso
Zabari
Zara International

Zero
Zora

Stores by Category

Women's Custom Tailoring

Arthur Gluck Shirtmakers
Couture by Jennifer Dule
Domenico Vacca
Lee Anderson
John Anthony
Maggie Norris
Pierre Garroudi

Women's Designer

Alexander McQueen
Anna Sui
Anne Klein
Barbara Bui

Betsey Johnson
Calvin Klein
Carolina Herrera
Celine

Cerruti
Chanel
Chloé
Christian Dior

Commes Des Garçons
Costume National
Cynthia Rowley
D&G

Diane von Furstenberg
Dolce & Gabbana
Donna Karan
Emanuel Ungaro

Escada
Fendi
Francis Hendy
Genny

Geoffrey Beene
Gianfranco Ferré
Giorgio Armani
Givenchy

Gucci
Helmut Lang
Hugo Boss
Issey Miyake

Jean Paul Gaultier
Jill Stuart
Kenzo

Kors
Krizia
Laura Biagiotti
Les Copains

Louis Féraud
Louis Vuitton
Maggie Norris
Marc Jacobs

MaxMara
Michael Kors
Missoni
Miu Miu

Morgane Le Fay
Moschino
Nicole Farhi
Nicole Miller

Norma Kamali
Philosophy by
  Alberta Ferretti
Prada

Pucci
Ralph Lauren
Roberto Cavalli
Salvatore Ferragamo

Shelly Steffee
Sonia Rykiel
Stella McCartney
Valentino

Vera Wang
Versace
Vivienne Tam
Vivienne Westwood

Y & Kei water the earth
Yohji Yamamoto
Yves Saint Laurent

Categories

Stores by Category

Women's Discount

Bolton's
Burlington Coat Factory
Century 21
Daffy's
Filene's Basement
Forman's
Loehmann's
TJ Maxx

Women's Ethnic

Do Kham
Hello Sari
Jungle Planet

Kinnu
Malatesta

Pan American Phoenix
Pearl River
Roberta Freymann

Tibet Arts & Crafts
Tibet Bazaar

Women's Evening & Special Occasion

Alicia Mugetti
Amsale
Angelo Lambrou
A. Tempo

Bergdorf Goodman
Bloomingdale's
Caché
Clifford Michael Design

Giorgio Armani
John Anthony
Lee Anderson
Lord & Taylor

Luca Luca
Maggie Norris
Makola

Marianne Novobatzky
Mary Adams
Morgane Le Fay
Pierre Garroudi

Pilar Rossi
Reva Mivasagar
Robert Danes
Saks Fifth Avenue

Sylvia Heisel
37 = 1
Thread
Valentino

Vera Wang
Vivaldi Boutique

Women's Furriers

Alexandros Furs
Alixandre
Ben Thylan Furs

Bergdorf Goodman
Bloomingdale's
Christie Brothers Furs

Denimax
Fendi
Helen Yarmak

J. Mendel
Ritz Furs
Saks Fifth Avenue

Women's Handbags & Leathergoods

Add
Amy Chan
Anya Hindmarch
Bally

Barneys New York
Bergdorf Goodman
Bloomingdale's
Bottega Veneta

Calypso St. Barths
Celine
Chanel
Coach

Crouch & Fitzgerald
Deco Jewels
Delfino
Dooney & Bourke

Fendi
Fine & Klein
Furla
Gabbriel Ichak

Ghurka
Gucci
Hans Koch
Helen Mariën

Hermès
Hunting World
Il Bisonte
J.S. Suarez

Judith Lieber
Kate Spade
Kazuyo Nakano

Lana Marks
Language
Lederer
LeSportSac

Longchamp
Lord & Taylor
Louis Vuitton
Lulu Guinness

Macy's
Me Too
Minette by Blue Bag
Patch NYC

Pelle Via Roma
Peter Hermann
Prada
Rafé New York

René Collections
Roberto Vascon
Roslyn
Ruco Line

Rugby North America
Saks Fifth Avenue
Salvatore Ferragamo
Shop Noir

Sigerson Morrison
T. Anthony
Tod's
TriBeCa Luggage & Leather

Verve
Yvone Christa

Women's Hats

Add
Amy Downs Hats
Barbara Feinman Millinery
Barneys New York

Bergdorf Goodman
Bloomingdale's
Calypso St. Barths
Destination

Eugenia Kim
The Hat Shop
Hatitude

Kelly Christy
Language
Lisa Shaub
Lord & Taylor

Macy's
Patch NYC
Roslyn
Saks Fifth Avenue

Samuel's Hats
Suzanne Couture Millinery
Tracey Tooker Hats

Stores by Category

Women's Hosiery

Barneys New York
Bergdorf Goodman
Bloomingdale's

Fogal
Legs Beautiful

Lord & Taylor
Macy's
Orva

Saks Fifth Avenue
Wolford

Women's Juniors

A. Tempo
Abercrombie & Fitch
American Eagle Outfitters
Betwixt

Bloomingdale's
Eclipse
Express
Fiorucci

Forreal Basics
Gap
Hennes & Mauritz
Infinity

Lester's
Levi Strauss
Lord of the Fleas
Macy's

Marsha D.D.
Miss Sixty
Old Navy Clothing Co.
Peter Elliot Kids

Reminiscence
Wet Seal
Z' Girl

Women's Leather

Behrle
Bridge
Buffalo Chips USA
Denimax

Leather Corner
The Leather and Suede
  Workshop

Lost Art
North Beach Leather
Original Leather
Rugby North America

Silverado
Studio 109
Tardini

Women's Lingerie & Sleepwear

Allure Lingerie
Barneys New York
Bergdorf Goodman
Bloomers

Bloomingdale's
Bra Smythe
Brief Encounters
D. Porthault

Enerla
Eres
Joovay
La Perla

La Petite Coquette
Le Corset
Laina Jane Lingerie

Lingerie on Lex
Lord & Taylor
Macy's
Makie

Martier
Mixona
Nisa
Nocturne

Only Hearts
Ripplu
Saks Fifth Avenue
37 = 1

Takashimaya
Victoria's Secret

Stores by Category

Maternity

Barneys New York
Cadeau
Liz Lange Maternity

Maternity Work
Michele Saint-Laurent
Mimi Maternity

Mommy Chic
Mom's Night Out
Motherhood Maternity

A Pea in the Pod
Pumpkin Maternity
Veronique Maternity

Women's Petite Size

Ann Taylor
Bloomingdale's
Dana Buchman
Liz Claiborne
Lord & Taylor

Macy's
Saks Fifth Avenue
Tahari
Talbots

Women's Plus Size

Bloomingdale's
Daphne
Lane Bryant

Lord & Taylor
Macy's

Marina Rinaldi
Old Navy Clothing Co.
Richard Metzger

Saks Fifth Avenue
Soho Woman

Women's Shirts

agnès b.
Anne Fontaine
A.P.C.

Banana Republic
Barneys New York
Bergdorf Goodman

Bloomingdale's
Brooks Brothers
J. Crew

Leggiadro
Ralph Lauren
Saks Fifth Avenue

Scoop
Seize sur Vingt
The Shirt Shop

Thomas Pink
Turnbull & Asser

Women's Shoes

Aboud Mimi
Aerosoles
Aldo
Antoin

Arche
A. Testoni
Avitto
Bally

Banana Republic
Barbara Shaum
Barneys New York

Bati
Belgian Shoes
Bergdorf Goodman
Bloomingdale's

Bottega Veneta
Botticelli
Bruno Magli
Camper

Cesare Paciotti
Chanel
Charles Jourdan

Categories

249

Women's Shoes (continued)

Christian Louboutin
Chuckies
Cole Haan
David Aaron

Easy Spirit
Edmundo Castillo
Enzo Angiolini
Eric Shoes

Fortuna Valentino
Fratelli Rossetti
French Sole
Galo

Geraldine
Giordano's
Giraudon
Giuseppe Zanotti Design

Goffredo Fantini
Gucci
Helene Arpels
Hogan

Hollywould
Iramo
Jeffrey New York
Jenny B.

Jimmy Choo
J.M. Weston
John Fluevog
Juno

Jutta Neumann
Kenneth Cole
Kerquelen
Lord & Taylor

Luichiny
Macy's
Make 10
Manolo Blahnik

Maraolo
Mare
Mark Schwartz
Martinez Valero

Maud Frizon
Me Too
Michel Perry

Milen Shoes
Nahbee
Nancy Geist
Nine West

Omari
Orva
Ottiva
Otto Tootsi Plohound

Peter Fox Shoes
Petit Peton
Prada
Rapax

René Mancini
Robert Clergerie
Rockport
Ruco Line

Sacco
Saks Fifth Avenue
Salvatore Ferragamo
Santoni

Sergio Rossi
Shoe
The Shoe Box
Sigerson Morrison

Skechers USA
Stephane Kélian
Steve Madden
Stuart Weitzman

Stubbs & Wootton
Tani
Tanino Crisci
Terra Plana

Timberland
Tod's
Unisa
Vanessa Noel

Varda
Via Spiga
Vincent & Edgar
  (custom only)

Walter Steiger
Warren Edwards

Stores by Category

Women's Swimwear

Barneys New York
Bergdorf Goodman
Bloomingdale's
Bra Smythe

Calypso St. Barths
Canyon Beachwear
Eres
J. Crew

Keiko's
La Perla
Leggiadro
Lord & Taylor

Macy's
Malatesta
Malia Mills
Martier

Nisa
Norma Kamali
Prada Sport
Pucci

Quiksilver
Ralph Lauren
Saks Fifth Avenue
Speedo Authentic Fitness

Women's Tweens

Abercrombie & Fitch
Betwixt
Bloomingdale's

Gap
Infinity
Lester's

Macy's
Marsha D.D.
Old Navy Clothing Co.

Space Kiddets
Wet Seal

Women's Vintage & Retro

Alice Underground
Allan & Suzi
Amarcord Vintage Fashion

Andy's Chee-pees
Antique Boutique
Atomic Passion

Canal Jeans Co.
Chelsea Girl
Cherry

David Owen
Decollage
Double RL

Eleven
Filth Mart
Flood

Foley & Corinna
Harriet Love

Keni Valenti
Legacy
Marmalade

Mary Efron
Minium New York
The 1909 Company

99X
Patina
Reminiscence

Resurrection Vintage
RRL
Screaming Mimi's

The Village Scandal
What Comes Around
    Goes Around

Yona Lee

Women's Wearable Art

Gallery of Wearable Art
Julie Artisan's Gallery

MarcoArt

Stores by Category

Women's Young & Trendy

Afterlife
Alife
Barneys New York
Bloomingdale's

Built by Wendy
DDC Lab
Detour
Hennes & Mauritz

Hotel Venus
Lord of the Fleas
Macy's
99X

Patricia Field
Urban Outfitters
Z' Girl

Men's Business Apparel—European

Barneys New York
Beau Brummel
Bergdorf Goodman Men
Bloomingdale's

Brioni
Cerruti
Davide Cenci

Domenico Vacca
Emporio Armani
Ermenegildo Zegna

Etro
Façonnable
Frank Stella
Hugo Boss

Jeffrey New York
Paul Smith
Saks Fifth Avenue

Sean
Seize sur Vingt
Tristan & America

Men's Business Apparel—Discount

Eisenberg and Eisenberg
Harry Rothman's

Men's Wearhouse
Today's Man

Men's Business Apparel—Traditional

Alfred Dunhill
Barneys New York
Bergdorf Goodman Men

Bloomingdale's
Brooks Brothers
Burberry

H. Herzfeld
Hickey-Freeman
Jay Kos

Jos. A. Banks
J. Press
Oxxford Clothes

Paul Stuart
Peter Elliot
Ralph Lauren

Saint Laurie, Ltd
Turnbull & Asser

Men's Cashmere

Barneys New York
Bergdorf Goodman Men
Berk
Best of Scotland

Bloomingdale's
Cashmere Cashmere
Cashmere New York
Jennifer Tyler

Loro Piana
Malo
Manrico
N. Peal

Ralph Lauren
Saks Fifth Avenue
Tse Cashmere

Stores by Category

Men's Casual

Abercrombie & Fitch
American Eagle Outfitters
Avirex
A/X Armani Exchange

Banana Republic
Barneys New York
Benetton
Bloomingdale's

Canal Jean Company
Diesel
Eddie Bauer
Fossil

Gant
Gap
Guess?
J. Crew

Lacoste
Levi Strauss
Lord & Taylor
Lucky Brand Dungarees

Macy's
Nautica
Old Navy Clothing Co.
A Perfect Day In Paradise

Phat Farm
Quiksilver
Ralph Lauren
Replay Country Store

Rugby North America
Tommy Hilfiger
Utility Canvas

Men's Vintage/Consignment

Fisch for the Hip
Ina
Tokio 7

Tokyo Joe
Transfer International

Men's Custom Tailoring

Alan Flusser
Arthur Gluck Shirtmakers
Ascot Chang
Borrelli

Cheo Tailors
Domenico Spano
Domenico Vacca
Frank Shattuck

H. Herzfeld
Hickey-Freeman
Jay Kos
Leonard Logsdail

Rosa Custom Ties
Vincent Nicolosi
William Fioravanti

Men's Designer

Burberry
Calvin Klein
Cerruti
Commes des Garçons

Costume National
D&G
Dolce & Gabbana
Donna Karan

Fendi
Francis Hendy
Gianfranco Ferré
Giorgio Armani

Gucci
Helmut Lang
Issey Miyake
Jean Paul Gaultier

Kenzo
Krizia
Louis Vuitton
Marc Jacobs

Missoni
Moschino
Nicole Farhi
Prada

Ralph Lauren
Salvatore Ferragamo
Valentino
Versace

Vivienne Westwood
Yohji Yamamoto
Yves Saint Laurent

Stores by Category

Men's Discount
Burlington Coat Factory
Century 21
Daffy's
Filene's Basement
Forman's
Loehman's
TJ Maxx

Men's Ethnic
Pan American Phoenix
Shanghai Tang

Men's Formal Wear & Tuxedos

A.T. Harris Formalwear, Ltd
Baldwin Formalwear
Hickey-Freeman
Jack Silver Formal Wear
Zeller Tuxedo

Men's Hats
Barneys New York
Bergdorf Goodman Men
Bloomingdale's

Brooks Brothers
Lord & Taylor

Jay Kos
Macy's
Paul Stuart

Saks Fifth Avenue
Young's Hat Corner

Men's Juniors
Abercrombie & Fitch
American Eagle Outfitters
Bloomingdale's
Brooks Brothers

Gant
Gap
Hennes & Mauritz
Lester's

Levi Strauss
Lord & Taylor
Macy's
Old Navy Clothing Co.

Patagonia
Peter Elliot Kids
Quiksilver

Men's Large Sizes
Rochester Big & Tall

Men's Leather
Behrle
Bridge
Buffalo Chips USA

Denimax
Leather Corner

The Leather Man
Lost Art
North Beach Leather

Silverado
Studio 109

Stores by Category

Men's Leathergoods & Briefcases

Bally
Barneys New York
Bergdorf Goodman Men
Bloomingdale's

Bottega Veneta
Coach
Crouch & Fitzgerald
Fendi

Ghurka
Gucci
Hermès

Hunting World
Il Bisonte
Jack Spade

Lancel
Lederer
Longchamp
Lord & Taylor

Louis Vuitton
Macy's
Peter Hermann
Prada

Rugby North America
Saks Fifth Avenue
Salvatore Ferragamo

T. Anthony
Tribeca Luggage & Leather

Men's Shirts

Addison On Madison
Alfred Dunhill
Ascot Chang
Barneys New York

Bergdorf Goodman Men
Bloomingdale's
Borrelli
Brooks Brothers

Burberry
Davide Cenci
Domenico Vacca
Façonnable

Frank Stella
H. Herzfeld
Hickey-Freeman

Hugo Boss
Jay Kos
Lord & Taylor
Macy's

Men's Wearhouse
Paul Stuart
Robert Talbott
Saks Fifth Avenue

Sean
Seize sur Vingt
The Shirt Shop
Thomas Pink

Today's Man
Turnbull & Asser

Men's Shoes

Aboud Mimi
Aerosoles
Aldo
Alife Rivington Club

Allen Edmonds
A. Testoni
Avitto
Bally

Barbara Shaum
Barneys New York
Belgian Shoes

Bergdorf Goodman Men
Bloomingdale's
Bostonian

Bottega Veneta
Botticelli
Bruno Magli
Camper

Cesare Paciotti
Church's English Shoes
Citishoes
Cole Haan

Fratelli Rossetti
Giraudon
Goffredo Fantini

Gucci
Hogan
Iramo

255

Stores by Category

Men's Shoes *(continued)*

Jenny B.
J.M. Weston
John Fluevog
John Lobb

Johnston & Murphy
Juno
Jutta Neumann
Kenneth Cole

Kerquelen
Lord & Taylor
Macy's
Make 10

Maraolo
Mare
Milen Shoes
99X

Omari
Ottiva
Otto Tootsi Plohound

Petit Peton
Prada
Robert Clergerie

Rockport
Ruco Line
Saks Fifth Avenue
Salvatore Ferragamo

Santoni
Sergio Rossi
Shoe
Skechers USA

Stephane Kélian
Steve Madden
Stubbs & Wootton
Tanino Crisci

Terra Plana
Timberland
Tod's
Tupli

Varda
Via Spiga
Vincent & Edgar
   (custom only)
Walter Steiger
Warren Edwards

Men's Sportswear—Contemporary

Adidas
agnès b. homme
Afterlife
A.P.C.

Atrium
Camouflage
Club Monaco
DieselStyleLab

DKNY
D/L Cerney
Emporio Armani
Final Home

Flying A
French Connection
Hennes & Mauritz

Hugo Boss
Hugo Hugo Boss
If
J. Lindeberg

Joseph
Lynn Park NY
Parke & Ronen
Paul & Joe

Rugby North America
Sisley
Ted Baker London
Triple Five Soul

Tristan & America
Unis
Zara International

Stores by Category

Men's Sportswear—Traditional

Barneys New York
Bergdorf Goodman Men
Beretta
Borrelli

Brooks Brothers
Burberry
Davide Cenci
Domenico Vacca

Etro
H. Herzfeld
Hermès
Hickey-Freeman

Holland & Holland
Hunting World
Jay Kos
J. McLaughlin

Lord & Taylor
Loro Piana
Paul & Shark
Paul Stuart

Peter Elliot
Ralph Lauren
Saks Fifth Avenue

Men's Swimwear

Barneys New York
Bergdorf Goodman Men
Bloomingdale's

J. Crew
Lord & Taylor
Macy's

Polo Sport
Prada Sport
Quiksilver

Saks Fifth Avenue
Speedo Authentic Fitness
Vilebrequin

Men's Ties

Alfred Dunhill
Barneys New York
Bergdorf Goodman Men
Bloomingdale's

Borrelli
Brioni
Brooks Brothers
Burberry

Domenico Vacca
Ermenegildo Zegna
Etro
Façonnable

Hermès
Hugo Boss
J. Press

Jay Kos
Jos. A. Banks
Lord & Taylor
Macy's

Men's Wearhouse
Paul Stuart
Ralph Lauren
Robert Talbott

Saks Fifth Avenue
Salvatore Ferragamo
Seigo
Thomas Pink

Today's Man
Turnbull & Asser

Stores by Category

Men's Vintage & Retro

Alice Underground
Andy's Chee-pees
Antique Boutique

Atomic Passion
Canal Jeans
Cherry

David Owen
Double RL
Filth Mart

99X
Reminiscence
Resurrection Vintage

Screaming Mimi's
Timtoum
The Village Scandal

What Comes Around
   Goes Around

Men's Young & Trendy

Alife
Bloomingdale's
DDC Lab
Hennes & Mauritz

Hotel Venus
Lord of the Fleas
Klurk
Macy's

Mêmes
99X
Patricia Field
Stackhouse

Stüssy
Supreme
Union
Urban Outfitters

Unisex Athletic

Adidas
Athlete's Foot
Champs
Crunch

Foot Locker
Modell's
New Balance
Niketown

Paragon
The Puma Store
Reebok
Speedo Authentic Fitness

Sports Authority
Super Runners Shop
Training Camp

Unisex Department Stores

Barneys New York
Bergdorf Goodman
Bergdorf Goodman Men

Bloomingdale's
Brooks Brothers

Henri Bendel (women only)
Lord & Taylor
Macy's

Saks Fifth Avenue
Takashimaya

Stores by Category

Unisex Golf

Champs
J. Lindeberg
Lacoste

New York Golf Center
Niketown
Prada Sport

Ralph Lauren
Richard Metz Golf
   Equipment

Walter Steiger (shoes only)
World of Golf

Unisex Jeans

Abercrombie & Fitch
A/X Armani Exchange
Barneys New York

Bloomingdale's
Canal Jean Company
Diesel

Earl Jean
Fiorucci (women only)
45rpm

Gap
Guess?
Henry Lehr

Levi Strauss
Lucky Brand Dungarees
Old Navy Clothing Co.

Replay Store
Selvedge

Unisex Outdoor Sports Equipment & Apparel

Adidas
Athlete's Foot (shoes only)
Bicycle Habitat
Bicycle Renaissance

Blades Board and Skate
Champs
Conrad's Bike Shop
Diesel

Eastern Mountain Sports
Gerry Crosby & Co.
Lacoste
Lady Foot Locker

Masons Tennis
Metro Bicycle

Miller Harness Shop
Modell's
Niketown
Orvis

Paragon Sporting Goods
Patagonia
Powers Court Tennis Outlet
Prada Sport

Princeton Ski Shop
The Puma Store
Reebok
Scandinavian Ski Shop

Sports Authority
Toga Bike Shop

Unisex Outerwear

Barneys New York
Bergdorf Goodman
Bloomingdale's

Brooks Brothers
Burberry
Davide Cenci

Denimax
Lord & Taylor
Macy's

Paul Stuart
Saks Fifth Avenue
Searle

Stores by Category

Unisex Tennis

Champs
Mason's Tennis Mart
Modell's
Niketown
Paragon Sporting Goods

Powers Court Tennis Outlet
Ralph Lauren
Reebok
Sports Authority

Unisex Western

Billy Martin
Buffalo Chips USA

Western Spirit
Whiskey Dust

Children's Clothing

April Cornell
Au Chat Botté
Bambini
Barneys New York

Basiques
Bebe Thompson
Bloomingdale's
Bonpoint

Bu and the Duck
Calypso Enfant
Catimini
The Children's Place

Coco & Z
Erica Tanov
Gap Kids & Baby Gap
Granny-Made

Greenstones & Cie
Gymboree
Hoofbeats, Ltd
Jacadi

Julian & Sara
Just for Tykes
Koh's Kids
La Layette

La Petite Etoile
Laura Ashley
Laura Beth's Baby
   Collection

Lester's
Lilliput / SoHo Kids
Lord & Taylor
Macy's

Magic Windows
Miss Pym (custom only)
Nursery Lines
Oilily

Old Navy Clothing Co.
OshKosh B'Gosh
Patagonia
Peanutbutter & Jane

Peter Elliot Kids
Petit Bateau
Saks Fifth Avenue
San Francisco Clothing

Shanghai Tang
Small Change
SoHo Baby
Space Kiddets

Spring Flowers
Talbots Kids
Tartine et Chocolat
The Stork Club

The Wicker Garden
Vilebrequin
Z' Baby Company
Zitomer

Stores by Category

Children's Discount
Century 21
Daffy's
TJ Maxx

Children's Shoes
Bambini
East Side Kids
Galo

Great Feet
Heun
Hogan

Jacadi
Juno
Kids Footlocker

Lester's
Little Eric Shoes
Shoofly

Skechers USA
Spring Flowers
Tip Top Kids

Timberland
Tod's
Training Camp (sneakers)

Stores by Neighborhood

Manhattan Maps

Upper East Side

Upper West Side

Midtown East

Midtown West

Fifth Avenue

Flatiron

Chelsea

East Village / Lower East Side

NoHo / West Village

SoHo / NoLiTa

Lower Manhattan / TriBeCa

Harlem

Brooklyn

Manhattan Walking Maps

Harlem

Manhattan Walking Maps

East Harlem, Spanish Harlem

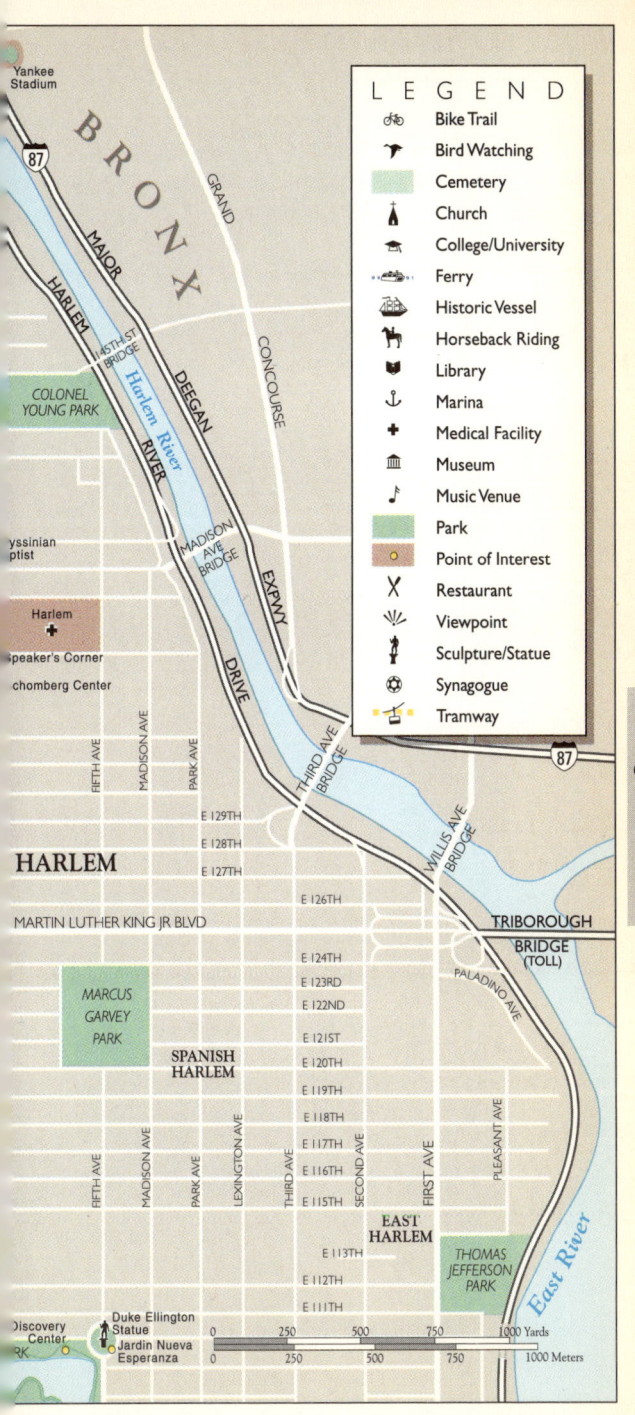

LEGEND	
⚲	Bike Trail
🦃	Bird Watching
	Cemetery
⛪	Church
🎓	College/University
⛴	Ferry
🚢	Historic Vessel
🐎	Horseback Riding
	Library
⚓	Marina
✚	Medical Facility
🏛	Museum
♪	Music Venue
	Park
⊙	Point of Interest
✕	Restaurant
☀	Viewpoint
🗿	Sculpture/Statue
✡	Synagogue
▬	Tramway

Neighborhoods

Yankee Stadium

BRONX

87

MAJOR DEEGAN

GRAND CONCOURSE

Harlem River

145TH ST BRIDGE

COLONEL YOUNG PARK

MADISON AVE BRIDGE

yssinian ptist

Harlem ✚

peaker's Corner

chomberg Center

FIFTH AVE
MADISON AVE
PARK AVE

HARLEM RIVER DRIVE

THIRD AVE BRIDGE

WILLIS AVE BRIDGE

87

E 129TH
E 128TH
E 127TH

HARLEM

MARTIN LUTHER KING JR BLVD

E 126TH

TRIBOROUGH BRIDGE (TOLL)

E 124TH
E 123RD
E 122ND

PALADINO AVE

MARCUS GARVEY PARK

SPANISH HARLEM

E 121ST
E 120TH
E 119TH
E 118TH

LEXINGTON AVE
THIRD AVE
SECOND AVE
FIRST AVE
PLEASANT AVE

FIFTH AVE
MADISON AVE
PARK AVE

E 117TH
E 116TH
E 115TH

EAST HARLEM

E 113TH
E 112TH
E 111TH

THOMAS JEFFERSON PARK

East River

Discovery Center

Duke Ellington Statue
Jardin Nueva Esperanza

0 250 500 750 1000 Yards
0 250 500 750 1000 Meters

265

Manhattan Walking Maps

Upper West Side

Manhattan Walking Maps

Upper East Side

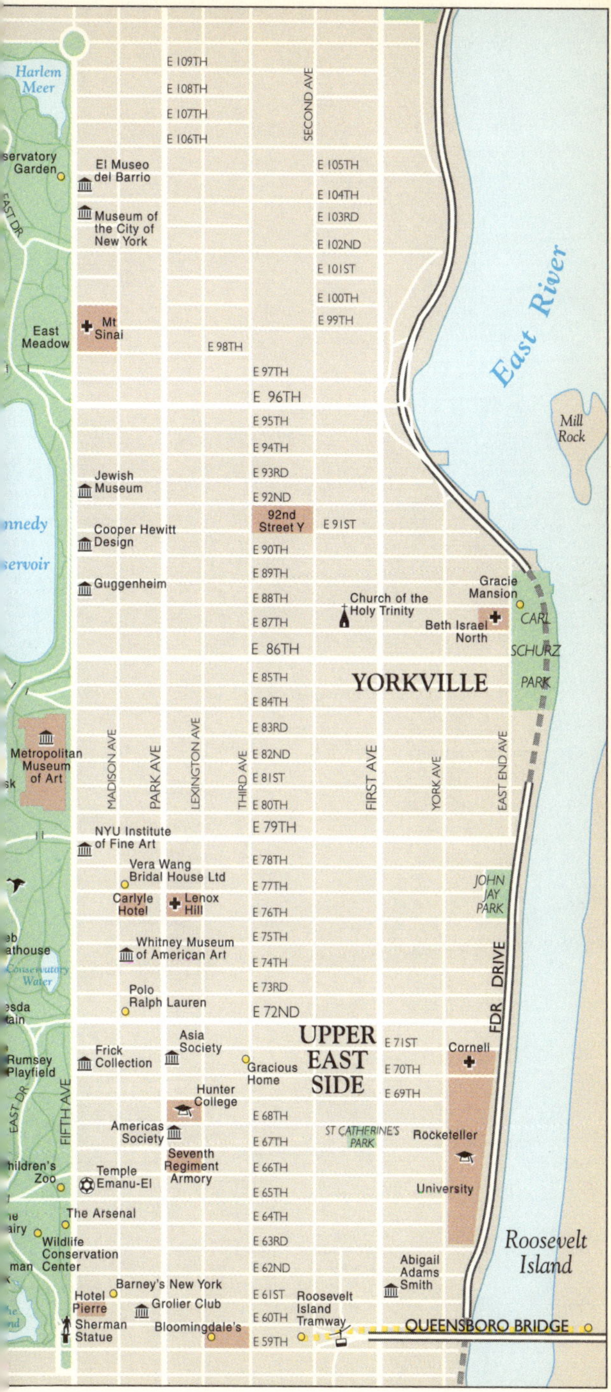

Neighborhoods

267

Manhattan Walking Maps

Midtown West, Chelsea

Manhattan Walking Maps

Midtown East, Fifth Avenue

Manhattan Walking Maps

Chelsea, Flatiron, West Village, SoHo

Manhattan Walking Maps

East Village, NoHo, NoLiTa, Lower East Side

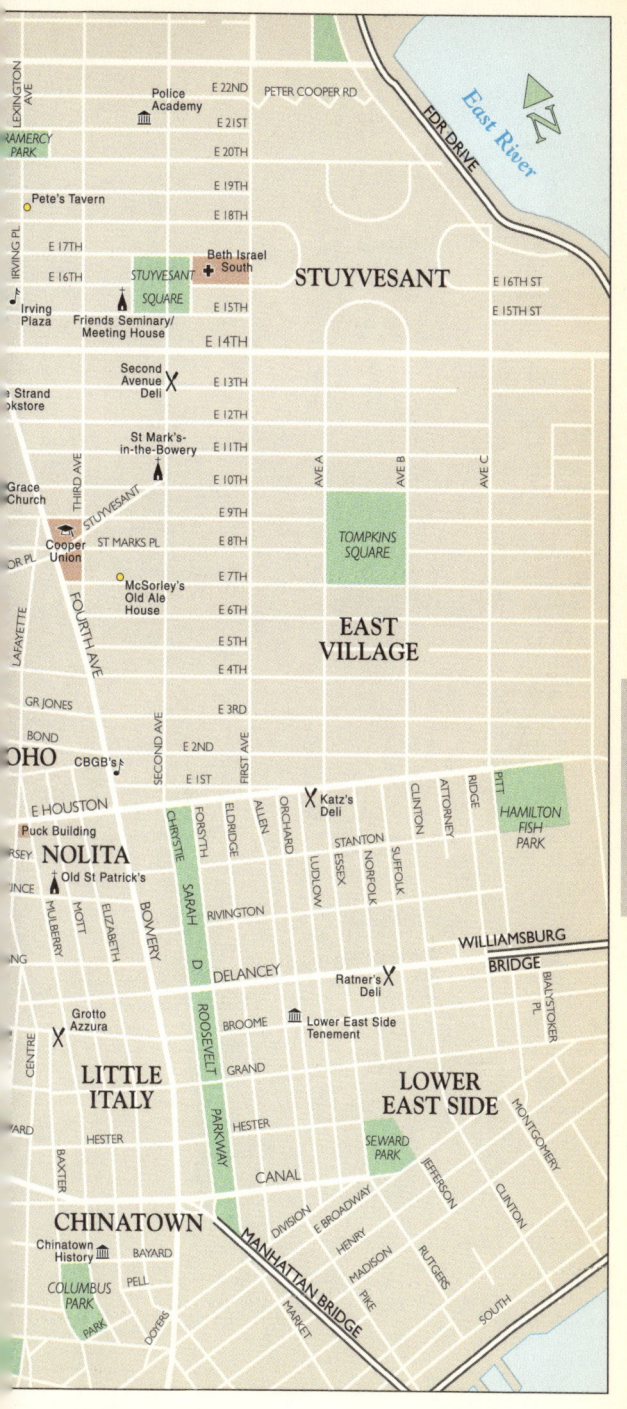

Manhattan Walking Maps

TriBeCa

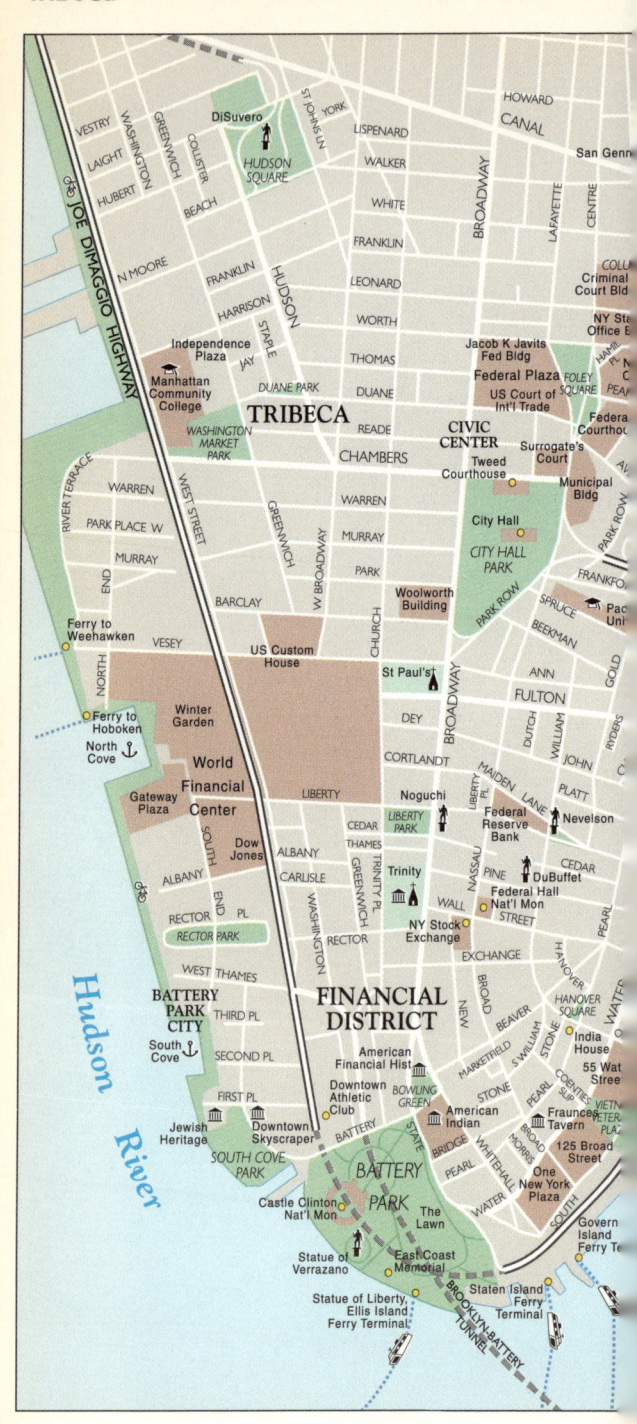

Manhattan Walking Maps

Lower Manhattan

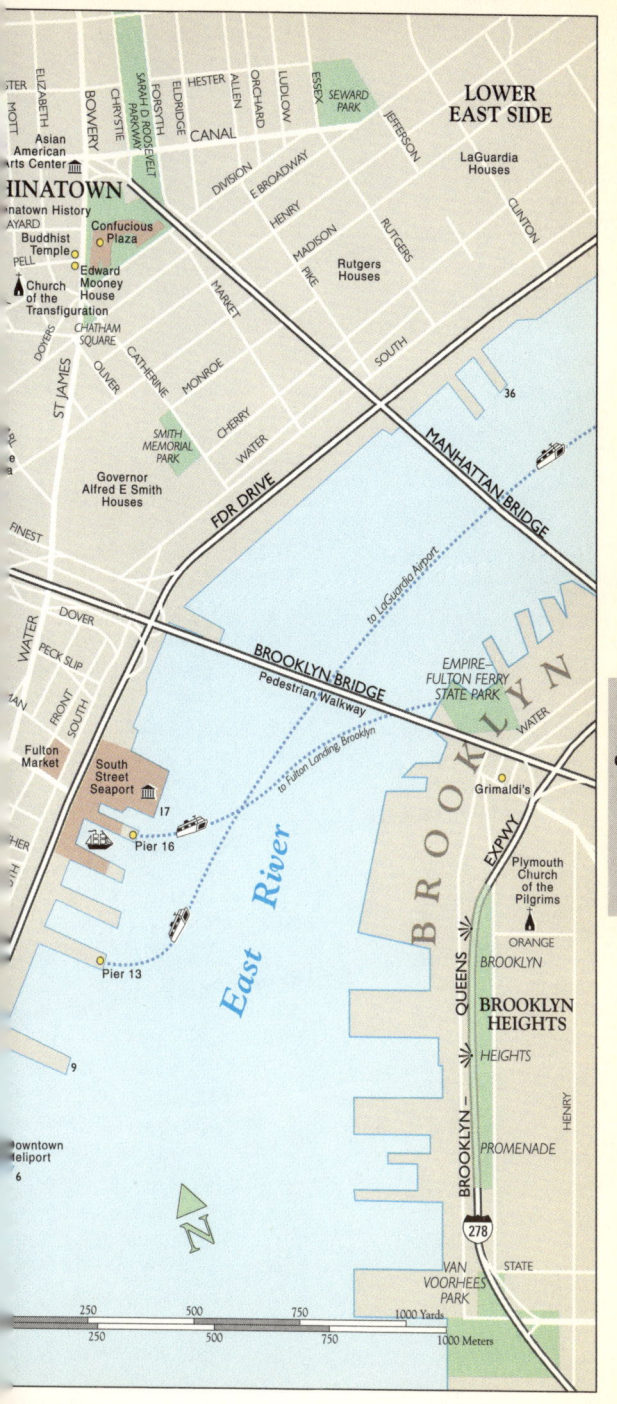

Upper East Side

Upper East Side *See map page 267.*

EAST 90'S

Bonpoint	1269 Madison at 91 St.
Capezio	1651 Third bet. 93/94 St.
Catimini	1284 Madison bet. 91/92 St.
Diana & Jeffries	1310 Madison bet. 92/93 St.
East Side Kids	1298 Madison at 92 St.
Jacadi	1281 Madison bet. 91/92 St.
J. McLaughlin	1311 Madison bet. 92/93 St.
Nocturne	1711 First bet. 90/91 St.
René Collection	1325 Madison bet. 93/94 St.
Veronique Maternity	1321 Madison at 93 St.
Wicker Garden	1327 Madison bet. 93/94 St.

EAST 80'S

agnès b.	1063 Madison bet. 80/81 St.
Aldo	157 E. 86 bet. Third/Lex. Ave.
Allure	1324 Lexington bet. 88/89 St.
Anik	1122 Madison bet. 83/84 St.
Ann Taylor	1055 Madison at 80 St.
Ann Taylor Loft	1492 Third bet. 84/85 St.
Au Chat Botté	1192 Madison bet. 87/88 St.
Banana Republic	1136 Madison bet. 84/85 St.
Banana Republic	1529 Third at 86 St.
Bebe Thompson	1216 Lexington bet. 82/83 St.
Betsey Johnson	1060 Madison bet. 80/81 St.
Bis	1134 Madison bet. 84/85 St.
Blades Board and Skate	160 E. 86 bet. Third/Lex. Ave.
Bolton's	1180 Madison at 86 St.
Cashmere New York	1100 Madison bet. 82/83 St.
The Children's Place	173 E. 86 bet. Lex./Third Ave.
Coach	1145 Madison at 85 St.
Cose Belle	7 E. 81 bet. Mad./Fifth Ave.
Easy Spirit	1518 Third bet. 85/86 St.
Encore	1132 Madison bet. 84/85 St.
Eric Shoes	1222 Madison at 88 St.
Foot Locker	159 E. 86 bet. Third/Lex. Ave.
Forreal	1200 Lexington bet. 81/82 St.
Gap	1511 Third at 85 St.
Gap Kids and Baby Gap	1535 Third bet. 86/87 St.
Gap	1164 Madison at 86 St.
Gap Kids and Baby Gap	1164 Madison at 86 St.
Great Feet	1241 Lexington at 84 St.
Greenstones & Cie.	1184 Madison bet. 86/87 St.
Gymboree	1120 Madison bet. 83/84 St.
Infinity	1116 Madison at 83 St.
LeSportSac	1065 Madison bet. 80/81 St.
Lester's	1534 Second at 80 St.
Little Eric Shoes	1118 Madison at 83 St.
Magic Windows	1186 Madison bet. 86/87 St.
Marsha D.D.	342 Lexington bet. 88/89 St.

Upper East Side

Metro Bicycle	1311 Lexington at 88 St.
Mimi Maternity	1125 Madison at 84 St.
Miss Pym	1025 Fifth bet. 83/84 St.
Modell's	1535 Third bet. 86/87 St.
Motherhood Maternity	1449 Third at 82 St.
Nancy & Co.	1242 Madison at 89 St.
Nellie M.	1309 Lexington at 88 St.
Nine West	184 E. 86 bet. Lex./Third Ave.
Original Leather	1100 Madison bet. 86/83 St.
Orva	155 E. 86 bet. Lex./Third Ave.
Peter Elliot	1070 Madison at 81 St.
Peter Elliot Kids	1067 Madison bet. 80/81 St.
Petit Bateau	1100 Madison at 82 St.
Rapax	1100 Madison bet. 82/83 St.
Searle	1124 Madison at 84 St.
Steve Madden	150 E. 86 bet. Lex./Third Ave.
Super Runners Shop	1337 Lexington at 89 St.
Tartine et Chocolat	1047 Madison at 80 St.
Tracey Tooker Hats	1211 Lexington at 82 St.
Vilebrequin	1070 Madison at 81 St.
Women by Peter Elliot	1071 Madison bet. 80/81 St.

EAST 70'S

Alexandre de Paris	971 Madison bet. 75/76 St.
Alicia Mugetti	999 Madison bet. 77/78 St.
Anik	1355 Third bet. 77/78 St.
Ann Taylor	1320 Third bet. 75/76 St.
Annika Inez	243 E. 78 bet. 2/3rd Ave.
Antoin	1110 Lexington bet. 77/78 St.
Arche	995 Madison at 77 St.
Bambini	1367 Third at 78 St.
Barami	1404 Second at 73 St.
Bebe	1044 Madison bet. 79/80 St.
Betsey Bunky Nini	980 Lexington bet. 71/72 St.
Big Drop	1321 Third bet. 75/76 St.
Bisou Bisou	1295 Third bet. 74/75 St.
Bloomers	1042 Lexington bet. 74/75 St.
Bra Smythe	905 Madison bet. 72/73 St.
Calypso St. Barths	935 Madison bet. 74/75 St.
Carolina Herrera	954 Madison at 75 St.
Cashmere Cashmere	965 Madison bet. 75/76 St.
Cashmere New York	1052 Lexington at 75 St.
Chloé	850 Madison at 70 St.
Christian Louboutin	941 Madison bet. 74/75 St.
Clyde's on Madison	926 Madison bet. 73/74 St.
Delfino	1351A Third bet. 77/78 St.
Eileen Fisher	1039 Madison bet. 79/80 St.
Eric Shoes	1333 Third at 76 St.
Forreal	1369 Third bet. 78/79 St.
Forreal Basics	1335 Third bet. 76/77 St.

Neighborhoods

Upper East Side

French Sole	985 Lexington bet. 71/72 St.
Gamine	1322 Third bet. 75/76 St.
Gap	1066 Lexington at 75 St.
Gap Kids and Baby Gap	1037 Lexington at 74 St.
Gianfranco Ferré	845 Madison at 70 St.
Gymboree	1332 Third at 76 St.
Hoofbeats, Ltd	232 E. 78 bet. 2/3rd Ave.
Intermix	1003 Madison bet. 77/78 St.
Issey Miyake	992 Madison at 77 St.
Jane	1025 Lexington bet. 73/74 St.
Jay Kos	986 Lexington bet. 72/73 St.
Jennifer Tyler	986 Madison bet. 76/77 St.
J. McLaughlin	1343 Third at 77 St.
Judith Leiber	987 Madison bet. 76/77 St.
Kids Foot Locker	1504 Second bet. 78/79 St.
Lady Foot Locker	1504 Second bet. 78/79 St.
Laura Beth's Baby Collection	300 E. 75 at Second Ave.
Little Eric Shoes	1331 Third at 76 St.
Liz Lange Maternity	958 Madison bet. 75/76 St.
Luca Luca	1011 Madison at 78 St.
Make 10	1227 Third bet. 70/71 St.
Makola	1045 Madison bet. 79/80 St.
Maraolo	1321 Third bet. 75/76 St.
Martino Midali	1015 Madison bet. 78/79 St.
Maud Frizon	1023 Lexington Avenue bet. 73/74th St.
Michael Kors	974 Madison at 76 St.
Michael's Resale	1041 Madison bet. 79/80 St.
Michele Saint-Laurent	1028 Lexington bet. 73/74 St.
Missoni	1009 Madison at 78 St.
Miu Miu	831 Madison Avenue bet. 69/70th St.
Mom's Night Out	147 E. 72 bet. Lex./Third Ave.
Noriko Maeda	985 Madison bet. 76/77 St.
Nursery Lines	1034 Lexington at 74 St.
Oilily	870 Madison bet. 70/71 St.
A Pea in the Pod	860 Madison at 70 St.
Pelle Via Roma	1322 Third bet. 75/76 St.
A Perfect Day In Paradise	153 E. 70 bet. Lex./Third Ave.
Polo Ralph Lauren	867 Madison at 72 St.
Pookie & Sebastian	249 E. 77 bet. 2/3rd Ave.
Prada	841 Madison at 70 St.
Precision	1310 Third at 75 St.
Ralph Lauren	888 Madison at 72 St.
René Collection	1007 Madison bet. 77/78 St.
Roberta Freymann	23 E. 73 St. Apt 5F bet. Fifth/Madison Ave.
San Francisco Clothing	975 Lexington bet. 70/71 St.
Santoni	864 Madison bet. 70/71 St.
Scoop	1275 Third bet. 73/74 St.
Searle	1296 Third at 74 St.

Upper East Side

Searle	1035 Madison at 79 St.
Shen	1005 Madison bet. 77/78 St.
The Shoe Box	1349 Third at 77 St.
Small Change	964 Lexington bet. 70/71 St.
Sonia Rykiel	849 Madison bet. 70/71 St.
Spring Flowers	905 Madison bet. 72/73 St.
Steven Stolman	22 E. 72 bet. Mad./Fifth Ave.
Stubbs & Wootton	22 E. 72 bet. Mad./Fifth Ave.
Super Runners Shop	1244 Third bet. 71/72 St.
Talbots	1251 Third at 72 St.
Talbots Kids	1523 Second at 79 St.
Vera Wang	991 Madison at 77 St.
Vera Wang Maids on Madison	980 Madison bet. 76/77 St.
Victoria's Secret	1240 Third at 71/72 St.
Vincent and Edgar	972 Lexington at 71 St.
Vivaldi Boutique	1288 Third at 74 St.
Wolford	996 Madison bet. 77/78 St.
Xelle	1300 Third bet. 74/75 St.
Yumi Katsuri	907 Madison bet. 72/73 St.
Yves Saint Laurent	855 Madison bet. 70/71 St.
Z' Baby & Co.	996 Lexington at 72 St.
Z' Girl	976 Lexington bet. 71/72 St.
Zitomer	969 Madison bet. 75/76 St.

EAST 60'S

Addison On Madison	698 Madison bet. 62/63 St.
Aerosoles	1555 Second at 61 St.
Ann Taylor	645 Madison at 60 St.
Ann Taylor Loft	1155 Third at 68 St.
Anne Fontaine	791 Madison at 67 St.
Anya Hindmarch	29 E. 60 bet. Mad./Park Ave.
Arche	1045 Third bet. 61/62 St.
Athlete's Foot	1031 Third at 61 St.
Banana Republic	1110 Third at 66 St.
Barneys New York	660 Madison at 61 St.
Bati	1052 Third bet. 62/63 St.
BCBG by Max Azria	770 Madison at 66 St.
Bebe	1127 Third at 66 St.
Beretta	718 Madison bet. 63/64 St.
Berk	781 Madison bet. 66/67 St.
Betsey Johnson	251 E. 60 bet. 2/3rd Ave.
Billy Martins	220 E. 60 at Third Ave.
Bonpoint	811 Madison at 68 St.
Borrelli	16 E. 60 bet. Mad./Fifth Ave.
Boyds	655 Madison bet. 60/61 St.
Calvin Klein	654 Madison at 60 St.
Canyon Beachwear	1136 Third bet. 66/67 St.
Capezio	136 E. 61 bet. Lex./Park Ave.
Celine	667 Madison bet. 60/61 St.
Cerruti	789 Madison at 67 St.
Cesare Paciotti	833 Madison bet. 69/70 St.

Upper East Side

Cheo Tailors	30 E. 60 bet. Mad./Park Ave.
Chuckies	1073 Third bet. 63/64 St.
Clifford Michael Design	45 E. 60 bet. Mad./Park Ave.
Club Monaco	1111 Third at 65 St.
Coach	710 Madison at 63 St.
Cole Haan	667 Madison at 61 St.
Davide Cenci	801 Madison bet. 67/68 St.
Diesel	770 Lexington at 60 St.
DKNY	665 Madison at 60 St.
Dolce & Gabbana	825 Madison bet. 68/69 St.
Donna Karan	819 Madison bet. 68/69 St.
Dooney & Bourke	28 E. 60 bet. Mad./Park Ave.
D. Porthault	11 E. 69 bet. Mad./Fifth Ave.
Eddie Bauer	1172 Third bet. 68/69 St.
Emanuel Ungaro	792 Madison at 67 St.
Entre Nous	1124 Third bet. 65/66 St.
Etro	720 Madison bet. 63/64 St.
Fogal	680 Madison bet. 61/62 St.
Foot Locker	1187 Third at 69 St.
Furla	727 Madison bet. 63/64 St.
Gallery of Wearable Art	34 E. 67 bet. Mad./Park Ave.
Galo	692 Madison bet. 62/63 St.
Galo	825 Lexington at 63 St.
Gap	1131-49 Third at 66 St.
Gap Kids and Baby Gap	1131-49 Third at 66 St.
Giordano's	1150 Second bet. 60/61 St.
Giorgio Armani	760 Madison at 65 St.
Giuseppe Zanotti Design	806 Madison bet. 67/68 St.
Givenchy	710 Madison at 63 St.
Gymboree	1049 Third bet. 61/62 St.
Hermès	691 Madison bet. 62/63 St.
Il Bisonte	22 E. 65 bet. Mad./Fifth Ave.
Jacadi	781 Madison bet. 66/67 St.
Jaeger	818 Madison at 68/69 St.
Jean Paul Gaultier	759 Madison bet. 65/66 St.
John Lobb	680 Madison bet. 61/62 St.
J. Mendel	723 Madison bet. 63/64 St.
J.M. Weston	812 Madison at 68 St.
Julie Artisan's Gallery	762 Madison bet. 65/66 St.
Krizia	769 Madison bet. 65/66 St.
La Layette	170 E. 61 bet. Third/Lex. Ave.
La Perla	777 Madison bet. 66/67 St.
La Petite Etoile	746 Madison bet. 64/65 St.
Lee Anderson	23 E. 67 bet. Mad./Fifth Ave.
Leggiadro	680 Madison bet. 61/62 St.
Legs Beautiful	1025 Third at 61 St.
Les Copains	807 Madison bet. 67/68 St.
Lingerie on Lex.	831 Lexington bet. 63/64 St.
Longchamp	713 Madison bet. 63/64 St.

Upper East Side

Loro Piana	821 Madison bet. 68/69 St.
Luca Luca	690 Madison at 62 St.
Malo	814 Madison at 68 St.
Manrico	802 Madison bet. 67/68 St.
Maraolo	782 Lexington bet. 60/61 St.
Maraolo	835 Madison bet. 69/70 St.
Marina Rinaldi	800 Madison bet. 67/68 St.
Martier	1010 Third at 60 St.
Martinez Valero	1029 Third at 61 St.
MaxMara	813 Madison at 68 St.
Morgane Le Fay	746 Madison bet. 64/65 St.
Moschino	803 Madison bet. 67/68 St.
Nicole Farhi	10 E. 60 bet. Mad./Fifth Ave.
Nicole Miller	780 Madison bet. 66/67 St.
Nine West	1195 Third bet. 69/70 St.
Oilily For Women	820 Madison bet. 68/69 St.
Olive & Bette's	1070 Madison bet. 81/82 St.
Pan American Phoenix	857 Lexington bet. 64/65 St.
Paul & Shark	772 Madison at 66 St.
Pilar Rossi	784 Madison bet. 66/67 St.
Pucci	24 E. 64 bet. Mad./Fifth Ave.
Reem Acra	10 E. 60 bet. Mad./Fifth Ave.
Roberto Cavalli	711 Madison at 63 St.
Robert Clergerie	681 Madison bet. 61/62 St.
Robert Talbott	680 Madison bet. 61/62 St.
Saada	1159 Second bet. 60/61 St.
Searle	805 Madison bet. 67/68 St.
Searle	1051 Third at 62 St.
Sergio Rossi	772 Madison at 66 St.
Shanghai Tang	714 Madison at 63 St.
Spring Flowers	1050 Third at 62 St.
Stephane Kélian	717 Madison bet. 63/64 St.
Suzanne	27 E. 61 bet. Madison/Park Ave.
Tanino Crisci	795 Madison bet. 67/68 St.
Tatiana Resale Boutique	767 Lexington bet. 60/61 St.
Timberland Shoes	709 Madison at 63 St.
Toto	870 Lexington Avenue at 65 St.
Tse Cashmere	827 Madison at 69 St.
Unisa	701 Madison bet. 62/63 St.
Valentino	747 Madison at 65 St.
Vanessa Noel	158 E. 64 bet. Lex./Third Ave.
Varda	786 Madison bet. 66/67 St.
Ventilo	810 Madison bet. 67/68 St.
Versace	815 Madison bet. 68/69 St.
Vertigo	755 Madison bet. 65/66 St.
Via Spiga	765 Madison bet. 65/66 St.
Warren Edwards	107 E. 60 bet. Lex./Park Ave.
Zeller Tuxedo	1010 Third bet. 60/61 St.

Upper West Side *See map page 266.*

Aerosoles	310 Columbus bet. 74/75 St.
Allan & Suzi	416 Amsterdam at 80 St.
Alskling	228 Columbus bet. 70/71 St.
Ann Taylor	2380 B'way at 87 St.
Ann Taylor	2015-17 B'way at 69 St.
April Cornell	487 Columbus bet. 83/84 St.
Assets London	464 Columbus bet. 82/83 St.
A. Tempo	290 Columbus bet. 73/74 St.
Athlete's Foot	2265 B'way bet. 81/82 St.
Athlete's Foot	2563 B'way bet. 96/97 St.
Banana Republic	215 Columbus bet. 69/70 St.
Banana Republic	2360 B'way at 86 St.
Barbara Gee Danskin Center (outlet)	2282 1/2 B'way bet. 82/83 St.
Barbara Gee Danskin Center (outlet)	2487 B'way bet. 92/93 St.
Bati	2323 B'way bet. 84/85 St.
Betsey Johnson	248 Columbus bet. 71/72 St.
Bicycle Renaissance	430 Columbus at 81 St.
Blades Board and Skate	120 W. 72 bet. Columbus/B'way
Brief Encounters	239 Columbus at 71 St.
Central Park West	2124 B'way bet. 74/75 St.
The Children's Place	2187 B'way at 77 St.
The Children's Place	2039 bet. B'way/Amsterdam Ave.
Club Monaco	2376 B'way at 87 St.
Coach	2321 B'way at 84 St.
CP Shades	300 Columbus at 74 St.
Crunch	162 W. 83 bet. Columbus/Amsterdam Ave.
Danskin	159 Columbus bet. 67/68 St.
Daphne	467 Amsterdam bet 82/83 St.
Darryl's	492 Amsterdam bet. 83/84 St.
Diana & Jeffries	2062 B'way bet. 70/71 St.
Eastern Mountain Sports	20 W. 61 bet. B'way/9th Ave.
Easy Spirit	2251 B'way bet. 80/81 St.
Eddie Bauer	1960 B'way at 67 St.
Eileen Fisher	341 Columbus bet. 76/77 St.
Express	321 Columbus bet. 75/76 St.
Filene's Basement	2222 B'way at 79 St.
Frank Stella	440 Columbus at 81 St.
French Connection	304 Columbus bet. 74/75 St.
Gap	2109 B'way at 73 St.
Gap	2373 B'way at 86 St.
Gap Kids and Baby Gap	1988 B'way at 67 St.
Gap Kids and Baby Gap	341 Columbus bet. 76/77 St.
Gap Kids and Baby Gap	2300 B'way at 83 St.
Gap (Women)	335 Columbus at 76 St.
Granny-Made	381 Amsterdam bet. 78/79 St.
Greenstones & Cie	442 Columbus bet. 81/82 St.

Gymboree	2271 B'way at 82 St.
Gymboree	2015 B'way bet. 68/69 St.
Intermix	210 Columbus at 69 St.
Kenneth Cole	353 Columbus at 77 St.
Laina Jane Lingerie	416 Amsterdam at 80 St.
Laura Ashley	398 Columbus at 79 St.
Liana	324 Columbus bet. 75/76 St.
Lord of the Fleas	2142 B'way bet. 75/76 St.
Lucky Brand Dungarees	216 Columbus at 70 St.
Maraolo (outlet)	131 W. 72 bet. Amsterdam/Columbus Ave.
Mimi Maternity	2005 B'way bet. 68/69 St.
Montmartre	247 Columbus bet. 71/72 St.
Montmartre	2212 B'way bet. 78/79 St.
Nautica	216 Columbus at 70 St.
The New York Look	30 Lincoln Plaza bet. 62/63 St.
The New York Look	2030 B'way bet. 69/70 St.
Nine West	2305 B'way at 83/84 St.
Olive & Bette's	252 Columbus bet. 71/72 St.
Only Hearts	386 Columbus bet. 78/79 St.
Original Leather	256 Columbus at 72 St.
Patagonia	426 Columbus bet. 80/81 St.
Really Great Things	284-A Columbus bet. 73/74 St.
Reebok	160 Columbus bet. 67/68 St.
Roberto Vascon	140 W. 72 bet. B'way/Columbus Ave.
Roslyn	276 Columbus at 73 St.
Sacco	324 Columbus bet. 75/76 St.
Sean	224 Columbus bet. 70/71 St.
Shoofly	465 Amsterdam bet. 82/83 St.
Sisley	2308 B'way bet. 83/84 St.
Skechers USA	2169 B'way bet. 76/77 St.
Speedo Authentic Fitness	150 Columbus at 66 St.
Steve Madden	2315 B'way at 84 St.
Super Runners Shop	360 Amsterdam bet. 77/78 St.
Talbots	2289-2291 B'way bet. 82/83 St.
Tani	2020 B'way bet. 69/70 St.
Tibet Bazaar	473 Amsterdam bet. 82/83 St.
Tip Top Kids	155 W. 72 bet. B'way/Columbus Ave.
Toga Bike Shop	110 West End Ave. at 64 St.
Varda	2080 B'way bet. 71/72 St.
Variazioni	309 Columbus bet. 74/75 St.
Victoria's Secret	1981 B'way at 67 St.
Z' Baby Company	100 W. 72 at Columbus Ave.

Midtown East *See map page 269.*

Aldo	730 Lexington bet. 58/59 St.
Alfred Dunhill	450 Park at 57 St.
Allen Edmonds	551 Madison bet. 55/56 St.
Allen Edmonds	24 E. 44 bet. Mad./Fifth Ave.

Midtown East

Alexandros Furs	5 E. 57 bet. Mad./Fifth Ave.
Amsale	625 Madison at 58 St.
Ann Taylor	850 Third at 52 St.
Ann Taylor	330 Madison Avenue at 43rd St.
Ann Taylor Loft	150 E. 42 at Lexington Ave.
Ann Taylor loft	488 Madison at 52 St.
A.T. Harris Formalwear	11 E. 44 bet. Mad./Fifth Ave.
Athlete's Foot	41 E. 42 bet. Mad./Vanderbilt Ave.
Athlete's Foot	655 Lexington at 55 St.
Bally	628 Madison at 59 St.
Banana Republic	130 E. 59 at Lexington Ave.
Barami	136 E. 57 at Lexington Ave.
Barami	375 Lexington at 41 St.
Bebe	805 Third at 50 St.
Belgian Shoes	110 E. 55 bet. Park/Lex. Ave.
Benetton	666 Third at 42 St.
Bloomingdale's	1000 Third bet. 59/60 St.
Bolton's	4 E. 34 bet. Mad./Fifth Ave.
Bolton's	109 E. 42 at Lexington Ave.
Bostonian	515 Madison at 53 St.
Bostonian	363 Madison at 43 St.
Bottega Veneta	635 Madison bet. 59/60 St.
Brioni	57 E. 57 bet. Mad./Park Ave.
Brioni	55 E. 52 bet. Mad./Park Ave.
Brooks Brothers	346 Madison bet. 44/45 St.
Caché	805 Third bet. 49/50 St.
Chanel	15 E. 57 bet. Mad./Fifth Ave.
Charles Jourdan	612 Madison bet. 58/59 St.
Christian Dior	21 E. 57 bet. Mad./Fifth Ave.
Church's English Shoes	428 Madison at 49 St.
Citishoes	445 Park bet. 56/57 St.
Coach	342 Madison bet. 43/44 St.
Coach	595 Madison at 57 St.
Conrad's Bike Shop	25 Tudor City Pl. at 41 St.
Crouch & Fitzgerald	400 Madison bet. 47/48 St.
Crunch	1109 Second bet. 58/59 St.
Daffy's	335 Madison at 44 St.
Daffy's	125 E. 57 bet. Lex./Park Ave.
Dana Buchman	65 E. 57 bet. Mad./Park Ave.
Denimax	444 Madison bet. 49/50 St.
Domenico Spano	611 Fifth Ave. at 50 St.
Easy Spirit	555 Madison at 56 St.
Eddie Bauer	711 Third bet. 44/45 St.
Eileen Fisher	521 Madison bet. 53/54 St.
Emporio Armani	601 Madison at 57/58 St.
Enzo Angiolini	551 Madison at 55 St.
Enzo Angiolini	331 Madison at 43 St.
Eres	621 Madison bet. 58/59 St.
Express	477 Madison bet. 51/52 St.

Midtown East

Express	722-728 Lexington bet. 58/59 St.
Express	733 Third at 46 St.
Fogal	510 Madison at 53 St.
Forman's	145 E. 42 bet. Lex./Third Ave.
Frank Shattuck	18 E. 53 bet. Mad./Fifth Ave.
Fratelli Rossetti	625 Madison at 58 St.
Gap	572 Madison at 54 St.
Gap	657-659 Third at 42 St.
Gap	900 Third at 54 St.
Gap	734 Lexington bet. 58/59 St.
Gap	757 Third at 47 St.
Gap Kids and Baby Gap	545 Madison at 55 St.
Gap Kids and Baby Gap	757 Third at 47 St.
Gap Kids and Baby Gap	657-659 Third at 42 St.
Geiger	505 Park at 59 St.
Ghurka	41 E. 57 bet. Mad./Park Ave.
H. Herzfeld	507 Madison at 52 St.
Helene Arpels	470 Park bet. 57/58 St.
Holland & Holland	50 E. 57 bet. Mad./Park Ave.
Hunting World	16 E. 53 bet. Mad./Fifth Ave.
John Anthony	130 W 57 bet. Sixth/Seventh Ave.
Johnston & Murphy	520 Madison at 54 St.
Johnston & Murphy	345 Madison bet. 44/45 St.
J. Press	7 E. 44 bet. Mad./Fifth Ave.
Jos. A. Banks	366 Madison bet. 46/47 St.
J. S. Suarez	450 Park bet. 56/57 St.
Kavanagh's Designer Resale Shop	146 E. 49 bet. Third/Lex. Ave.
Kenneth Cole	107 E. 42 at Park Ave.
Lacoste	543 Madison bet. 54/55 St.
Lana Marks	645 Madison bet. 59/60 St.
The Leather and Suede Workshop	107 E. 59 bet. Lex./Park Ave.
Lederer	457 Madison at 51 St.
Legs Beautiful	153 E. 53 at Lexington Ave.
Legs Beautiful	200 Park bet. 44/45 St.
Leonard Logsdail	9 E. 53 bet. Mad./Fifth Ave.
Levi Strauss	750 Lexington bet. 59/60 St.
Levi Strauss	3 E. 57 bet. Mad./Fifth Ave.
Linda Dresner	484 Park at 58 St.
Louis Vuitton	49 E. 57 bet. Mad./Park Ave.
Lucky Brand Dungarees	216 Columbus at 70 St.
Maraolo	551 Madison at 55 St.
Mason's Tennis Mart	56 E. 53 bet. Mad./Park Ave.
Men's Wearhouse	380 Madison at 46 St.
Michel Perry	320 Park at 51 St.
Modell's	51 E. 42 bet.Vanderbilt/Mad. Ave.
New Balance	821 Third at 50 St.
Niketown	6 E. 57 bet. Mad./Fifth Ave.
Nine West	750 Lexington bet. 58/59 St.

Neighborhoods

Midtown West

Nine West	757 Third bet. 47/48 St.
Otto Tootsi Plohound	38 E. 57 bet. Mad./Park. Ave.
Oxxford Clothes	36 E. 57 bet. Mad./Park Ave.
Paul Stuart	Madison at 45 St.
A Pea in the Pod	625 Madison bet. 58/59 St.
Precision	522 Third at 35 St.
Prada	45 E. 57 bet. Mad./Park Ave.
Reaction Kenneth Cole	130 E. 57 at Lexington Ave.
René Mancini	470 Park at 58 St.
Richard Metz Golf Equipment	12 E. 46 bet. Mad./Fifth Ave.
Richard Metzger	325 W. 38 bet. 8/9th Ave.
Saint Laurie, Ltd.	350 Park bet. 51/52 St.
Searle	609 Madison bet 57/58 St.
The Shirt Store	51 E. 44 at Vanderbilt Ave.
Speedo Authentic Fitness	90 Park at 39 St.
Sports Authority	845 Third at 51 St.
Stuart Weitzman	625 Madison bet. 58/59 St.
Talbots	525 Madison bet. 53/54 St.
T. Anthony	445 Park at 56 St.
Tartine et Chocolat	475 Park bet. 57/58 St.
Thomas Pink	520 Madison bet. 53/54 St.
Tod's	650 Madison bet. 59/60 St.
Tokyo Joe	240 E. 28 bet. 2/3rd Ave.
Turnbull & Asser	42 E. 57 bet. Mad./Park Ave.
Victoria's Secret	34 E. 57 bet. Mad./Park Ave.
Vincent Nicolosi	510 Madison at 53 St.
Walter Steiger	417 Park at 55 St.
Wolford	619 Madison bet. 58/59 St.
World of Golf	147 E. 47 bet. Third/Lex. Ave.
Zara International	750 Lexington at 59 St.

Midtown West *See map page 268.*

Aldo	29 W. 34 bet. Fifth/Sixth Ave.
Alixandre	150 W. 30 bet. Sixth/Seventh Ave.
Ann Taylor	1166 Sixth at 46 St.
Ann Taylor Loft	1290 Sixth at 52 St.
Arche	128 W. 57 bet. Sixth/Seventh Ave.
Arthur Gluck Shirtmakers	47 W. 57 bet. Fifth/Sixth Ave.
Ascot Chang	7 W. 57 bet. Fifth/Sixth Ave.
Athlete's Foot	46 W. 34 bet. Fifth/Sixth Ave.
Athlete's Foot	1568 B'way at 47 St.
Baldwin Formalwear	52 W. 56 bet. Fifth/Sixth Ave.
Banana Republic	17 W. 34 bet. Fifth/Sixth Ave.
Banana Republic	107 E. 42 at Madison at Grand Central
Barami	901 Sixth bet. 33/34 St.
Barami	85 Seventh bet 36/37 St.
Blades Board and Skate	901 Sixth at 32 St.
Bolton's	27 W. 57 bet. Fifth/Sixth Ave.
Bolton's	110 W. 51 at Sixth Ave.

Midtown West

Bolton's	1700 B'way at 54 St.
Burberry	9 E. 57 bet. Sixth/Madison Ave.
Capezio	1776 B'way at 57 St.
Capezio	1650 B'way at 51 St.
Champs	1381-1399 Sixth at 56 St.
The Children's Place	1460 B'way bet. 41/42 St.
The Children's Place	901 Sixth bet. 32/33 St.
Christie Brothers Furs	333 Seventh bet. 28/29 St.
Club Monaco	37 W. 57 bet. Fifth/Sixth Ave.
Crunch	144 W. 38 bet. B'way/ Seventh Ave.
Crunch	560 W. 43 at Eleventh Ave.
Daffy's	1311 B'way bet. 33/34 St.
Delfino	56 W. 50 at Rockefeller Ctr.
Easy Spirit	1166 Sixth at 46 St.
Enzo Angiolini	901 Sixth bet. B'way/33 St.
Express	7 W. 34 bet. Fifth/Sixth Ave.
Express	901 Sixth bet. B'way/33 St.
Fame	512 Seventh Avenue bet. 37/38 St.
Fiona Walker	451 W. 46 bet. Ninth/Tenth Ave.
Foot Locker	901 Sixth at 33 St.
Foot Locker	120 W. 34 bet. Sixth/Seventh Ave.
Foot Locker	43 W. 34 bet. Fifth/Sixth Ave.
Frank Stella	921 Seventh at 58 St.
French Connection	1270 Sixth at 51 St.
Gap	60 W. 34 at B'way
Gap	1212 Sixth bet. 47/48 St.
Gap Kids and Baby Gap	1212 Sixth bet. 47/48 St.
Gap	1466 B'way at 42 St.
Gap Kids and Baby Gap	1466 B'way at 42 St.
Gap	250 W. 57 bet. B'way/Eighth Ave.
Geoffrey Beene	37 W. 57 bet. Fifth/Sixth Ave.
Gerry Cosby & Co.	3 Penn Plaza at MSG
H&M (Hennes & Mauritz)	1328 B'way at 34 St.
Jack Silver Formal Wear	1780 B'way bet. 57/58 St.
Keni Valenti	247 W. 30 bet. Seventh/Eighth Ave.
LaCrasia Gloves	304 Fifth at 32 in the Empire State Bld.
Lady Foot Locker	120 W. 34 at Sixth Ave.
Laura Biagiotti	4 W. 57 bet. Fifth/Sixth Ave.
Louis Féraud	3 W. 56 bet. Fifth/Sixth Ave.
Macy's	Herald Sq. at B'way at 34 St.
Maggie Norris	24 West 40 bet. Fifth/Sixth Ave.
Make 10	1386 Sixth bet. 56/57 St.
Manolo Blahnik	31 W. 54 bet. Fifth/Sixth Ave.
Maternity Work	16 W. 57 bet. Fifth/Sixth Ave.
Metro Bicycle	360 W. 47 at Ninth Ave.
Michelle Roth & Co.	24 W. 57 bet. Fifth/Sixth Ave.
Modell's	1293 Broadway at 34 St.
Motherhood Maternity	901 Sixth at 33 St.
Motherhood Maternity outlet	16-18 W. 57 St. bet. Fifth/Sixth Ave.

Neighborhoods

Fifth Avenue

New Balance	51 W. 42 bet. Fifth/Sixth Ave.
New York Golf Center	131 W. 35 bet. B'way/Seventh Ave.
The New York Look	570 Seventh at 41 St.
Nine West	1230 Sixth at 49 St.
Norma Kamali	11 W. 56 bet. Fifth/Sixth Ave.
N. Peal	5 W. 56 bet. Fifth/Sixth Ave.
Old Navy Clothing Co.	150 W. 34 bet. Sixth/Seventh Ave.
Ritz Furs	107 W. 57 bet. Sixth/Seventh Ave.
Rochester Big & Tall	1301 Sixth at 52 St.
Rosa Custom Ties	30 W. 57 bet. Fifth/Sixth Ave.
Scandinavian Ski Shop	40 W. 57 bet. Fifth/Sixth Ave.
Skechers	140 W. 34 bet Sixth/Seventh Ave.
Soho Woman	32 W. 40 bet. Fifth/Sixth Ave.
Sports Authority	57 W. 57 at Sixth Ave.
Steve Madden	45 W. 34 bet. Fifth/Sixth Ave.
Thomas Pink	1155 Sixth at 44 St.
Training Camp	25 W. 45 bet. Fifth/Sixth Ave.
Training Camp	1079 Sixth at 41 St.
Tristan & America	1230 Sixth at 49 St.
Variazioni	37 W. 57 bet. Fifth/Sixth Ave.
Victoria's Secret	901 Sixth at 33rd at Manhattan Mall
Victoria's Secret	Herald Square at 34th St.
Wet Seal	901 Sixth at 33rd at Manhattan Mall
William Fioravanti	45 W. 57 bet. Fifth/Sixth Ave.
Zara International	39 W. 34 bet. Fifth/Sixth Ave.

Fifth Avenue *See map page 269.*

Alfred Dunhill	711 Fifth Ave. bet. 55/56 St.
Ann Taylor	575 Fifth Ave. at 47 St.
A.Testoni	665 Fifth Ave. bet. 52/53 St.
A/X Armani Exchange	645 Fifth Ave. at 51 St.
Banana Republic	655 Fifth Ave. at 52 St.
Banana Republic	626 Fifth Ave. at Rockefeller Ctr.
Barami	535 Fifth Ave. at 45 St.
Benetton	597 Fifth Ave. bet. 48/49 St.
Bergdorf Goodman Men	745 Fifth Ave. at 58 St.
Bergdorf Goodman Women	754 Fifth Ave. bet. 57/58 St.
Best of Scotland	581 Fifth Ave. bet. 47/48 St.
Botticelli	666 Fifth Ave. at Rockefeller Ctr.
Botticelli	522 Fifth Ave. bet. 43/44 St.
Botticelli (women only)	620 Fifth Ave. bet. 49/50 St.
Brooks Brothers	666 Fifth Ave. bet. 52/53 St.
Bruno Magli	677 Fifth Ave. at 53 St.
Coach	620 Fifth Ave. at Rockefeller Ctr.
Cole-Haan	620 Fifth Ave. at 50 St.
Domenico Spano	611 Fifth Ave at 50 St.
Domenico Vacca	781 Fifth Ave. bet. 59/60th St.
Ermenegildo Zegna	743 Fifth Ave. bet. 57/58 St.
Escada	715 Fifth Ave. bet. 55/56 St.

Flatiron

Façonnable	689 Fifth Ave. at Rockefeller Ctr.
Fendi	720 Fifth Ave. at 56 St.
Forman's	560 Fifth Ave. at 46 St.
Gant	645 Fifth Ave. bet. 51/52 St.
Gap	680 Fifth Ave. at 54 St.
Gucci	685 Fifth Ave. at 54 St.
Helen Yarmak	730 Fifth Ave. bet. 56/57 St.
H&M (Hennes & Mauritz)	640 Fifth Ave. at 51 St.
Henri Bendel	712 Fifth Ave. at 56 St.
Hickey-Freeman	666 Fifth Ave. bet. 52/53 St.
Hugo Boss	717 Fifth Ave. 56 St.
Jimmy Choo	645 Fifth Ave. at 51 St.
Kenneth Cole	610 Fifth Ave. at Rockefeller Ctr.
Liz Claiborne	650 Fifth Ave. at 52 St.
Lord & Taylor	424 Fifth Ave. bet. 38/39 St.
Louis Vuitton	703 Fifth Ave. at 55 St.
Maggie Norris	754 Fifth Ave. at Bergdorf Goodman
Make 10	366 Fifth Ave. bet. 34/35 St.
Nautica	50 Rockefeller Ctr. bet. 49/50 St.
The New York Look	551 Fifth Ave. at 45 St.
Nine West	675 Fifth Ave. bet. 53/54 St.
Orvis	522 Fifth Ave. at 44 St.
Oshkosh B'Gosh	586 Fifth Ave. bet. 47/48 St.
Prada	724 Fifth Ave. bet. 56/57 St.
Ripplu	575 Fifth Ave. bet. 46/47 St.
Saks Fifth Avenue	611 Fifth Ave. bet. 49/50 St.
Salvatore Ferragamo Men	725 Fifth Ave. bet. 56/57 St.
Salvatore Ferragamo Women	661 Fifth Ave. bet. 52/53 St.
Speedo Authentic Fitness	500 Fifth Ave. at 42 St.
St. John	665 Fifth Ave. at 53 St.
Takashimaya	693 Fifth Ave. bet. 54/55 St.
Today's Man	529 Fifth Ave. at 44 St.
Versace	647 Fifth Ave. bet. 51/52 St.

Flatiron *See map pages 270–271.*

agnès b.	13 E. 16 bet. Fifth Ave./Union Sq. West
Ann Taylor	149 Fifth Ave. at 21 St.
Anthropologie	85 Fifth Ave. at 16 St.
Banana Republic Women	89 Fifth Ave. bet. 16/17 St.
Banana Republic Men	114 Fifth Ave. bet. 17/18 St.
Bebe	100 Fifth Ave. at 15 St.
The Children's Place	36 Union Sq. East at 16 St.
Club Monaco	160 Fifth Ave. bet. 20/21 St.
Couture by Jennifer Dule	133 Fifth Ave. at 20 St.
Crunch	54 E. 13 bet. B'way/Univ. Pl.
Daffy's	111 Fifth Ave. at 18 St.
Eileen Fisher	103 Fifth Ave. bet. 17/18 St.
Emporio Armani	110 Fifth Ave. at 16 St.
Express	130 Fifth Ave. at 18 St.

Chelsea

Foot Locker	853 B'way at 14 St.
Gap	122 Fifth Ave. bet. 17/18 St.
Gap Kids and Baby Gap	122 Fifth Ave. bet. 17/18 St.
Harry Rothman's	200 Park Ave. South at Union Sq.
Himaya	551 Fifth Ave. at 45 St.
Intermix	125 Fifth Ave. bet. 19/20 St.
J. Crew	91 Fifth Ave. bet. 16/17 St.
J. Crew	30 Rockefeller Ctr. at 50 St.
Juno	170 Fifth Ave. at 22 St.
Kenneth Cole	95 Fifth Ave. at 17 St.
La Gallerie La Rue	12 W. 23 bet. Fifth/Sixth Ave.
Lucky Brand Dungarees	172 Fifth Ave. at 22 St.
Miller Harness Company	117 E. 24 bet. Park/Lex. Ave.
Nine West	115 Fifth Ave. at 19 St.
Otto Tootsi Plohound	137 Fifth Ave. bet. 20/21 St.
Paragon Sporting Goods	867 B'way at 18 St.
Paul Smith	108 Fifth Ave. at 16 St.
Princeton Ski Shop	21 E. 22 bet. B'way/Park Ave. South
Sacco	14 E. 17 bet. Broadway/Fifth Ave.
Skechers USA	150 Fifth Ave. bet. 19/20 St.
Space Kiddets	46 E. 21 bet. B'way/Park Ave.
Threads	26 W. 17 bet. Fifth/Sixth Ave.
Victoria's Secret	115 Fifth Ave. bet. 18/19 St.
Warehouse	150 Fifth Ave. bet. 19/20 St.
Zara International	101 Fifth Ave. bet. 17/18 St.

Chelsea *See map page 270.*

Alexander McQueen	413 W. 14 bet. Ninth/Washington
Alexandros Furs	213 W. 28 bet. Seventh/Eighth Ave.
Banana Republic (M)	111 Eighth Ave. bet. 15/16 St.
Benetton	120 Seventh Ave. at 17 St.
Ben Thylan Furs	345 Seventh Ave. bet. 29/30 St.
Blades Board and Skate	23rd and West St. at Chelsea Pier 62
Burlington Coat Factory	707 Sixth Ave. at 23 St.
Camouflage	139/141 Eighth Ave. at 17 St.
Comme des Garçons	520 W. 22 bet. Tenth/Eleventh Ave.
Destination	32-36 Little West 12 St. bet. Wash./Ninth Ave.
Eisenberg & Eisenberg	16 W. 17 bet. Fifth/Sixth Ave.
Fan Club	22 W. 19 bet. Fifth/Sixth Ave.
Filene's Basement	620 Sixth Ave. bet. 18/19 St.
Find Outlet	361 W. 17 bet. Eighth/Ninth Ave.
Fisch for the Hip	153 W. 18 bet. Sixth/Seventh Ave.
Giraudon	152 Eighth Ave. bet. 17/18 St.
Jeffrey New York	449 W. 14 bet. Ninth/Tenth Ave.
Loehmann's	101 Seventh Ave. bet. 16/17 St.
Lost Art	515 W. 29 bet. Tenth/Eleventh Ave.
Lucy Barnes	422 W. 15 bet. Ninth/Tenth Ave.

East Village/Lower East Side

Men's Wearhouse	655 Sixth Ave. at 20 St.
Metro Bicycle	546 Sixth Ave. at 15 St.
Motherhood Maternity	641 Sixth Ave. at 20 St.
Old Navy Clothing Co.	610 Sixth Ave. bet. 17/18 St.
Parke & Ronen	176 Ninth Ave. bet. 20/21 St.
Powers Court Tennis Outlet	132 1/2 W. 24 St. bet. Sixth/Seventh Ave.
Reminiscence	50 W. 23 bet. Fifth/Sixth Ave.
Sacco	94 Seventh Ave bet. 15/16 St.
Shelly Steffee	34 Gainsvoort Street at 9th Ave.
Sports Authority	636 Sixth Ave.at 19 St.
Stella McCartney	429 W. 14 bet. Ninth/Washington
TJ Maxx	620 Sixth Ave. bet. 18/19 St.
Today's Man	625 Sixth Ave. bet. 18/19 St.
Urban Outfitters	526 Sixth Ave. at 14 St.

East Village/Lower East Side *See map page 271.*

A. Cheng	443 E. 9 bet. Ave. A/First Ave.
Alife	178 Orchard bet Houston/Stanton
Alife Rivington Club	158 Rivington Street bet. Clinton/Suffolk
Alpana Bawa (outlet)	70 E. 1 bet. First/Second Ave.
Amarcord Vintage Fashion	84 E. 7 bet. First/Second Ave.
Amy Downs Hats	227 E. 14 bet Second/Third Ave.
Angelo Lambrou	96 E. 7 bet. Ave. A/First Ave.
Anna	150 E. 3 bet. Ave. A/B
Atomic Passion	430 E. 9 bet Ave. A/First Ave.
Barbara Feinman Millinery	66 E. 7 bet. First/Second Ave.
Barbara Shaum	60 E. 4 bet. Bowery/Second Ave.
Bridge	98-100 Orchard bet. Broome/Delancey
DDC Lab	180 Orchard bet. Stanton/Houston
D/L Cerney	13 E. 7 bet. Second/Third Ave.
Do Kham	304 E. 5 bet. First/Second Ave.
Doyle & Doyle	189 Orchard Street bet. Houston/Stanton
Eileen Fisher	314 E. 9 bet. First/Second Ave.
Enerla	48 1/2 E. 7 bet. First/Second Ave.
Eugenia Kim	203 E. 4 bet. Ave. A/B
Fabulous Fanny's	335 E. 9 bet. First/Second Ave.
February Eleventh	315 E. 9 bet. First/Second Ave.
Filth Mart	531 E. 13 bet. Avenue A/B
Fine & Klein	119 Orchard at Delancey
Flood	26 First Ave. bet. 1/2 St.
Foley & Corinna	108 Stanton bet. Ludlow/Essex
Foot Locker	252 First Ave. at 15 St.
Foot Locker	94 Delancey bet. Ludlow/Orchard
Forman's	82 Orchard bet. Broome/Grand
Gabbriel Ichak	430 E. 9 bet. First/Ave. A
Gap (Men)	750 B'way bet. Astor Pl./8 St.
Gap	1 Astor Pl. at B'way

Neighborhoods

289

NoHo/West Village

The Gown Company	326 E. 9 bet. First/Second Ave.
Hello Sari	261 Broome bet. Allen/Orchard
Huminska New York	315 E. 9 bet. First/Second Ave.
Jill Anderson	331 E. 9 bet. First/Second Ave.
Johnson	179 Orchard bet. Houston/Stanton
Jutta Neumann	158 Allen bet. Stanton/Rivington
Klein's of Monticello	105 Orchard at Delancey
Lara Nabulsi	101 Stanton Street at Ludlow
Leather Corner	144 Orchard at Rivington
Lord of the Fleas	305 E. 9 bet. First/Second Ave.
MarcoArt	181 Orchard bet. Houston/Stanton
Mark Montano	434 E. 9 bet. First/Ave. A
Marmalade	172 Ludlow bet Houston/Stanton
Martin	206 E. 6 bet. Second/Third Ave.
Mary Adams	128 Ludlow bet. Stanton/Delancey
Meg	312 E. 9 bet. First/Second Ave
Metro Bicycle	332 E. 14 bet. First/Second Ave.
Miracle	100 St. Mark's Place bet. First/Second Ave.
Mshop	177 Orchard bet. Houston/Stanton
99X	84 E. 10 bet. 3/4 St.
No. 436	436 E. 9 bet. First/Ave. A
The Open Door Gallery	27 E. 3 bet. Second Ave./Bowery
Peacock NYC	440 E. 9 bet. First/Ave. A
Project	175 Orchard Street at Stanton
Resurrection Vintage	123 E. 7 bet. First/Ave. A
Selia Yang	328 E. 9 bet. First/Second Ave.
Skella	156 Orchard St. bet. Rivington/Stanton
Shop	105 Stanton at Ludlow
Stanley	169 Ludlow bet Houston/Stanton
Studio 109	115 St. Mark's Place bet. First/Ave. A
TG-170	170 Ludlow bet. Houston/Stanton
Tokio 7	64 E. 7 bet. First/Second Ave.
Tokyo Joe	334 E. 11 bet. First/Second Ave.
Urban Outfitters	162 Second Ave. bet. 10/11 St.
The Village Scandal	19 E. 7 bet. Second/Third Ave.
Vlada	101 Stanton at Ludlow
Võ	169 Ludlow bet Houston/Stanton
Yona Lee	412 E. 9 bet. First/Ave. A

NoHo/West Village *See map pages 270-271.*

Aerosoles	63 E. 8 bet. B'way/University Pl.
Aldo	700 B'way at W. 4 St.
Andy's Chee-pees	691 B'way bet. 3/4 St.
Ann Taylor Loft	770 B'way at 9 St.
Antique Boutique	712-714 B'way bet. 4 St./Astor Pl.
Arche	10 Astor Place bet. Lafayette/B'way
Arleen Bowman	353 Bleecker bet. W. 10/Charles
Athlete's Foot	60 E. 8 at B'way
Atrium	644 B'way at Bleecker

NoHo/West Village

Banana Republic	205 Bleecker at Sixth Ave.
Basiques	380 Bleecker Street bet. Perry/Charles
Basis Basic	710 B'way bet. Wash. Pl./4 St.
Benetton	749 B'way bet. 8 St./Astor Pl.
Betwixt	245 W. 10 bet. Bleecker/Hudson
Blades Board and Skate	659 B'way bet. 3 St./Bleecker
Bond 07	7 Bond bet. B'way/Lafayette
Cherry	19 8th Avenue bet. W. 12/James
Crunch	404 Lafayette bet. Astor/4 St.
Crunch	152 Christopher St. bet. Wash./Greenwich
Decollage	23 Eighth Avenue bet.12/James
Diane von Furstenberg	385 W. 12 bet. Wash./W. Side Highway
Diesel	1 Union Sq. West at 14 St.
Eastern Mountain Sports	611 B'way bet. Houston/Bleecker
Eclipse	400 Lafayette at E. 4 St.
Eye Candy	329 Lafayette Street bet. Bleecker/Houston
Flight 001	96 Greenwich Avenue at 12 St.
Foot Locker	734 Broadway at 8 St.
French Connection	700 B'way bet. Wash. Pl./4 St.
Gap	345 Sixth Ave. at 4 St.
Gap Kids and Baby Gap	354 Sixth Ave. at Washington Pl.
Gerry's	353 Bleecker Street bet. 10th/Charles
Ghost	28 Bond bet. Lafayette/Bowery
Jungle Planet	175 W. 4 bet Sixth/Seventh Ave.
Katayone Adeli	35 Bond bet. Lafayette/Bowery
KD Dance	339 Lafayette at Bleecker
La Gallerie la Rue	385 Bleecker at Perry
La Petite Coquette	51 University Pl. bet 9/10 St.
The Leather Man	111 Christopher bet. Bleecker/Hudson
Luichiny	21 W. 8 bet. Fifth/Sixth Ave.
Make 10	680 B'way bet. Bond/W. 3 St.
Make 10	49 W. 8 bet. Fifth/Sixth Ave.
Marc Jacobs	403 Bleecker bet. W. 11/Hudson
Marc Jacobs	405 Bleecker bet. W.11/Hudson
Memes	3 Great Jones bet. Lafayette/B'way
Milen Shoes	23 W. 8 bet. Fifth/Sixth Ave.
1 on G	55 Great Jones Street bet. Bowery/Broadway
Original Leather	171 W. 4 bet Sixth/Seventh Ave.
Sleek on Bleecker	361 Bleecker bet. W. 10/Charles
Patricia Field	10 E. 8 bet. Fifth/University Pl.
Petit Peton	27 W. 8 bet. Fifth/Sixth Ave.
Rafé New York	1 Bleecker at Bowery
Screaming Mimi's	382 Lafayette bet. Great Jones/4 St.
Skechers USA	55 W. 8 bet. Fifth/Sixth Ave.
Tibet Arts & Crafts	197 Bleecker bet. MacDougal/Sixth Ave.
Tupli	378 Bleecker bet. Charles/Perry
Untitled	26 W. 8 bet. Fifth/Sixth Ave.
Urban Outfitters	374 6th Ave. bet. Waverly/Wash. Pl.

Neighborhoods

SoHo/NoLiTa

Urban Outfitters	628 B'way bet. Houston/Bleecker
Verve Shoes	105 Christopher bet. Bleecker/Hudson
Wet Seal	670 B'way at Bond St.
Whiskey Dust	526 Hudson bet. 10th St./Charles

SoHo/NoLiTa *See map pages 270–271.*

Aboud Mimi	137 Thompson bet. Prince/Houston
Add	461 W. B'way bet. Houston/Prince
A Détacher	262 Mott bet. Houston/Prince
Adidas	136 Wooster bet Prince/Spring
Afterlife	450 B'way bet. Houston/Prince
agnès b.	76 Greene Street bet. Spring/Broome
agnès b. hommes	79 Greene at Spring
Alpana Bawa	41 Grand bet. W. B'way/Thompson
American Colors	232 Elizabeth bet. Prince/Houston
Amy Chan	247 Mulberry bet. Prince/Spring
Anna Sui	113 Greene bet. Prince/Spring
Anne Fontaine	93 Greene bet. Prince/Spring
Anne Klein	417 W. B'way bet. Prince/Spring
Anthropologie	375 W. B'way bet. Broome/Spring
A.P.C.	131 Mercer bet. Prince/Spring
Avirex	652 B'way bet. Bleecker/Bond
A/X Armani Exchange	568 B'way at Prince
Baby Blue Line	238 Mott bet. Prince/Spring
Bagutta	402 W. B'way at Spring
Banana Republic Men	528 B'way at Spring
Banana Republic Women	552 B'way bet. Prince/Spring
Barbara Bui	117 Wooster bet. Prince/Spring
Barneys Co-op	116 Wooster bet. Prince/Spring
Beau Brummel	421 W. B'way bet. Prince/Spring
Benetton	555 B'Way bet Prince/Spring
Betsey Johnson	138 Wooster bet. Prince/Houston
Big Drop	174 Spring bet. Thompson/W. B'way
Big Drop	425 W. B'way bet. Prince/Spring
Bisou-Bisou	474 W. B'way bet. Houston/Prince
Bicycle Habitat	244 Lafayette bet. Prince/Spring
Blue Bag	266 Elizabeth at Houston
Boudoir	244 Mulberry bet. Prince/Spring
Buffalo Chips Bootery	355 W. B'way bet. Broome/Grand
Built by Wendy	7 Centre Market Place bet. Broome/Gran
Cadeau	254 Elizabeth bet. Houston/Prince
Calypso Enfant	284 Mulberry bet. Houston/Prince
Calypso Enfant	280 Mulberry bet. Houston/Prince
Calypso Hommes	405 Broome bet. Crosby/Lafayette
Calypso St. Barths	280 Mott bet. Houston/Prince
Calypso St. Barths	424 Broome bet. Crosby/Lafayette
Canal Jean Company	504 B'way bet. Spring/Broome
Catherine	468 Broome at Greene
Chanel	139 Spring at Wooster

SoHo/NoLiTa

Chelsea Girl	63 Thompson bet. Broome/Spring
Christopher Totman	262 Mott bet. Houston/Prince
Chuckies	399 B'way bet. Broome/Spring
Club Monaco	121 Prince bet. Wooster/Greene
Club Monaco	520 B'way at Spring
Coach	143 Prince at W. B'way
C.P. Shades	154 Spring bet. Wooster/W. B'way
C. Ronson	269 Elizabeth bet. Houston/Prince
Crunch	623 B'way at Houston
Cynthia Rowley	112 Wooster bet. Prince/Spring
Deborah Moorfield	466 Broome bet. Mercer/Greene
Deco Jewels	131 Thompson bet. Prince/Houston
Detour	472 W. B'way bet. Houston/Prince
Detour	154 Prince bet. W. B'way/Thompson
Detour	425 W. B'way bet. Prince/Spring
D&G	434 W. B'way bet. Prince/Spring
Dinosaur Designs	250 Mott bet. Houston/Prince
DKNY	420 W. B'way bet. Prince/Spring
Dosa	107 Thompson bet. Spring/Prince
Earl Jean	160 Mercer bet. Houston/Prince
Eastern Mountain Sports	611 B'way at Houston
Eddie Bauer	578 B'way bet. Houston/Prince
Edmundo Castillo	219 Mott bet. Houston/Prince
Emporio Armani	410 W. B'way at Prince
Eres	98 Wooster at Spring
Flying A	169 Spring bet. W. B'way/Thompson
45rpm	169 Mercer at Houston
Fossil	541 B'way at Prince
Francis Hendy	65 Thompson bet. Spring/Broome
French Connection	435 W. B'way bet. Prince/Spring
Furla	430 W. B'way bet. Spring/Prince
Gas	238 Mott bet. Prince/Spring
Geraldine	246 Mott bet. Houston/Prince
Gi Gi	15 Prince at Elizabeth
Girlprops.com	153 Prince at W. B'way
Guess?	537 B'way bet. Prince/Spring
H&M	588 B'way bet. Prince/Spring
Hans Koch	174 Prince bet. Sullivan/Thompson
Harriet Love	126 Prince bet. Wooster/Greene
The Hat Shop	120 Thompson bet. Prince/Spring
Hedra Prue	281 Mott bet. Houston/Prince
Helen Mariën	250 Mott bet. Prince/Houston
Helmut Lang	80 Greene bet. Spring/Broome
Henry Lehr	232 Elizabeth bet. Prince/Lafayette
Henry Lehr	268 Elizabeth bet. Houston/Prince
Hiponica	238 Mott bet. Prince/Spring
Hogan	134 Spring bet. Greene/Wooster
Hollywould	284 Mulberry bet. Prince/Houston
Hotel Venus	382 W. B'way bet. Broome/Spring

Neighborhoods

SoHo/NoLiTa

Hugo Hugo Boss	132 Greene bet. Prince/Houston
If	94 Grand bet. Mercer/Greene
Il Bisonte	72 Thompson bet. Broome/Spring
Ina	101 Thompson bet. Spring/Prince
Institut	97 Spring bet. Mercer/Greene
Jade	280 Mulberry bet. Houston/Prince
Janet Russo	262 Mott bet. Houston/Prince
J. Crew	99 Prince at Mercer
J. Lindeberg	126 Spring at Greene
Jenne Maag	29 Spring at Mott
Jenny B.	118 Spring bet. Mercer/Greene
Jill Stuart	100 Greene bet. Prince/Spring
John Fluevog	250 Mulberry at Prince
Joovay	436 W. B'way at Prince
Joseph	115 Greene bet. Spring/Prince
Joseph	106 Greene bet. Spring/Prince
Julian and Sara	103 Mercer bet. Prince/Spring
Juno	543 B'way bet. Prince/Spring
Juno	444 B'way bet. Grand/Canal
Just for Tykes	83 Mercer bet. Spring/Broome
Kate Spade	454 Broome at Mercer
Keiko	62 Greene bet. Spring/Broome
Kelly Christy	235 Elizabeth bet. Houston/Prince
Kenneth Cole	597 B'way bet. Prince/Houston
Kenzo	80 Wooster bet. Spring/Broome
Kirna Zabête	96 Greene bet. Spring/Prince
Klurk	360 Broome bet. Mott/Elizabeth
Language	238 Mulberry bet. Prince/Spring
Laundry by Shelli Segal	97 Wooster bet. Prince/Spring
Le Corset	80 Thompson bet. Spring/Broome
Legacy	109 Thompson bet. Prince/Spring
LeSportSac	176 Spring bet. W. B'way/Thompson
Lisa Shaub	232 Mulberry bet. Prince/Spring
Louis Vuitton	116 Greene bet. Spring/Prince
Lucky Brand Dungarees	38 Greene at Grand
Lynn Park NY	51 Wooster at Broome
Malatesta	115 Grand bet. B'way/Mercer
Malia Mills	199 Mulberry bet. Spring/Kenmare
Malo	125 Wooster bet. Prince/Spring
Marc Jacobs	163 Mercer bet. Houston/Prince
Mare	426 W. B'way bet. Prince/Spring
Marianne Novobatzky	65 Mercer bet. Spring/Broome
Marni	161 Mercer bet. Houston/Prince
Martino Midali	160 Spring bet. W. B'way/Wooster
Mary Efron	68 Thompson bet. Broome/Spring
Max Studio	415 W. B'way bet. Prince/Spring
Me & Ro	239 Elizabeth bet. Houston/Prince
Me Too	500 Broome at West Broadway
Minium New York	49 Prince bet. Lafayette/Mulberry
Miu Miu	100 Prince bet. Greene/Mercer

SoHo/NoLiTa

Miss Sixty	246 Mulberry bet Prince/Spring
Miss Sixty	386 W. B'way bet Spring/Broome
Mixona	262 Mott bet. Houston/Prince
Mommy Chic	235 Mulberry bet. Spring/Prince
Morgane Le Fay	67 Wooster bet. Spring/Broome
Nahbee	262 Mott bet. Houston/Prince
New & Almost New	65 Mercer bet. Spring/Broome
Nicole Miller	134 Prince bet. Wooster/W. B'way
Nine West	577 B'way at Prince
The 1909 Company	63 Thompson bet. Broome/ Spring
Old Navy Clothing Co.	503 B'way bet. Spring/Broome
Olive & Bette's	158 Spring bet. Wooster/W. B'way
Omari	68 Spring bet. Crosby/Lafayette
Only Hearts	230 Mott bet. Prince/Spring
Onward Soho	172 Mercer at Houston
Ottiva	192 Spring bet. Thompson/Sullivan
Otto Tootsi Plohound	413 W. B'way bet. Spring/Prince
Patagonia	101 Wooster bet. Prince/Spring
Patina	451 Broome bet. B'way/Mercer
Peter Fox Shoes	105 Thompson bet. Spring/Prince
Peter Hermann	118 Thompson bet. Spring/Prince
Philosophy di Alberta Ferretti	452 W. B'way bet. Houston/Prince
Pierre Garroudi	139 Thompson bet. Prince/Houston
Pleats Please	128 Wooster at Prince
Prada	575 B'way at Prince
The Puma Store	521 Broadway bet. Spring/Broome
Pumpkin Maternity	407 Broome bet. Lafayette/Center
Quiksilver	109 Spring at Mercer
Ralph Lauren	381 W. B'way bet. Broome/Spring
Rampage	127 Prince at Wooster
Red Wong	181 Mulberry bet. Kenmare/Broome
Replay Store	109 Prince at Greene
Resurrection Vintage	217 Mott bet. Prince/Spring
Rockport	565 W. B'way bet. Houston/Prince
Rugby North America	115 Mercer bet. Prince/Spring
Sacco	111 Thompson bet. Spring/Prince
Salvatore Ferragamo	124 Spring at Greene
Scoop	532 B'way bet. Prince/Spring
Sean	132 Thompson bet. Houston/Prince
Seize sur Vingt	243 Elizabeth bet. Houston/Prince
Selvedge	250 Mulberry bet. Prince/Spring
Shin Choi	19 Mercer bet. Prince/Spring
Shop Noir	246 Mott bet Prince/Houston
Sigerson Morrison	242 Mott bet. Houston/Prince
Sigerson Morrison	28 Prince bet. Mott/Elizabeth
Sisley	469 W. B'way bet. Prince/Houston
Skechers USA	530 B'way at Spring
Smaak	219 Mulberry bet. Prince/Spring
SoHo Baby	247 Elizabeth bet.Houston/Prince

Neighborhoods

Lower Manhattan/TrBeCa

Stackhouse	282 Lafayette bet. Prince/Houston
Stephane Kélian	158 Mercer bet. Houston/Prince
Steve Madden	540 B'way bet. Prince/Spring
Steven Alan	60 Wooster bet. Broome/Spring
The Stork Club	142 Sullivan bet. Prince/Houston
Stüssy	140 Wooster bet. Houston/Prince
Supreme	274 Lafayette bet. Prince/Houston
37 = 1	37 Crosby bet. Grand/Broome
Tommy Hilfiger	372 W. B'way bet. Spring/Broome
Tracy Feith	209 Mulberry bet. Spring/Kenmare
Triple Five Soul	290 Lafayette bet. Houston/Prince
Union	172 Spring bet. W. B'way/Thompson
Unis	226 Elizabeth bet. Houston/Prince
Varda	149 Spring bet. Wooster/W. B'way
Victoria's Secret	565 B'way bet. Prince/Spring
Vivienne Tam	99 Greene bet. Spring/Prince
Vivienne Westwood	71 Greene bet. Spring/Broome
Wang	219 Mott bet. Prince/Spring
Warehouse	581 B'way bet. Houston/Prince
Western Spirit	486 B'way at Broome
What Comes Around Goes Around	351 W. B'way bet. Broome/Grand
Wolford	122 Greene at Prince
Yohji Yamamoto	103 Grand at Mercer
Y & Kei water the earth	125 Greene bet. Prince/Spring
Zara International	580 B'way at Prince

Lower Manhattan/TriBeCa *See map pages 272-273.*

Abercrombie & Fitch	119 Water at S.S.S.
Aerosoles	18 John bet. B'way/Nassau
American Eagle Outfitters	89 South at S.S.S.
Assets London	152 Franklin bet. Hudson/Varick
Behrle	89 Franklin bet. Church/Broadway
Benetton	10 Fulton at S.S.S.
Brooks Brothers	1 Liberty Plaza at Church
Century 21	22 Cortland bet. Church/B'way
Champs	89 S.S.S at Pier 17
D/L Cerney	222 W. B'way bet. Franklin/White
Easy Spirit	182 B'way bet. John/Maiden Lane
Foot Locker	89 S.S.S. at Pier 17
Gap	89 S.S.S. at Pier 17
Gap Kids and Baby Gap	89 S.S.S. at Pier 17
Gotham Bikes	112 W. B'way bet. Duane/Reade
Guess?	23-25 Fulton at S.S.S.
Issey Miyake	119 Hudson at N. Moore
J. Crew	203 Front at S.S.S.
Koh's Kids	311 Greenwich bet. Chambers/Reade
Legs Beautiful	225 Liberty at World Fin. Ctr.

Metro Bicycle	417 Canal at Sixth Ave.
Mika Inatome	11 Worth bet. W. B'way/Hudson
Min Lee	7 Prince bet. Elizabeth/Bowery
Modell's	200 B'way bet. Fulton/John
Modell's	280 B'way at Chambers
Peanutbutter and Jane	617 Hudson bet. Jane/12 St.
Samuel's Hats	74 Nassau at John
Shoofly	42 Hudson bet. Duane/Thomas
Sorelle Firenze	139 1/2 Reade Street bet. Hudson/Greenwich
Steven Alan	103 Franklin bet. Hudson/Varick
Talbots	189-191 Front at S.S.S.
TriBeCa Luggage & Leather	90 Hudson at Harrison
Victoria's Secret	Pier 17 at S.S.S.
Young's Hat Corner	139 Nassau at Beekman

Harlem *See map pages 264-265.*

Lane Bryant   222 W. 125 bet. Seventh/Eighth Ave.

Brooklyn

Kleinfeld & Son   8202 Fifth Ave. at 82 St.

Health & Beauty

Barbers

Haircuts—Unisex

Haircuts—Children

Hair Salons

Hair Removal

Beauty Treatments

Eyebrow Grooming

Manicures/Pedicures

Day Spas

Fitness Studios

Pilates/Mat Classes

Yoga

Massage Therapists

Tanning

Bridal Consultants

Make-up Artists

Personal Shoppers

Health & Beauty

Barbers

Chelsea Barbers
465 West 23rd Street
NYC 10011
212-741-2254
bet. 9/10th Ave.
Mon-Fri 9-7, Sat 9-6

Delta Men's Hair Stylist
992 Lexington Avenue
NYC 10021
212-628-5723 or 212-650-9055
Mon-Sat 8-7

Jerry's Salon
50 Rockefeller Plaza
NYC 10020
212-246-3151
enter bet. 5/6th Ave.
Mon-Fri 8-6

Paul Mole
1031 Lexington Avenue
NYC 10021 Mon-Fri 7:30-6:30, Sat 7:30-5:30, Sun 9-3:30
212-535-8461
bet. 73/74th St.

York Barber
981 Lexington Avenue
NYC 10021
212-988-6136
bet. 70/71st St.
Mon-Fri 8-7, Sat 8-6

Haircuts—Unisex

Astor Place Hair Designers ($14 cuts)
2 Astor Place
NYC 10003
212-475-9854
bet. B'way/8th Ave.
Mon-Sat 8-8, Sun 9-6

Ginger Rose on Bleecker ($20 cuts)
154 Bleecker Street
NYC 10012
212-677-6511
bet. Thompson/LaGuardia
Mon-Sat 10-7, Sun 12-6

Jean Louis David ($23-$36 cuts)
2111 Broadway
NYC 10023
212-873-1850
at 73rd St.
Mon-Sat 10-7, Sun 11-5

Jean Louis David ($23-$36 cuts)
783 Lexington Avenue
NYC 10021
212-838-7372
at 61st St.
Mon-Fri 10-7, Sat 9-7

Jean Louis David ($23-$36 cuts)
1180 Sixth Avenue
NYC 10011
212-944-7389
at 46th St.
Mon-Sat 10-7

Jean Louis David ($23-$36 cuts)
30 Vesey Street
NYC 10007
212-732-4938
at Church
Mon-Fri 10-7

Haircuts—Children

Cozy's Cuts for Kids
1125 Madison Avenue
NYC 10028
212-744-1716
at 84/85th St.
Mon-Sat 10-6

Cozy's Cuts for Kids
448 Amsterdam Avenue
NYC 10024
212-579-2600
bet. 81/82nd St.
Mon-Sat 10-5:30

Kids Cuts
201 East 31st Street
NYC 10016
212-684-5252
bet. 2/3rd Ave.
Tues-Sat 10-6

Health & Beauty

Hair Salons

A.K.S.   **212-888-0707**
694 Madison Avenue
NYC 10021
bet. 62/63rd St.
Mon-Sat 9-6, Wed & Thurs 9-8

Antonio Prieto Salon   **212-255-3741**
25 West 19th Street
NYC 10011
bet. 5/6th Ave.
Mon-Sat 9-9

Bollei   **212-759-7985**
115 East 57th Street
NYC 10022
bet. Lex./Park Ave.
Mon-9-4, Tues, Wed & Fri 8-5
Thurs 8-7, Sat 9-4

Bumble & Bumble   **212-521-6500**
146 East 56th Street
NYC 10022
bet. Lexington/3rd Ave.
Tues-Fri 9:30-8, Sat 8-6

Devachan Hair Salon & Day Spa   **212-274-8686**
560 Broadway
NYC 10012
bet. Spring/Prince
Tues-Fri 11-7, Sat 10-5

Donsuki   **212-826-3397**
19 East 62nd Street
NYC 10021
bet. Madison/5th Ave.
Tues-Sat 9-6

Dop Dop Salon   **212-965-9540**
170 Mercer Street
NYC 10012
bet. Houston/Prince
Mon-Wed 11-5, Thur-Sat 11-7

Eiji (specializes in dry cuts)   **212-570-1151**
768 Madison Avenue, 2nd Fl.
NYC 10021
bet. 65/66th St.
Tues-Sat 9-6

Frederic Fekkai   **212-753-9500**
15 East 57th Street,
Level T1
NYC 10022
bet. Madison/5th
in the Chanel Bldg.
Mon, Tues & Sat 9-6
Wed & Fri 9-7, Thur 9-8

Garren Salon at Henri Bendel   **212-841-9400**
712 Fifth Avenue
NYC 10019
bet. 55/56th St.
Mon-Sat 9-7, Thur 9-8

John Barrett Salon   **212-872-2700**
754 Fifth Avenue, 9th Fl.
NYC 10019
at Bergdorf Goodman
Mon-Wed & Fri 10-7, Thur 10-8
Sat 9-7, Sun 12-6

John Frieda   **212-879-1000**
797 Madison Avenue, 2nd Fl.
NYC 10021
bet. 67/68th St.
Mon-Sat 8:30-6:30, Thur 8:30-7

John Masters Organic Haircare   **212-343-9590**
77 Sullivan Street
NYC 10012
bet. Spring/Broome
Mon-Fri 11-6:30, Sat 10-6:30, Sun 12-5

John Sahag   **212-750-7772**
425 Madison Avenue, 2nd Fl.
NYC 10017
at 49th St.
Tues-Sat 8:30-8

Health & Beauty

Julien Farel
605 Madison Avenue
NYC 10022
212-888-8988
bet. 57-58th St.
Mon-Wed 9-5:30, Thur-Sat 9-7

Julius Caruso Salon
22 East 62nd Street
NYC 10021
212-759-7574
bet. Madison/5th Ave.
Mon-Sat 9-5

Kenneth Salon
301 Park Avenue
NYC 10022
212-752-1800
at The Waldorf Astoria Hotel
Mon-Sat 9-6, Wed 9-8

Louis Licari Color Group
693 Fifth Avenue
NYC 10021
212-758-2090
at Takashimaya bet. 53/54th St.
Mon & Tues 8:30-7, Wed & Sat 7:30-5:30
Thur & Fri 7:30-8

Miano Viel
16 East 52nd Street
NYC 10022
212-980-3222
bet. Madison/5th Ave.
Tues 9-6, Wed, Fri & Sat 9-5, Thur 9-7

Minardi Salon
29 East 61st Street
NYC 10021
212-308-1711
bet. Park/Madison Ave.
Mon 9-7, Tues 8-9, Wed & Fri 8-7
Thur 9-9, Sat 9-5

Oribe
691 Fifth Avenue
NYC 10022
212-319-3910
at Elizabeth Arden bet. 54/55th St.
Mon-Sat 9-6

Oscar Blandi
768 Fifth Avenue
NYC 10019
212-593-7930
at The Plaza Hotel at 58th St.
Mon-Sat 8-6, Thur 8-7

Oscar Bond
42 Wooster Street
NYC 10013
212-334-3777
bet. Broome/Grand
Tues & Wed 10-8
Thur & Fri 11-9, Sat 10-6, Sun 11-6

Peter Coppola
746 Madison Avenue
NYC 10021
212-988-9404
bet. 64/65th St.
Mon-Sat 9-6, Thur 9-7

Pierre Michel
131 East 57th Street
NYC 10022
212-593-1460
bet. Lex./Park Ave.
Mon-Sat 8:30-6

Prive at The Soho Grand
310 West Broadway
NYC 10013
212-274-8888
bet. Grand/Canal
Mon 11-5, Tues & Fri 10-7
Wed & Thur 10-9, Sat 10-6, Sun 12-6

Red Salon
323 West 11th Street
NYC 10014
212-924-1444
bet. Greenwich/Washington
Mon-Fri 12-8, Sat 11-5

Robert Kree Salon
375 Bleecker Street
NYC 10014
212-989-9547
bet. Charles/Perry
Mon & Sun 12-7, Tues-Fri 11-8, Sat 10-6

Simon
22 East 66th Street
NYC 10021
212-517-4566
bet. Madison/5th Ave.
Mon-Sat 10-6

Health & Beauty

Soon Beauty Lab 212-260-4423
318 East 11th Street bet. 1st/2nd Ave.
NYC 10003 Mon-Fri 11-8, Sat-Sun 10-5

Space 212-647-8588
155 Sixth Avenue at Spring
NYC 10013 Tues-Fri 11-8, Sat 10-7

Suite 303 at The Chelsea Hotel 212-633-1011
222 West 23rd Street bet. 7/8th Ave.
NYC 10011 Tues-Fri 12-6:45, Sat 12-4:45

Thomas Morrissey Salon 212-772-1111
787 Madison Avenue bet. 66/67th St.
NYC 10021 Mon-Sat 9-5, Thur 9-6

Yann Varin 212-734-9055
142 East 73rd Street bet. Park/Lex. Ave.
NYC 10021 Mon-Fri 10-7, Sat 9-6

Hair Removal

Bernice Electrolysis 212-355-7055
29 East 61st Street, 2nd Fl. bet. Park/Madison Ave.
NYC 10021 Mon, Tues., Fri & Sat 8-6
  Wed & Thur 8-8

Completely Bare 212-717-9300
764 Madison Avenue bet. 65/66th St.
NYC 10021 Mon-Thurs 10-9, Fri 10-7, Sat 10-6

Expert Electrolysis Inc. 212-755-0671
57 West 57th Street, Suite 810 bet. 5/6th Ave.
NYC 10022 by appointment

Isabella Electrolysis 212-832-0431
794 Lexington Avenue bet. 61/62nd St.
NYC 10021 Mon-Fri 10-7, Thur 10-8, Sat 10-6

Miriam Vasicka 212-734-1017
897 Park Avenue at 79th St.
NYC 10021 daily 730-7:30 by appointment

Smooth 212-759-6997
133 East 58th Street, Suite 507 bet. Park/Lexington Ave.
NYC 10022 Mon-Fri 12-7

Steven Victor, M.D. 212-249-3050
30 East 76th Street bet. Park/Madison Ave.
NYC 10021 daily by appointment

Beauty Treatments

Beauty Basics Skincare 212-288-7781
1166 Lexington Avenue at 80th St.
NYC 10028 by appointment

Bernice 212-355-7055
29 East 61st Street, 2nd Floor bet. Park/Madison Ave.
NYC 10021 Mon, Tues, Fri & Sat 8-6, Wed & Thur 8-8

Health & Beauty

Diane Young — 212-753-1200
38 East 57th Street, 8th Fl.   bet. Park/Madison Ave.
NYC 10022   Mon-Thur 10-8, Fri 10-6, Sat 9-5

Eastside Massage Therapy Center — 212-249-2927
351 East 78th Street   bet. 1st/2nd Ave.
NYC 10021   Mon-Fri 10-9:30, Sat 9-8, Sun 10-8

Elena Pociu Skin Care — 212-754-9866
815 Fifth Avenue   bet. 62/63rd St.
NYC 10021   Tues-Sat 9:30-5:30

Elizabeth Arden — 212-546-0200
691 Fifth Avenue   at 54th St.
NYC 10022   Mon, Tues & Sat 8-6:30, Wed 8-7:30
Thur & Fri 8-8, Sun 9-6

Erbe — 212-966-1445
196 Prince Street   bet. MacDougal/Sullivan
NYC 10012   Sun & Mon 11-6, Tues-Sat 11-7

Gemayel Salon — 212-787-5555
2030 Broadway   at 70th St.
NYC 10023   Mon-Fri 10-8, Sat 9-7, Sun 10-6

Janet Sartin — 212-751-5858
500 Park Avenue   bet. 58/59th St.
NYC 10022   Mon-Fri 10-7, Sat 10-6, Sun 11-6

Lia Schorr Skin Care — 212-486-9670
686 Lexington Avenue, 4th Fl.   bet. 56/57th St.
NYC 10022   Mon-Fri 11-7, Sat & Sun 9-5

Ling Skin Care — 212-989-8833
12 East 16th Street   bet. 5th Ave./Union Sq.
NYC 10003   Mon-Thurs 10-9, Fri 11-7
Sat 9:30-5:30, Sun 12-5:30

Mario Badescu — 212-758-1065
320 East 52nd Street   bet. 1st/2nd Ave.
NYC 10022   Mon & Fri 8:30-6, Tues-Thur 8:30-8:30
Sat 9-5, Sun 10-5

The Mezzanine Spa — 212-431-1600
@ SoHo Integrated Health
62 Crosby Street   bet. Spring/Broome
NYC 10012   Sun 10-6, Tues & Wed 12-8
Thur & Fri 9-8, Sat 10-6

Miano Viel — 212-980-3222
16 East 52nd Street   bet. Madison/5th Ave.
NYC 10022   Tues 9-6, Wed, Fri & Sat 9-5, Thur 9-7

Oasis Day Spa — 212-254-7722
108 East 16th Street   bet. Irving Pl./Union Sq.
NYC 10003   Mon-Fri 10-10, Sat & Sun 9-9

Skinklinic — 212-521-3100
800B Fifth Avenue   at 61st St
NYC 10021   Mon-Tues 11-7, Wed-Thur 8-8
Fri 8-7, Sat 9-4

Health & Beauty

Soho Sanctuary   212-334-5550
119 Mercer Street   bet. Prince/Spring
NYC 10012   Mon 3-9, Tues-Fri 10-9, Sat 10-6, Sun 12-6

Tracie Martyn   212-206-9333
59 Fifth Avenue   bet. 12th/13th St
NYC 10003   Mon-Sun 9-5
(hours vary according to client)

Wellpath   212-737-9604
1100 Madison Avenue   at 83rd St.
NYC 10028   Mon-Sat 9-5

Yasmine Djerradine   212-588-1771
30 East 60th Street   bet. Park/Madison Ave.
NYC 10022   Mon-Sat 9-7

Eyebrow Grooming

Ramy Gafni at Bergdorf Goodman's   212-684-9889
at Ramy counter   on the lower level
754 Fifth Avenue   at 58th St.
NYC 10019   by appointment on Fri & Sat

Eliza's Eyes at Avon Salon and Spa   212-755-2866
725 Fifth Avenue   bet. 56/57th St.
NYC 10022   Mon, Tues & Sat 8-6, Wed-Fri 8-8

Oama at Pierre Michel   212-593-1460
131 East 57th Street   Mon-Sat 9-5:30, Thur 9-7
NYC 10022

Manicures/Pedicures

Acqua Beauty Bar   212-620-4329
7 East 14th Street   bet. Fifth Ave./Union Sq.
NYC 10003   Mon-Wed 10-9, Thur & Fri 10-8
Sat & Sun 10-7

Buff Spa @ Bergdorf Goodman   212-753-7300
754 Fifth Avenue   at 58th Street
NYC 10019   Mon-Sat 10-7, Sun 12-6, Thur 10-8

Ellegee Nail Salon   212-472-5063
22 East 66th Street   bet. Madison/5th Ave.
NYC 10021   Mon-Fri 9-6, Sat 9-4

Four Seasons Fitness Center   212-350-6420
57 East 57th Street   bet. Park/Madison Ave.
NYC 10022   Mon-Sun 10-6

Josephine Beauty Treatment   212-223-7157
200 East 62nd Street   bet. 2nd/3rd Ave.
NYC 10021   Mon & Thur 10-7
Tues, Wed & Fri 9:30-6:30, Sat 9:30-6

Nails by Nina   212-288-8130
129 East 80th Street   bet. Lexington/Park Ave.
NYC 10021   Mon-Fri 10-6

Health & Beauty

167 Nail Plaza　　　　　　　　　　　**212-496-7155**
167 Amsterdam Avenue　　　　　　bet. 67/68th St.
NYC 10023　　　　　　　　　　　　Mon-Fri 9:30-8
　　　　　　　　　　　　　　Sat 9-7:30, Sun 10:30-7

Paul LaBrecque　　　　　　　　　**212-595-0099**
160 Columbus Avenue　　　　　　　bet. 67/68th St.
NYC 10023　　　　　Mon-Fri 8-11, Sat 9-8, Sun 10-8

Rescue Beauty Lounge　　　　　**212-431-0449**
8 Centre Market Place　　　　　　bet. Broome/Grand
NYC 10012　　　　　　　　　Tues-Fri 11-8, Sat-Sun 10-6

Resue Aromatherapy Nail Spa　**212-431-3805**
NYC 10012　　　　　　　Mon-Fri 11-8, Sat & Sun 10-6

Warren-Tricomi　　　　　　　　　**212-262-8899**
16 West 57th Street　　　　　　　　bet. 5/6th Ave.
NYC 10019　　　　　　　　　　　Mon 9-6, Tues 8-5
　　　　　　　　　　　　　　Wed-Fri 7:30-7, Sat 9-5

Day Spas—Women

Ajune　　　　　　　　　　　　　　**212-628-0044**
1294 Third Avenue　　　　　　　　　at 74/75th St.
NYC 10021　　Mon 10-4, Tues-Fri 9-8, Sat 9-6, Sun 11-5

Allure Day Spa　　　　　　　　　**212-644-5500**
139 East 55th Street　　　　　　　bet. 3rd/Lex. Ave.
NYC 10022　　　　　Mon-Fri 10:30-7:30, Sat & Sun 10-6

Anushka Institute　　　　　　　　**212-355-6404**
241 East 60th Street　　　　　　　bet. 2/3rd Ave.
NYC 10022　　　　　　　　Mon 9-6, Tues & Thur 10-8
　　　　　　　　　　　　　　Wed & Fri 10-7, Sat 9-6

The Avon Center　　　　　　　　**212-755-2866**
725 Fifth Avenue, 14th Fl.　at Trump Tower bet. 56/57th St
NYC 10022　　　　Mon, Tues & Sat 8-6, Wed & Fri 8-8

Away　　　　　　　　　　　　　　**212-407-2970**
541 Lexington Avenue, 4th Fl.　　bet. 49/50th St.
NYC 10022　　　　　　　　　　　　at the W Hotel
　　　　　　　Mon-Fri 5:30-9:30, Sat 8:30-8, Sun 8:30-7

Bliss Spa　　　　　　　　　　　　**212-219-8970**
19 East 57th Street, 3rd Fl.　bet. Madison/Fifth Ave.
NYC 10022　　　　　　　　　　　Mon-Fri 9:30-8:30
　　　　　　　　　　　Wed 12:30-8:30, Sat 9:30-6:30

Bliss Spa　　　　　　　　　　　　**212-219-8970**
568 Broadway　　　　　　　　　　at Prince
NYC 10012　　　　　Mon-Fri 9:30-8:30, Sat 9:30-6:30

Brigitte Mansfield European Spa　**212-366-0706**
37 Union Square West　　　　　　bet. 16/17th St.
NYC 10003　　　　　Tues-Fri 11-10, Sat 12-8, Sun 12-6

Dorit Baxter Day Spa　　　　　　**212-371-4542**
47 West 57th Street, 3rd Fl.　　　bet. 5/6th Ave.
NYC 10019　　　　　　Mon-Fri 9-8, Sat 9-7, Sun 11-6

Health & Beauty

Eden Day Spa　　　　　　　　　　**212-226-0515**
388 Broadway　　　　　　　　　bet. Walker/White
NYC 10013　　　　　　　　　　　Mon-Sun 9:30-9

Faina European Spa　　　　　　**212-245-6557**
315 West 57th Street　　　　　　　bet. 8/9th Ave.
NYC 10019　　　Mon-Fri 10-8, Sat 9-6, Sun 10-6

Gemayel Salon & Spa　　　　　**212-787-5555**
2030 Broadway　　　　　　　　　　　at 70th St.
NYC 10023　　　Mon-Fri 10-8, Sat 9-7, Sun 10-6

Georgette Klinger　　　　　　　**212-838-3200**
501 Madison Avenue　　　　　　　bet. 52/53rd St.
NYC 10022　　　　　　　　Mon-Thurs 9-8, Fri 9-6
　　　　　　　　　　　　　　　　　Sat & Sun 9-5

Glow Skin Spa　　　　　　　　　**212-319-6654**
41 East 57th Street, Suite 1206　bet. Madison/Park Ave.
NYC 10022　　　　　Mon-Sun by appointment only

The Greenhouse Day Spa　　　**212-644-4449**
127 East 57th Street　　　　　bet. Lexington/Park Ave.
NYC 10022　　　　Mon-Fri 9-9, Sat & Sun 10-6

Haven　　　　　　　　　　　　　**212-343-3515**
150 Mercer Street　　　　　　　bet. Prince/Houston
NYC 10012　　　　　　　Mon-Fri 11-7, Sat 10-6

The HR Beauty Gallery　　　　　**212-343-9963**
135 Spring Street　　　　　　　bet. Greene/Wooster
NYC 10012　　Mon & Tues 11-7, Wed 11-9, Thur-Fri 11-8
　　　　　　　　　　　　　　　Sat 10-6, Sun 12-6

Karen Wu Beauty & Wellness Spa　**212-585-2044**
1377 Third Avenue　　　　　　　　bet. 78/79th St.
NYC 10021　　　Mon-Fri 10-9, Sat 10-8, Sun 10:30-7

Maximus　　　　　　　　　　　　**212-431-3333**
15 Mercer Street　　　　　　　　bet. Grand/Canal
NYC 10013　　　　　　　　　Tues, Wed & Fri 10-7
　　　　　　　　　　　　　　Thur 11-8:30, Sat 9-6

The Mezzanine Spa　　　　　　　**212-431-1600**
@ SoHo Integrated Health
62 Crosby Street　　　　　　　bet. Spring/Broome
NYC 10012　　　　　Sun 10-6, Tues & Wed 12-8
　　　　　　　　　　　　Thur & Fri 9-8, Sat 10-6

Millefleurs (organic spa)　　　　**212-966-3656**
130 Franklin Street　　　　　　　　　　at Varick
NYC 10013　　　　　　　　　　　　Mon-Sun 10-8

Oasis Day Spa　　　　　　　　　**212-254-7722**
108 East 16th Street　　　bet. Irving Pl./Union Sq. E.
NYC 10003　　　Mon-Fri 10-10, Sat & Sun 9-9

The Peninsula Spa　　　　　　　**212-903-3910**
700 Fifth Avenue, 21st Fl.　　　　　　at 55th St.
NYC 10022　　Mon-Fri 6-9:30, Sat & Sun 7-7:30

Health & Beauty

Qiora Spa — 212-527-0400
535 Madison Avenue — bet. 54/55th St.
NYC 10022   Mon-Wed & Fri 10-8, Thur 11-8, Sat 12-6

Repechage Spa de Beaute — 212-751-2500
115 East 57th Street — bet. Park/Lex. Ave.
NYC 10022   Mon & Thur 10-8
Tues, Wed & Fri 10-6:30, Sat 10-6

Shiseido Studio — 212-625-8821
155 Spring Street — bet. Wooster/W. B'way
NYC 10012   Sun & Mon 12-6, Tues 11-6, Wed-Sat 11-7

SkinCareLab — 212-334-3142
568 Broadway — at Prince
NYC 10012   Mon-Sat 11-8, Sat 10-7, Sun 12-6

Susan Ciminelli Day Spa — 212-872-2650
754 Fifth Avenue — at Bergdorf Goodman
NYC 10019   Mon-Wed & Fri 10-7, Thur 10-8
Sat 11-7, Sun 11-4

The Townhouse Day Spa — 212-439-6664
East 76th Street — bet. Madison/5th Ave.
NYC 10021   Mon-Fri 9-5, Thur 9-8

Ula's Day Spa — 212-343-2376
8 Harrison — bet. Greenwich/Hudson
NYC 10013   Tues-Fri 11-7, Sat 10-6

Day Spas—Men

Aveda Institute — 212-807-1492
233 Spring Street — bet. 6th Ave./Varick
NYC 10013   Mon-Sun 10-6

Bliss Spa — 212-219-8970
19 East 57th Street, 3rd Fl. — bet. Madison/5th Ave.
NYC 10022   Mon-Fri 9:30-8:30, Sat 9:30-6:30

Bliss Spa — 212-219-8970
568 Broadway — at Prince
NYC 10012   Mon-Fri 9:30-8:30, Sat 9:30-6:30

Carapan Spa — 212-633-6220
5 West 16th Street — bet. 5/6th Ave.
NYC 10001   Mon-Sun 10-9:45

Eden Day Spa — 212-226-0515
388 Broadway — bet. Walker/White
NYC 10013   Mon-Sun 9:30-9

Equinox Spa — 212-396-9611
205 East 85th Street — bet. 2/3rd Ave.
NYC 10028   Mon & Tues 9-10, Wed-Fri 9-9,
Sat & Sun 9-8

Equinox Spa — 212-750-4671
140 East 63rd Street — at Lex. Ave.
NYC 10021   Mon-Tues 9-10, Wed-Fri 9-9
Sat & Sun 9-8

Health & Beauty

Glow Skin Spa   **212-319-6654**
41 East 57th Street, Suite 1206   bet. Madison/Park Ave.
NYC 10022   by appointment only

Kozue Aesthetic Spa   **212-734-8600**
795 Madison Avenue, 2nd Fl.   bet. 67/68th St.
NYC 10021   Mon-Sun 10-10

Nickel Day Spa   **212-242-3203**
77 Eighth Avenue   at 14th St.
NYC 10014   Mon 3-9, Tues-Fri 11-9
Sat 10-9, Sun 2-9

Paul Lebrecque at Reebok   **212-595-0099**
160 Columbus Avenue   bet. 68th/69th St.
NYC 10023   Mon-Fri 8-11, Sat 9-8, Sun 10-8

Prema NoLiTa (holistic skincare)   **212-226-3972**
252 Elizabeth Street   bet. E. Houston/Prince
NYC 10012   Tues-Sun 11-7:30

Qiora Spa   **212-527-0400**
535 Madison Avenue   bet. 54/55th St.
NYC 10022   Mon-Wed & Fri 10-7, Thur 11-8, Sat 11-6

SkinCareLab   **212-334-3142**
568 Broadway   at Prince
NYC 10012   Mon-Fri 11-8, Sat 10-7, Sun 12-6

Fitness Studios

Casa Fitness (Personal training only)   **212-717-1998**
48 East 73rd Street   bet. Madison/Park Ave.
NYC 10021

Classic Bodies   **212-737-8440**
189 East 79th Street   at Lex. Ave.
NYC 10021   call for class schedule

Crunch   **212-875-1902**
162 West 83rd Street   bet. Amsterdam/Columbus Ave.
NYC 10024   Mon-Thur 5:30-11, Fri 5:30-10
Sat & Sun 8-9

Crunch   **212-758-3434**
1109 Second Avenue   bet. 58/59th St.
NYC 10022   Mon-Fri 5-11, Sat & Sun 8-9

Crunch   **212-594-8050**
560 West 43rd Street   at 11th Ave.
NYC 10036   Mon-Fri 6-10, Sat & Sun 9-7

Crunch   **212-869-7788**
144 West 38th Street   bet. B'way/7th Ave.
NYC 10018   Mon-Fri 5:30-10, Sat & Sun 8-6

Crunch   **212-475-2018**
54 East 13th Street   bet. B'way/University Pl.
NYC 10003   Mon-Fri 6-10, Sat & Sun 8-8

Crunch   **212-614-0120**
404 Lafayette Street   bet. Astor/E. 4th St.
NYC 10003   Mon-Fri open 24 hrs, Sat to 9, Sun 8-9

Health & Beauty

Crunch
623 Broadway
NYC 10012
212-420-0507
bet. Houston/Bleecker
Mon-Fri 6-12, Sat 8-8, Sun 9-8

Crunch
152 Christopher Street
NYC 10014
212-366-3725
bet. Washington/Greenwich
Mon-Fri 6-11, Sat & Sun 8-9

David Barton Gym
30 East 85th Street
NYC 10028
212-517-7577
bet. Madison/5th Ave.
Mon-Fri 5:30-11, Sat & Sun 8-9

David Barton Gym
552 Sixth Avenue
NYC 10011
212-727-0004
bet. 15/16th St.
Mon-Fri 6-12, Sat 9-9, Sun 10-11

The Equinox
2465 Broadway
NYC 10025
212-799-1818
bet. 91/92nd St.
Mon-Thur 5:30-11
Fri 5:30-10, Sat & Sun 8-9

The Equinox
205 East 85th Street
NYC 10028
212-439-8500
bet. 2/3rd Ave.
Mon-Thur 5:30-10:30
Fri 5:30-10, Sat & Sun 8-9

The Equinox
344 Amsterdam Avenue
NYC 10024
212-721-4200
at 76th St.
Mon-Thur 5:30-11
Fri 5:30-10, Sat & Sun 8-9

The Equinox
140 East 63rd Street
NYC 10021
212-750-4900
at Lex. Ave.
Mon-Thur 5:30-11
Fri 5:30-10, Sat & Sun 8-9

The Equinox
250 East 54th Street
NYC 10022
212-277-5400
at 2nd Ave.
Mon-Thur 5:30-11
Fri 5:30-10, Sat & Sun 8-9

The Equinox
897 Broadway
NYC 10003
212-780-9300
bet. 19/20th St.
Mon-Fri 5:15-11, Sat & Sun 8-5

The Equinox
97 Greenwich Avenue
NYC 10012
212-620-0103
at West 12th St
Mon-Thur 5:30-11, Fri 5:30-10
Sat & Sun 8-9

Lotte Berk Method
23 East 67th Street
NYC 10021
212-288-6613
bet. Madison/5th Ave.
Mon-Fri 6-9, Sat & Sun 8-3

Radu
24 West 57th Street, 2nd Fl.
NYC 10019
212-581-1995
bet. 5/6th Ave.
Mon & Wed 7-7, Tues & Thur 8-7
Fri 5:30-10, Sat & Sun 8-9

Reebok
160 Columbus Avenue
NYC 10023
212-362-6800
at 67th St.
Mon-Thur 5-11
Fri 5-10, Sat & Sun 7-9

Health & Beauty

The Sports Ctr. at Chelsea Piers   **212-336-6000**
Pier 60, West Side Hwy.   at W. 23rd St.
NYC 10011   Mon-Fri 6-11, Sat & Sun 8-9

The Sports Club LA (private membership)   **212-355-5100**
330 East 61st Street   bet. 1st/2nd Ave.
NYC 10021   Mon-Fri 5-11, Sat & Sun 7-9

The Sports Club/LA (membership)   **212-218-8600**
45 Rockefeller Plaza   at 51st Street
NYC 10111   Mon-Thur 5-11
  Fri 5-10, Sat & Sun 9-4

Studio Uma   **212-249-7979**
20 East 68th Street   bet. Madison/5th Ave.
NYC 10021   Mon-Fri 7-9, Sat 7-9, Sun 9-6

Synergy Fitness Center   **212-879-6013**
1438 Third Avenue   bet. 81/82nd St.
NYC 10028   Mon-Fri 5:30-11, Sat & Sun 8-8

Synergy Fitness Center   **212-545-9590**
4 Park Avenue   bet. 33/34th St.
NYC 10016   Mon-Fri 5-11, Sat & Sun 8-7

Pilates/Mat Classes

Contemporary Fitness   **212-687-8885**
501 Fifth Avenue, Suite 22   at 42nd St.
NYC 10017   Mon-Thurs 7-9, Fri 7-7
  Sat & Sun 10-4

Drago's Gymnasium, Inc   **212-757-0724**
50 West 57th Street, 6th Fl.   bet. 5/6th Ave.
NYC 10019   Mon-Fri 7-7, Sat 9-2

The Kane School of Core Integration   **212-463-8308**
7 East 17th Street, 5th Fl.   bet. 5th Ave./B'way
NYC 10003   Mon-Fri 9-8 by appointment

Power Pilates   **212-627-5852**
49 West 23rd Street, 10th Fl.   bet. 5/6th Ave.
NYC 10011   Mon-Fri 7-8, Sat & Sun 9-4

re: AB   **212-420-9111**
33 Bleecker Street   at Mott
NYC 10012   Mon-Fri 7-8, Sat 9-2, Sun 10-4

Tribeca Bodyworks   **212-625-0777**
177 Duane Street   bet. Greenwich/Hudson
NYC 10013   Mon-Thur 7-9, Fri 7-8
  Sat 10-4, Sun 11-4

Yoga

Integral Yoga Institute   **212-721-4000**
200 West 72nd Street, Room 41   at Broadway
NYC 10023   call for class times

Integral Yoga Institute   **212-929-0586**
227 West 13th Street   bet. 7/8th Ave.
NYC 10011   Mon-Fri 10-8:30, Sat 9-5, Sun 10-2

Health & Beauty

Jivamukti Yoga Center   212-353-0214
404 Lafayette Street
NYC 10003
bet. W. 4th St./Astor Pl.
Mon-Sun 7-8:30

Om Yoga Center   212-229-0267
135 West 14th Street
NYC 10011
bet. 6/7th Ave.
Mon-Fri 7:30-8, Sat 9-6, Sun 9-6:30

Pantajali Yoga Shala   212-431-3738
430 Broome Street
NYC 10012
at Crosby
(call for class hours)

Soho Sanctuary   212-334-5550
119 Mercer Street, 3rd Fl.
NYC 10012
bet. Prince/Spring
Tues-Fri 10-9, Sat 10-6, Sun 12-6

The Sports Club LA (private membership)   212-355-5100
330 East 61st Street
NYC 10021
bet.1st/2nd Ave.
Mon-Fri 5-11, Sat & Sun 7-9

The Sports Club LA (private membership)   212-218-8600
45 Rockefeller Plaza
NYC 10111
at 51st Street
Mon-Thur 5-11
Fri 5-10, Sat & Sun 8-6

Yoga (private lessons)

Kristin Leigh/Barbara Verrochi   212-334-4176
mskristinleigh@hotmail.com

Massage Therapists (office & home visits)

Hands   212-219-9186
18 Harrison Street
NYC 10013
bet. Hudson/Grand
Mon-Fri 1-9, Sat & Sun 10-9

Lisa Smith   212-969-8718

Massage - Massage   212-696-9069
$60 to $80 per hour

Marcelo Countinho   212-924-3741
201 West 11th Street, Suite 5G
comcountinhom@aol.com.
bet 8th/9th

Osaka   212-956-3422
50 West 56th Street, 2nd Fl.
NYC 10019
bet. 5/6th Ave.
Mon-Sun 10-3

Physical Advantage   212-460-1879
$70 to $95 per hour

New York Massage Company   212-427-8175
$60 per hour

Salon de Tokyo   212-757-2187
200 West 57th Street, Suite 1308
NYC 10019
at 7th Avenue
Mon-Sat 11-midnight

Health & Beauty

Tui Na
171 Sullivan Street
$50 per hour, $20 per 20 min.
$10 for 10 min.
212-387-0733
bet. Houston/Bleecker
call for opening hours

Tanning Salons

Portofino Sun Center
1300 Third Avenue
NYC 10021
212-988-6300
at 75th St.
Mon-Fri 8-10, Sat 9-9, Sun 10-7

Portofino Sun Center
104 West 73rd Street
NYC 10023
212-769-0200
at Columbus Ave.
Mon-Fri 8:15-9, Sat 9-8, Sun 10-6

Portofino Sun Center
38 East 58th Street
NYC 10022
212-355-2772
bet. Park/Madison Ave.
Mon-Fri 8-8:15, Sat 9-7, Sun 10-6

Portofino Sun Center
462 West Broadway
NYC 10012
212-473-7600
bet. Houston/Prince
Mon-Sat 9-8:15, Sun 11-5:15

Portofino Sun Center
64 Greenwich Avenue
NYC 10011
212-627-4775
at 7th Ave.
Mon-Fri 9-10, Sat 9-9, Sun 10-7

Bridal Consultants

Ober, Onet & Associates
205 East 95th Street
NYC 10128
212-876-6775
bet. 2/3rd Ave.
Contact: Polly Onet

Marcy Blum Associates
251 East 51st Street
NYC 10022
212-929-9814
bet. 2/3rd Ave.
Contact: Marcy Blum

Saved by the Bell
11 Riverside Drive
NYC 10023
212-874-5457
bet. 73/74th St.
Contact: Susan Bell

Make-up Artists

Carlos Solano
Shu Uemura counter
212-872-2750
@ Bergdorf Goodman

Madina Milano
151 Spring Street
646-613-0838
Mon-Thur 11-7
Fri & Sat 11-8, Sun 12-7

Kathy Pomerantz
518 East 80th Street
212-772-3865
call for opening hours

Kimara Ahnert
1113 Madison Avenue
212-452-4252
Mon-Sat 10-7, Sun 12-5

Rochelle Weithorn
431 East 73rd Street
212-472-8668
call for appointment

Health & Beauty

Personal Shoppers

Barneys New York   212-826-8900 or 212-833-2105
660 Madison Avenue, 4th Fl.   bet. 60/61st St.
NYC 10021   Mon-Sat 10-6:30
Contact: Jose Parron

Bergdorf Goodman   212-872-8772
754 Fifth Avenue   bet. 57/58th St.
NYC 10019   Mon-Fri 9:30-5:30
Contact: "Solutions" by Betty Halbreich

Bloomingdale's   212-705-2000
1000 Third Avenue   at 59/60th St.
NYC 10022   Mon-Fri 10-8:30, Sat 10-7, Sun 11-7

Go Lightly   212-352-1153
405 West 23rd Street, Apt 3J   646-486-7475
NYC 10011   www.go-lightly.com
Contact: Jenny Gering

Henri Bendel   212-373-6353
712 Fifth Avenue   bet. 55/56th St.
NYC 10019   Mon-Sat 10-7
Contact: Michael Palladino

Lord & Taylor   212-391-3344
424 Fifth Avenue   bet. 38/39th St.
NYC 10018   Mon & Tues & Sat 10-7
Wed & Thur 9-8:30, Fri 10-8:30, Sun 11-7

Macy's   212-494-4181
Broadway   at Herald Sq.
NYC 10001   Mon-Sat 10-7:30, Sun 11-6
Contact: Linda Lee

Paul Stuart   212-682-0320
Madison Avenue   at 45th St.
NYC 10017   Mon-Fri 8-6:30, Thur 8-7
Sat 9-6, Sun 12-5

Saks Fifth Avenue   212-940-4145
611 Fifth Avenue   bet. 49/50th St.
NYC 10022   Mon-Sat 10-7, Thur 10-8, Sun 12-6
Contact: Cynthia Strickland

Visual Therapy   212-315-2233
24 West 57th Street, Suite 502   bet. 5/6th Ave.
NYC 10019   Mon-Fri 9-5:30
Contact: Jesse Garza, Joe Lupo, Lani Rosenstock

Repairs & Services

Dry Cleaners

Mending, Alterations & Custom Tailoring

Boutique Clothing Storage

Shoe Repair

Leather Repair

Trimmings

Thrift Shops

Repairs & Services

Dry Cleaners—Haute Couture & Bridal

Dunrite   212-221-9297
141 West 38th Street   bet. B'way/7th Ave.
NYC 10018   Mon-Fri 7:30-5:20

Fashion Award Cleaners   212-289-5623
1462 Lexington Avenue   bet. 94/95th St.
NYC 10128   Mon-Fri 7:30-6:30, Sat 9-3

Hallak Cleaners   212-879-4694
1232 Second Avenue   bet. 64/65th St.
NYC 10021   Mon-Fri 7-6:30, Sat 8-3

Jeeves of Belgravia   212-570-9130
39 East 65th Street   bet. Madison/Park Ave.
NYC 10021   Mon-Fri 8-6, Sat 10-3

Madame Paulette   212-838-6827
1255 Second Avenue   bet. 65/66th St.
NYC 10021   Mon-Fri 7:30-7, Sat 8-5

Montclair   212-289-2070
1331 Lexington Avenue   bet. 88/89th St.
NYC 10128   Mon-Fri 7-7, Sat 8-5

Dry Cleaners—Leather & Suede

Leathercraft Process of America   212-564-8980
Two locations in New York, call for information.   800-845-6155

Dry Cleaners—All-Purpose Cleaners

Anita Cleaners   212-717-6602
1380 First Avenue   bet. 73/74th St.
NYC 10021   Mon-Fri 8-6

Handy Cleaners   212-247-0922
301 East 75th Street   Mon-Fri 7-7, Sat 8-4
NYC 10019

Meurice Garment Care   212-475-2778
31 University Place   bet. 8/9th St.
NYC 10003   Mon-Fri 8-7, Sat 9-5

Meurice Garment Care & Tiecrafters   212-759-9057
245 East 57th Street   bet. 2/3rd Ave.
NYC 10022   Mon-Fri 8-6:30, Sat 9-3

Midnight Express   212-921-0111
38-38 Thirteenth Street   800-7-MIDNITE
Long Island City   Mon-Fri 8-6
Will pick up and deliver for a small minimum charge.

Montclair   212-289-2070
1331 Lexington Avenue   bet. 88/89th St.
NYC 10128   Mon-Fri 7-7, Sat 8-5

New York's Finest French Cleaners   212-431-4010
144 Reade Street   bet. Hudson/Greenwich
NYC 10013   Mon-Fri 7:30-6:30, Sat 8:30-5

Repairs & Services

Tiecrafters   212-629-5800
252 West 29th Street   bet. 7/8th Ave.
NYC 10001   Mon-Fri 8:30-5, Sat 10-2

Young's Cleaners and Launderers   212-473-6154
188 Third Avenue   at 17th St.
NYC 10003   Mon-Fri 7-7, Sat 8-5

Mending & Alterations

Alfonso Sciortino Custom Alteration   212-888-2846
57 West 57th Street, Suite 602   at 6th Ave.
NYC 10019   Mon-Sat 9-5:30 (closed lunchtime)

Bhambi Custom Tailors   212-935-5379
14 East 60th Street, Rm. 610   bet. Madison/5th Ave.
NYC 10022   Mon-Fri 10-7, Sat 10-7

Claudia Bruce (dressmaker)   212-685-2810
140 East 28th Street   bet. Lex./3rd Ave.
NYC 10016   Mon-Fri 10-5:30 by appointment only

Eddie Ugras   212-595-1596
125 West 72nd Street, 3rd Fl.   bet. Columbus Ave./B'way
NYC 10023   Mon-Fri 9:30-7, Sat 10-6

Fine Alterations-Sewing   212-254-0829
240 East 6th Street   at 2nd Ave.
NYC 10003   by appointment only

French American Weaving Co.   212-765-4670
119 West 57th Street, Rm. 1406   bet. 6/7th Ave.
NYC 10019   Mon-Fri 10:30-5:30, Sat 11-2

John's European Boutique & Tailoring   212-752-2239
118 East 59th Street, 2nd Fl.   bet. Park/Lex. Ave.
NYC 10022   Mon-Fri 9-6:30

Nelson Ferri   212-988-5085
766 Madison Avenue, 4th Fl.   bet. 65/66th St.
NYC 10021   Mon-Fri 9-6, Thur 10-6:30, Sat 10-5

Peppino   212-832-3844
780 Lexington Avenue   bet. 60/61st St.
NYC 10021   Mon-Fri 8:30-6:30, Sat 8:30-4
  (closed lunchtime)

Sebastian Tailors   212-688-1244
767 Lexington Avenue   bet. 60/61st St.
NYC 10021   Mon-Fri 8:30-5, Sat 9-4:30

Superior Repair Center (leather)   212-889-7211
7 West 30th Street, 9th Fl.   bet. 5/6th Ave.
NYC 10016   Mon-Fri 10-6, Sat 10-3 (winter only)

Three Star (leather apparel only)   212-879-4200
790 Madison Avenue, 5th Fl.   at 67th St.
NYC 10021   Mon-Sat 10-6:30

Repairs & Services

Custom Design Tailors

Albert Sakhai   **212-647-1241**
144 West 19th Street   bet. 6/7th Ave.
NYC 10011   by appointment only

Atelier Eva Devecsery   **212-751-6091**
201 East 61st Street   at 3rd Ave.
NYC 10021   Mon-Fri 9-6, Sat 10-4 by appointment

Dynasty Custom Tailoring   **212-679-1075**
6 East 38th Street   bet. Madison/5th Ave.
NYC 10016   Mon-Fri 9-6:30, Sat 10-4

Hong Kong Tailor Jack   **212-675-0818**
136 Waverly Place   at 6th Ave.
NYC 10014   Mon-Sat 10-7

Mr. Ned   **212-924-5042**
137 Fifth Avenue   at 20th St.
NYC 10010   Mon-Fri 8-4, Sat 8-1

Riviera Tailor   **212-533-3944**
144 East 22nd Street   bet. Lex./3rd Ave.
NYC 10010   Mon-Fri 9-5:30, Sat 9-4

Boutique Clothing Storage

Garde Robe   **212-227-7554**
137 Duane Street   bet. Church/West
NYC 10013   (call for an appointment)
www.garderobeonline.com.

Shoe Repair

Andrade Boot and Shoe Repair   **212-787-0465**
379 Amsterdam Avenue   bet. 78/79th St.
NYC 10024   Mon-Fri 7:30-7, Sat 9-7

Andrade Shoe Repair   **212-529-3541**
103 University Place   bet. 12/13th Street
NYC 10003   Mon-Fri 7:30-7, Sat 9-6:30

Angelos Shoe Repair   **212-757-6364**
666 Fifth Avenue, lower level   at 51st St.
NYC 10136   Mon-Fri 7-6:30, Sat 10-5

B. Nelson   **212-869-3552**
1221 Sixth Avenue   bet. 48/49th St.
NYC 10020 (Level C-2)   Mon-Fri 7:30-5

David's Shoe Repair   **212-867-4338**
Grand Central Corridor   at 45th St. and Vanderbilt
NYC 10017   Mon-Fri 6-6:30

Jim's Shoe Repair   **212-355-8259**
50 East 59th Street   bet. Park/Madison Ave.
NYC 10022   Mon-Fri 8-6, Sat 9-4

Shoe Service Plus   **212-262-4823**
15 West 55th Street   bet. 5/6th Ave.
NYC 10019   Mon-Fri 7-7, Sat 10-5

Repairs & Services

Top Service   212-765-3190
845 Seventh Avenue   bet. 54/55th St.
NYC 10019   Mon-Fri 8-6, Sat 9-3

Leather Repair (Handbags & Luggage)

Artbag Creations   212-744-2720
1130 Madison Avenue   at 84th St.
NYC 10028   Mon-Fri 9:30-5:45, Sat 10-5:15

John R. Gerardo   212-695-6955
30 West 31st Street   bet. 5th/B'way
NYC 10001   Mon-Fri 9-5:30,
Sat 10-3 (fall/winter only)

Modern Leather   212-947-7770
2 West 32nd Street, 4th Fl.   bet. 5th/B'way
NYC 10001   Mon-Fri 8:30-5, Sat 8:30-1 (winter only)

Superior Repair Center   212-889-7211
7 West 30th Street, 9th Fl.   bet. 5/6th Ave.
NYC 10016   Mon-Fri 10-6, Sat 10-3 (winter only)

Trimmings (Ribbons, Buttons, Feathers and Odds & Ends)

A.A. Feather Company   212-695-9470
16 West 36th Street, Eighth Floor   bet. 5/6th Ave.
NYC 10018   Mon-Thurs 8:30-5:30, Fri 8:30-5
Selection: Quality feathers like ostrich plumes and feather boas.

Feibusch—Zippers and Threads   212-226-3964
27 Allen Street   bet. Canal/Hester
NYC 10002   Mon-Fri 9-5, Sun 9-4 (winter only – call first)
Selection: Stocks zippers in every size, color and style with threads to match.

Greenberg & Hammer   212-246-2836
24 West 57th Street   bet. 5/6th Ave.
NYC 10019   Mon-Fri 9-6, Sat 10-5
Selection: Trims, notions, buttons, zippers and more.

Hyman Hendler and Sons   212-840-8393
67 West 38th Street   bet. 5/6th Ave.
NYC 10018   Mon-Fri 9-5
Selection: The highest quality ribbons from around the world.

M&J Trimming Co.   212-391-9072
1008-1014 Sixth Avenue   bet. 37/38th St.
NYC 10018   Mon-Fri 9-6, Sat 10-5
Selection: Ribbons, trimmings, buttons, rhinestones and more.

Margola   212-840-0644
48 West 37th Street   bet. 5/6th Ave.
NYC 10018   Mon-Fri 8:30-6, Sat 10-4
Selection: Feather trimmings, silk flowers, ribbons, veiling and netting, beading and stones.

Repairs & Services

Mokuba   **212-869-8900**
55 West 39th Street   bet. 5/6th Ave.
NYC 10018   Mon-Fri 9-5
*Selection: Super fancy ribbons. Find them in silk,
velvet, chiffon, fake fur and pleated.*

Tender Buttons   **212-758-7004**
143 East 62nd Street   bet. Lex./3rd Ave.
NYC 10021   Mon-Fri 10:30-6, Sat 10:30-5:30
*Selection: An exquisite collection of buttons,
from modern to antique.*

Tinsel Trading   **212-730-1030**
47 West 38th Street   bet. 5/6th Ave.
NYC 10018   Mon-Fri 11-3:30
Open some Saturdays—ring first
*Selection: Fabrics, ribbons, soutaches, trims, cords,
tassels, military braids and sword knots.*

Thrift Shops

Cancer Care Thrift Shop   **212-879-9868**
1480 Third Avenue   bet. 83/84th St.
NYC 10028   Mon, Tues & Fri 11-6, Wed & Thur 11-7
Sat 11-4:30, Sun 12:30-5

Housing Works Thrift Shop   **212-772-8461**
202 East 77th Street   bet. 2/3rd Ave
NYC 10021   Mon-Fri 11-7, Sat 10-6, Sun 12-5

Housing Works Thrift Shop   **212-579-7566**
306 Columbus Avenue   bet. 74th/75th
NYC 10023   Mon-Fri 11-7, Sat 10-6, Sun 12-5

Housing Works Thrift Shop   **212-529-5955**
157 East 23rd Street   bet. 3rd/Lexington Ave.
NYC 10004   Mon-Sat 10-6, Sun 12-5

Housing Works Thrift Shop   **212-366-0820**
143 West 17th Street   bet. 6th/7th Ave.
NYC 10004   Mon-Sat 10-6, Sun 12-5

Irvington Institute Thrift Shop   **212-879-4555**
(ring for new address and opening hours)

Memorial Sloan-Kettering Thrift Shop   **212-535-1250**
1440 Third Avenue   bet. 81/82nd St.
NYC 10028   Mon-Fri 10-5:15, Sat 11-5

Spence-Chapin Thrift Shop   **212-737-8448**
1473 Third Avenue   at 83rd St.
NYC 10028   Mon-Fri 11-6:45, Sat 11-6

Fashion Speak

Glossary of Terms

Avant-garde: forward-thinking or advanced. When referring to art or costume, sometimes implies erotic or startling. Derived from the French for "advance guard".

Bridge collection: a collection that is priced between designer and mass market.

Couture: French word used throughout fashion industry to describe the original styles, the ultimate in fine sewing and tailoring, made of expensive fabrics, by designers. The designs are shown in collections twice a year—spring/summer and fall/winter.

Custom-made/tailor-made, also called bespoke: garments made by tailor or couture house for an individual customer following couturier's original design. Done by either fitting a model form adjusted to the customer's measurements or by several personal fittings.

Diffusion line: a designer's second and less expensive collection.

Ensemble: an entire costume, including accessories, worn at one time. Two or more items of clothing designed and coordinated to be worn together.

Fashion trend: direction in which styles, colors and fabrics are moving. Trends may be influenced by political events, films, personalities, dramas, social and sporting events or indeed any human activity.

Faux: false or counterfeit, imitation: used in connection with gems, pearls and leathers. Faux fur (fake fur) is commonplace today, as is what is sometimes known as "pleather" (plastic leather). Artificial gems, especially pearls, are often made from a fine kind of glass known as "paste", and are accordingly sometimes called "paste" for short.

Haberdashery: a store that sells men's apparel and furnishings.

Knock-off: trade term for the copying of an item of apparel, e.g. a dress or a coat, in a lower price line. Similar to piracy.

Made-to-measure: clothing (dress, suit, shirt etc) made according to individual's measurement. No fittings required.

One-off: a unique, one-of-a-kind item that will not be found in any other store or produced again in the future, e.g. a customized denim skirt or a rare vintage cocktail dress. Can also refer to made-to-measure and couture garments designed for a particular person and/or event, such as a dress for the Oscars.

Prêt-à-porter: French term which literally means ready-to-wear, i.e. to take (or wear) straight out of the shop.

Ready-to-wear (rtw): apparel that is mass-produced in standard sizes. Records of the ready-to-wear industry tabulated in the U.S. Census of 1860 included hoop skirts, cloaks, and mantillas; from 1890 on, shirtwaists and wrappers were added; and, after 1930, dresses.

Notes

Notes

Notes

How to order *Where to Wear*

Where to Wear publishes guides to the following cities: *London, New York, Paris, Los Angeles, San Francisco* and *Italy* (which includes Florence, Milan and Rome). Each edition retails at £9.99, $12.95, €14.95.

There is also a gift box set available for £29.99, $49.99, €49.99 which includes the *London, New York, Paris* and *Italy* guides.

If you live in the UK or Europe you can order your copies of *Where to Wear* by contacting our London office at:

1st floor
571 King's Road
London SW6 2EB
TEL: 020 7371 9004
EMAIL: wheretowear@onetel.net.uk

If you live in the USA you can order your copies of *Where to Wear* by contacting our New York office at:

666 Fifth Avenue
PMB 377
New York, NY 10103
TEL: 212-969-0138
FAX: 914-763-0056
EMAIL: wheretowear@aol.com

Or simply log on to our website: www.wheretowear.com

Where to Wear accepts Visa/Mastercard and delivers worldwide.

Notes